FIRE FORCE

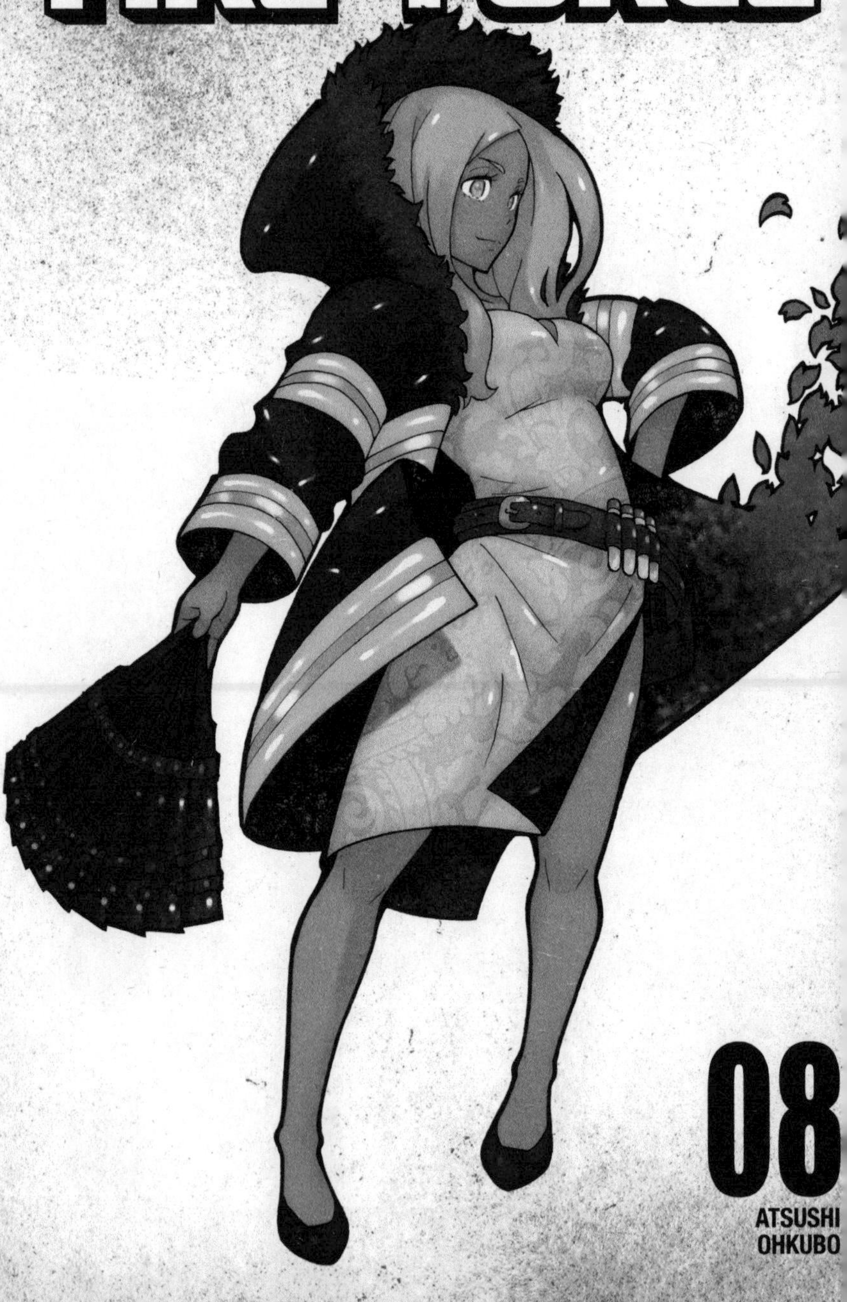

08

ATSUSHI
OHKUBO

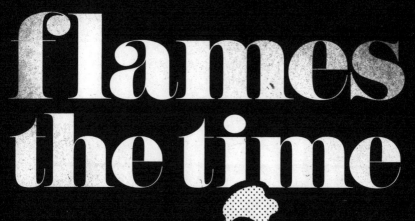

flames
the time
us.

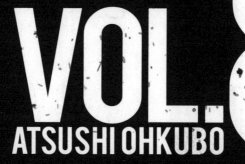

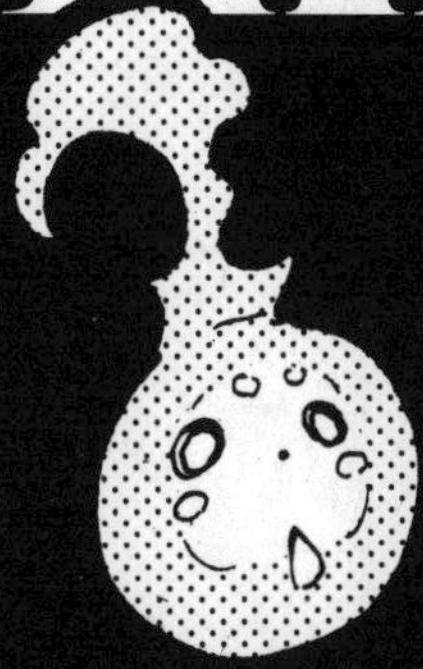

VOL.8
ATSUSHI OHKUBO

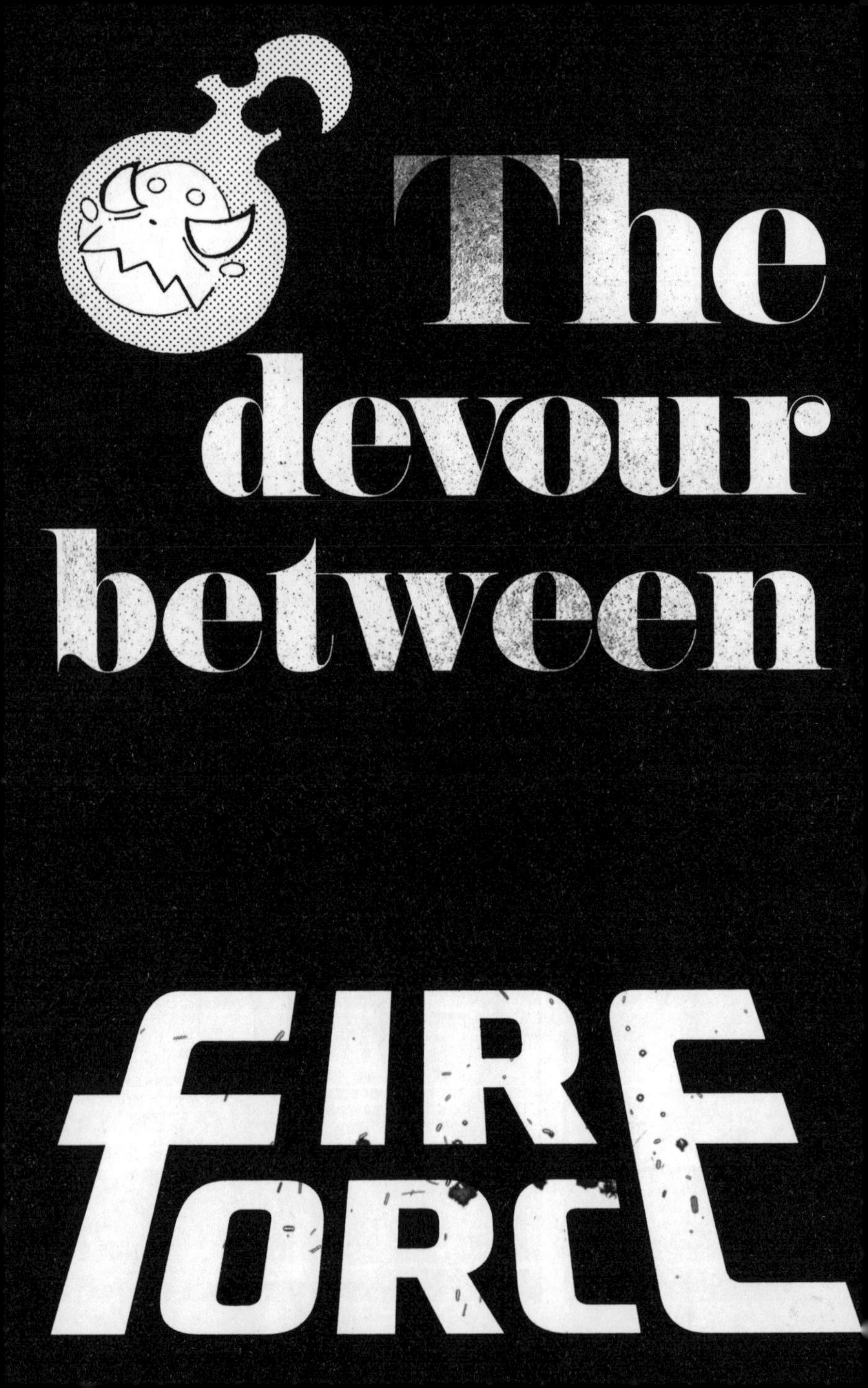

The devour between

FIRE FORCE

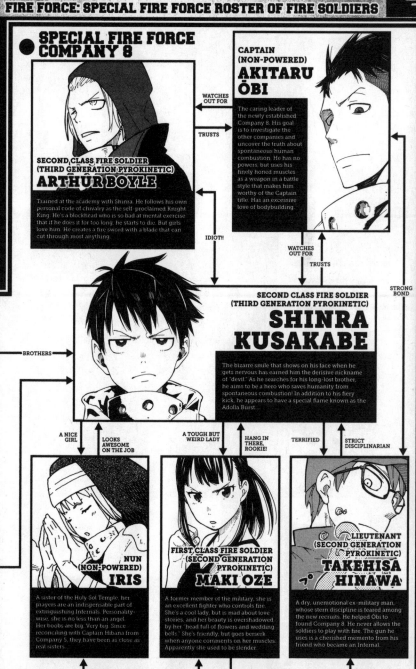

SPECIAL FIRE FORCE COMPANY 8

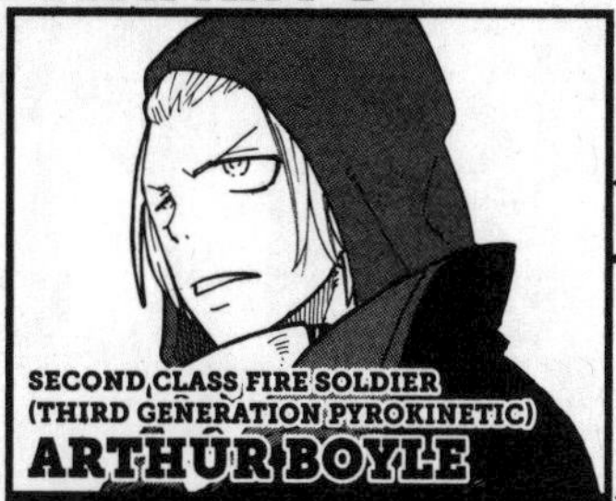

SECOND CLASS FIRE SOLDIER
(THIRD GENERATION PYROKINETIC)
ARTHUR BOYLE

Trained at the academy with Shinra. He follows his own personal code of chivalry as the self-proclaimed Knight King. He's a blockhead who is so bad at mental exercise that if he does it for too long, he starts to die. But girls love him. He creates a fire sword with a blade that can cut through most anything.

CAPTAIN
(NON-POWERED)
AKITARU ŌBI

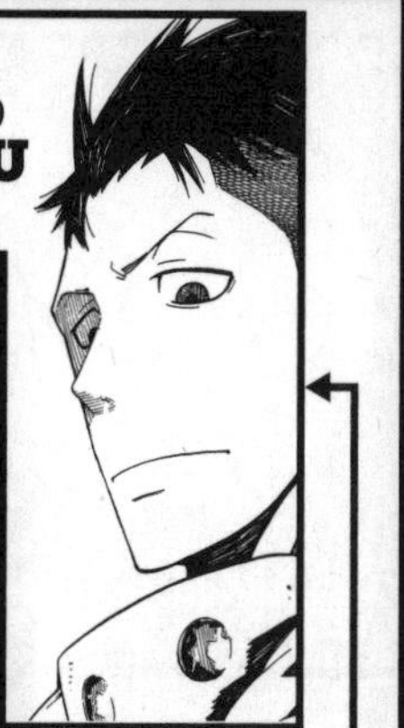

The caring leader of the newly established Company 8. His goal is to investigate the other companies and uncover the truth about spontaneous human combustion. He has no powers, but uses his finely honed muscles as a weapon in a battle style that makes him worthy of the Captain title. Has an excessive love of bodybuilding.

WATCHES OUT FOR

TRUSTS

IDIOT!!

WATCHES OUT FOR

TRUSTS

STRONG BOND

BROTHERS

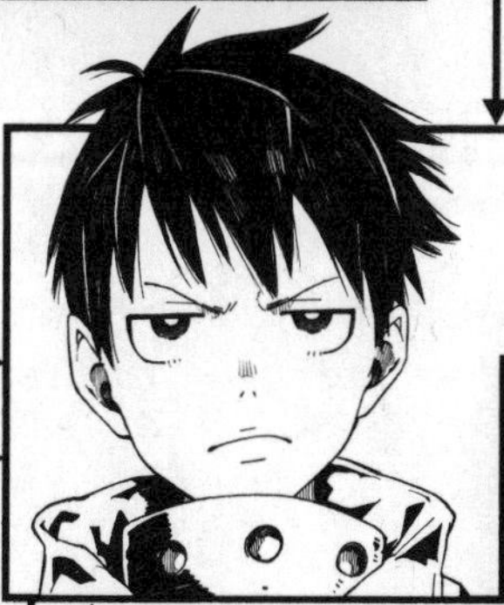

SECOND CLASS FIRE SOLDIER
(THIRD GENERATION PYROKINETIC)
SHINRA KUSAKABE

The bizarre smile that shows on his face when he gets nervous has earned him the derisive nickname of "devil." As he searches for his long-lost brother, he aims to be a hero who saves humanity from spontaneous combustion! In addition to his fiery kick, he appears to have a special flame known as the Adolla Burst....

A NICE GIRL

LOOKS AWESOME ON THE JOB

A TOUGH BUT WEIRD LADY

HANG IN THERE, ROOKIE!

TERRIFIED

STRICT DISCIPLINARIAN

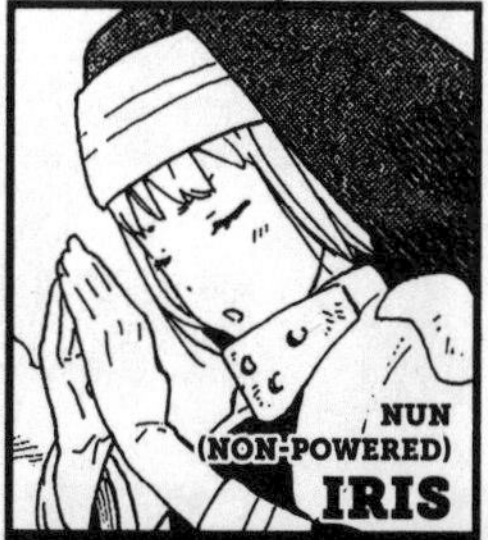

NUN
(NON-POWERED)
IRIS

A sister of the Holy Sol Temple, her prayers are an indispensable part of extinguishing Infernals. Personality-wise, she is no less than an angel. Her boobs are big. Very big. Since reconciling with Captain Hibana from Company 5, they have been as close as real sisters.

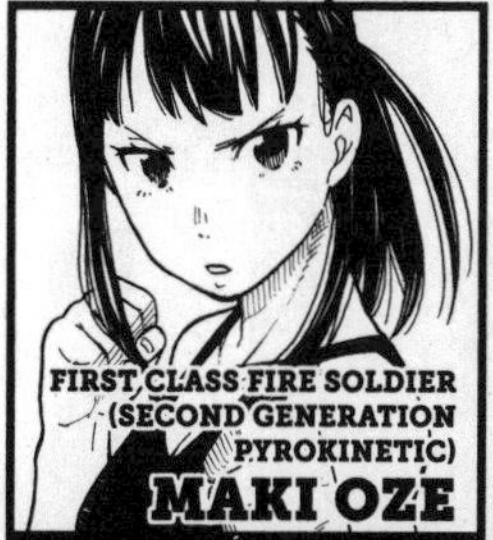

FIRST CLASS FIRE SOLDIER
(SECOND GENERATION PYROKINETIC)
MAKI OZE

A former member of the military, she is an excellent fighter who controls fire. She's a cool lady, but is mad about love stories, and her beauty is overshadowed by her "head full of flowers and wedding bells." She's friendly, but goes berserk when anyone comments on her muscles. Apparently she used to be slender.

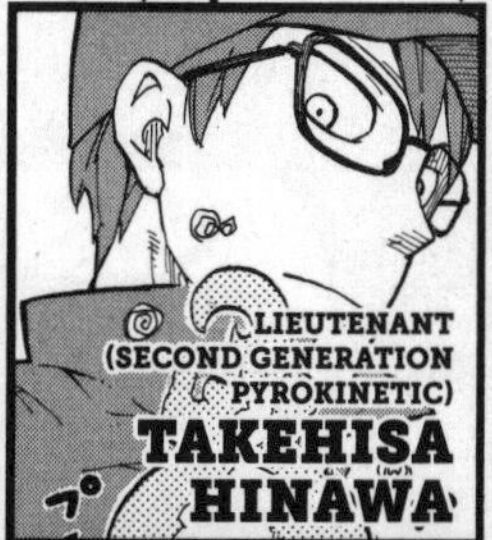

LIEUTENANT
(SECOND GENERATION PYROKINETIC)
TAKEHISA HINAWA

A dry, unemotional ex-military man, whose stern discipline is feared among the new recruits. He helped Ōbi to found Company 8. He never allows the soldiers to play with fire. The gun he uses is a cherished memento from his friend who became an Infernal.

THE GIRLS' CLUB

RESPECTS

FOLLOWERS OF THE EVANGELIST

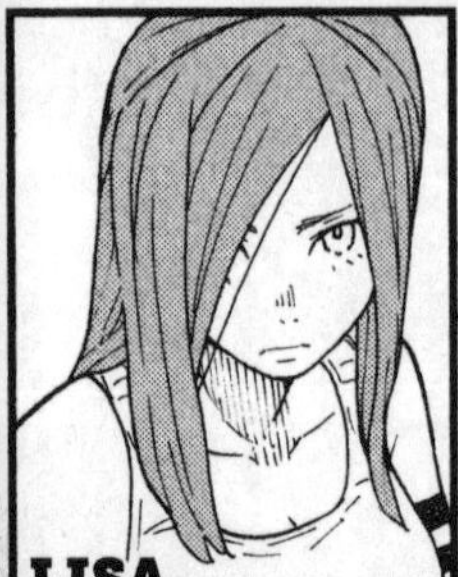

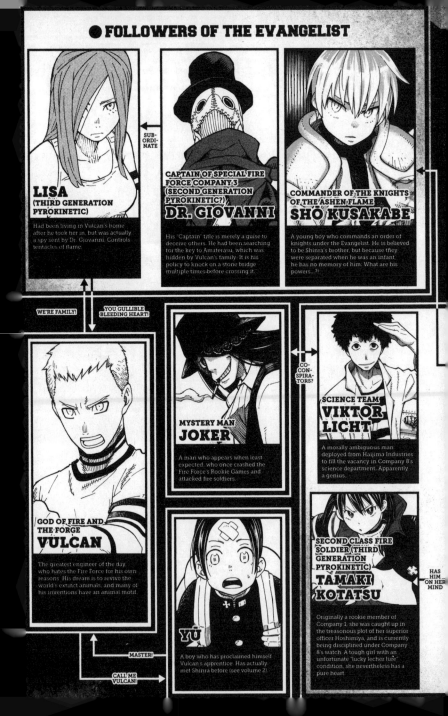

LISA
(THIRD GENERATION PYROKINETIC)

Had been living in Vulcan's home after he took her in, but was actually a spy sent by Dr. Giovanni. Controls tentacles of flame.

SUBORDINATE

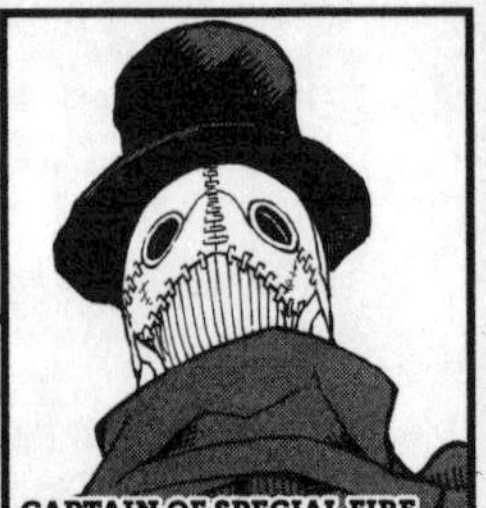

CAPTAIN OF SPECIAL FIRE FORCE COMPANY 3 (SECOND GENERATION PYROKINETIC?)
DR. GIOVANNI

His "Captain" title is merely a guise to deceive others. He had been searching for the key to Amaterasu, which was hidden by Vulcan's family. It is his policy to knock on a stone bridge multiple times before crossing it.

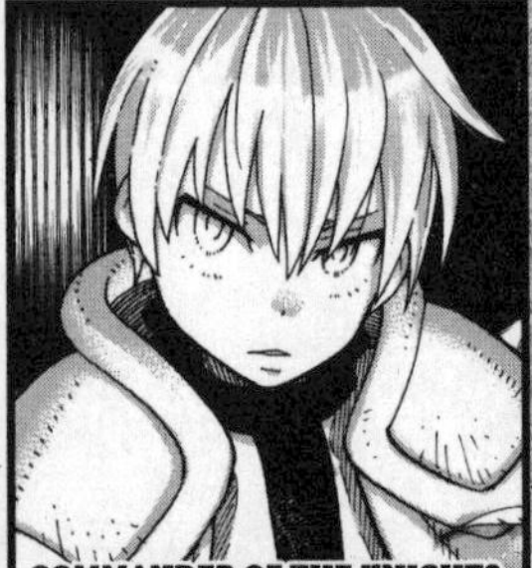

COMMANDER OF THE KNIGHTS OF THE ASHEN FLAME
SHŌ KUSAKABE

A young boy who commands an order of knights under the Evangelist. He is believed to be Shinra's brother, but because they were separated when he was an infant, he has no memory of him. What are his powers...?!

WE'RE FAMILY!

YOU GULLIBLE BLEEDING HEART!

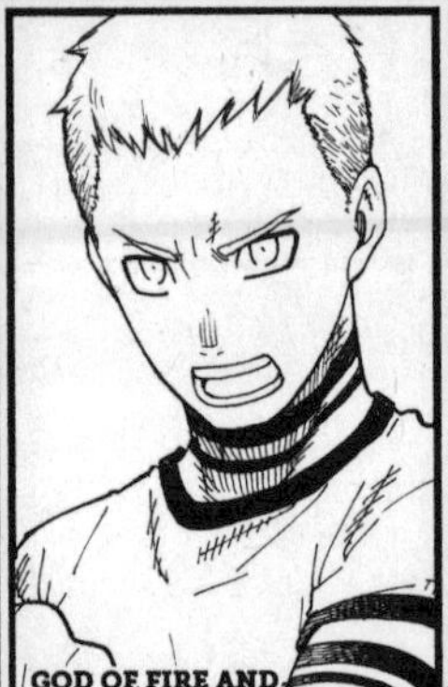

GOD OF FIRE AND THE FORGE
VULCAN

The greatest engineer of the day, who hates the Fire Force for his own reasons. His dream is to revive the world's extinct animals, and many of his inventions have an animal motif.

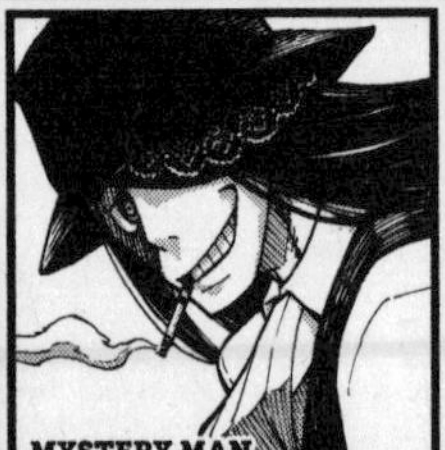

MYSTERY MAN
JOKER

A man who appears when least expected, who once crashed the Fire Force's Rookie Games and attacked fire soldiers.

CO-CONSPIRATORS?

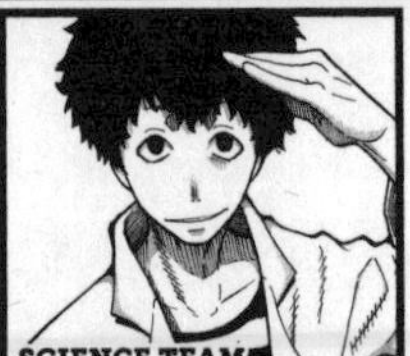

SCIENCE TEAM
VIKTOR LICHT

A morally ambiguous man deployed from Haijima Industries to fill the vacancy in Company 8's science department. Apparently a genius.

MASTER!

CALL ME VULCAN!

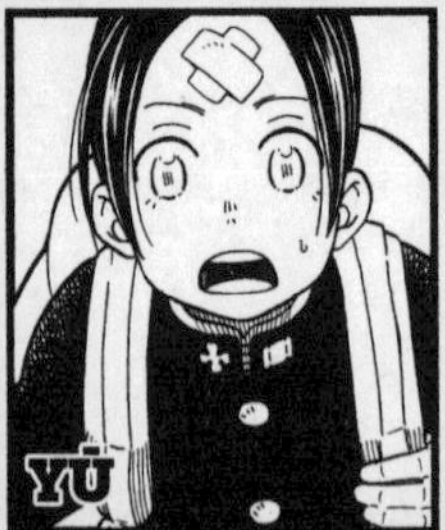

YŪ

A boy who has proclaimed himself Vulcan's apprentice. Has actually met Shinra before (see volume 2).

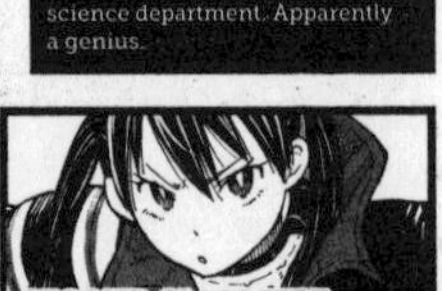

SECOND CLASS FIRE SOLDIER (THIRD GENERATION PYROKINETIC)
TAMAKI KOTATSU

Originally a rookie member of Company 1, she was caught up in the treasonous plot of her superior officer Hoshimiya, and is currently being disciplined under Company 8's watch. A tough girl with an unfortunate "lucky lecher lure" condition, she nevertheless has a pure heart.

HAS HIM ON HER MIND

FIRE FORCE 08
CONTENTS

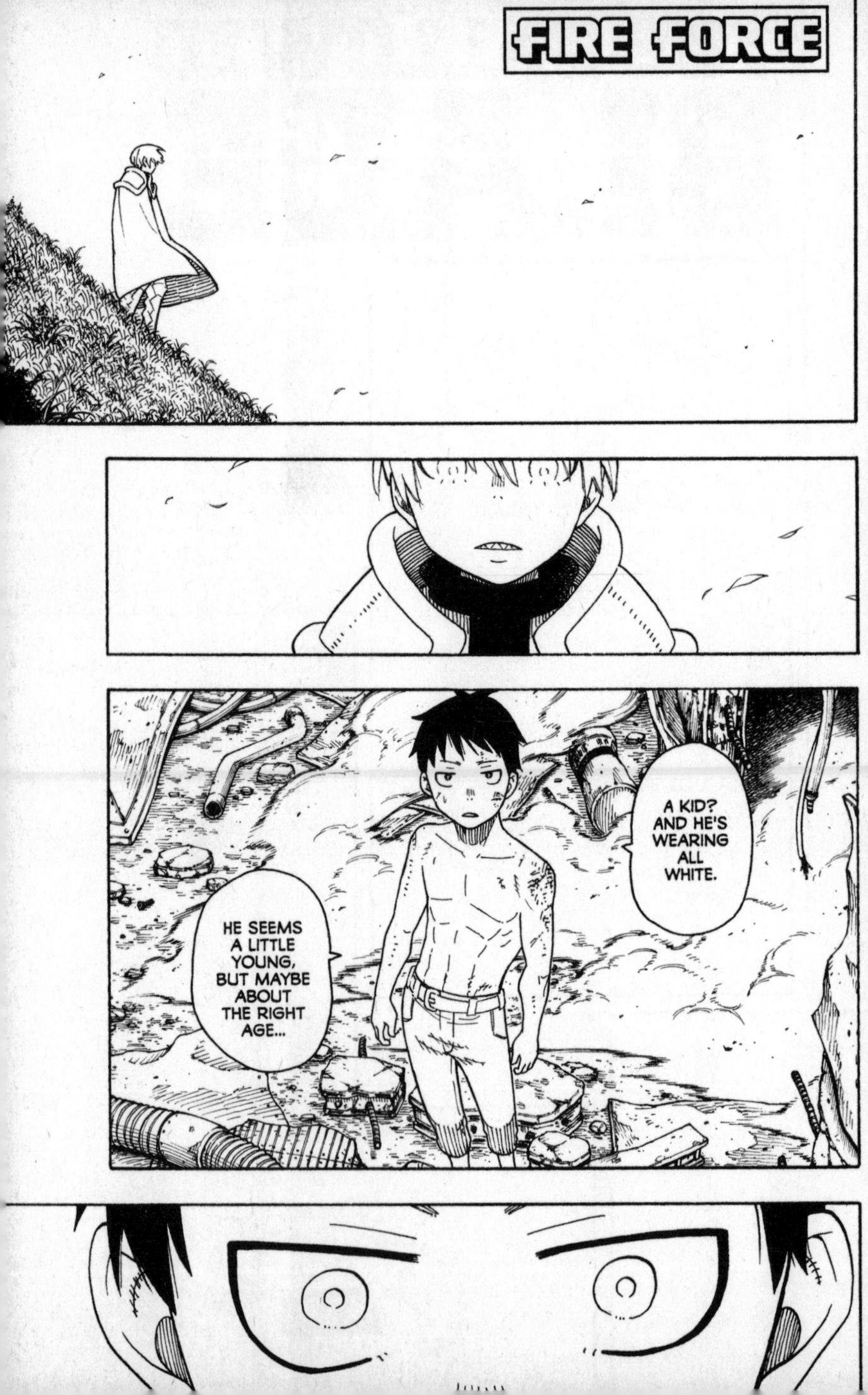
FIRE FORCE
A KID? AND HE'S WEARING ALL WHITE.
HE SEEMS A LITTLE YOUNG, BUT MAYBE ABOUT THE RIGHT AGE...

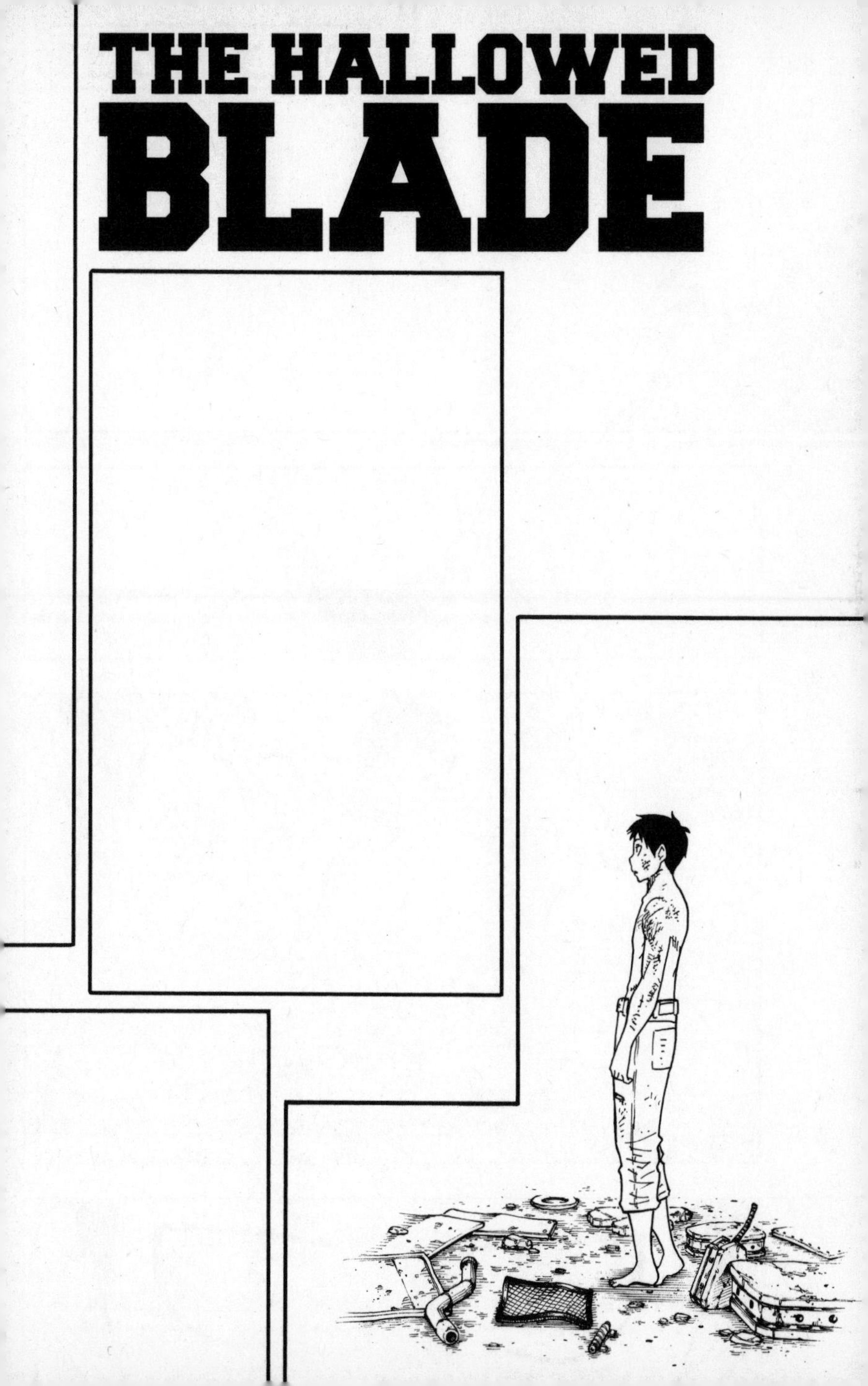
THE HALLOWED
BLADE

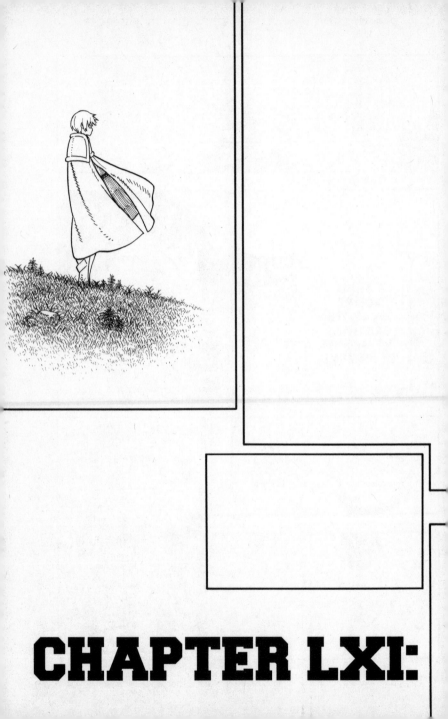

CHAPTER LXI:

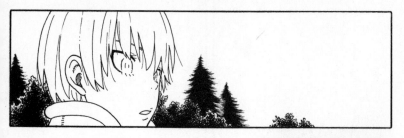

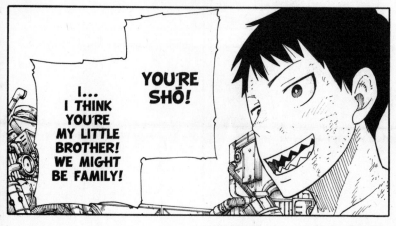

YOU'RE SHŌ!
I... I THINK YOU'RE MY LITTLE BROTHER! WE MIGHT BE FAMILY!
THAT'S THE BROTH-ER YOU TOLD US ABOUT?
YEAH, IT'S GOTTA BE!!
SHŌ!! SHŌ, IT'S YOU!!
YOU AND I? BROTH-ERS?
SPARKLE キラ
キラ SPARKLE

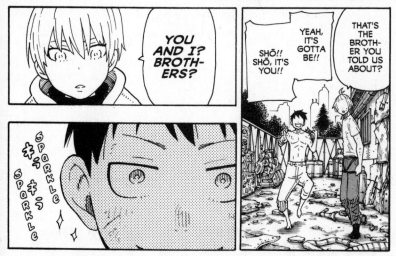

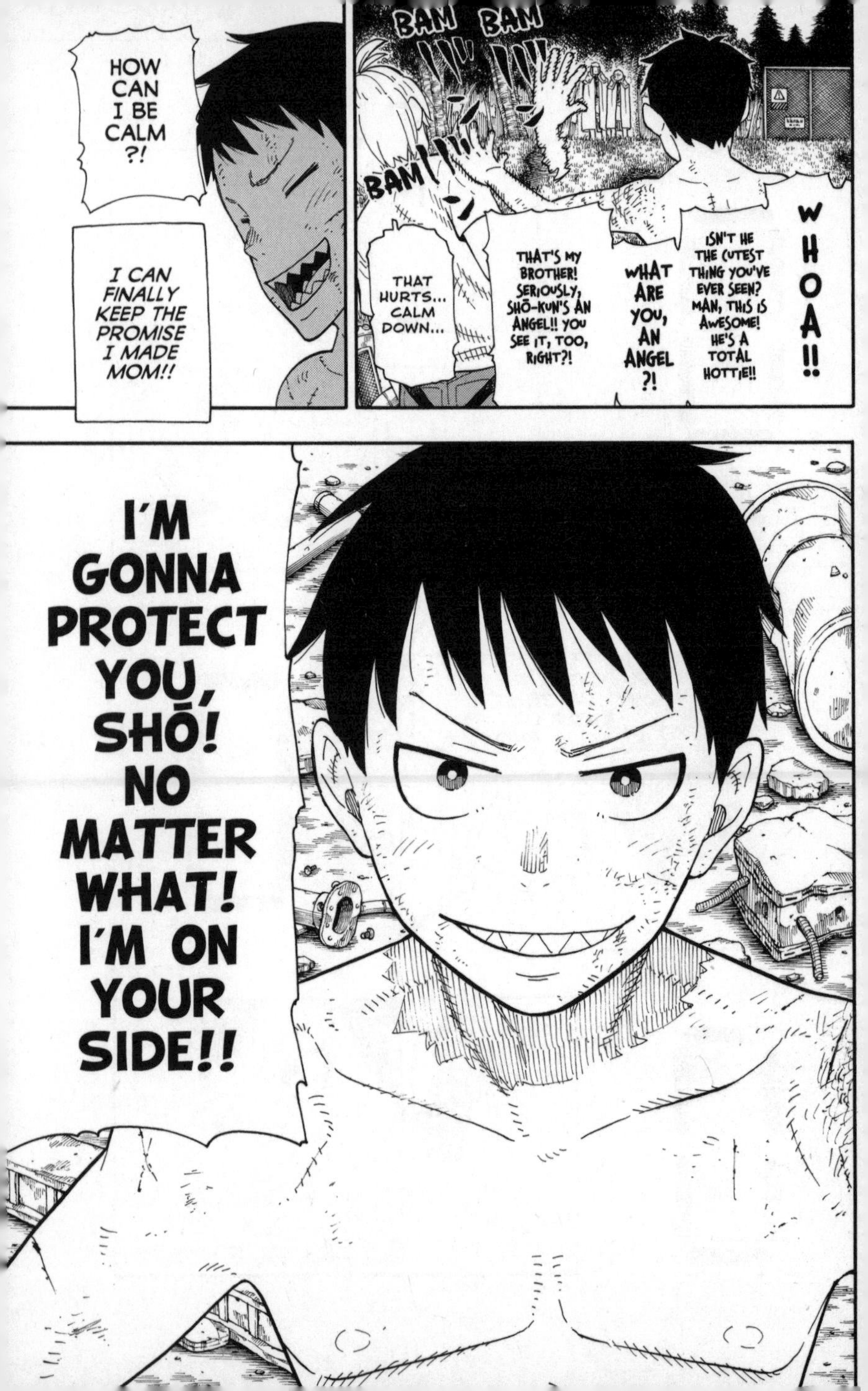
BAM BAM
WHOA!!
ISN'T HE THE CUTEST THING YOU'VE EVER SEEN? MAN, THIS IS AWESOME! HE'S A TOTAL HOTTIE!!
WHAT ARE YOU, AN ANGEL ?!
THAT'S MY BROTHER! SERIOUSLY, SHŌ-KUN'S AN ANGEL!! YOU SEE IT, TOO, RIGHT?!
BAM
THAT HURTS... CALM DOWN...
HOW CAN I BE CALM ?!
I CAN FINALLY KEEP THE PROMISE I MADE MOM!!
I'M GONNA PROTECT YOU, SHŌ! NO MATTER WHAT! I'M ON YOUR SIDE!!

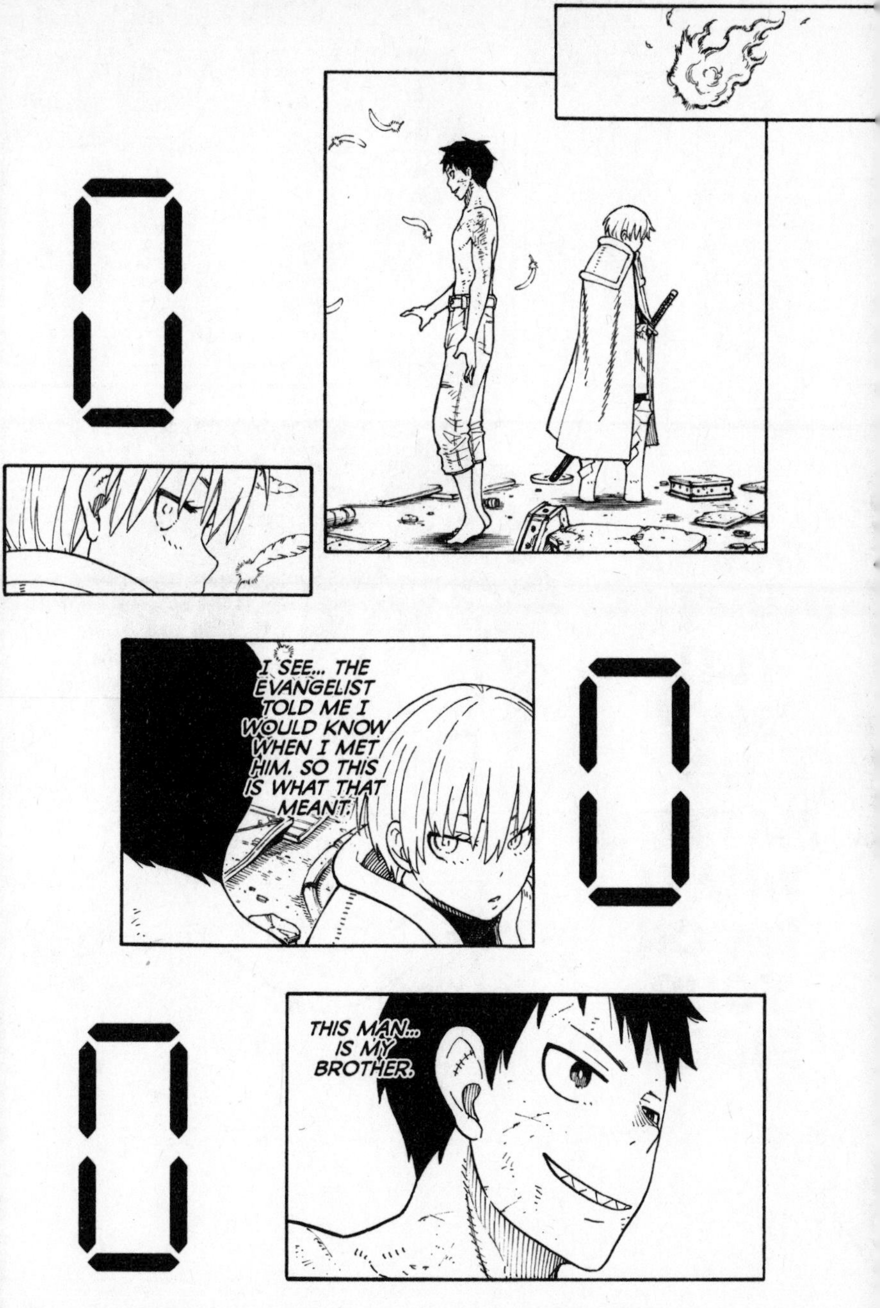
I SEE... THE EVANGELIST TOLD ME I WOULD KNOW WHEN I MET HIM. SO THIS IS WHAT THAT MEANT.
THIS MAN... IS MY BROTHER.

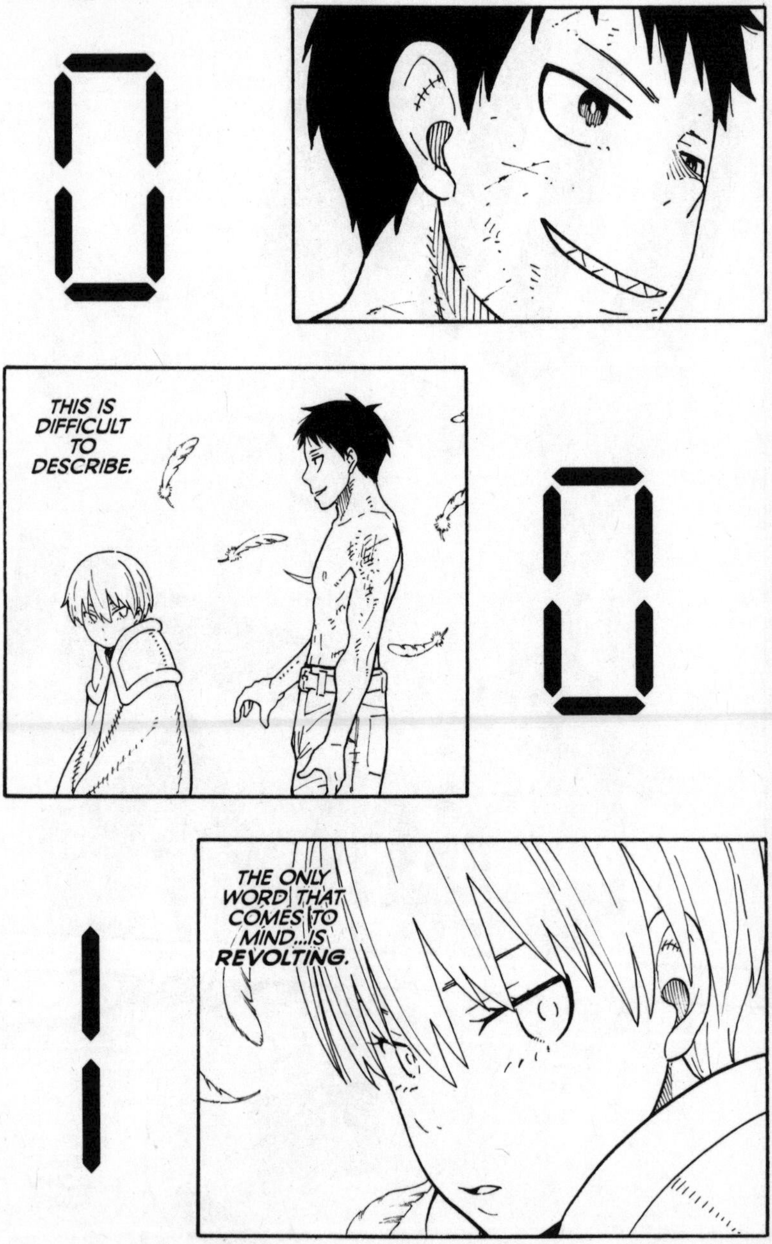
THIS IS DIFFICULT TO DESCRIBE.
THE ONLY WORD THAT COMES TO MIND...IS REVOLTING.

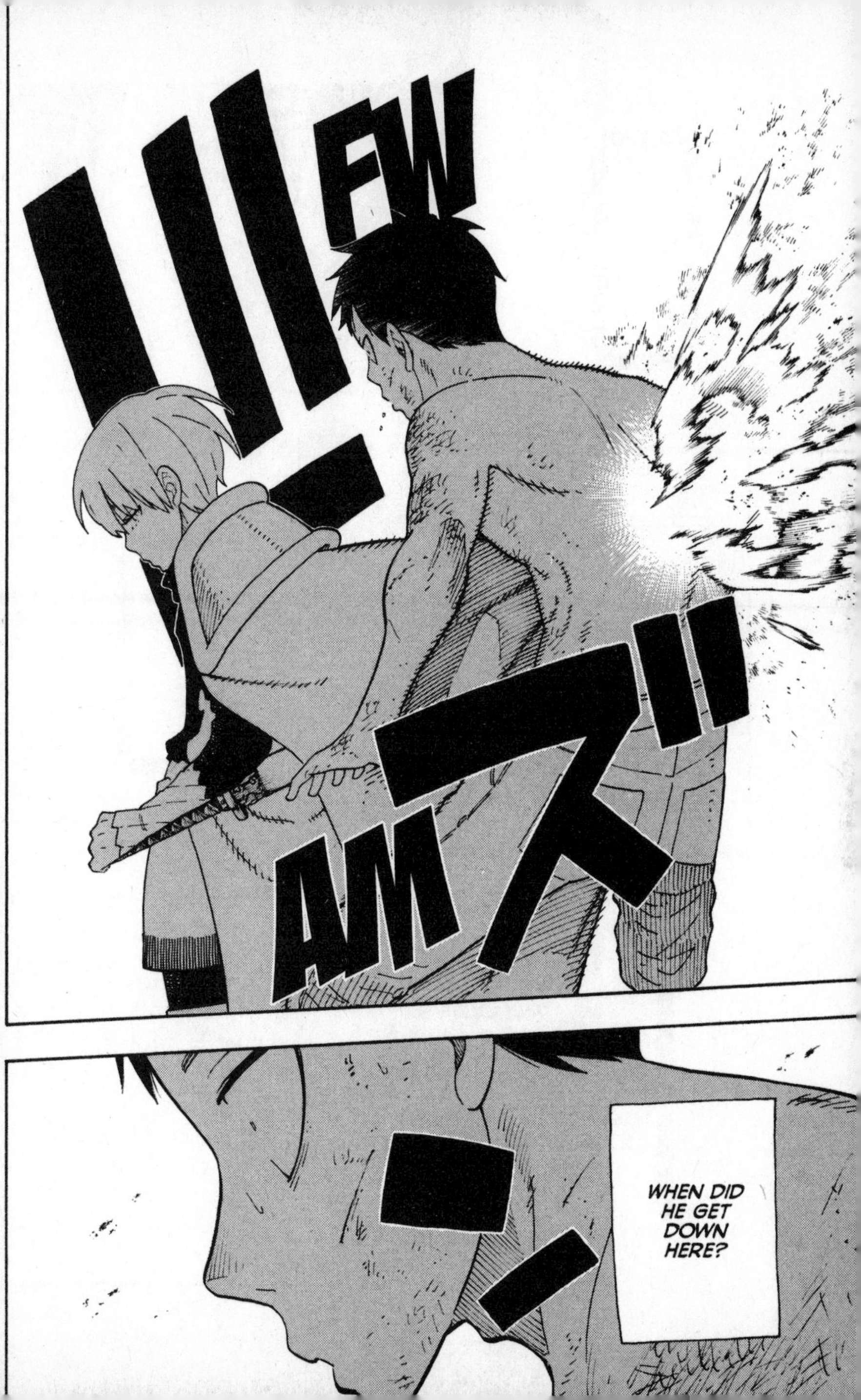
FW
ズ
AM
WHEN DID HE GET DOWN HERE?

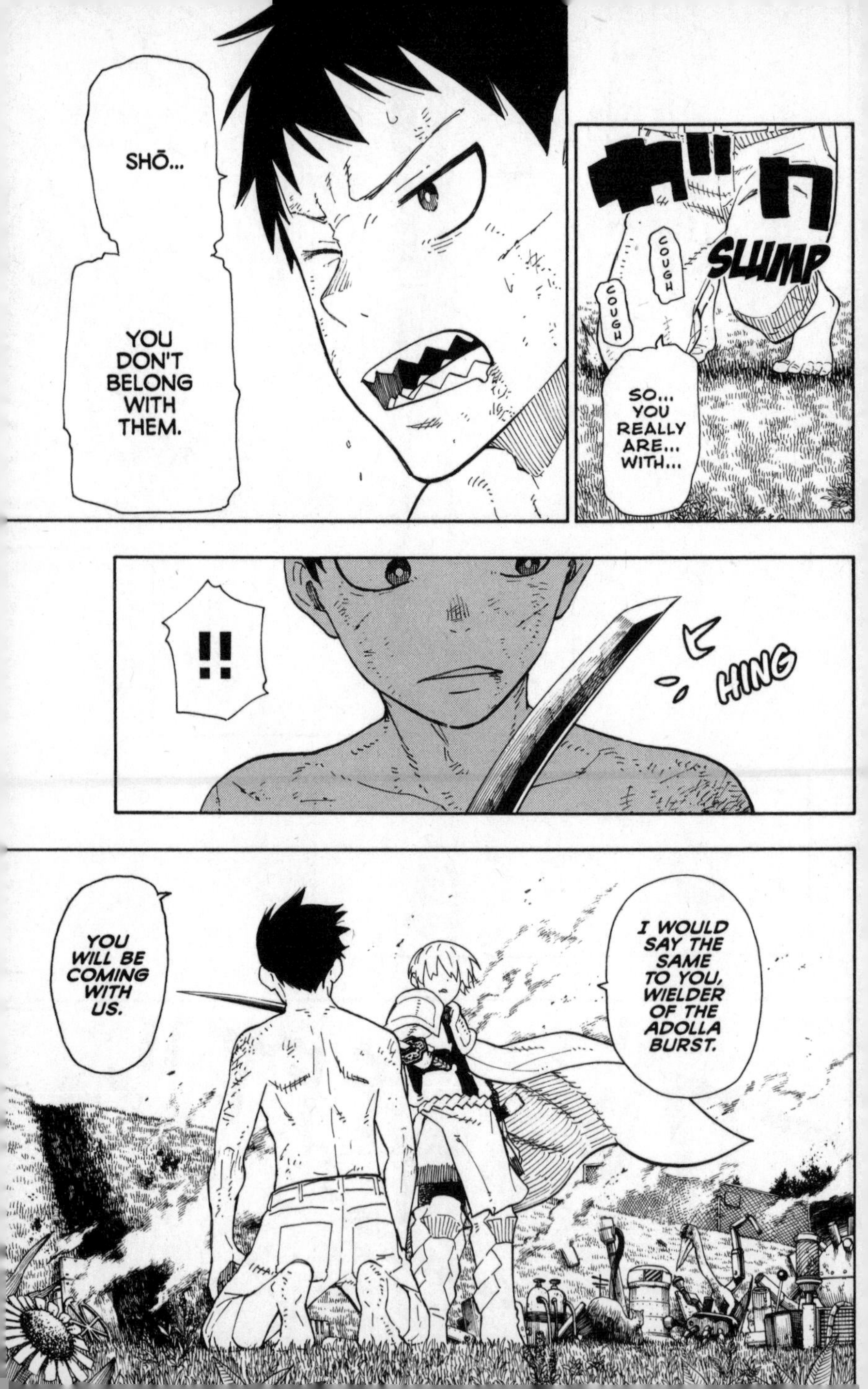
ガク
SLUMP
COUGH
COUGH
SO... YOU REALLY ARE... WITH...
SHŌ...
YOU DON'T BELONG WITH THEM.
HING
!!
I WOULD SAY THE SAME TO YOU, WIELDER OF THE ADOLLA BURST.
YOU WILL BE COMING WITH US.

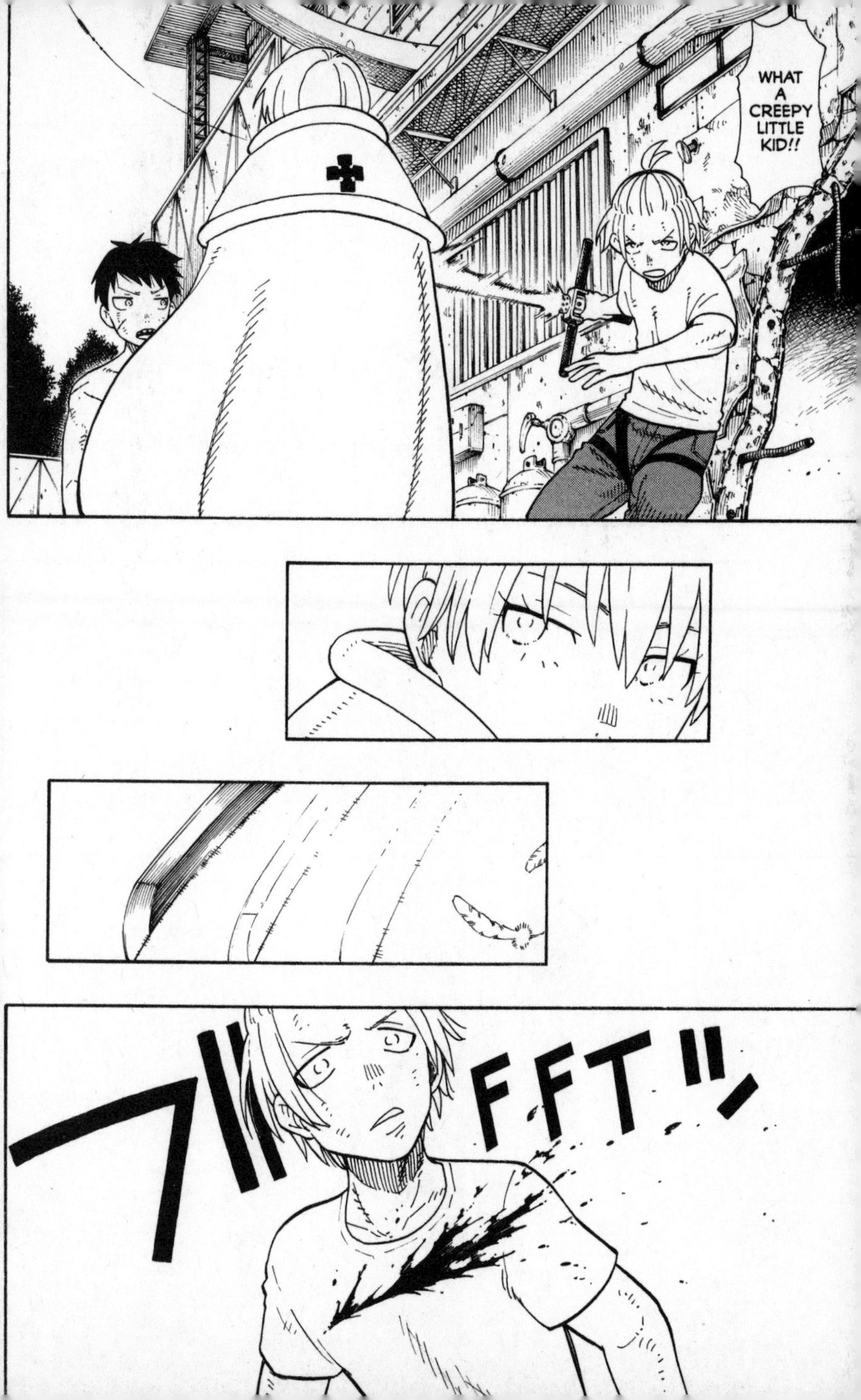
WHAT A CREEPY LITTLE KID!!
FFFT

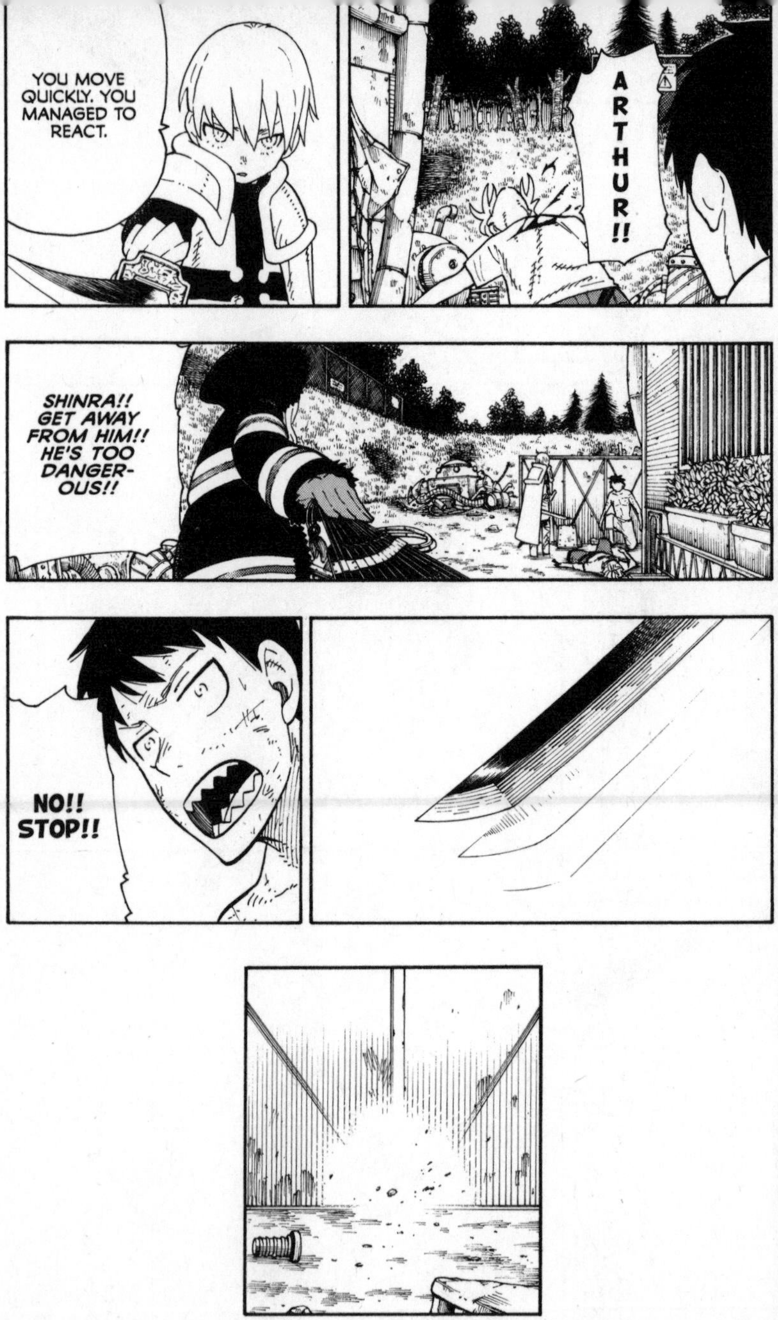
ARTHUR!!
YOU MOVE QUICKLY. YOU MANAGED TO REACT.
SHINRA!! GET AWAY FROM HIM!! HE'S TOO DANGER-OUS!!
NO!! STOP!!

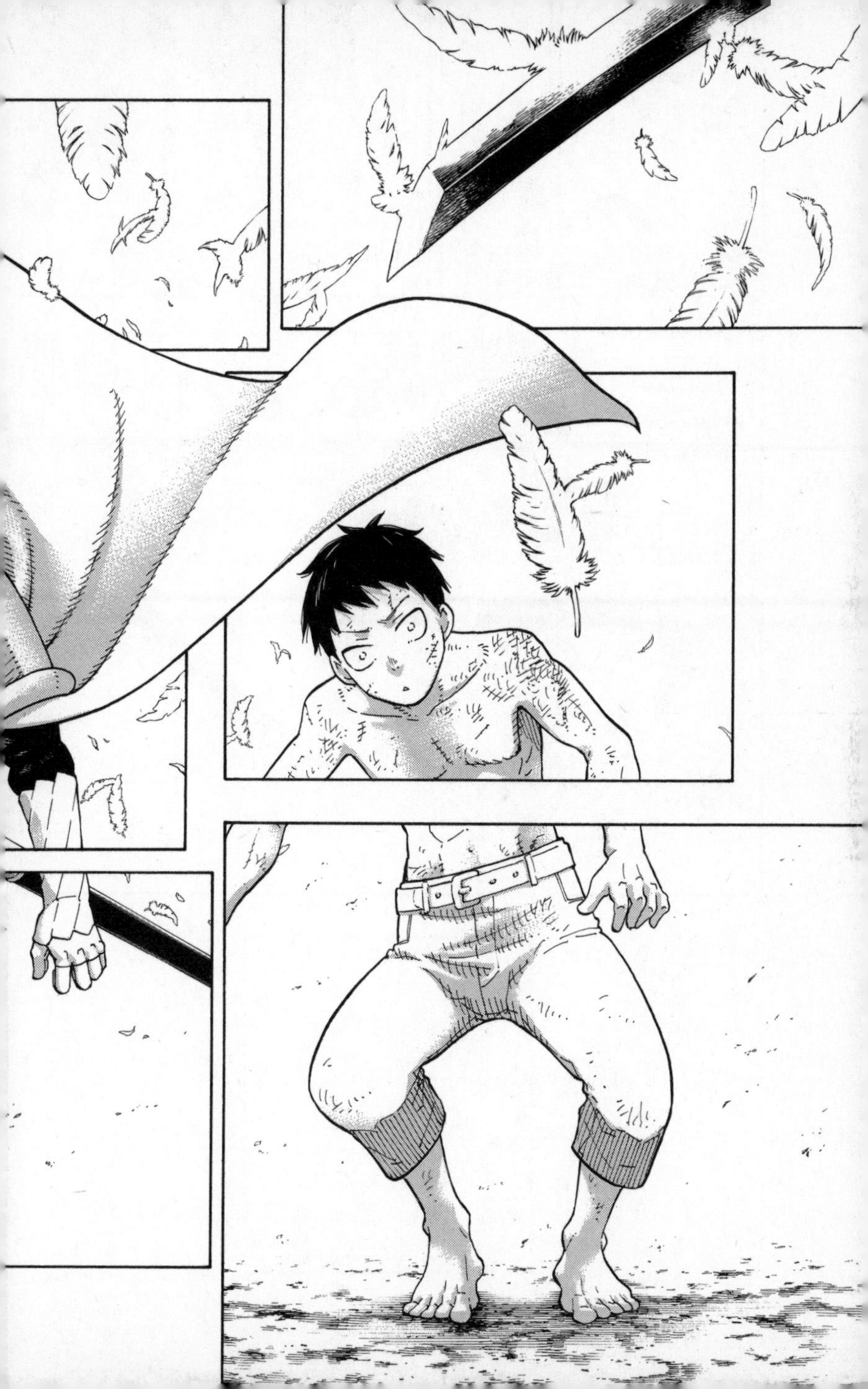

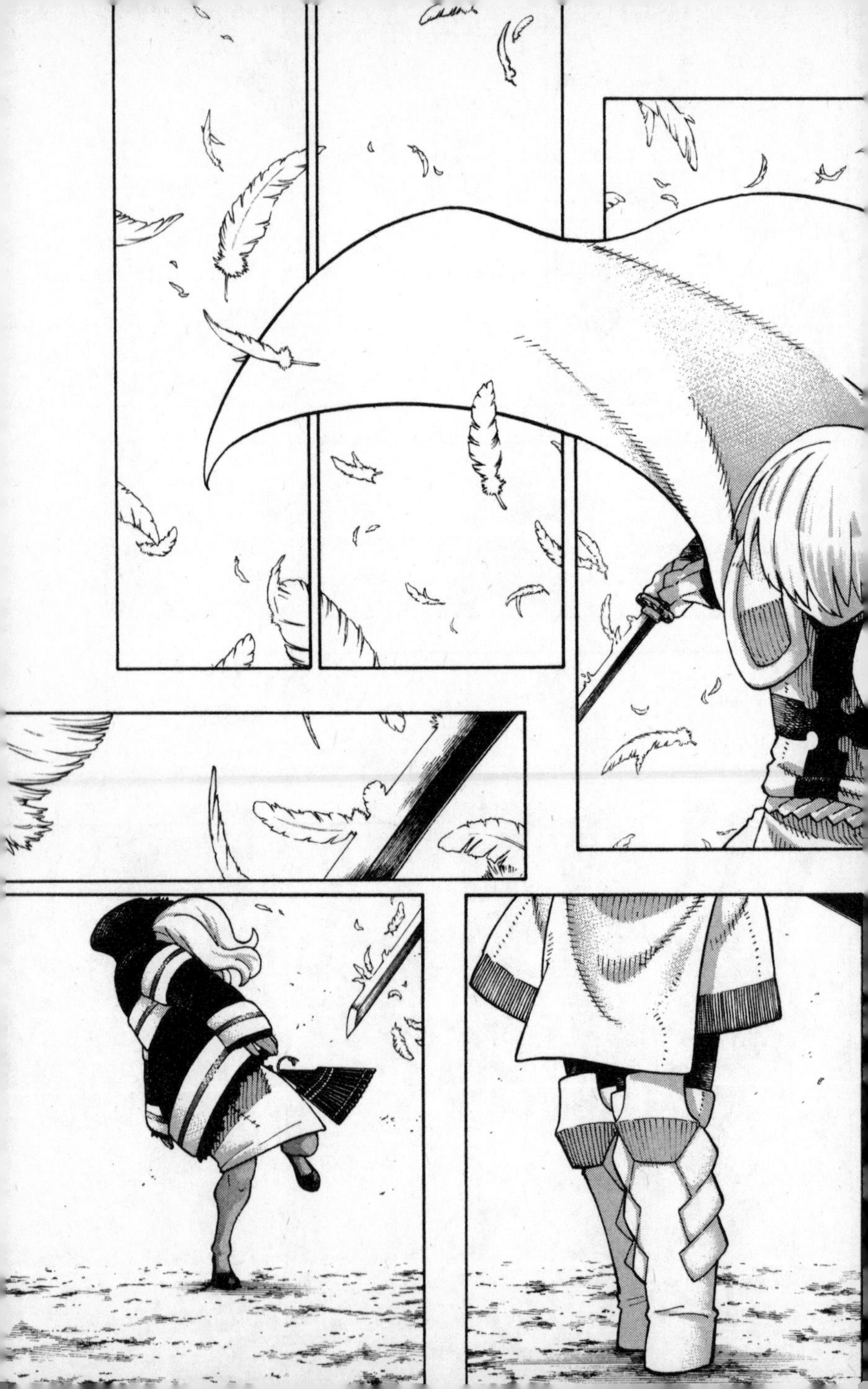

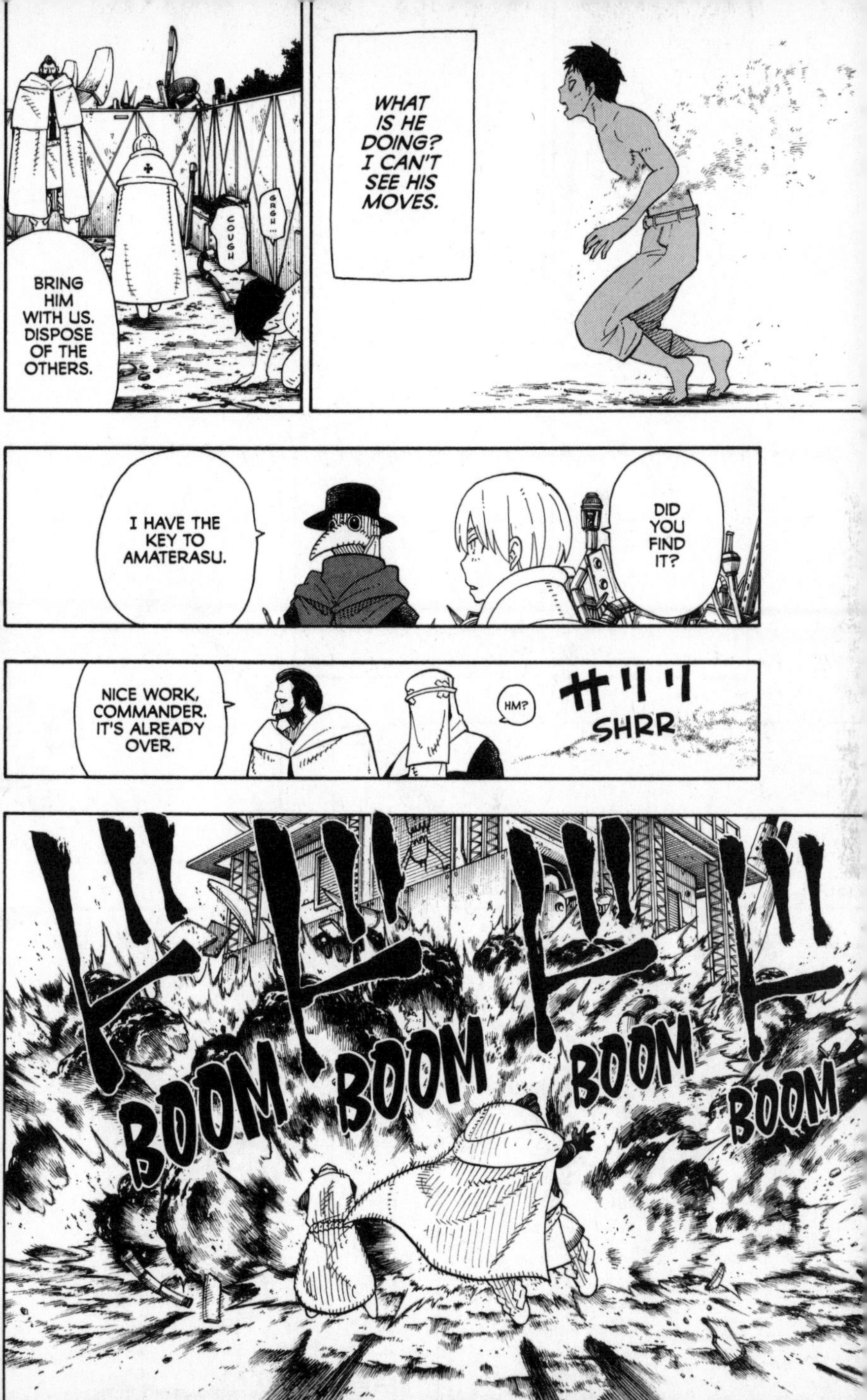
WHAT IS HE DOING? I CAN'T SEE HIS MOVES.
GRGH...
COUGH
BRING HIM WITH US. DISPOSE OF THE OTHERS.
DID YOU FIND IT?
I HAVE THE KEY TO AMATERASU.
サリリ
SHRR
HM?
NICE WORK, COMMANDER. IT'S ALREADY OVER.
ドドドド
BOOM BOOM BOOM BOOM

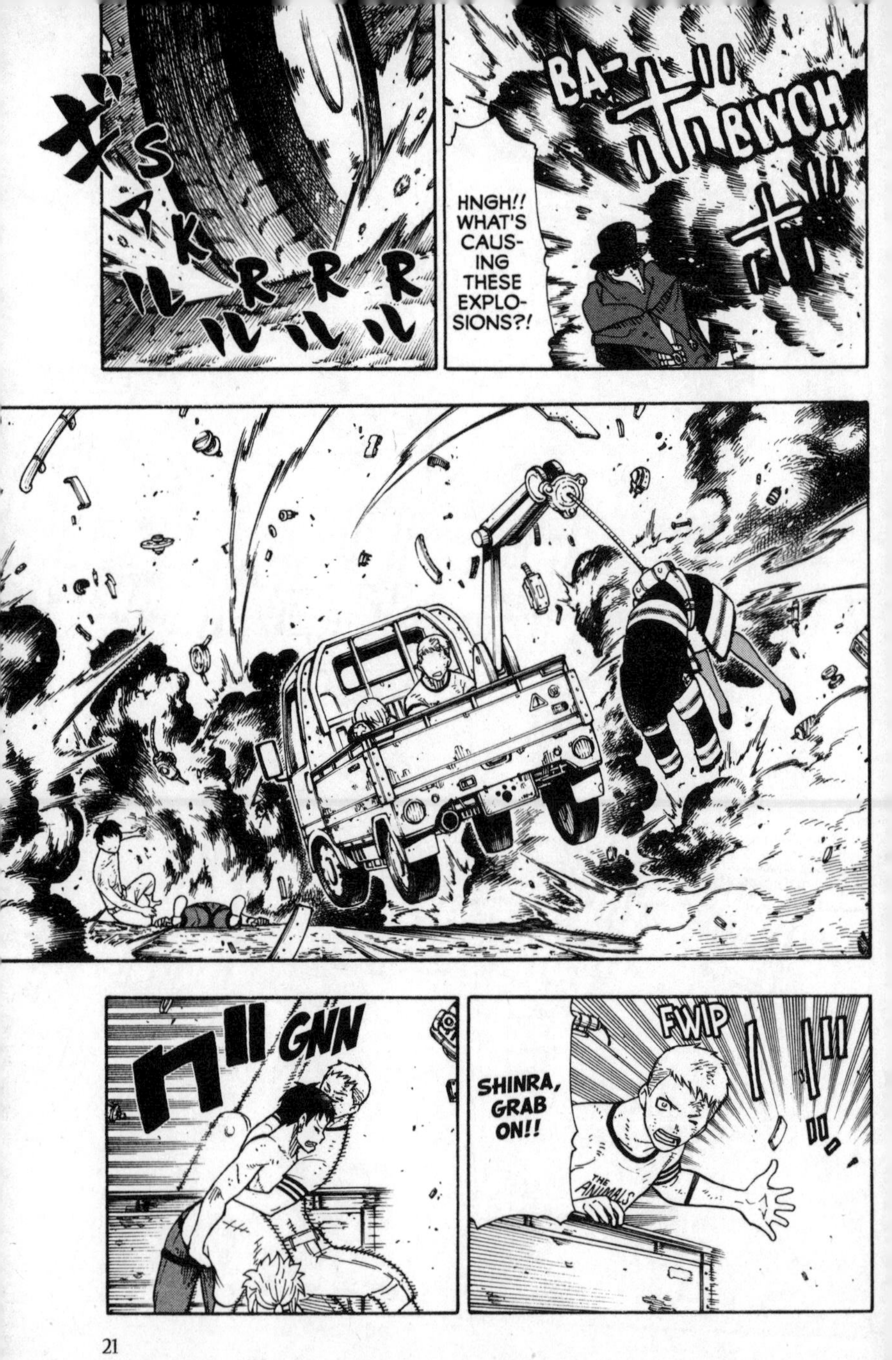
BA-BWOH
HNGH!! WHAT'S CAUSING THESE EXPLOSIONS?!
SKRRR
FWIP
SHINRA, GRAB ON!!
THE ANIMALS
GNN

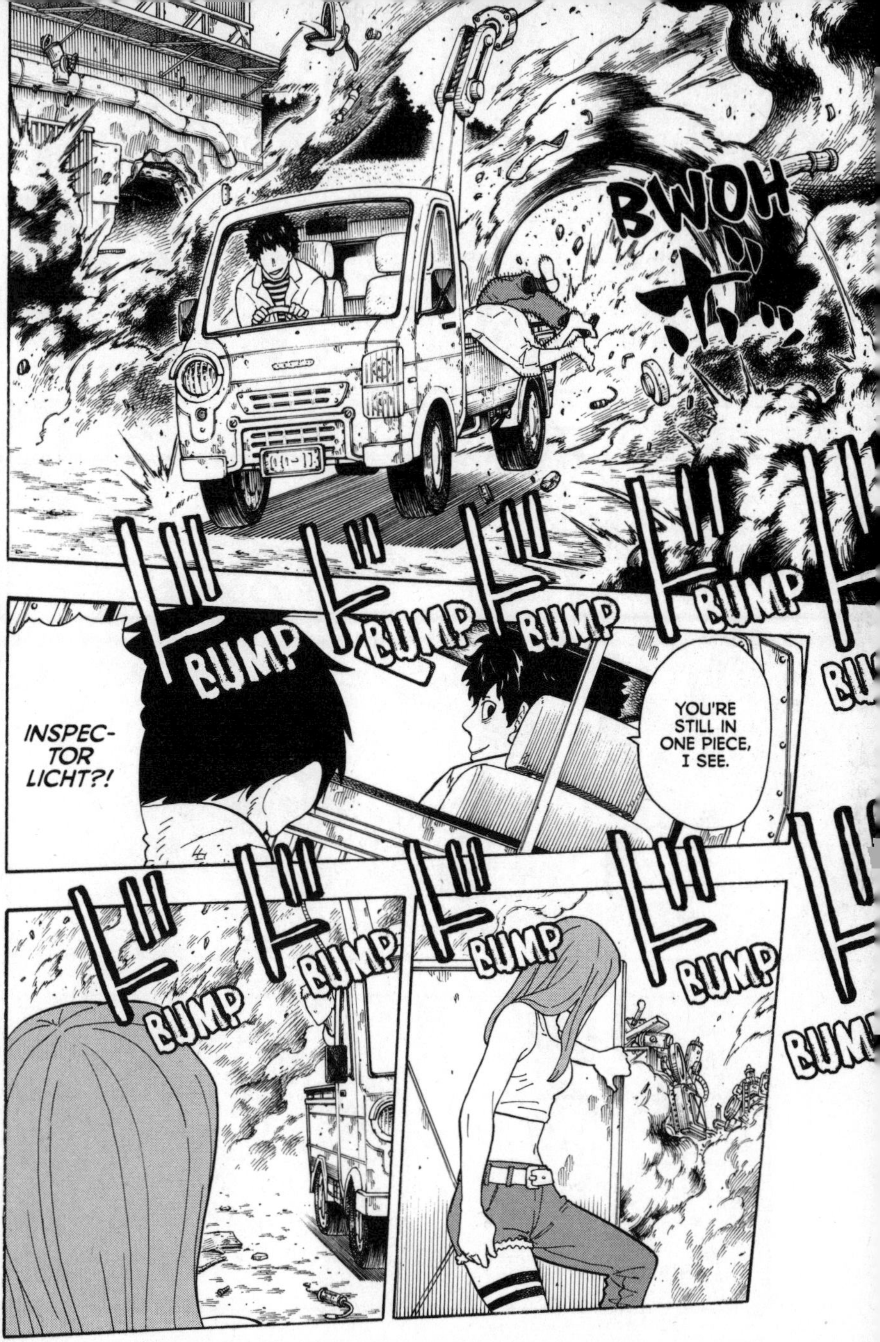
BWOH
BUMP
BUMP
BUMP
BUMP
YOU'RE STILL IN ONE PIECE, I SEE.
INSPECTOR LICHT?!
BUMP
BUMP
BUMP
BUMP

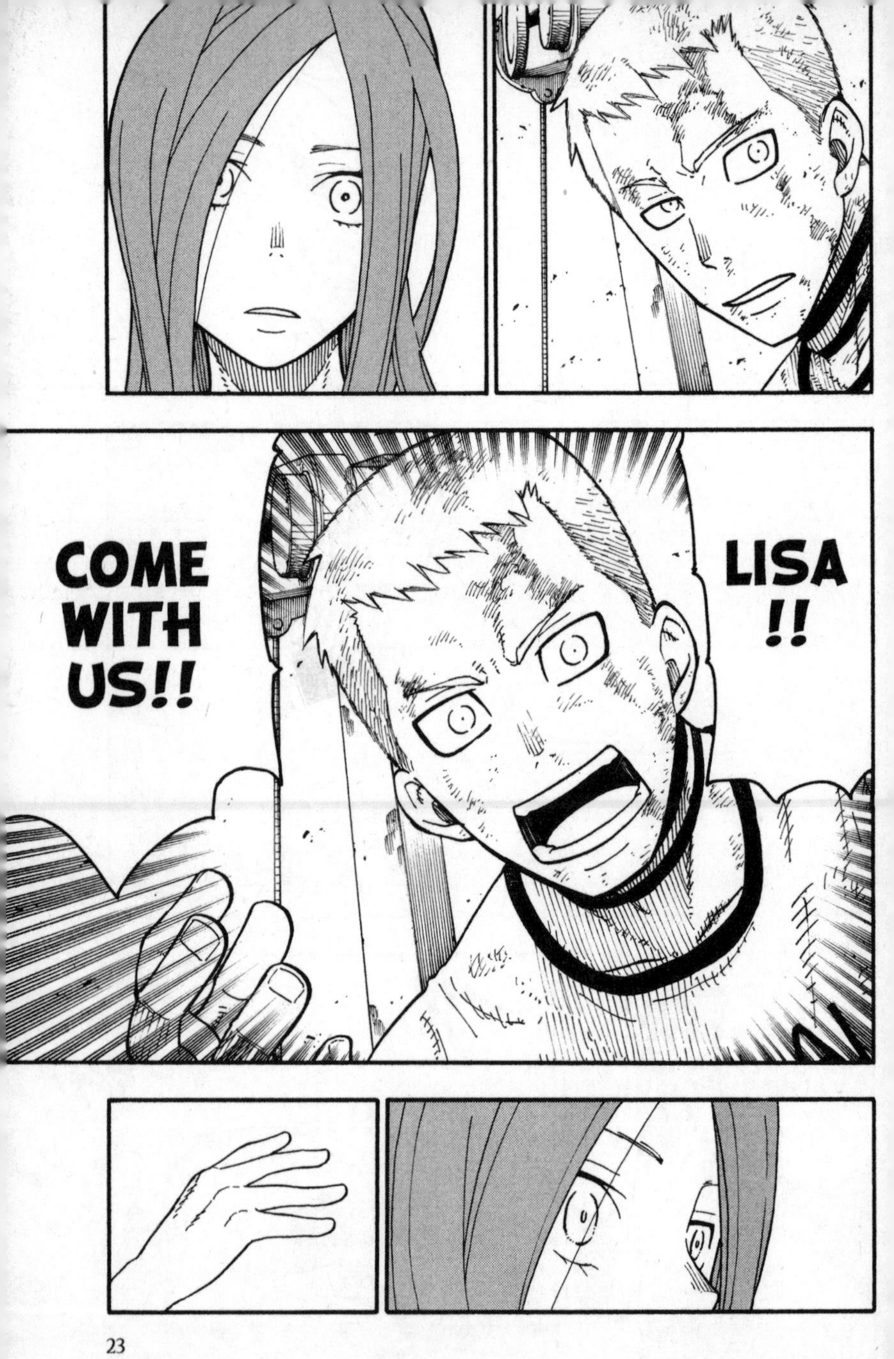
LISA!!
COME WITH US!!

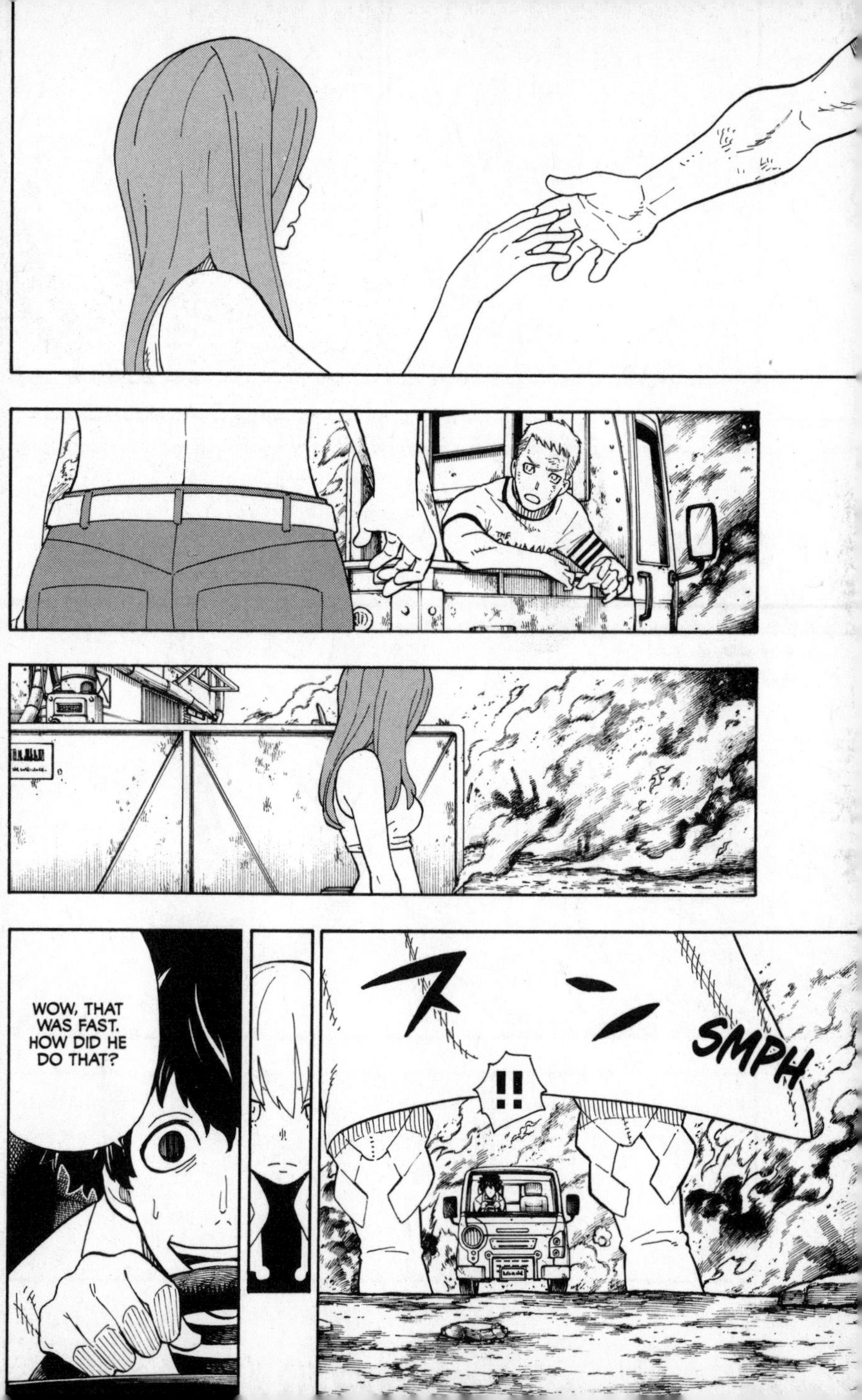
SMPH
!!
WOW, THAT WAS FAST. HOW DID HE DO THAT?

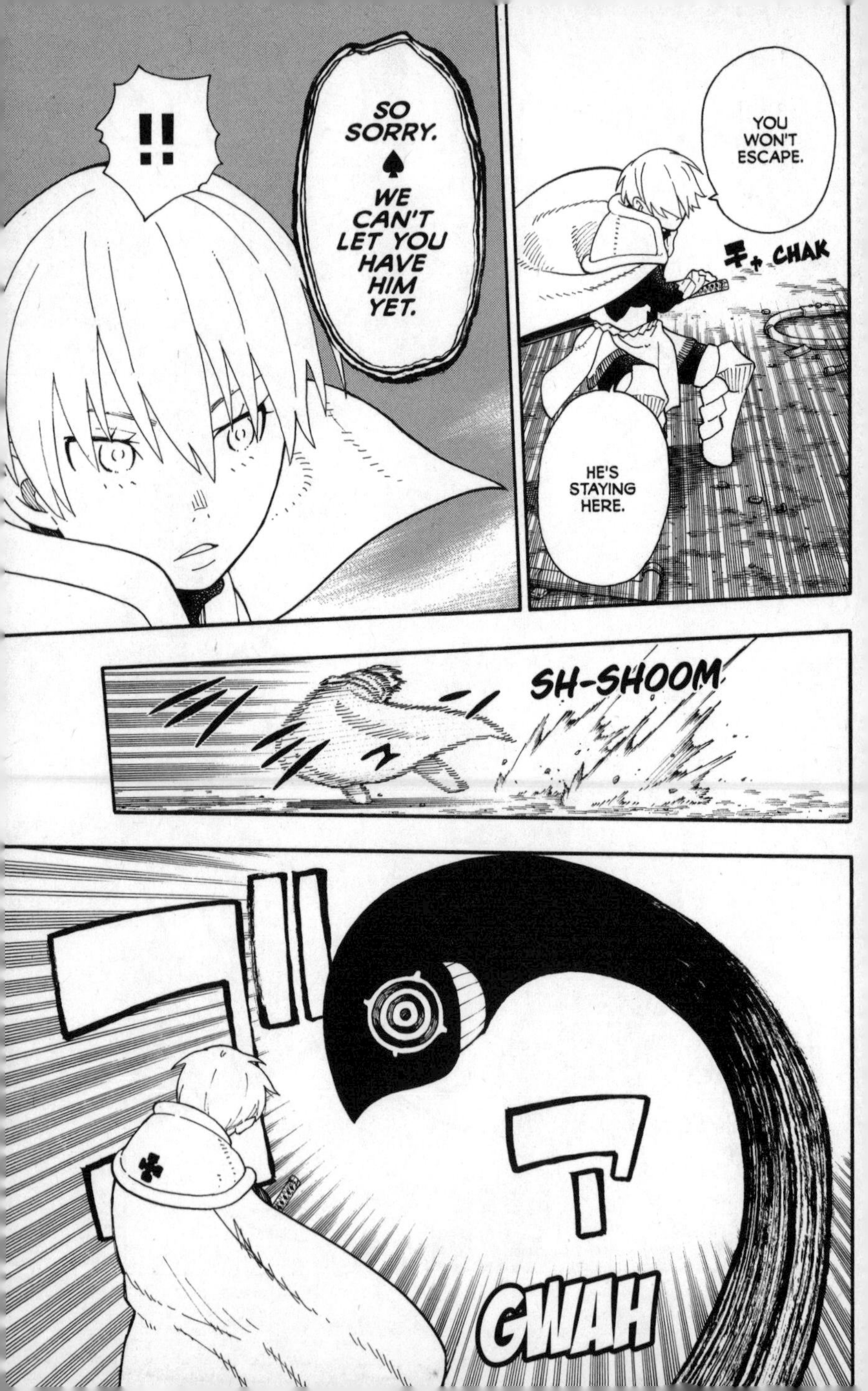
YOU WON'T ESCAPE.
CHAK
HE'S STAYING HERE.
!!
SO SORRY. ♠ WE CAN'T LET YOU HAVE HIM YET.
SH-SHOOM
GWAH

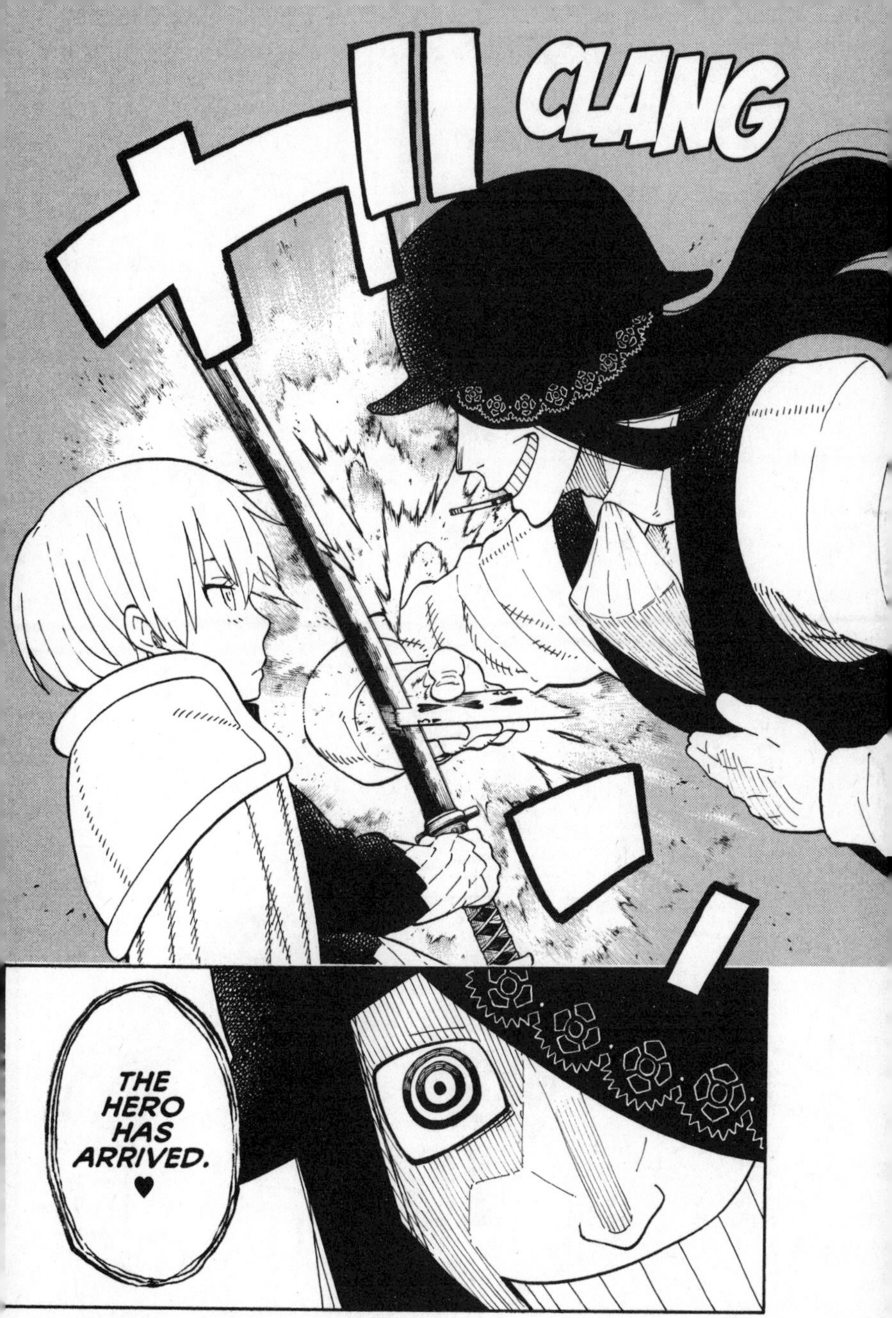
CLANG
THE HERO HAS ARRIVED. ♥

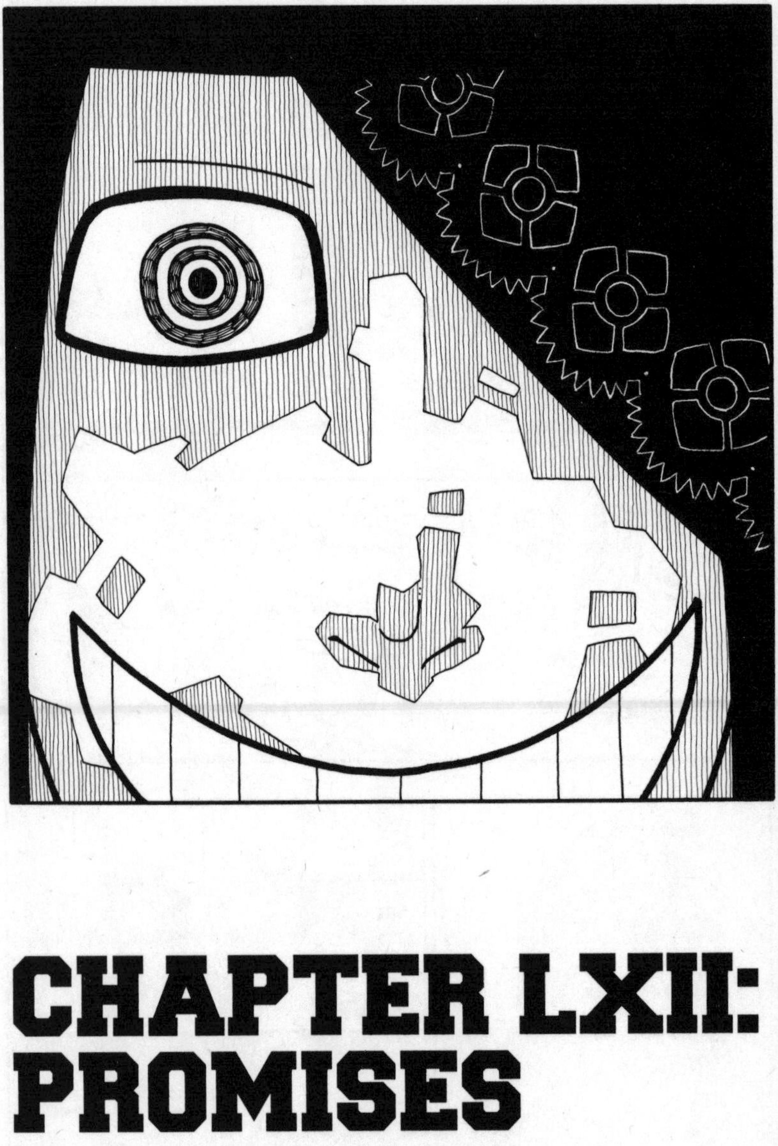

CHAPTER LXII: PROMISES

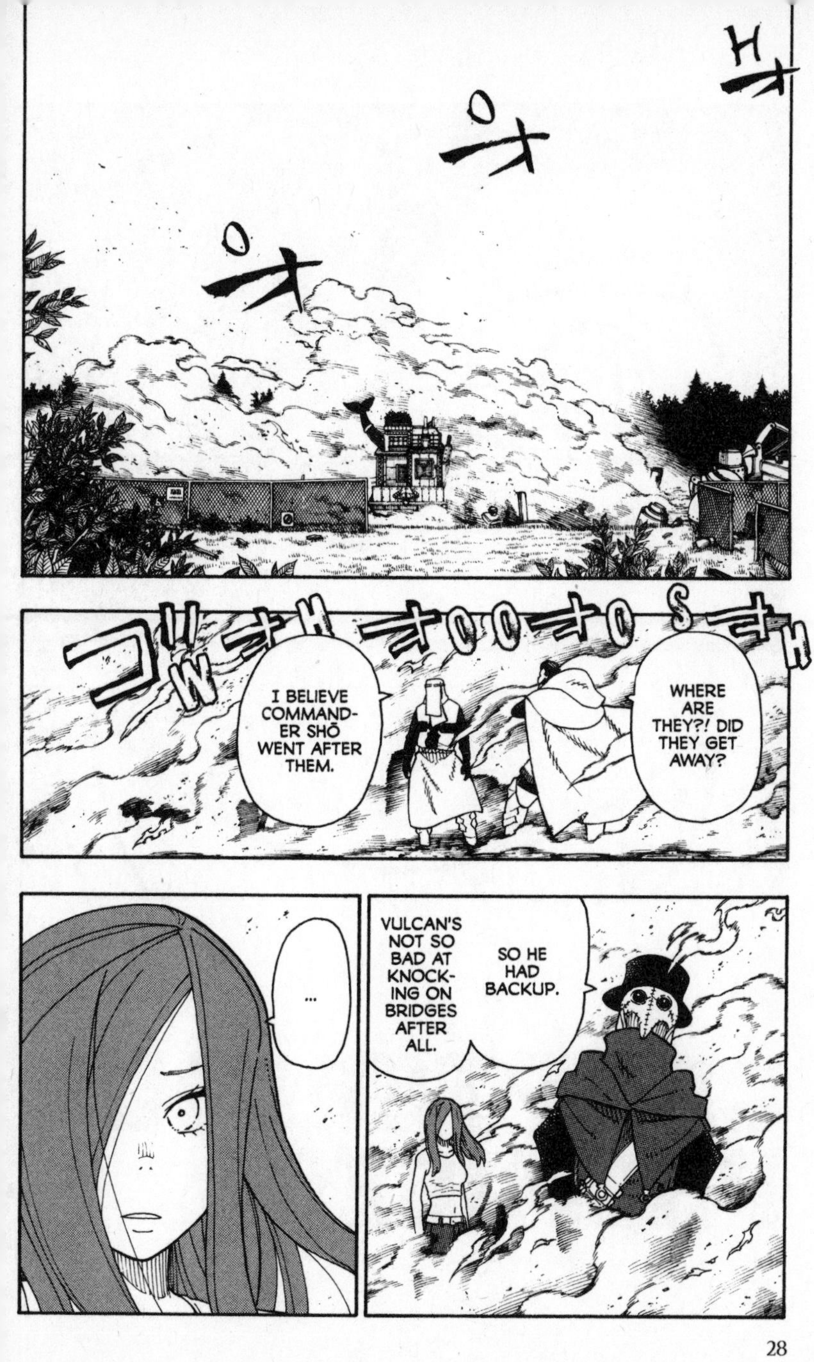
WHERE ARE THEY?! DID THEY GET AWAY?
I BELIEVE COMMANDER SHŌ WENT AFTER THEM.
SO HE HAD BACKUP.
VULCAN'S NOT SO BAD AT KNOCKING ON BRIDGES AFTER ALL.
...

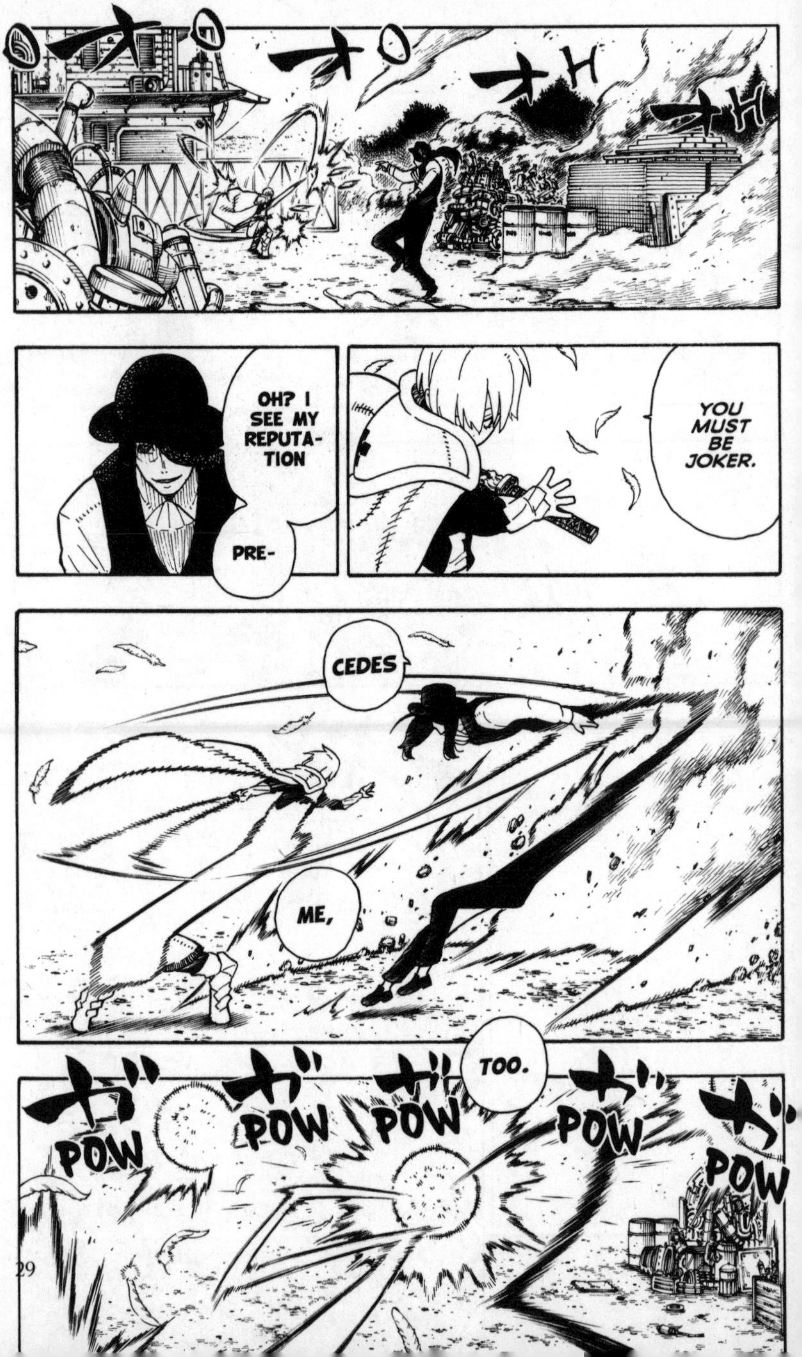
YOU MUST BE JOKER.
OH? I SEE MY REPUTATION
PRE-
CEDES
ME,
TOO.
POW
POW
POW
POW
POW

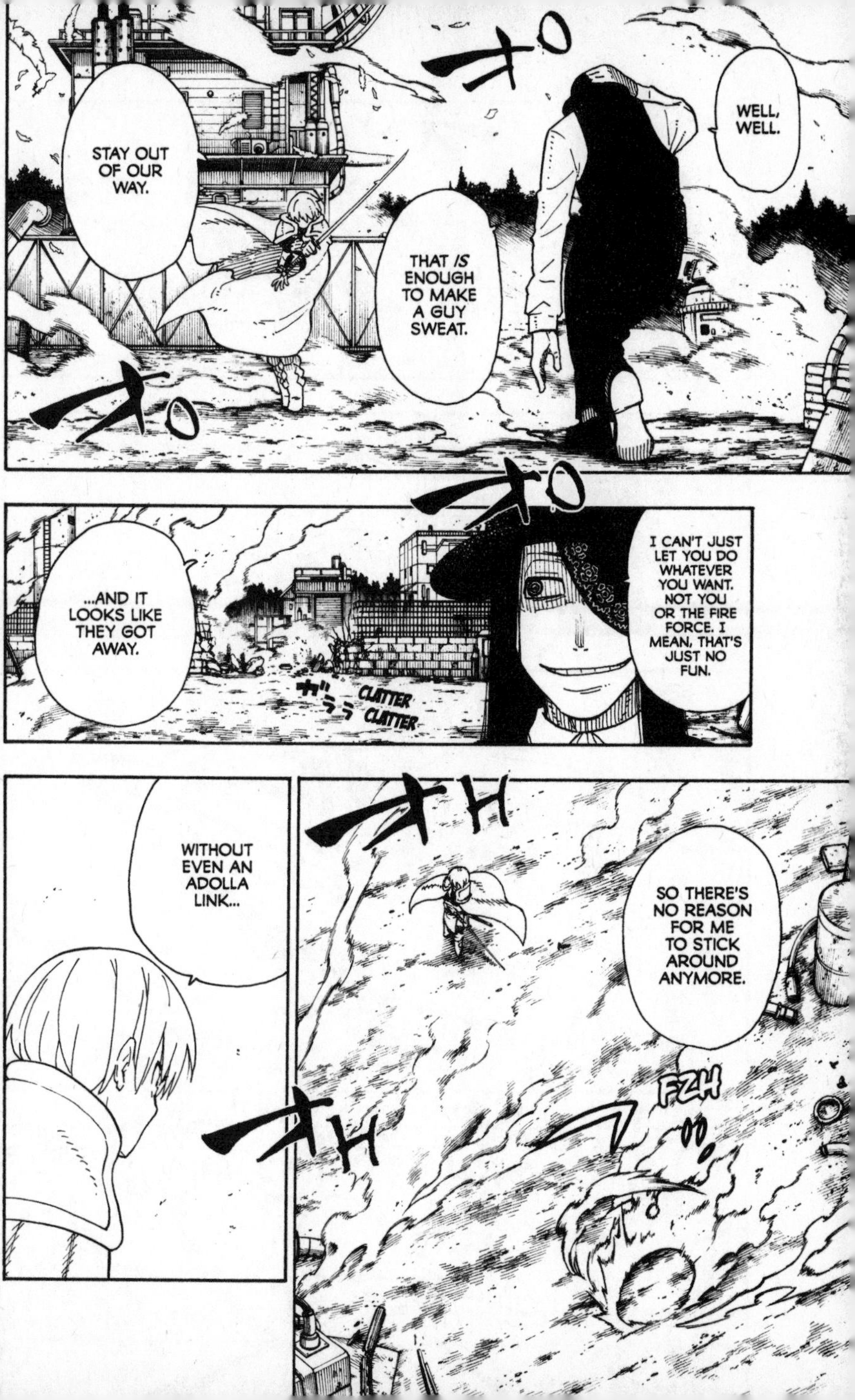
WELL, WELL.
THAT *IS* ENOUGH TO MAKE A GUY SWEAT.
STAY OUT OF OUR WAY.
I CAN'T JUST LET YOU DO WHATEVER YOU WANT. NOT YOU OR THE FIRE FORCE. I MEAN, THAT'S JUST NO FUN.
...AND IT LOOKS LIKE THEY GOT AWAY.
CLATTER CLATTER
SO THERE'S NO REASON FOR ME TO STICK AROUND ANYMORE.
FZH
WITHOUT EVEN AN ADOLLA LINK...

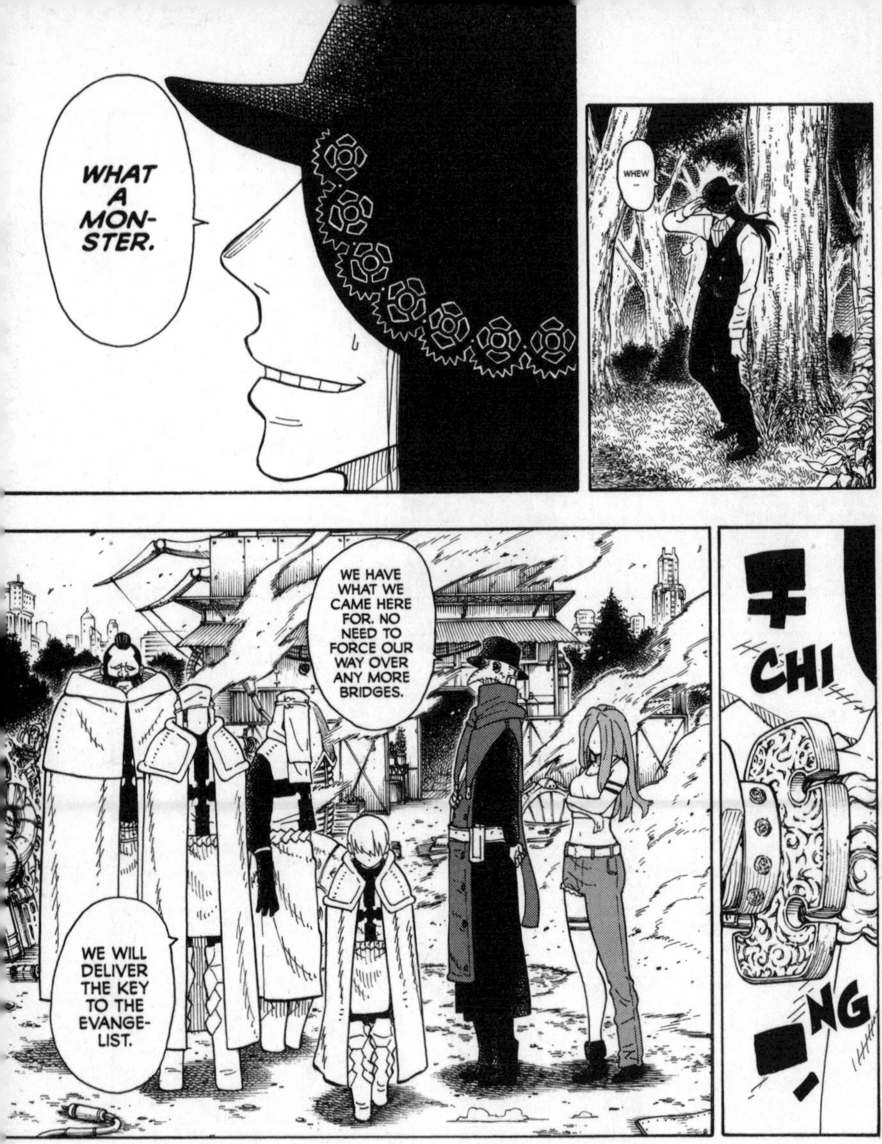
WHEW ...
WHAT A MON-STER.
CHI
NG
WE HAVE WHAT WE CAME HERE FOR. NO NEED TO FORCE OUR WAY OVER ANY MORE BRIDGES.
WE WILL DELIVER THE KEY TO THE EVANGE-LIST.

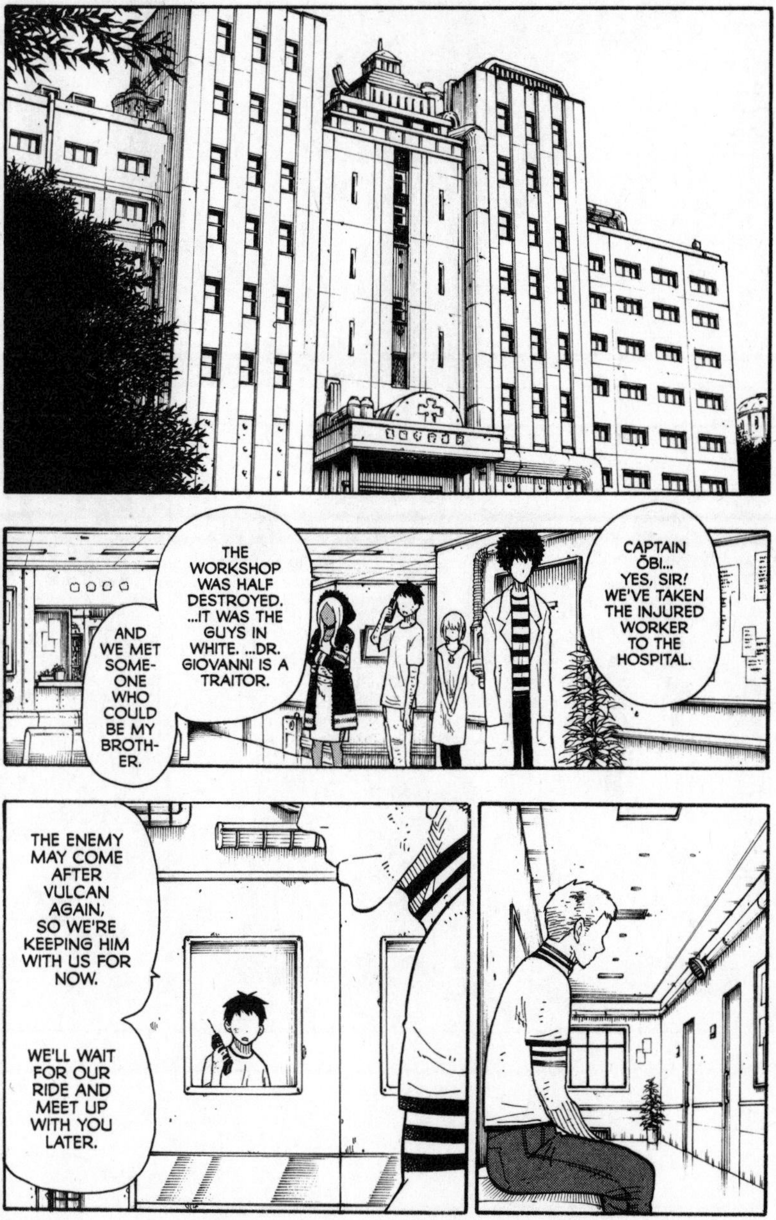
CAPTAIN ŌBI... YES, SIR! WE'VE TAKEN THE INJURED WORKER TO THE HOSPITAL.
THE WORKSHOP WAS HALF DESTROYED. ...IT WAS THE GUYS IN WHITE. ...DR. GIOVANNI IS A TRAITOR.
AND WE MET SOME-ONE WHO COULD BE MY BROTH-ER.
THE ENEMY MAY COME AFTER VULCAN AGAIN, SO WE'RE KEEPING HIM WITH US FOR NOW.
WE'LL WAIT FOR OUR RIDE AND MEET UP WITH YOU LATER.

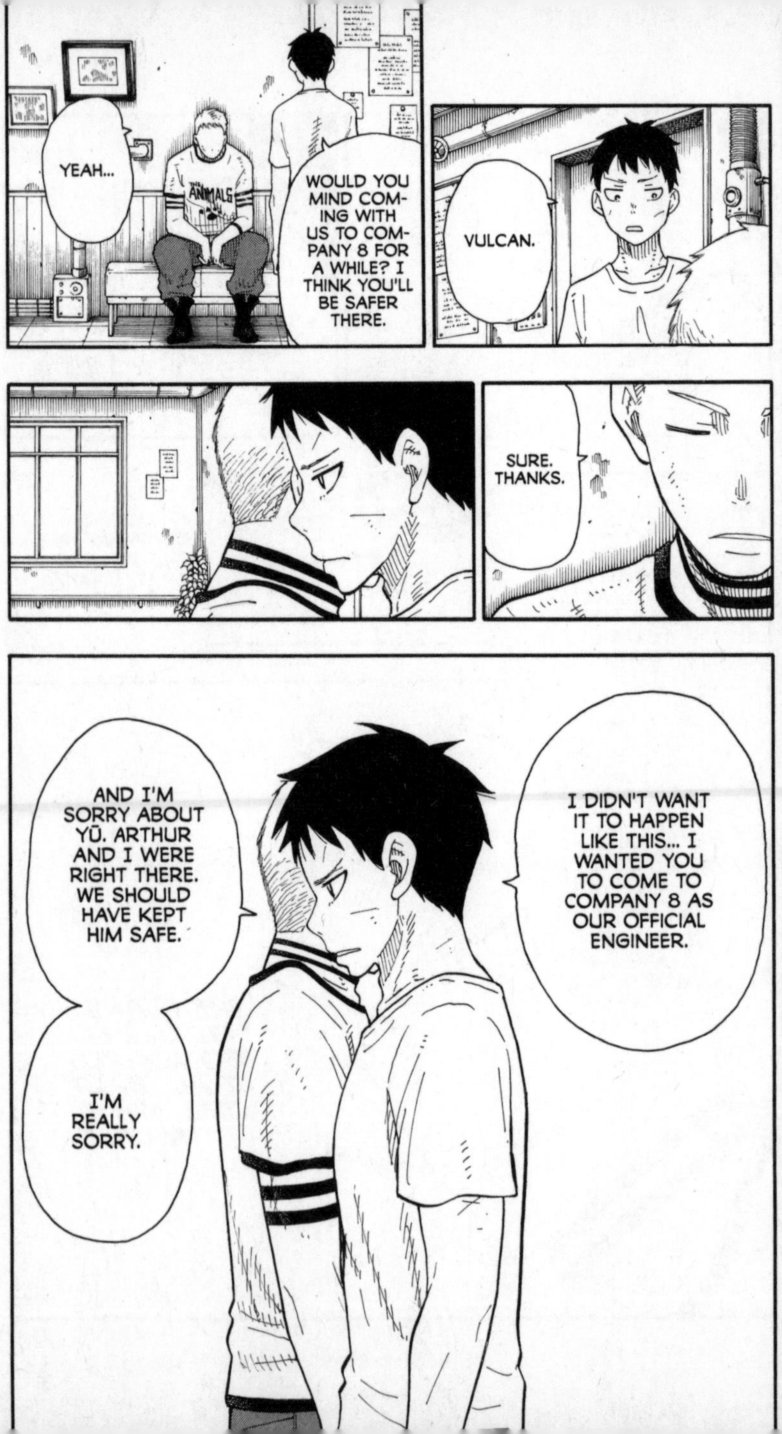
VULCAN.
WOULD YOU MIND COMING WITH US TO COMPANY 8 FOR A WHILE? I THINK YOU'LL BE SAFER THERE.
YEAH...
SURE. THANKS.
I DIDN'T WANT IT TO HAPPEN LIKE THIS... I WANTED YOU TO COME TO COMPANY 8 AS OUR OFFICIAL ENGINEER.
AND I'M SORRY ABOUT YŪ. ARTHUR AND I WERE RIGHT THERE. WE SHOULD HAVE KEPT HIM SAFE.
I'M REALLY SORRY.

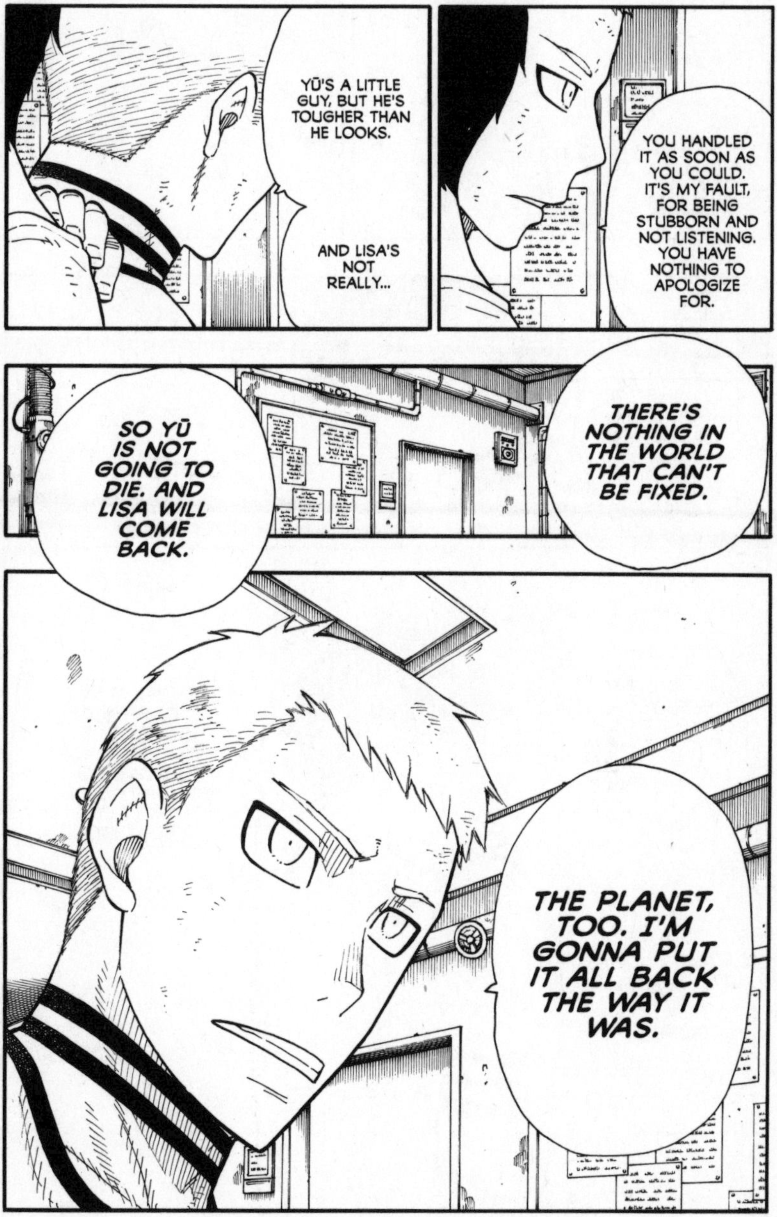
YOU HANDLED IT AS SOON AS YOU COULD. IT'S MY FAULT, FOR BEING STUBBORN AND NOT LISTENING. YOU HAVE NOTHING TO APOLOGIZE FOR.
YŪ'S A LITTLE GUY, BUT HE'S TOUGHER THAN HE LOOKS.
AND LISA'S NOT REALLY...
THERE'S NOTHING IN THE WORLD THAT CAN'T BE FIXED.
SO YŪ IS NOT GOING TO DIE. AND LISA WILL COME BACK.
THE PLANET, TOO. I'M GONNA PUT IT ALL BACK THE WAY IT WAS.

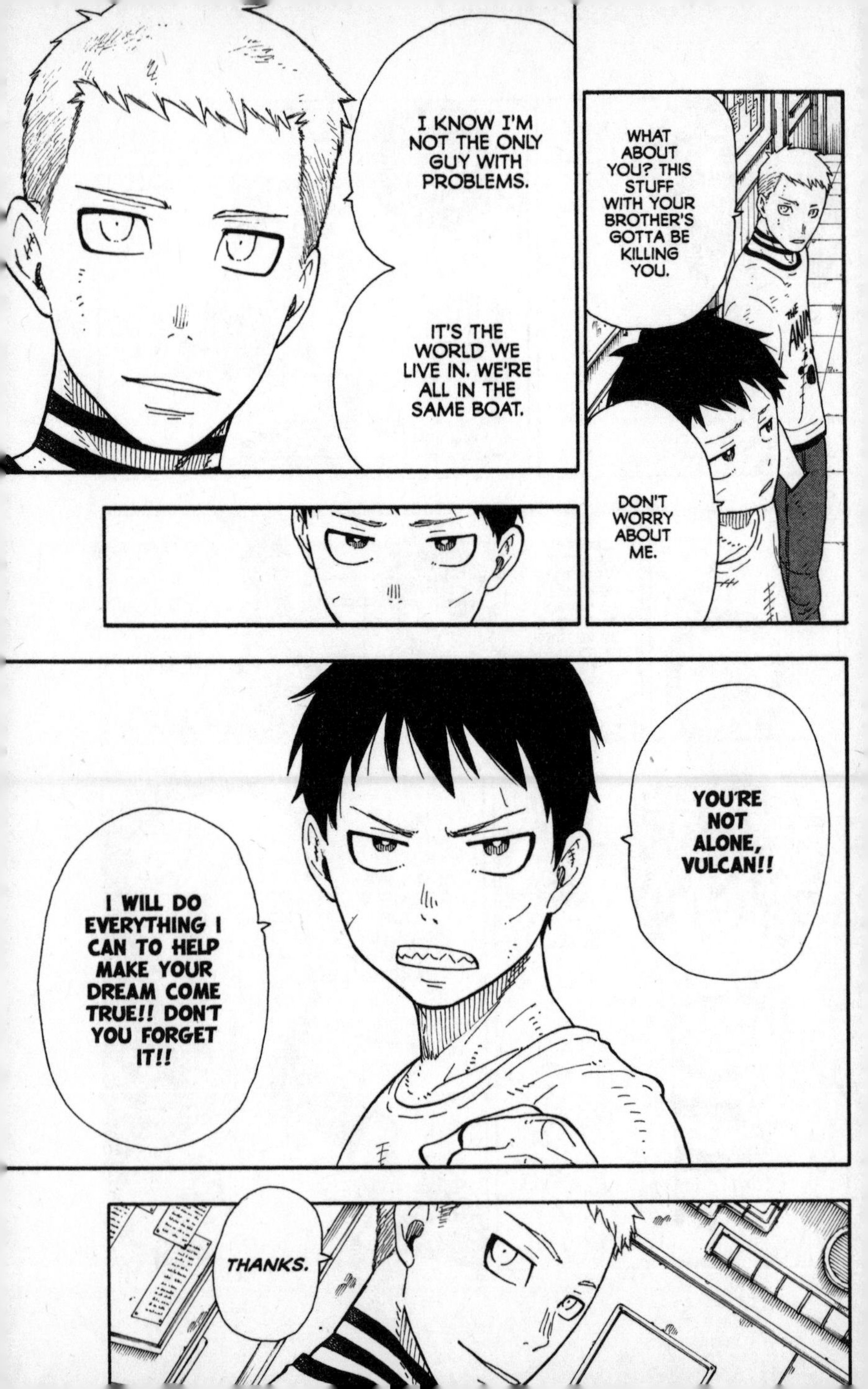
WHAT ABOUT YOU? THIS STUFF WITH YOUR BROTHER'S GOTTA BE KILLING YOU.
DON'T WORRY ABOUT ME.
I KNOW I'M NOT THE ONLY GUY WITH PROBLEMS.
IT'S THE WORLD WE LIVE IN. WE'RE ALL IN THE SAME BOAT.
YOU'RE NOT ALONE, VULCAN!!
I WILL DO EVERYTHING I CAN TO HELP MAKE YOUR DREAM COME TRUE!! DON'T YOU FORGET IT!!
THANKS.

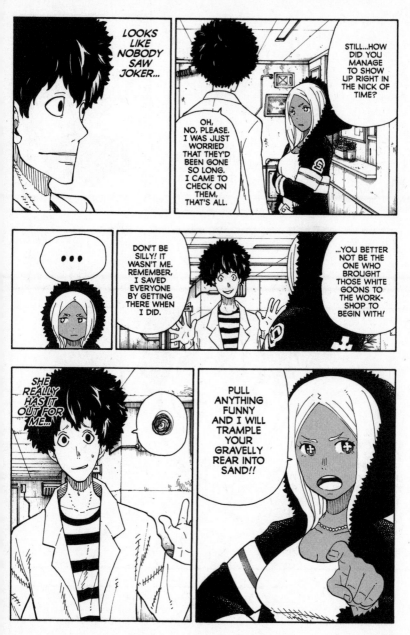

STILL...HOW DID YOU MANAGE TO SHOW UP RIGHT IN THE NICK OF TIME?
OH, NO, PLEASE. I WAS JUST WORRIED THAT THEY'D BEEN GONE SO LONG. I CAME TO CHECK ON THEM, THAT'S ALL.
LOOKS LIKE NOBODY SAW JOKER...
...YOU BETTER NOT BE THE ONE WHO BROUGHT THOSE WHITE GOONS TO THE WORK-SHOP TO BEGIN WITH!
DON'T BE SILLY! IT WASN'T ME. REMEMBER, I SAVED EVERYONE BY GETTING THERE WHEN I DID.
...
PULL ANYTHING FUNNY AND I WILL TRAMPLE YOUR GRAVELLY REAR INTO SAND!!
SHE REALLY HAS IT OUT FOR ME...

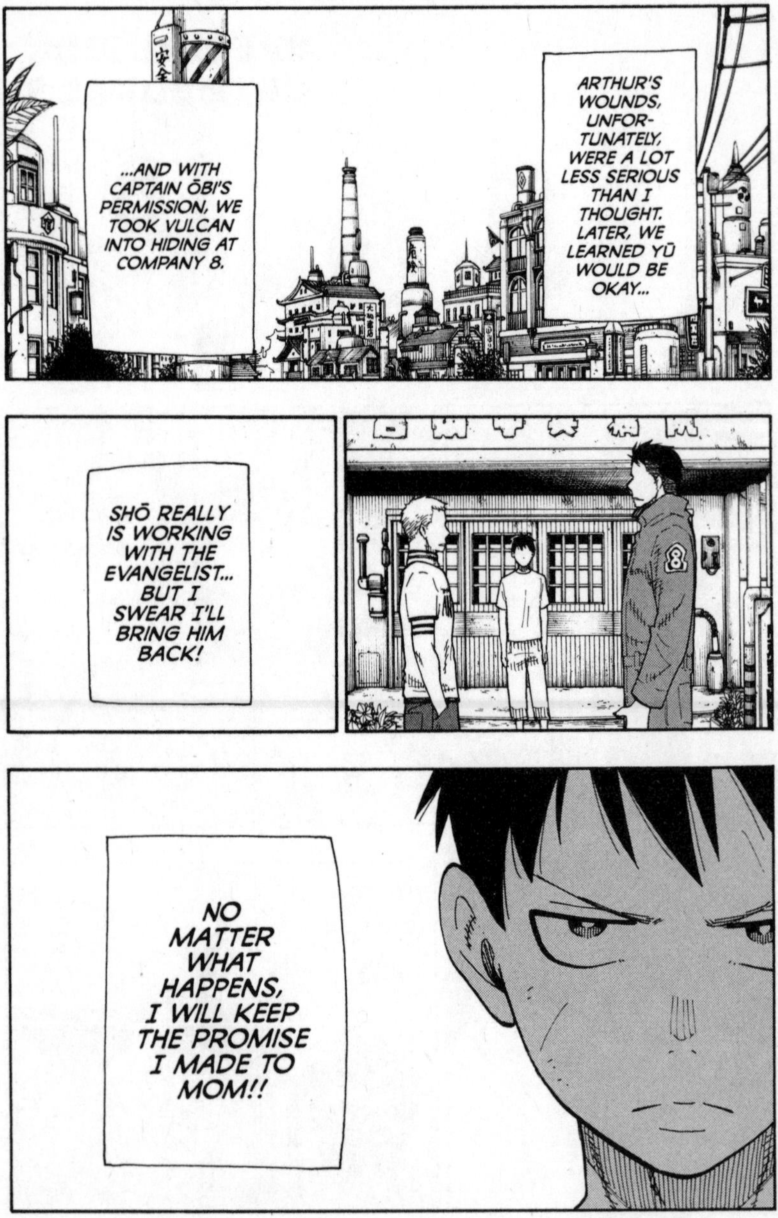
ARTHUR'S WOUNDS, UNFOR-TUNATELY, WERE A LOT LESS SERIOUS THAN I THOUGHT. LATER, WE LEARNED YŪ WOULD BE OKAY...
...AND WITH CAPTAIN ŌBI'S PERMISSION, WE TOOK VULCAN INTO HIDING AT COMPANY 8.
SHŌ REALLY IS WORKING WITH THE EVANGELIST... BUT I SWEAR I'LL BRING HIM BACK!
NO MATTER WHAT HAPPENS, I WILL KEEP THE PROMISE I MADE TO MOM!!

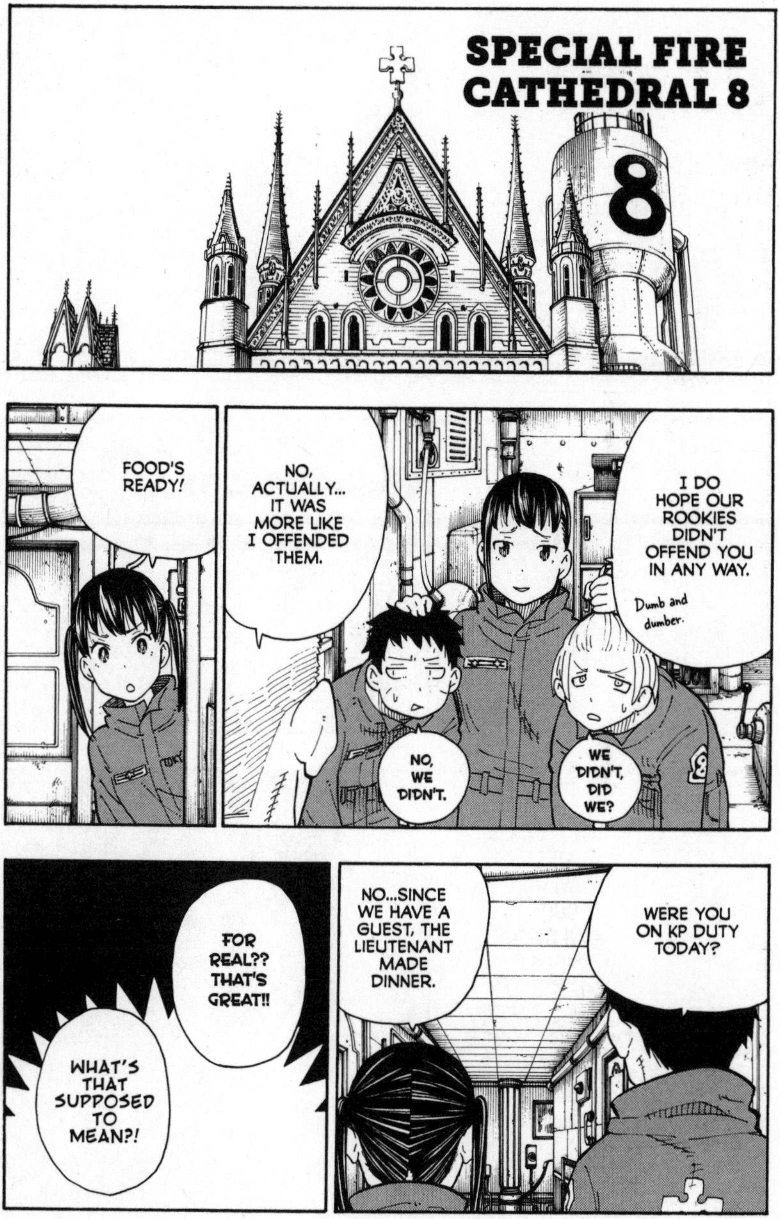
SPECIAL FIRE CATHEDRAL 8
8
I DO HOPE OUR ROOKIES DIDN'T OFFEND YOU IN ANY WAY.
Dumb and dumber.
NO, ACTUALLY... IT WAS MORE LIKE I OFFENDED THEM.
WE DIDN'T, DID WE?
NO, WE DIDN'T.
FOOD'S READY!
WERE YOU ON KP DUTY TODAY?
NO...SINCE WE HAVE A GUEST, THE LIEUTENANT MADE DINNER.
FOR REAL?? THAT'S GREAT!!
WHAT'S THAT SUPPOSED TO MEAN?!

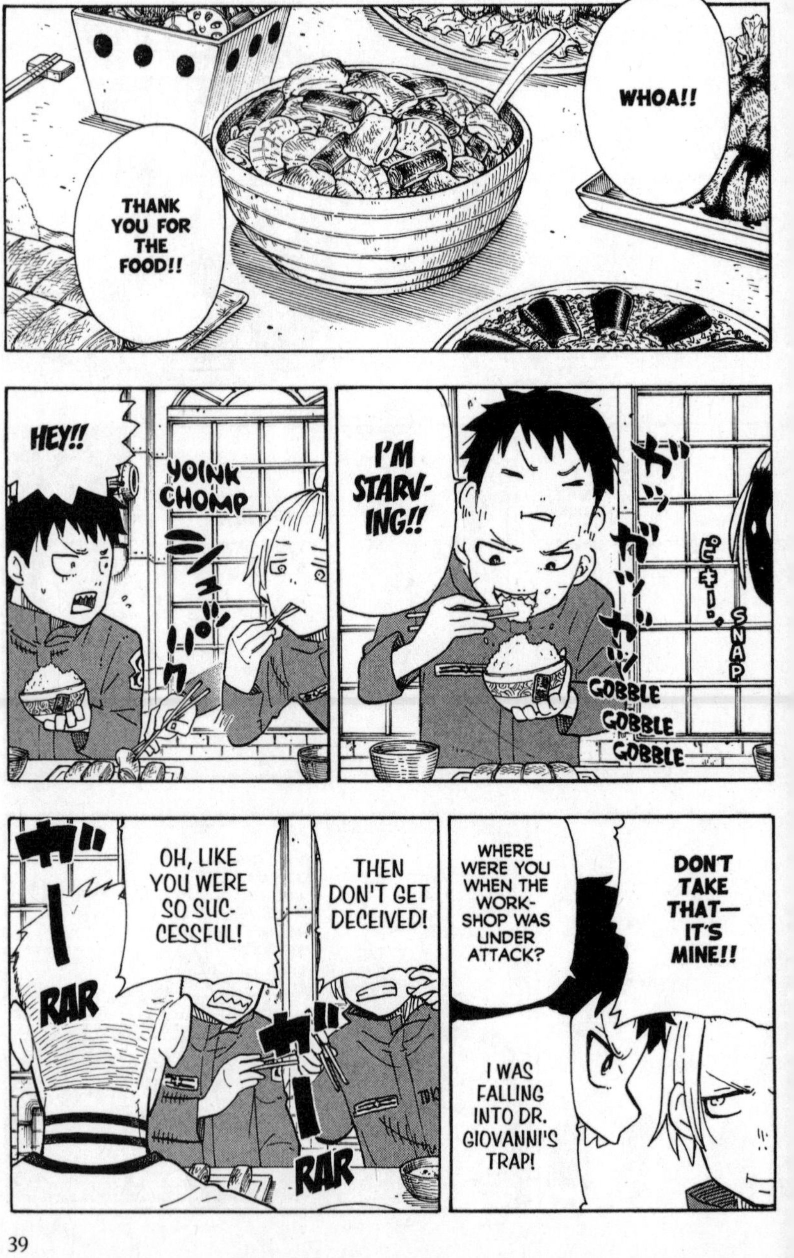
WHOA!!
THANK YOU FOR THE FOOD!!
I'M STARV-ING!!
GOBBLE GOBBLE GOBBLE
SNAP
HEY!!
YOINK CHOMP
DON'T TAKE THAT— IT'S MINE!!
WHERE WERE YOU WHEN THE WORK-SHOP WAS UNDER ATTACK?
I WAS FALLING INTO DR. GIOVANNI'S TRAP!
THEN DON'T GET DECEIVED!
OH, LIKE YOU WERE SO SUC-CESSFUL!
RAR
RAR

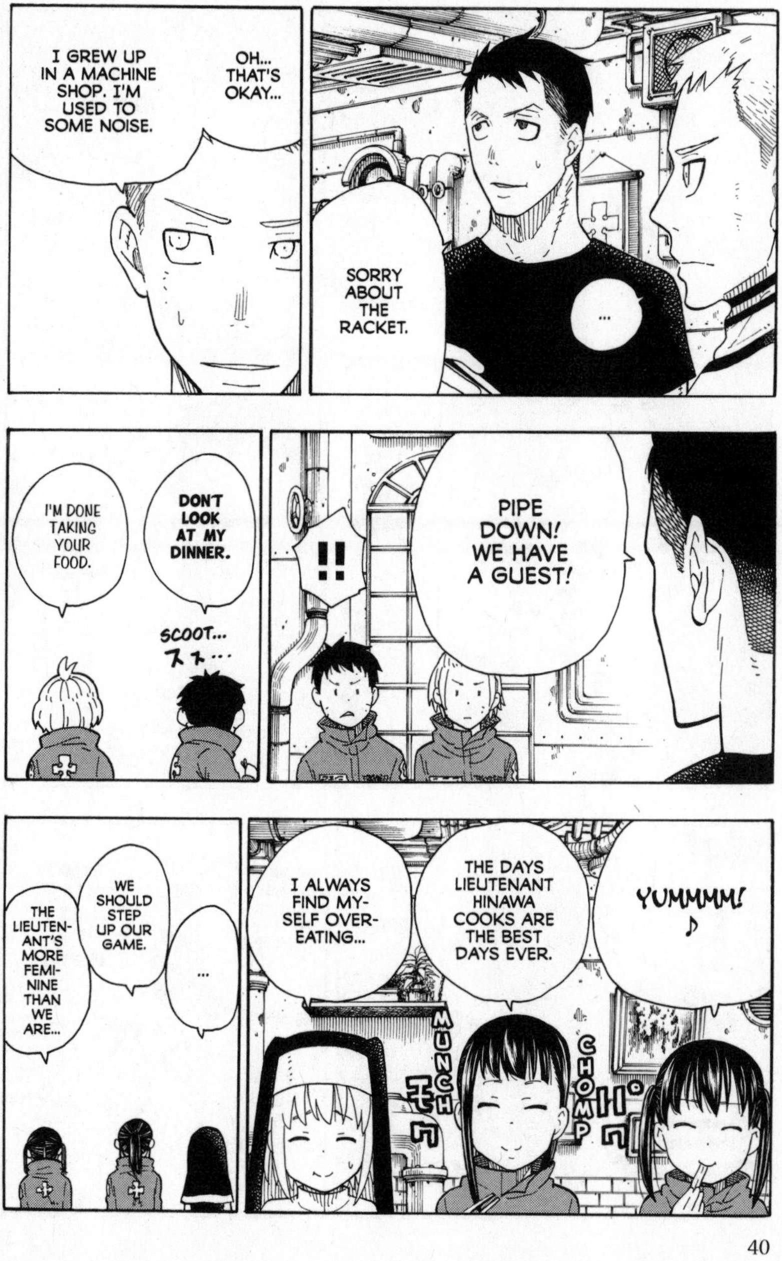
SORRY ABOUT THE RACKET.
...
OH... THAT'S OKAY...
I GREW UP IN A MACHINE SHOP. I'M USED TO SOME NOISE.
PIPE DOWN! WE HAVE A GUEST!
!!
DON'T LOOK AT MY DINNER.
SCOOT...
I'M DONE TAKING YOUR FOOD.
YUMMMM! ♪
THE DAYS LIEUTENANT HINAWA COOKS ARE THE BEST DAYS EVER.
CHOMP
I ALWAYS FIND MYSELF OVER-EATING...
MUNCH
...
WE SHOULD STEP UP OUR GAME.
THE LIEUTENANT'S MORE FEMININE THAN WE ARE...

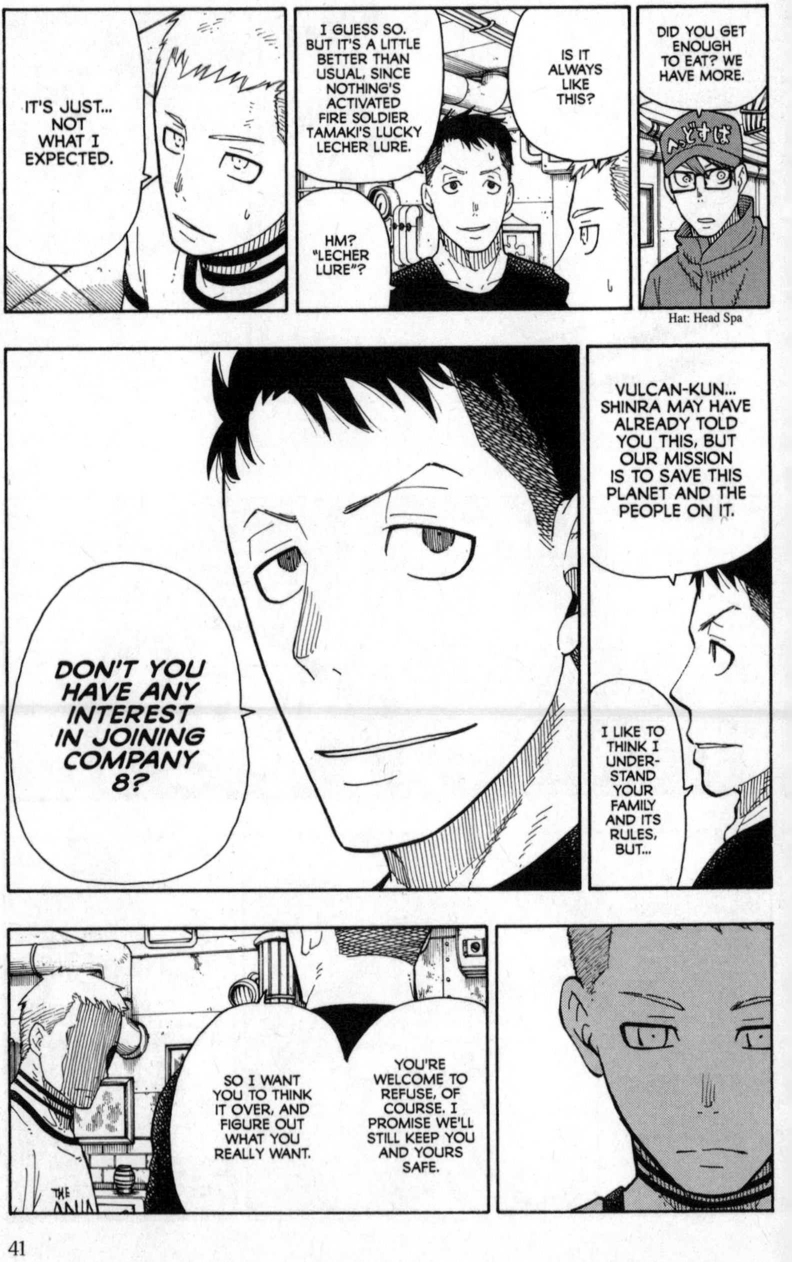
DID YOU GET ENOUGH TO EAT? WE HAVE MORE.
IS IT ALWAYS LIKE THIS?
I GUESS SO. BUT IT'S A LITTLE BETTER THAN USUAL, SINCE NOTHING'S ACTIVATED FIRE SOLDIER TAMAKI'S LUCKY LECHER LURE.
HM? "LECHER LURE"?
IT'S JUST... NOT WHAT I EXPECTED.
VULCAN-KUN... SHINRA MAY HAVE ALREADY TOLD YOU THIS, BUT OUR MISSION IS TO SAVE THIS PLANET AND THE PEOPLE ON IT.
I LIKE TO THINK I UNDER-STAND YOUR FAMILY AND ITS RULES, BUT...
DON'T YOU HAVE ANY INTEREST IN JOINING COMPANY 8?
YOU'RE WELCOME TO REFUSE, OF COURSE. I PROMISE WE'LL STILL KEEP YOU AND YOURS SAFE.
SO I WANT YOU TO THINK IT OVER, AND FIGURE OUT WHAT YOU REALLY WANT.

Hat: Head Spa

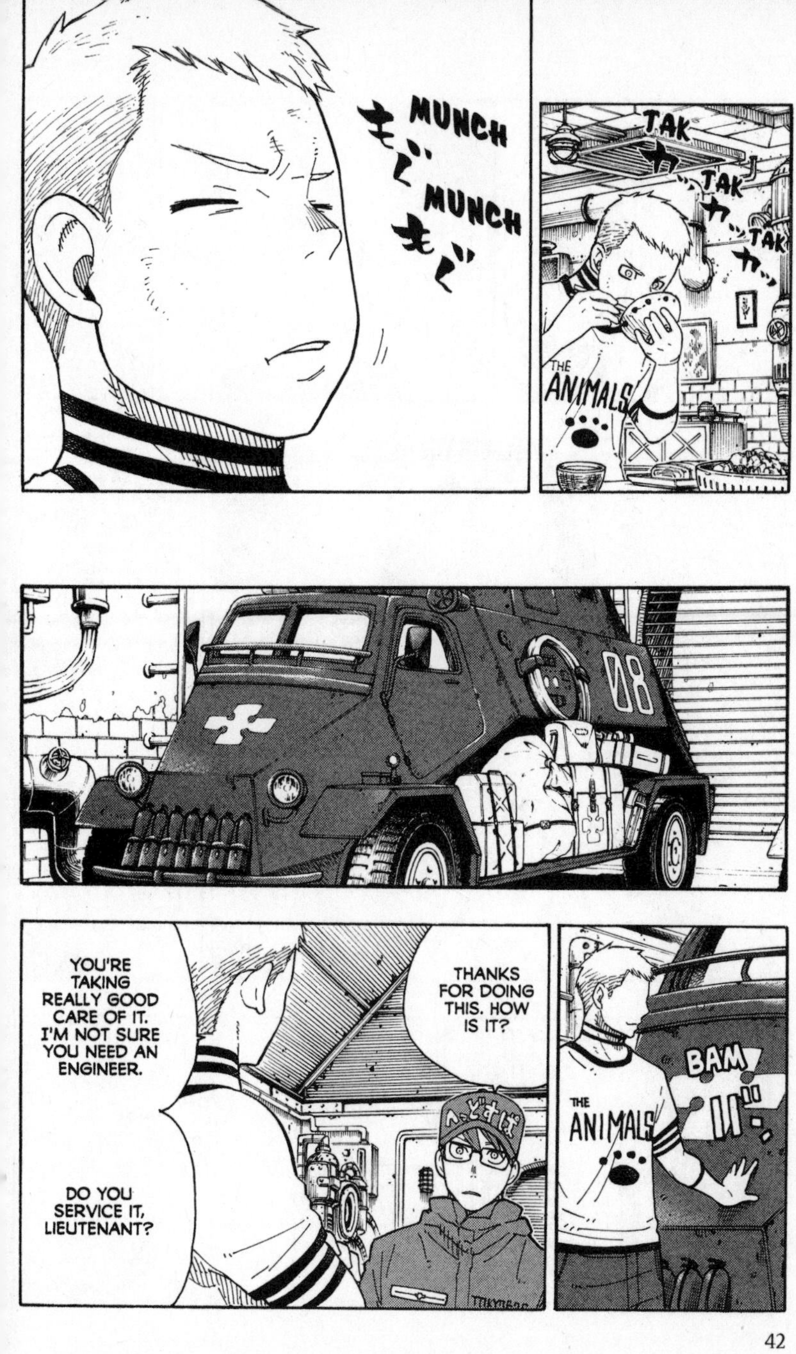
TAK
TAK
TAK
MUNCH
MUNCH
08
THE ANIMALS
BAM
THE ANIMALS
THANKS FOR DOING THIS. HOW IS IT?
YOU'RE TAKING REALLY GOOD CARE OF IT. I'M NOT SURE YOU NEED AN ENGINEER.
DO YOU SERVICE IT, LIEUTENANT?

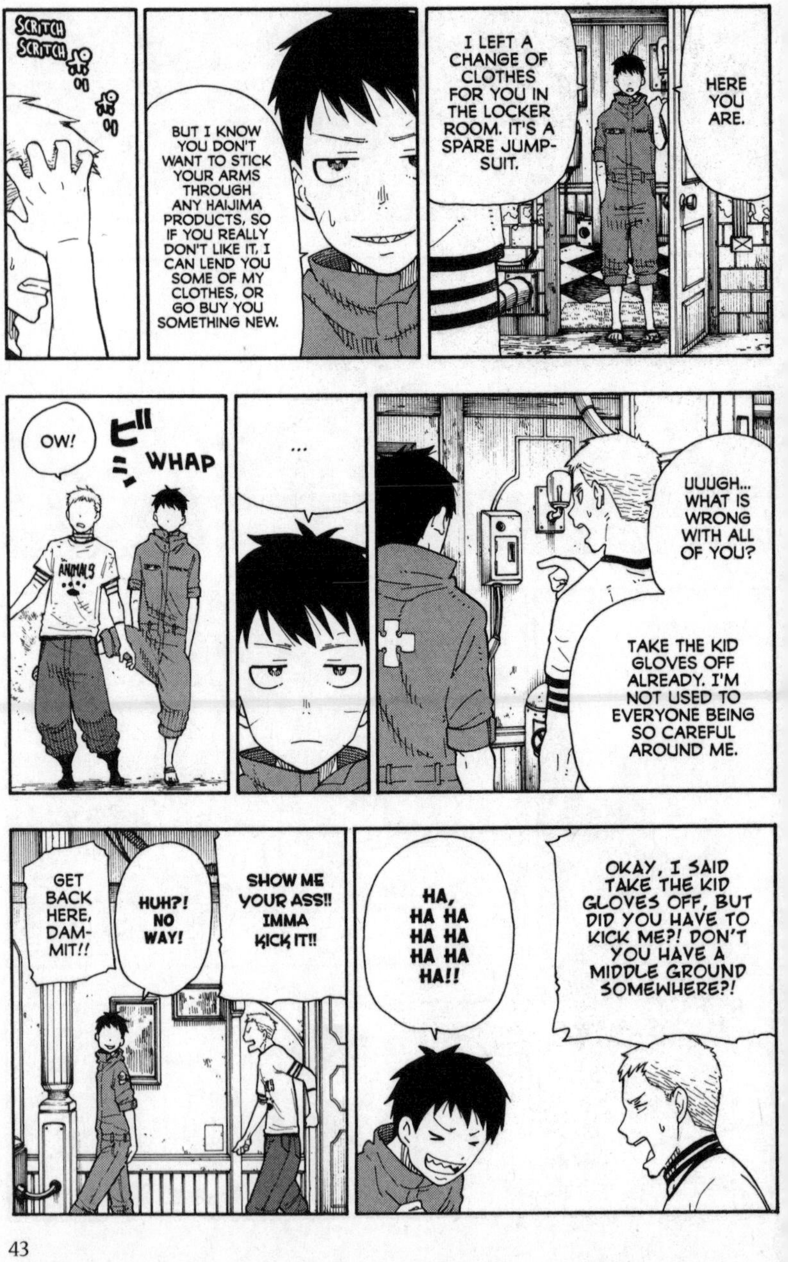
HERE YOU ARE.
I LEFT A CHANGE OF CLOTHES FOR YOU IN THE LOCKER ROOM. IT'S A SPARE JUMP-SUIT.
BUT I KNOW YOU DON'T WANT TO STICK YOUR ARMS THROUGH ANY HAIJIMA PRODUCTS, SO IF YOU REALLY DON'T LIKE IT, I CAN LEND YOU SOME OF MY CLOTHES, OR GO BUY YOU SOMETHING NEW.
SCRITCH SCRITCH
UUUGH... WHAT IS WRONG WITH ALL OF YOU?
TAKE THE KID GLOVES OFF ALREADY. I'M NOT USED TO EVERYONE BEING SO CAREFUL AROUND ME.
...
WHAP
OW!
OKAY, I SAID TAKE THE KID GLOVES OFF, BUT DID YOU HAVE TO KICK ME?! DON'T YOU HAVE A MIDDLE GROUND SOMEWHERE?!
HA, HA HA HA HA HA HA HA!!
SHOW ME YOUR ASS!! IMMA KICK IT!!
HUH?! NO WAY!
GET BACK HERE, DAM-MIT!!

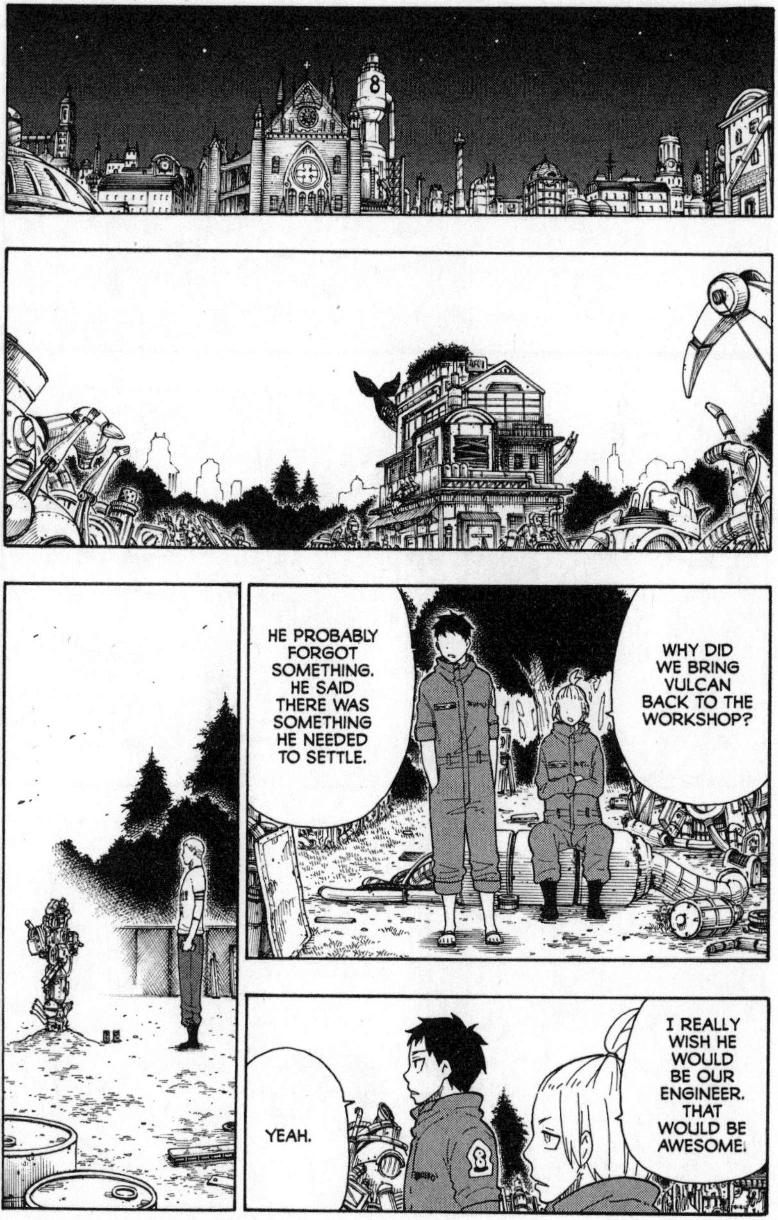
WHY DID WE BRING VULCAN BACK TO THE WORKSHOP?
HE PROBABLY FORGOT SOMETHING. HE SAID THERE WAS SOMETHING HE NEEDED TO SETTLE.
I REALLY WISH HE WOULD BE OUR ENGINEER. THAT WOULD BE AWESOME!
YEAH.

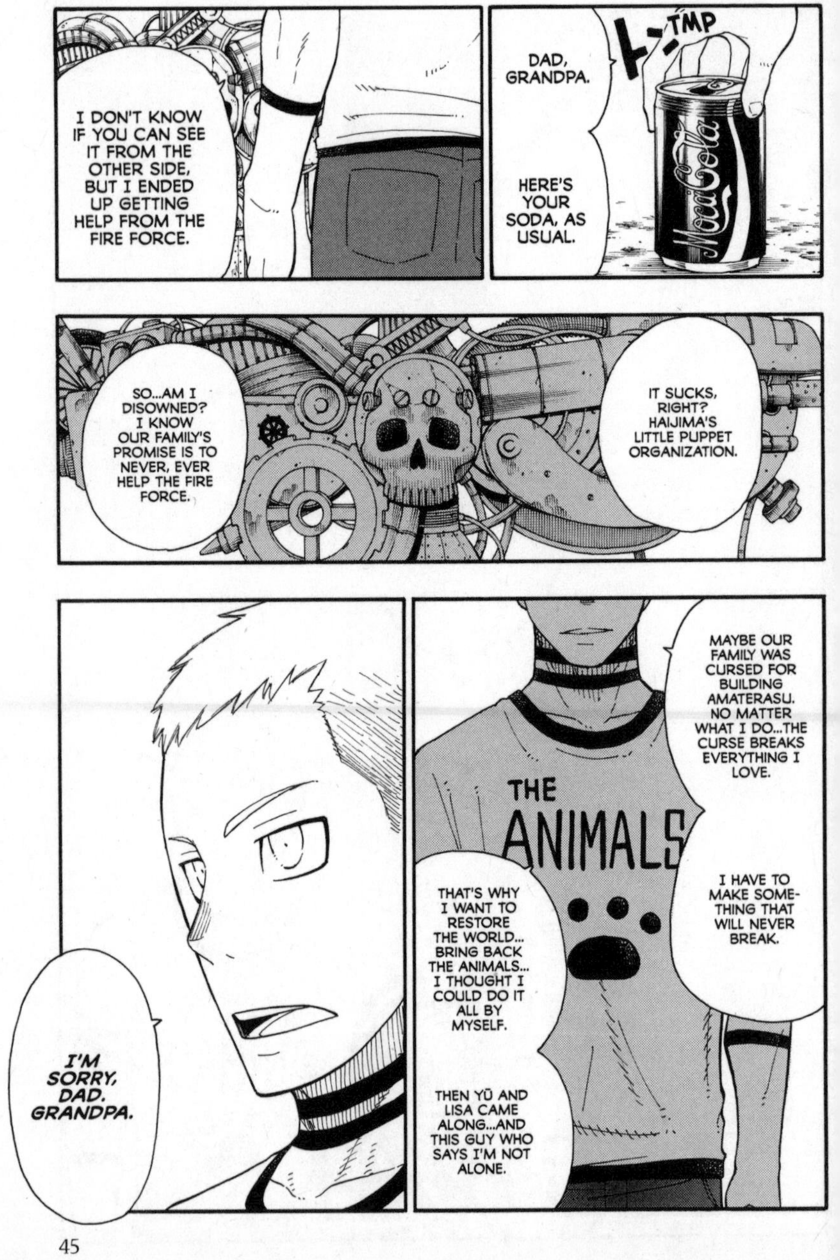
TMP
DAD, GRANDPA.
HERE'S YOUR SODA, AS USUAL.
MocaCola
I DON'T KNOW IF YOU CAN SEE IT FROM THE OTHER SIDE, BUT I ENDED UP GETTING HELP FROM THE FIRE FORCE.
IT SUCKS, RIGHT? HAIJIMA'S LITTLE PUPPET ORGANIZATION.
SO...AM I DISOWNED? I KNOW OUR FAMILY'S PROMISE IS TO NEVER, EVER HELP THE FIRE FORCE.
MAYBE OUR FAMILY WAS CURSED FOR BUILDING AMATERASU. NO MATTER WHAT I DO...THE CURSE BREAKS EVERYTHING I LOVE.
THE ANIMALS
I HAVE TO MAKE SOME-THING THAT WILL NEVER BREAK.
THAT'S WHY I WANT TO RESTORE THE WORLD... BRING BACK THE ANIMALS... I THOUGHT I COULD DO IT ALL BY MYSELF.
THEN YŪ AND LISA CAME ALONG...AND THIS GUY WHO SAYS I'M NOT ALONE.
I'M SORRY, DAD. GRANDPA.

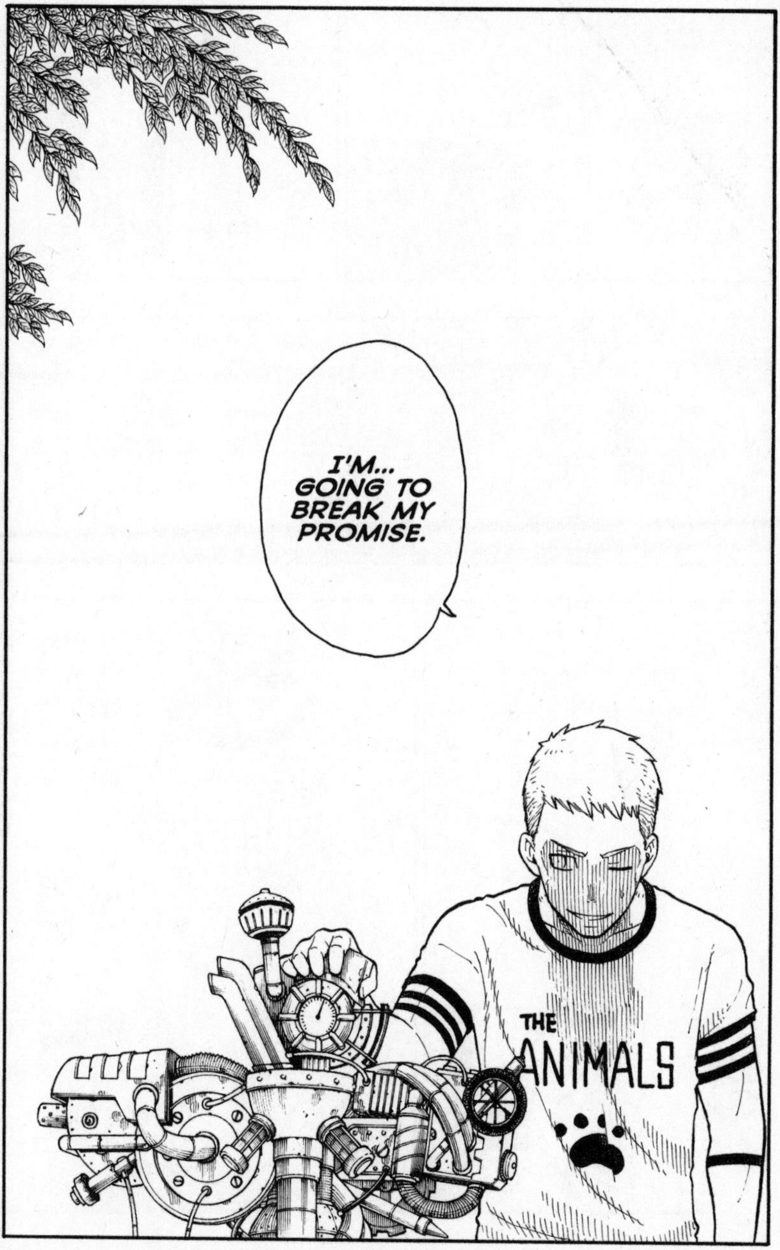
I'M... GOING TO BREAK MY PROMISE.
THE ANIMALS

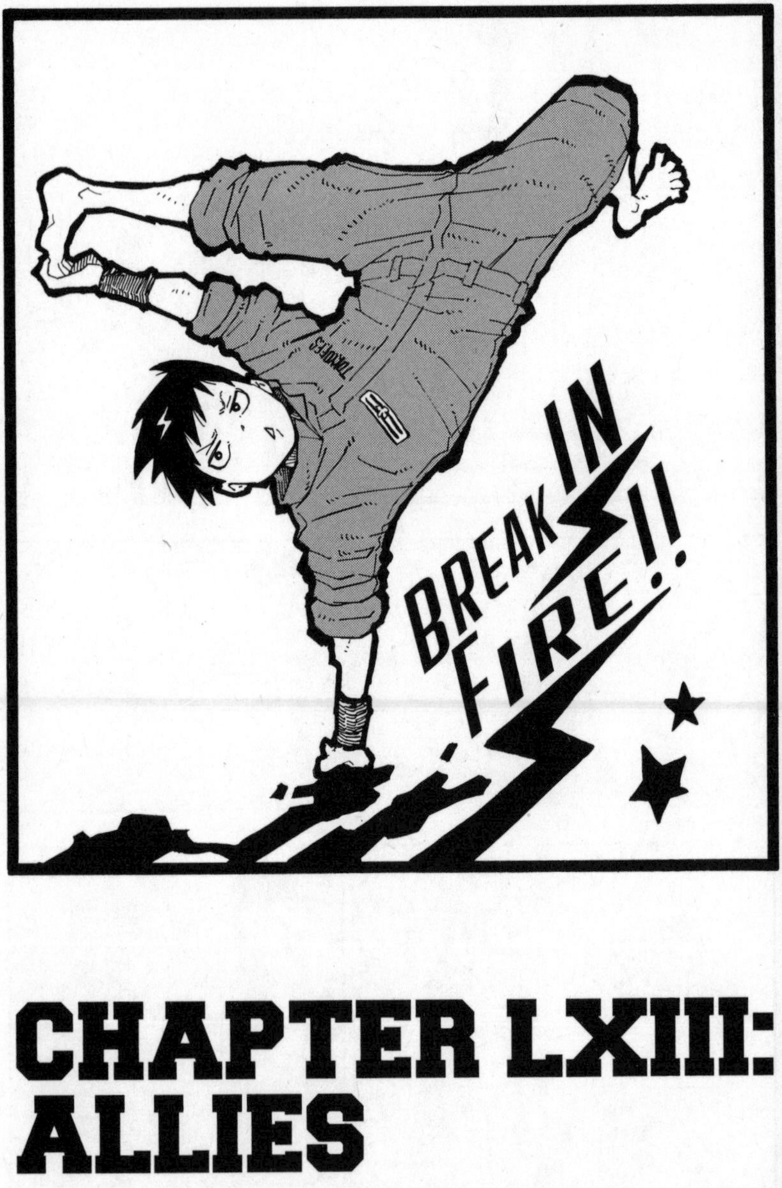
BREAK IN FIRE!!
TOKYO F.S

CHAPTER LXIII: ALLIES

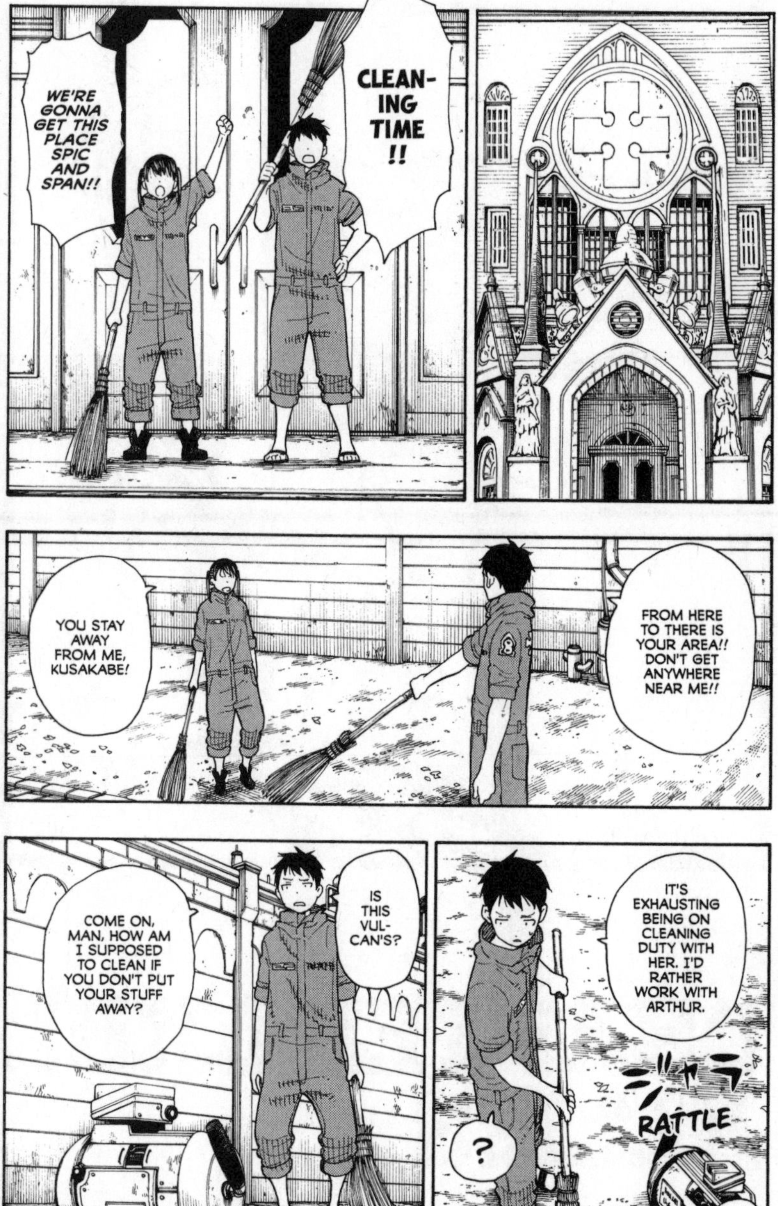
CLEAN-ING TIME!!
WE'RE GONNA GET THIS PLACE SPIC AND SPAN!!
FROM HERE TO THERE IS YOUR AREA!! DON'T GET ANYWHERE NEAR ME!!
YOU STAY AWAY FROM ME, KUSAKABE!
IT'S EXHAUSTING BEING ON CLEANING DUTY WITH HER. I'D RATHER WORK WITH ARTHUR.
RATTLE
?
IS THIS VUL-CAN'S?
COME ON, MAN, HOW AM I SUPPOSED TO CLEAN IF YOU DON'T PUT YOUR STUFF AWAY?

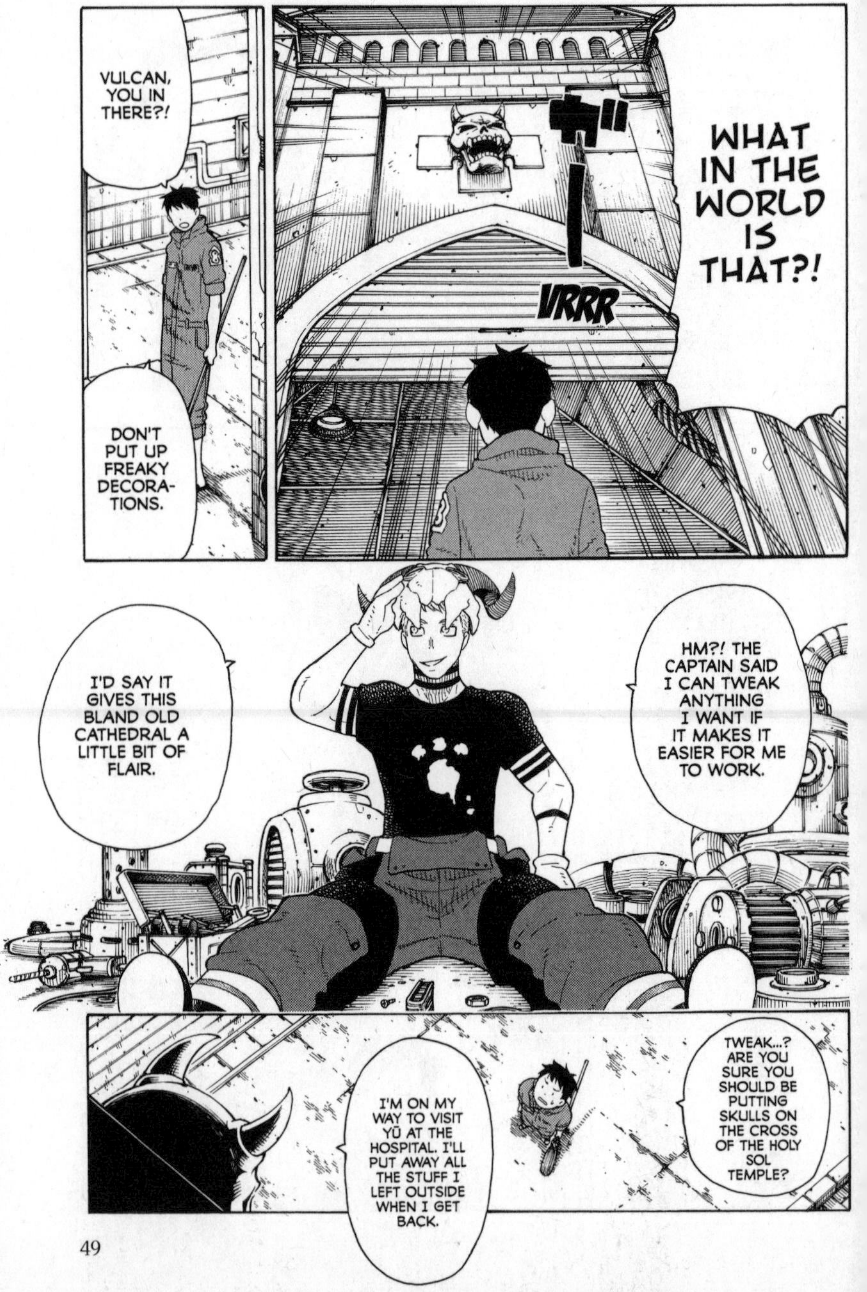
WHAT IN THE WORLD IS THAT?!
VRRR
VULCAN, YOU IN THERE?!
DON'T PUT UP FREAKY DECORA-TIONS.
HM?! THE CAPTAIN SAID I CAN TWEAK ANYTHING I WANT IF IT MAKES IT EASIER FOR ME TO WORK.
I'D SAY IT GIVES THIS BLAND OLD CATHEDRAL A LITTLE BIT OF FLAIR.
TWEAK...? ARE YOU SURE YOU SHOULD BE PUTTING SKULLS ON THE CROSS OF THE HOLY SOL TEMPLE?
I'M ON MY WAY TO VISIT YŪ AT THE HOSPITAL. I'LL PUT AWAY ALL THE STUFF I LEFT OUTSIDE WHEN I GET BACK.

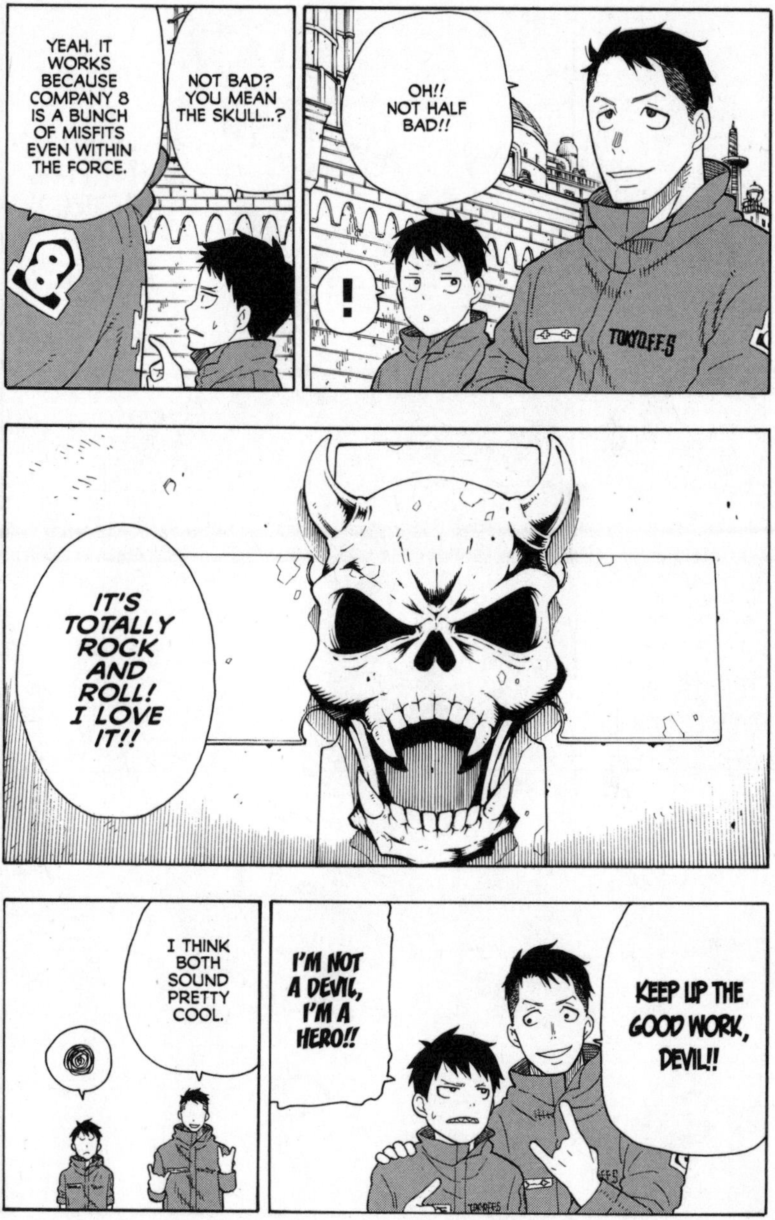
OH!! NOT HALF BAD!!
!
NOT BAD? YOU MEAN THE SKULL...?
YEAH. IT WORKS BECAUSE COMPANY 8 IS A BUNCH OF MISFITS EVEN WITHIN THE FORCE.
IT'S TOTALLY ROCK AND ROLL! I LOVE IT!!
KEEP UP THE GOOD WORK, DEVIL!!
I'M NOT A DEVIL, I'M A HERO!!
I THINK BOTH SOUND PRETTY COOL.

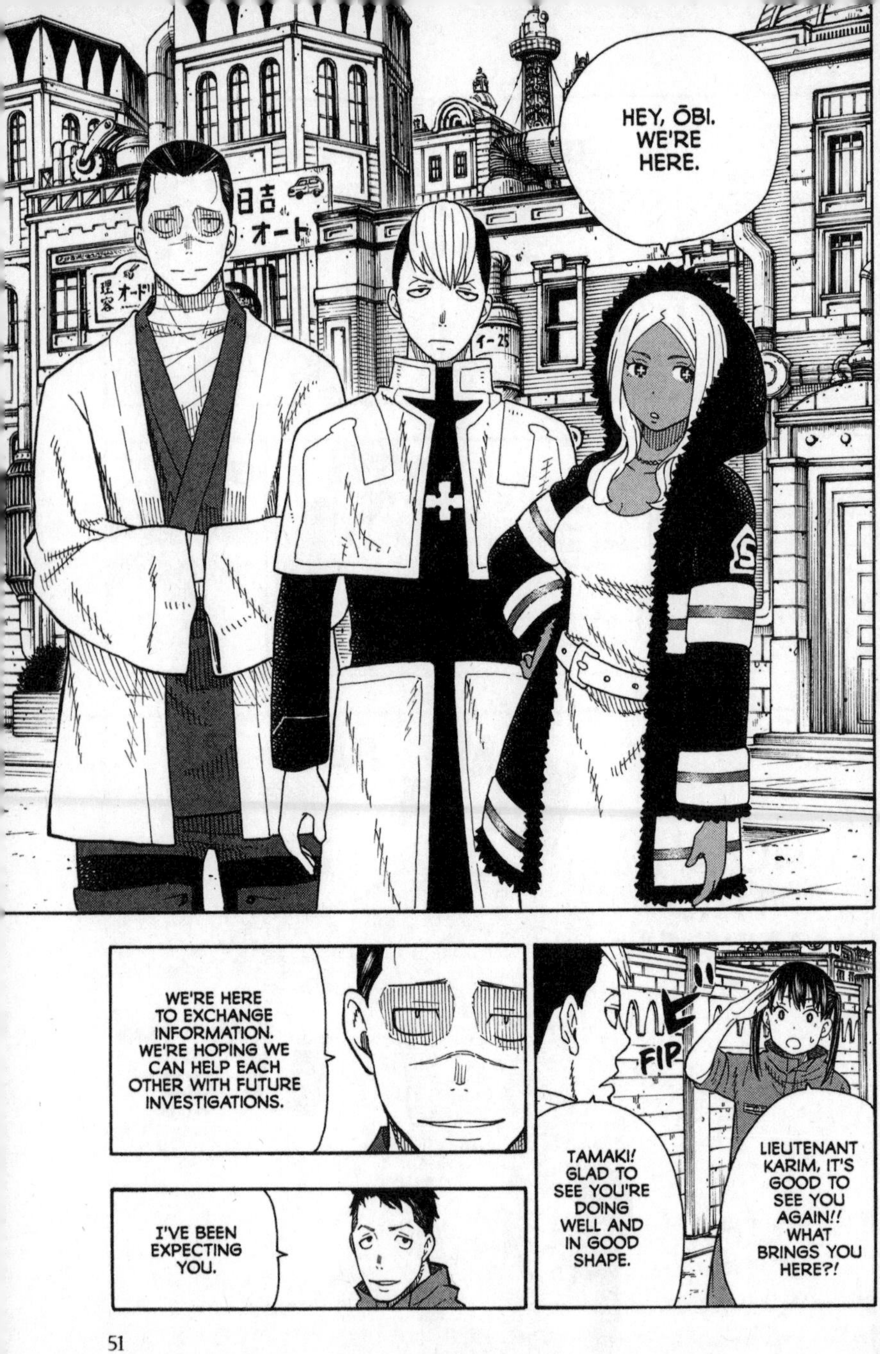
HEY, ŌBI. WE'RE HERE.
FIP
LIEUTENANT KARIM, IT'S GOOD TO SEE YOU AGAIN!! WHAT BRINGS YOU HERE?!
TAMAKI! GLAD TO SEE YOU'RE DOING WELL AND IN GOOD SHAPE.
WE'RE HERE TO EXCHANGE INFORMATION. WE'RE HOPING WE CAN HELP EACH OTHER WITH FUTURE INVESTIGATIONS.
I'VE BEEN EXPECTING YOU.

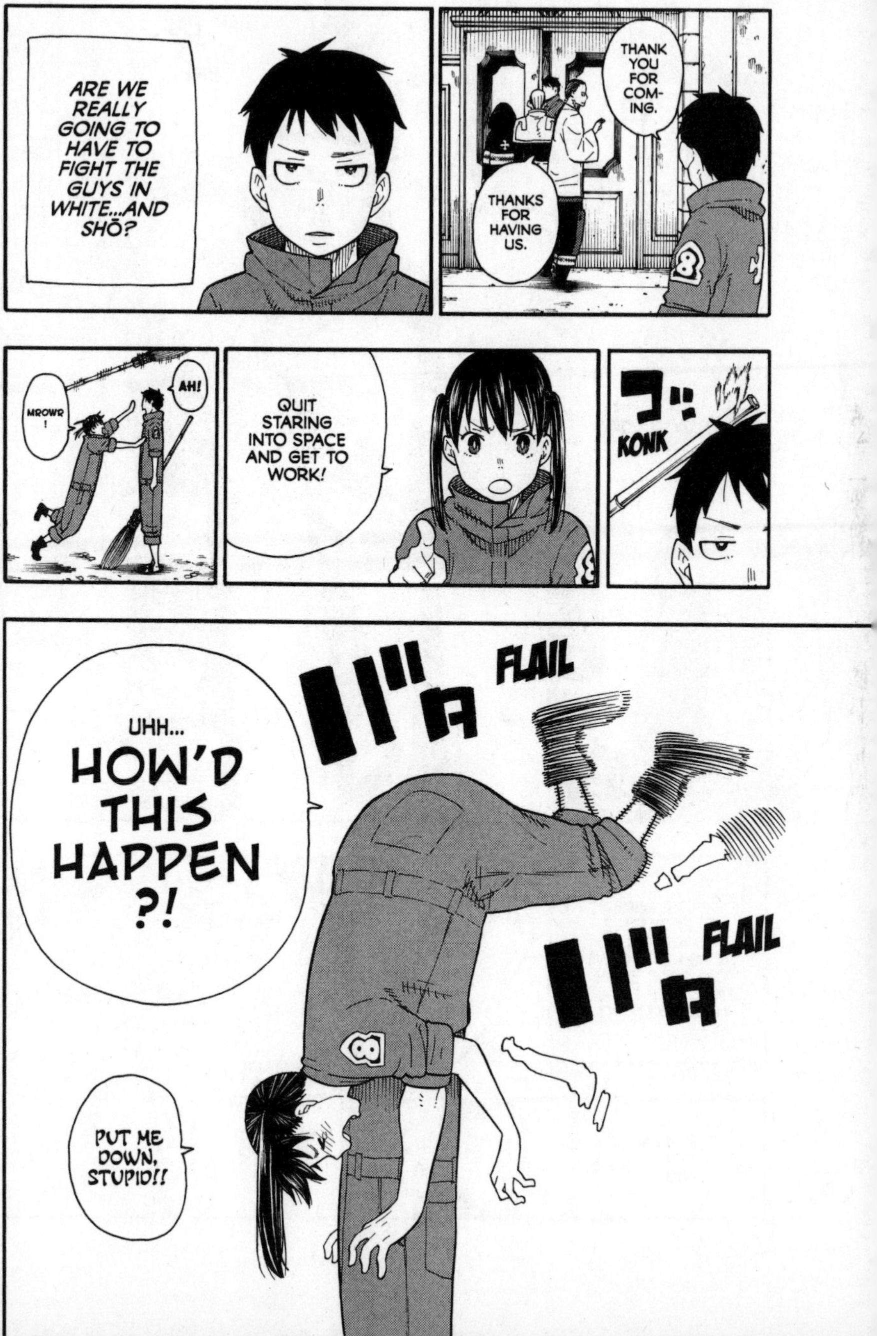
THANK YOU FOR COMING.
THANKS FOR HAVING US.
ARE WE REALLY GOING TO HAVE TO FIGHT THE GUYS IN WHITE...AND SHŌ?
コッ
KONK
QUIT STARING INTO SPACE AND GET TO WORK!
AH!
MROWR!
バタ
FLAIL
UHH... HOW'D THIS HAPPEN?!
バタ
FLAIL
PUT ME DOWN, STUPID!!

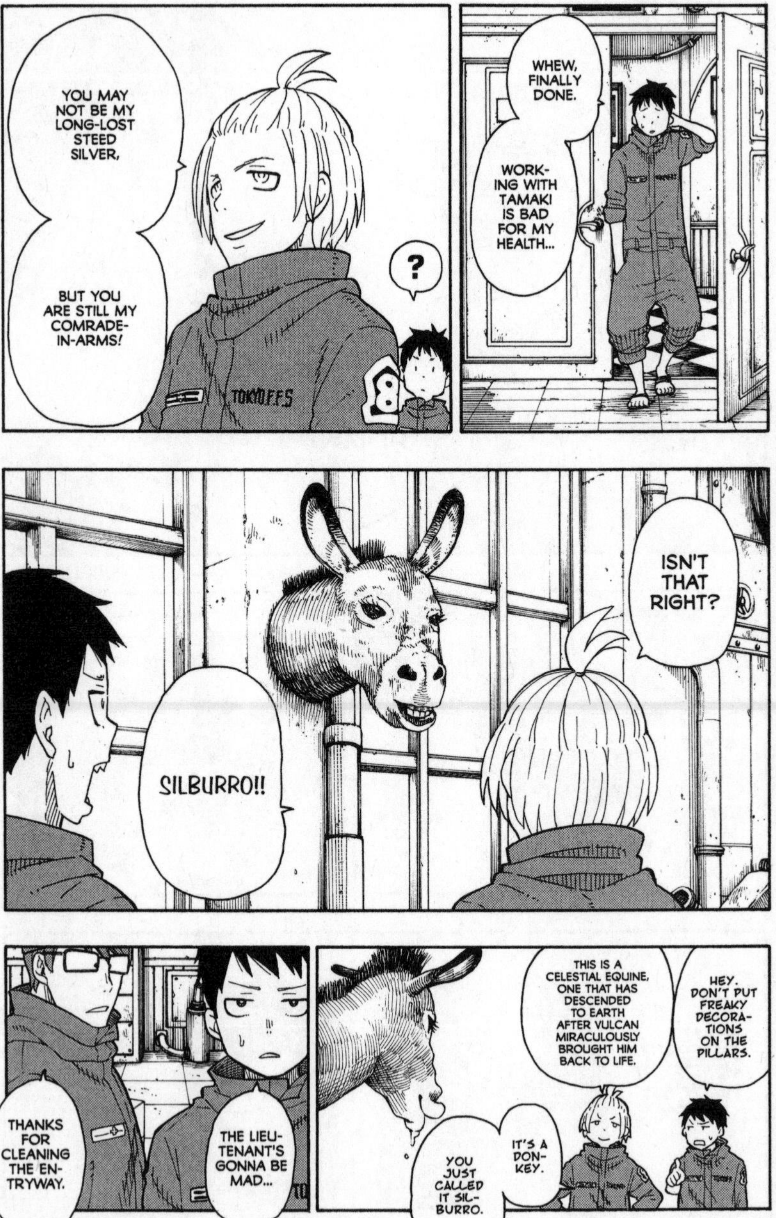
WHEW, FINALLY DONE.
WORKING WITH TAMAKI IS BAD FOR MY HEALTH...
YOU MAY NOT BE MY LONG-LOST STEED SILVER,
BUT YOU ARE STILL MY COMRADE-IN-ARMS!
?
TOKYO F.F.S
8
ISN'T THAT RIGHT?
SILBURRO!!
HEY. DON'T PUT FREAKY DECORATIONS ON THE PILLARS.
THIS IS A CELESTIAL EQUINE, ONE THAT HAS DESCENDED TO EARTH AFTER VULCAN MIRACULOUSLY BROUGHT HIM BACK TO LIFE.
IT'S A DONKEY.
YOU JUST CALLED IT SILBURRO.
THE LIEUTENANT'S GONNA BE MAD...
THANKS FOR CLEANING THE ENTRYWAY.

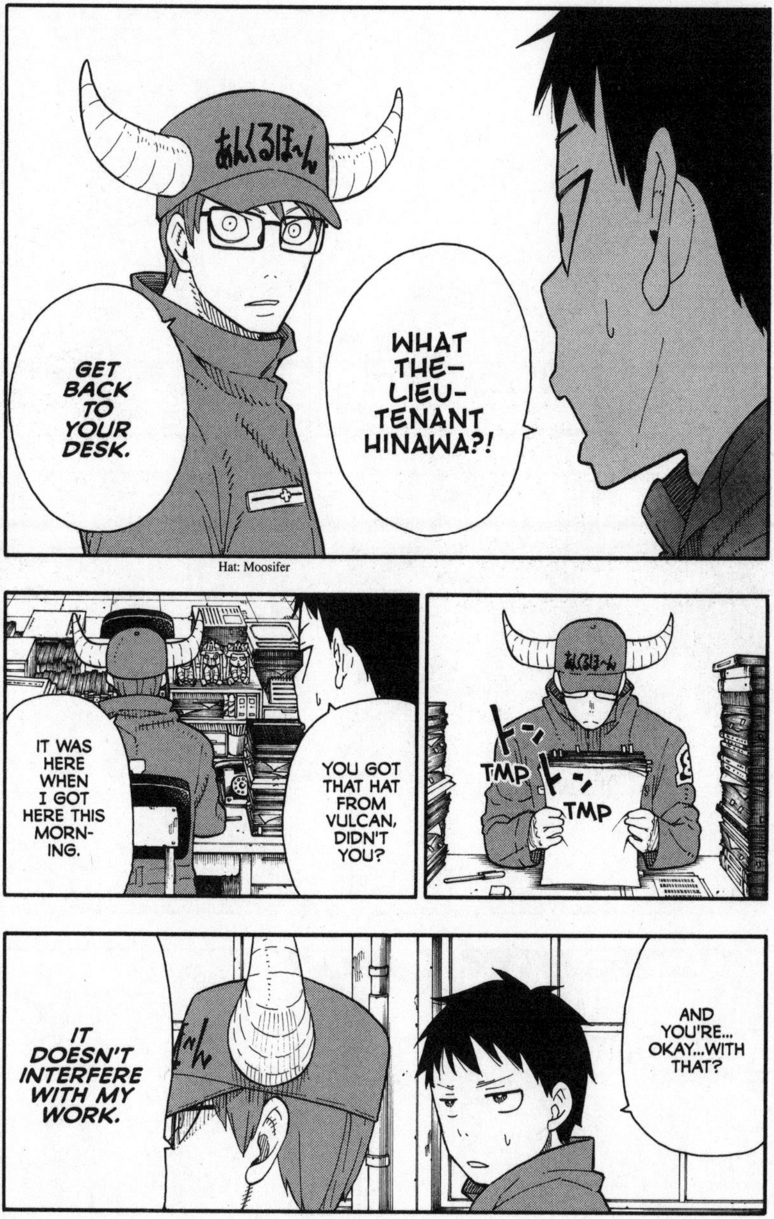
あんくるほ～ん
WHAT THE— LIEU- TENANT HINAWA?!
GET BACK TO YOUR DESK.
TMP
TMP
YOU GOT THAT HAT FROM VULCAN, DIDN'T YOU?
IT WAS HERE WHEN I GOT HERE THIS MORN- ING.
AND YOU'RE... OKAY...WITH THAT?
IT DOESN'T INTERFERE WITH MY WORK.

Hat: Moosifer

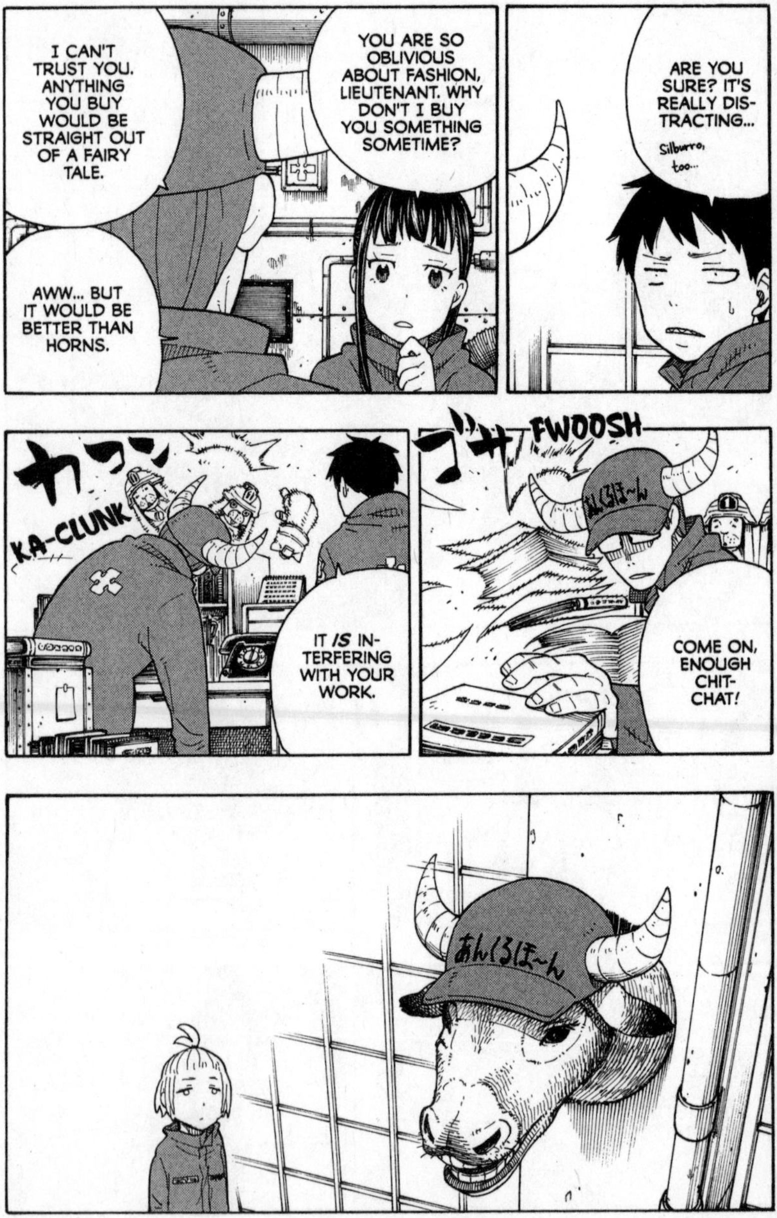
ARE YOU SURE? IT'S REALLY DISTRACTING...
Silburro, too...
YOU ARE SO OBLIVIOUS ABOUT FASHION, LIEUTENANT. WHY DON'T I BUY YOU SOMETHING SOMETIME?
I CAN'T TRUST YOU. ANYTHING YOU BUY WOULD BE STRAIGHT OUT OF A FAIRY TALE.
AWW... BUT IT WOULD BE BETTER THAN HORNS.
FWOOSH
COME ON, ENOUGH CHIT-CHAT!
KA-CLUNK
IT *IS* INTERFERING WITH YOUR WORK.
あんくろほ〜ん

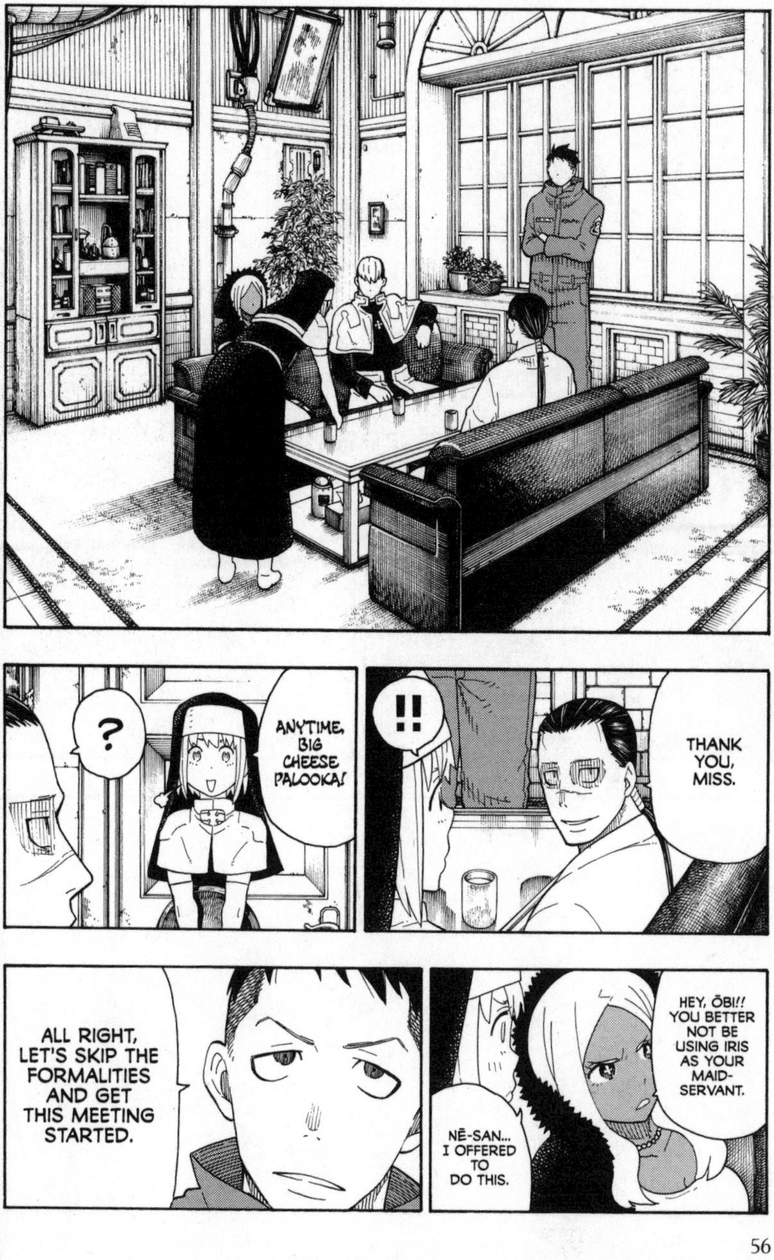
THANK YOU, MISS.
!!
ANYTIME, BIG CHEESE PALOOKA!
?
HEY, ŌBI!! YOU BETTER NOT BE USING IRIS AS YOUR MAID-SERVANT.
NĒ-SAN... I OFFERED TO DO THIS.
ALL RIGHT, LET'S SKIP THE FORMALITIES AND GET THIS MEETING STARTED.

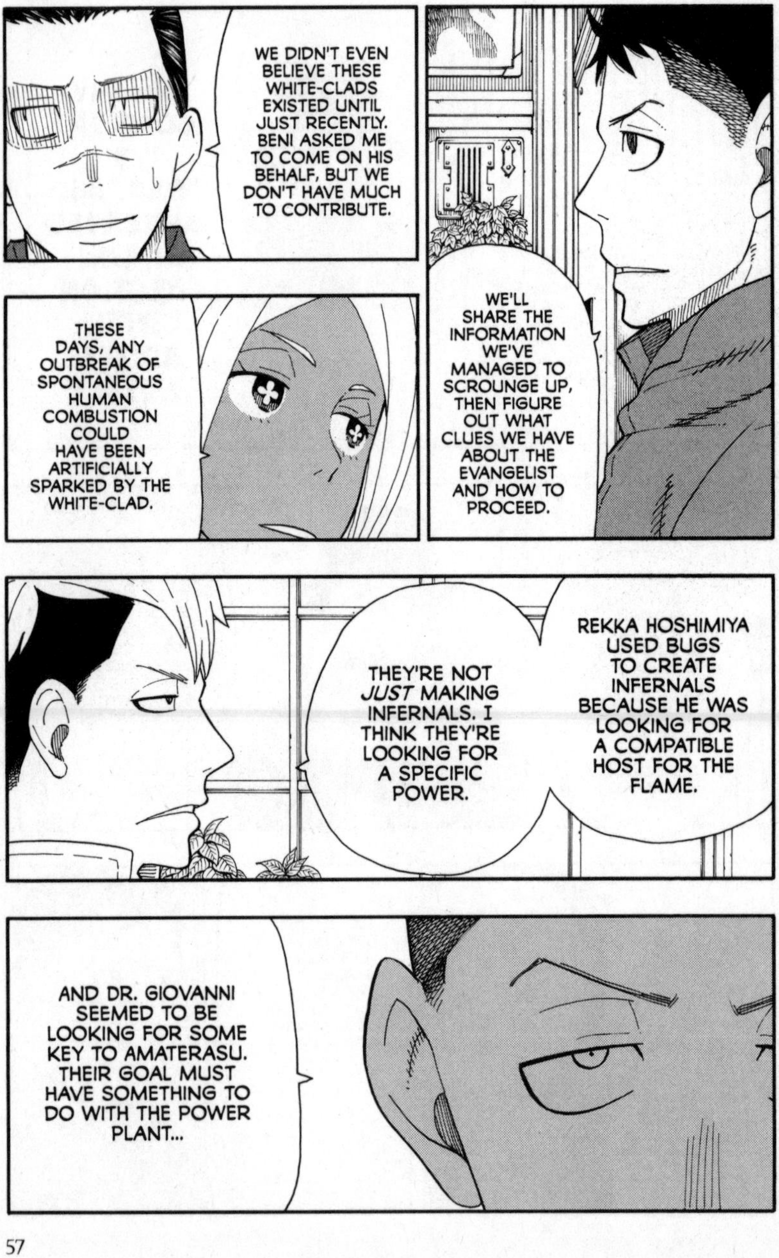
WE'LL SHARE THE INFORMATION WE'VE MANAGED TO SCROUNGE UP, THEN FIGURE OUT WHAT CLUES WE HAVE ABOUT THE EVANGELIST AND HOW TO PROCEED.
WE DIDN'T EVEN BELIEVE THESE WHITE-CLADS EXISTED UNTIL JUST RECENTLY. BENI ASKED ME TO COME ON HIS BEHALF, BUT WE DON'T HAVE MUCH TO CONTRIBUTE.
THESE DAYS, ANY OUTBREAK OF SPONTANEOUS HUMAN COMBUSTION COULD HAVE BEEN ARTIFICIALLY SPARKED BY THE WHITE-CLAD.
REKKA HOSHIMIYA USED BUGS TO CREATE INFERNALS BECAUSE HE WAS LOOKING FOR A COMPATIBLE HOST FOR THE FLAME.
THEY'RE NOT *JUST* MAKING INFERNALS. I THINK THEY'RE LOOKING FOR A SPECIFIC POWER.
AND DR. GIOVANNI SEEMED TO BE LOOKING FOR SOME KEY TO AMATERASU. THEIR GOAL MUST HAVE SOMETHING TO DO WITH THE POWER PLANT...

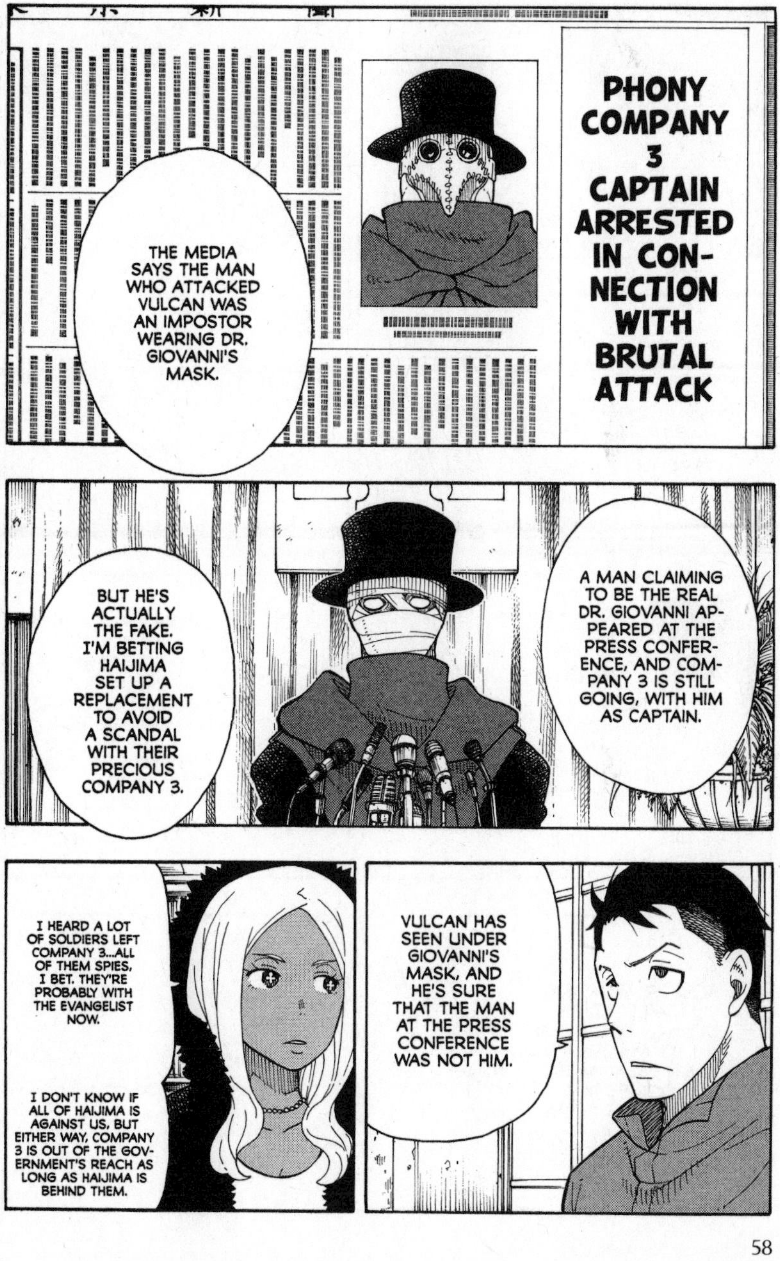
PHONY COMPANY 3 CAPTAIN ARRESTED IN CONNECTION WITH BRUTAL ATTACK
THE MEDIA SAYS THE MAN WHO ATTACKED VULCAN WAS AN IMPOSTOR WEARING DR. GIOVANNI'S MASK.
A MAN CLAIMING TO BE THE REAL DR. GIOVANNI APPEARED AT THE PRESS CONFERENCE, AND COMPANY 3 IS STILL GOING, WITH HIM AS CAPTAIN.
BUT HE'S ACTUALLY THE FAKE. I'M BETTING HAIJIMA SET UP A REPLACEMENT TO AVOID A SCANDAL WITH THEIR PRECIOUS COMPANY 3.
VULCAN HAS SEEN UNDER GIOVANNI'S MASK, AND HE'S SURE THAT THE MAN AT THE PRESS CONFERENCE WAS NOT HIM.
I HEARD A LOT OF SOLDIERS LEFT COMPANY 3...ALL OF THEM SPIES, I BET. THEY'RE PROBABLY WITH THE EVANGELIST NOW.
I DON'T KNOW IF ALL OF HAIJIMA IS AGAINST US, BUT EITHER WAY, COMPANY 3 IS OUT OF THE GOVERNMENT'S REACH AS LONG AS HAIJIMA IS BEHIND THEM.

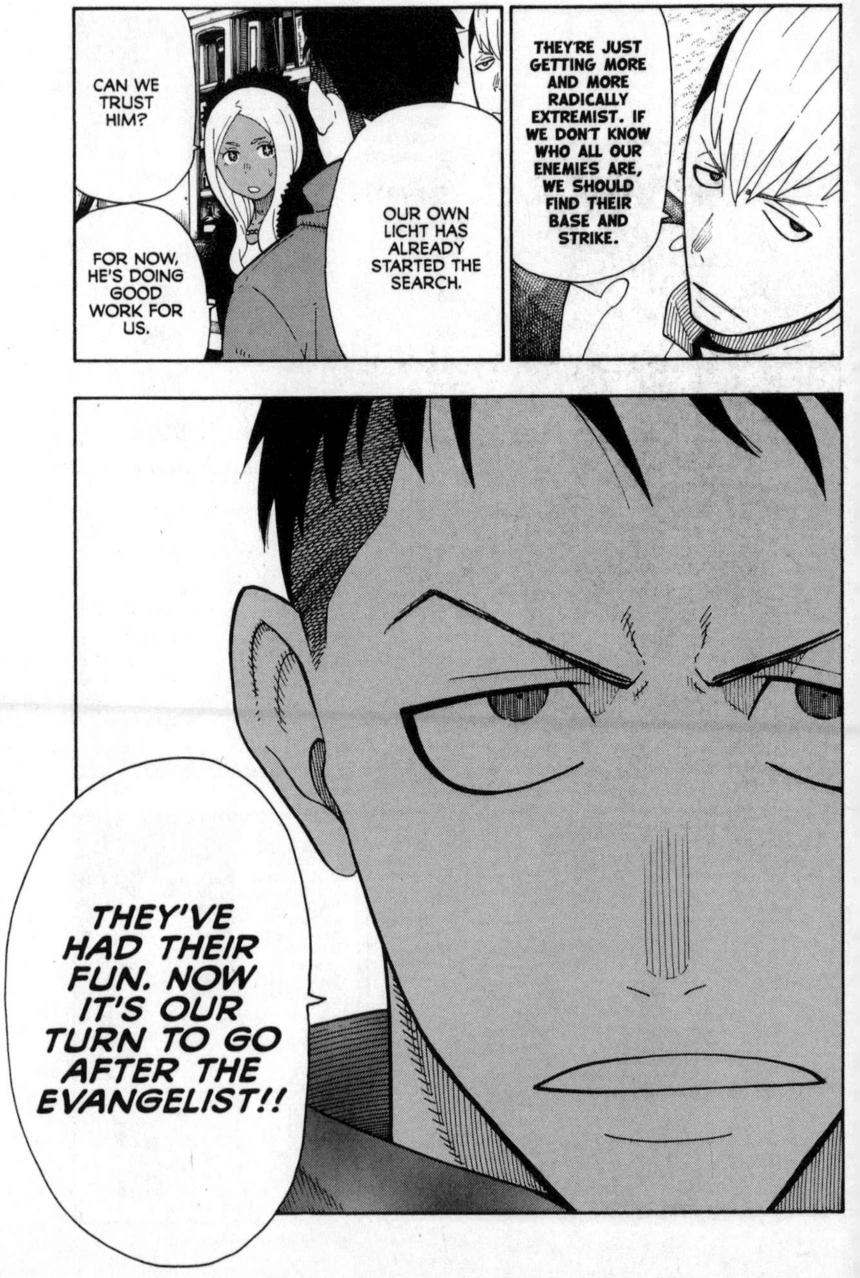
THEY'RE JUST GETTING MORE AND MORE RADICALLY EXTREMIST. IF WE DON'T KNOW WHO ALL OUR ENEMIES ARE, WE SHOULD FIND THEIR BASE AND STRIKE.
OUR OWN LICHT HAS ALREADY STARTED THE SEARCH.
CAN WE TRUST HIM?
FOR NOW, HE'S DOING GOOD WORK FOR US.
THEY'VE HAD THEIR FUN. NOW IT'S OUR TURN TO GO AFTER THE EVANGELIST!!

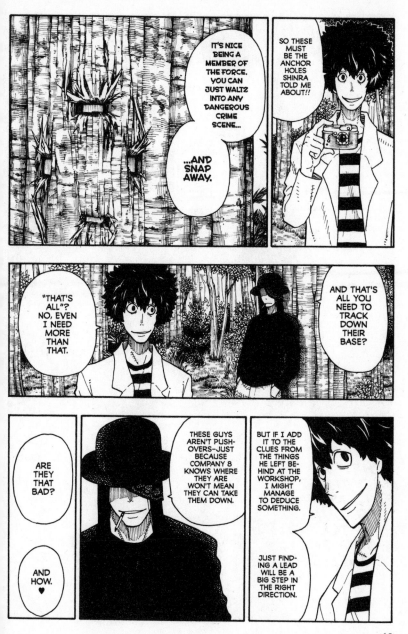

SO THESE MUST BE THE ANCHOR HOLES SHINRA TOLD ME ABOUT!!
IT'S NICE BEING A MEMBER OF THE FORCE. YOU CAN JUST WALTZ INTO ANY DANGEROUS CRIME SCENE...
...AND SNAP AWAY.
AND THAT'S ALL YOU NEED TO TRACK DOWN THEIR BASE?
"THAT'S ALL"? NO, EVEN I NEED MORE THAN THAT.
BUT IF I ADD IT TO THE CLUES FROM THE THINGS HE LEFT BE-HIND AT THE WORKSHOP, I MIGHT MANAGE TO DEDUCE SOMETHING.
JUST FIND-ING A LEAD WILL BE A BIG STEP IN THE RIGHT DIRECTION.
THESE GUYS AREN'T PUSH-OVERS–JUST BECAUSE COMPANY 8 KNOWS WHERE THEY ARE WON'T MEAN THEY CAN TAKE THEM DOWN.
ARE THEY THAT BAD?
AND HOW. ♥

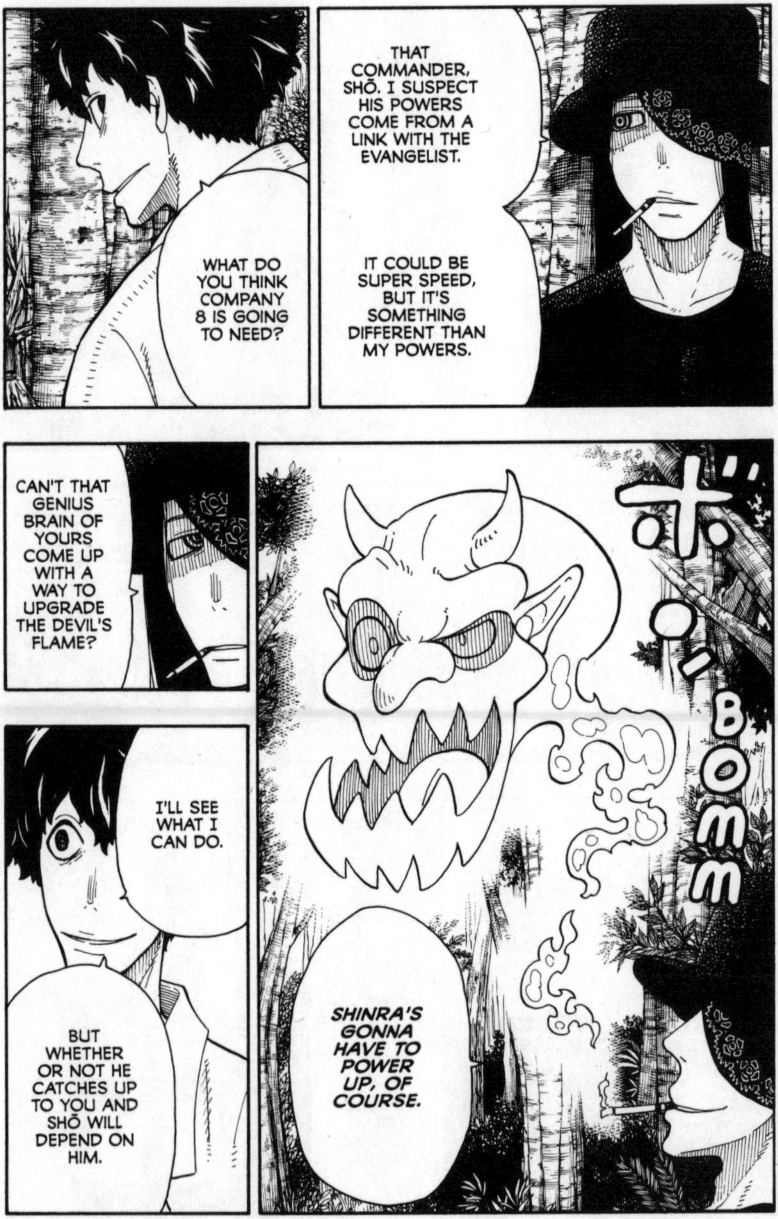
THAT COMMANDER, SHŌ. I SUSPECT HIS POWERS COME FROM A LINK WITH THE EVANGELIST.
IT COULD BE SUPER SPEED, BUT IT'S SOMETHING DIFFERENT THAN MY POWERS.
WHAT DO YOU THINK COMPANY 8 IS GOING TO NEED?
BOMM
SHINRA'S GONNA HAVE TO POWER UP, OF COURSE.
CAN'T THAT GENIUS BRAIN OF YOURS COME UP WITH A WAY TO UPGRADE THE DEVIL'S FLAME?
I'LL SEE WHAT I CAN DO.
BUT WHETHER OR NOT HE CATCHES UP TO YOU AND SHŌ WILL DEPEND ON HIM.

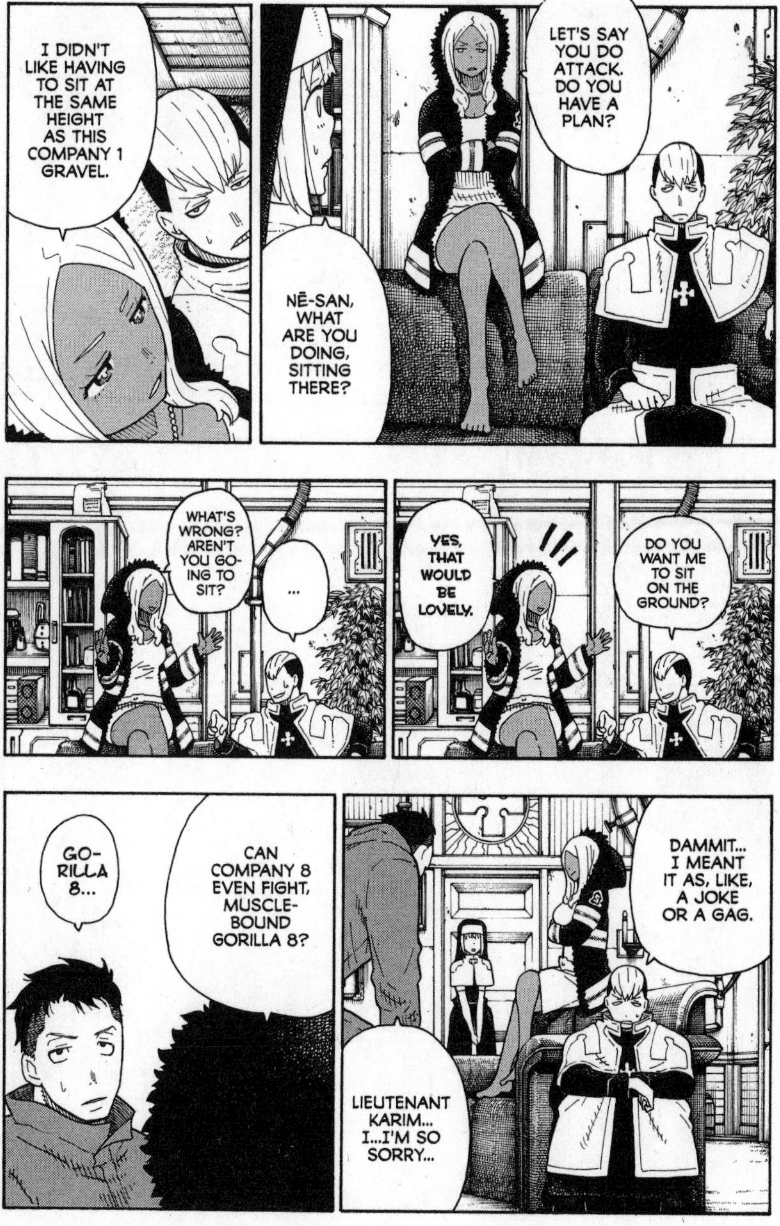
LET'S SAY YOU DO ATTACK. DO YOU HAVE A PLAN?
NĒ-SAN, WHAT ARE YOU DOING, SITTING THERE?
I DIDN'T LIKE HAVING TO SIT AT THE SAME HEIGHT AS THIS COMPANY 1 GRAVEL.
DO YOU WANT ME TO SIT ON THE GROUND?
YES, THAT WOULD BE LOVELY.
WHAT'S WRONG? AREN'T YOU GOING TO SIT?
...
DAMMIT... I MEANT IT AS, LIKE, A JOKE OR A GAG.
LIEUTENANT KARIM... I...I'M SO SORRY...
CAN COMPANY 8 EVEN FIGHT, MUSCLE-BOUND GORILLA 8?
GO-RILLA 8...

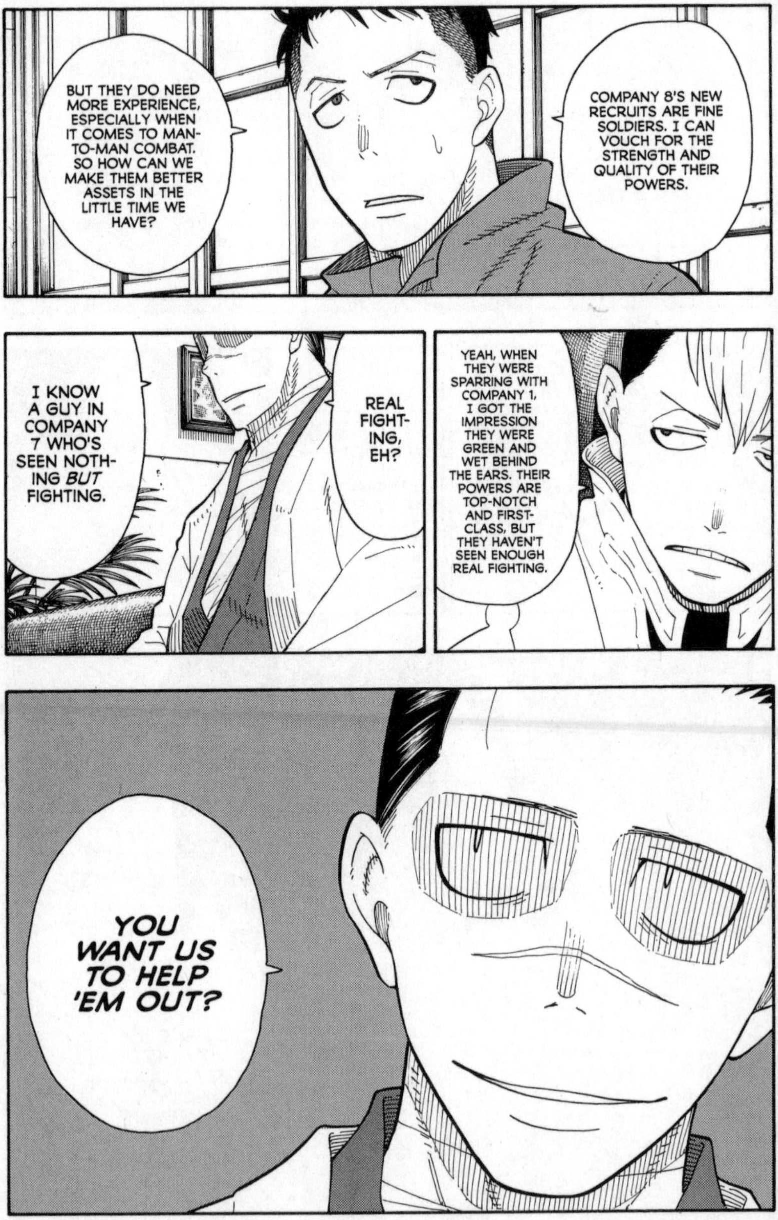
COMPANY 8'S NEW RECRUITS ARE FINE SOLDIERS. I CAN VOUCH FOR THE STRENGTH AND QUALITY OF THEIR POWERS.
BUT THEY DO NEED MORE EXPERIENCE, ESPECIALLY WHEN IT COMES TO MAN-TO-MAN COMBAT. SO HOW CAN WE MAKE THEM BETTER ASSETS IN THE LITTLE TIME WE HAVE?
YEAH, WHEN THEY WERE SPARRING WITH COMPANY 1, I GOT THE IMPRESSION THEY WERE GREEN AND WET BEHIND THE EARS. THEIR POWERS ARE TOP-NOTCH AND FIRST-CLASS, BUT THEY HAVEN'T SEEN ENOUGH REAL FIGHTING.
REAL FIGHTING, EH?
I KNOW A GUY IN COMPANY 7 WHO'S SEEN NOTHING *BUT* FIGHTING.
YOU WANT US TO HELP 'EM OUT?

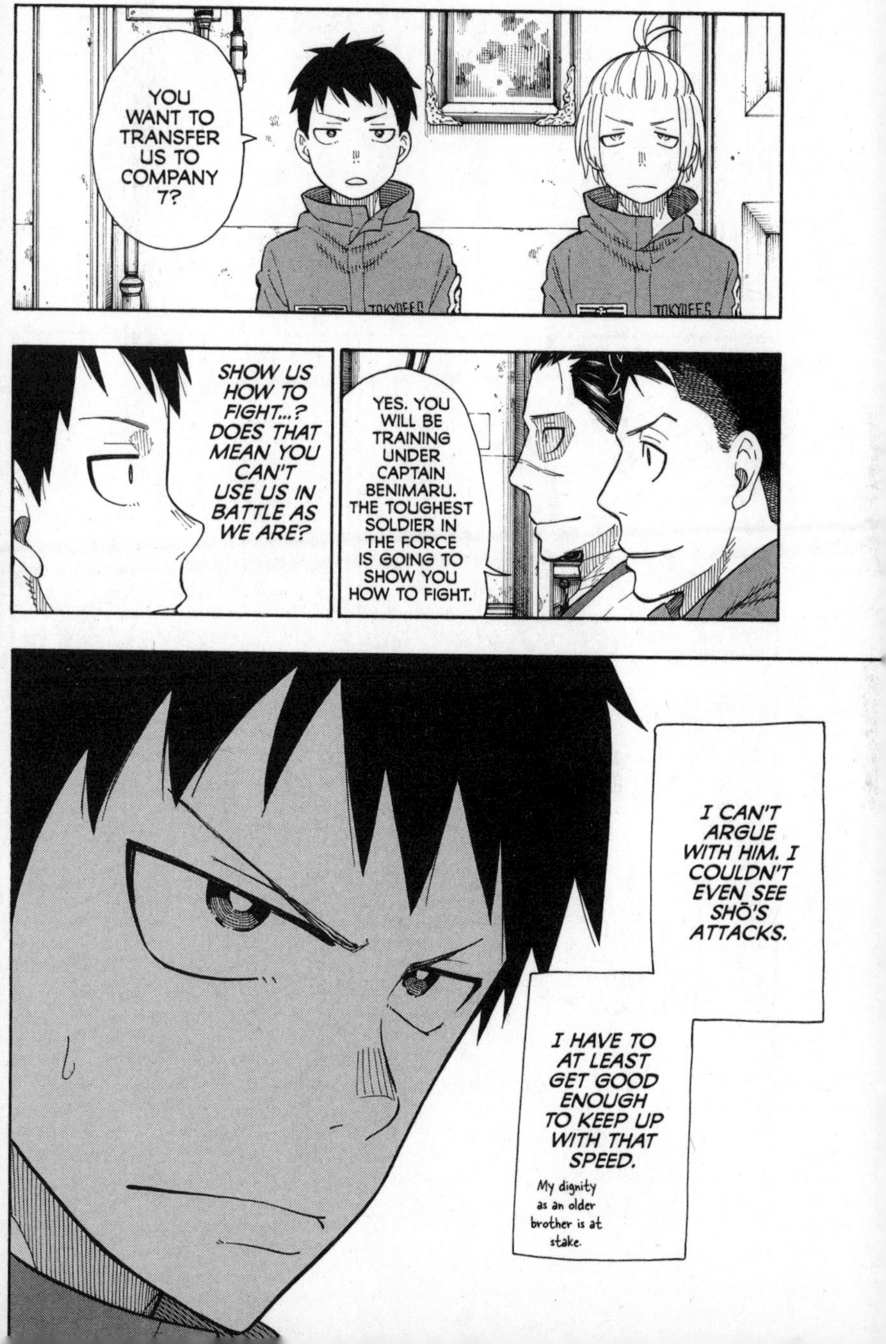
YOU WANT TO TRANSFER US TO COMPANY 7?
YES. YOU WILL BE TRAINING UNDER CAPTAIN BENIMARU. THE TOUGHEST SOLDIER IN THE FORCE IS GOING TO SHOW YOU HOW TO FIGHT.
SHOW US HOW TO FIGHT...? DOES THAT MEAN YOU CAN'T USE US IN BATTLE AS WE ARE?
I CAN'T ARGUE WITH HIM. I COULDN'T EVEN SEE SHŌ'S ATTACKS.
I HAVE TO AT LEAST GET GOOD ENOUGH TO KEEP UP WITH THAT SPEED.
My dignity as an older brother is at stake.
TOKYOFFS
TOKYOFFS

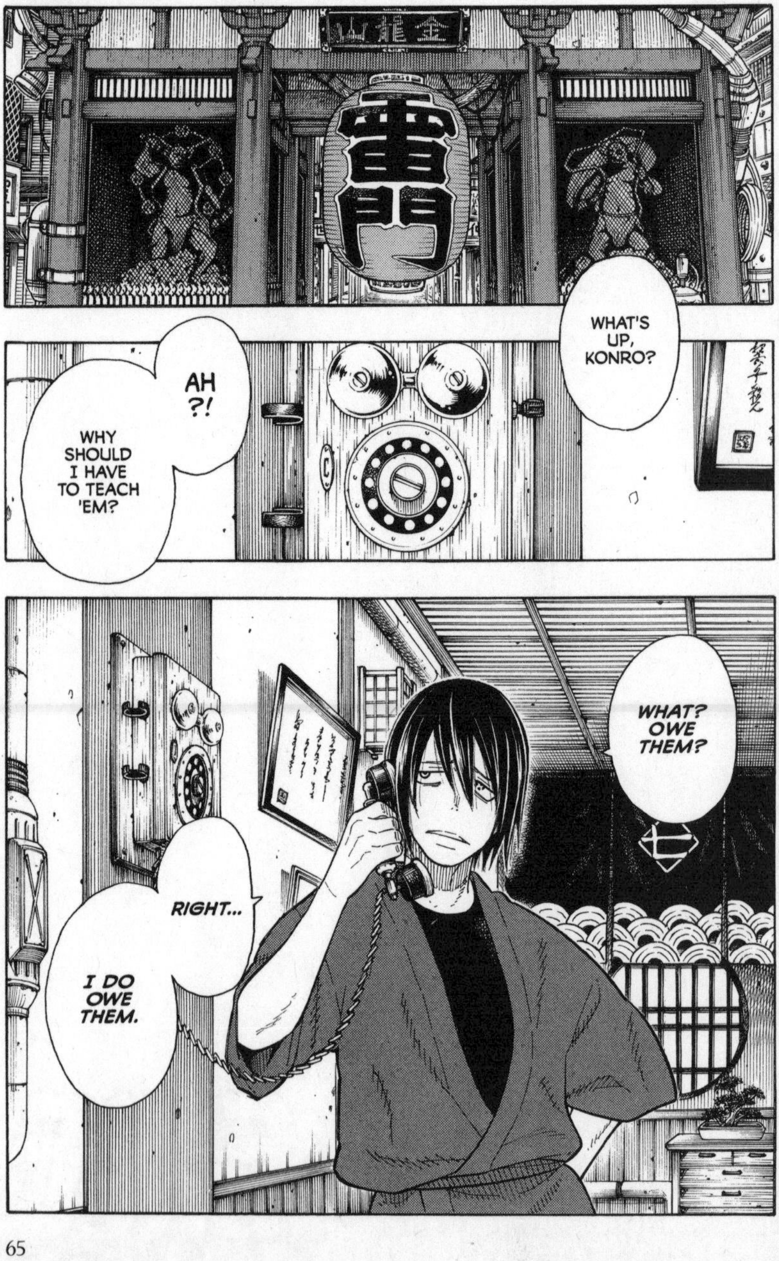
金龍山
雷門
WHAT'S UP, KONRO?
AH ?!
WHY SHOULD I HAVE TO TEACH 'EM?
WHAT? OWE THEM?
RIGHT...
I DO OWE THEM.

FIRE FORCE

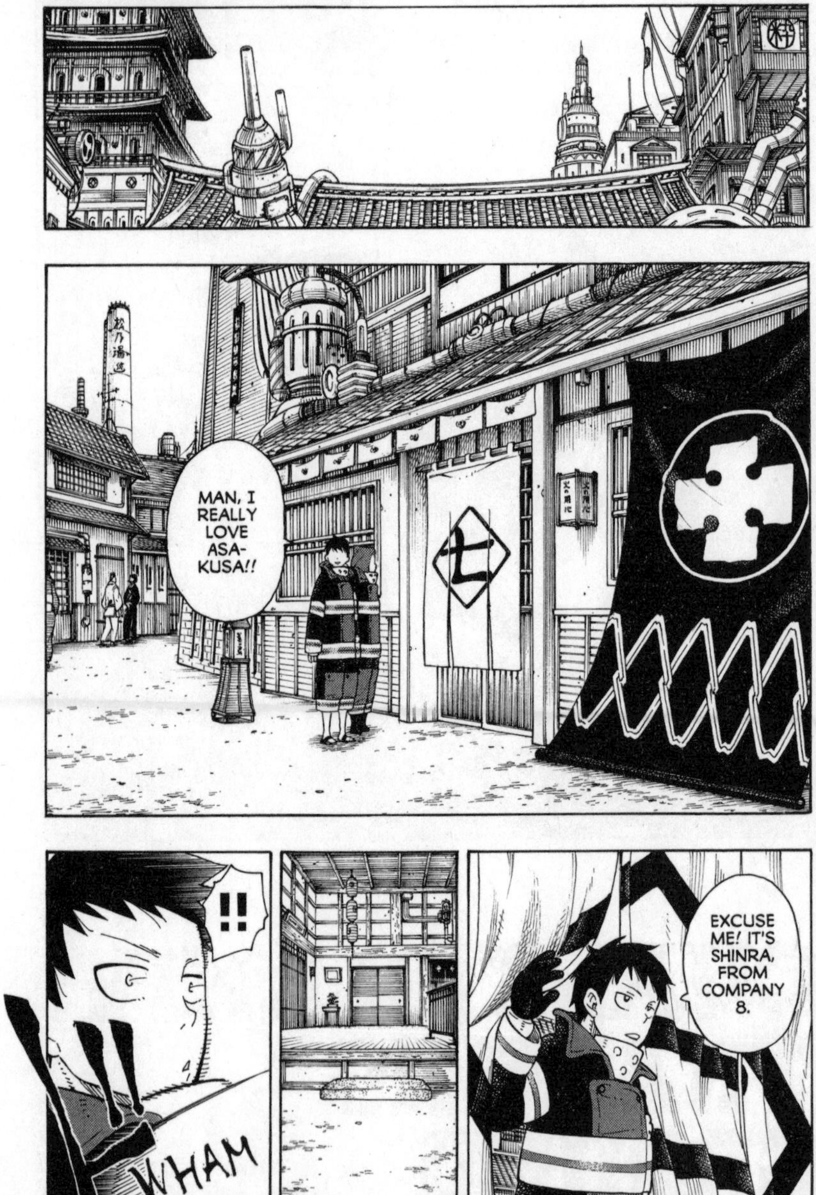
MAN, I REALLY LOVE ASA-KUSA!!
EXCUSE ME! IT'S SHINRA, FROM COMPANY 8.
!!
WHAM

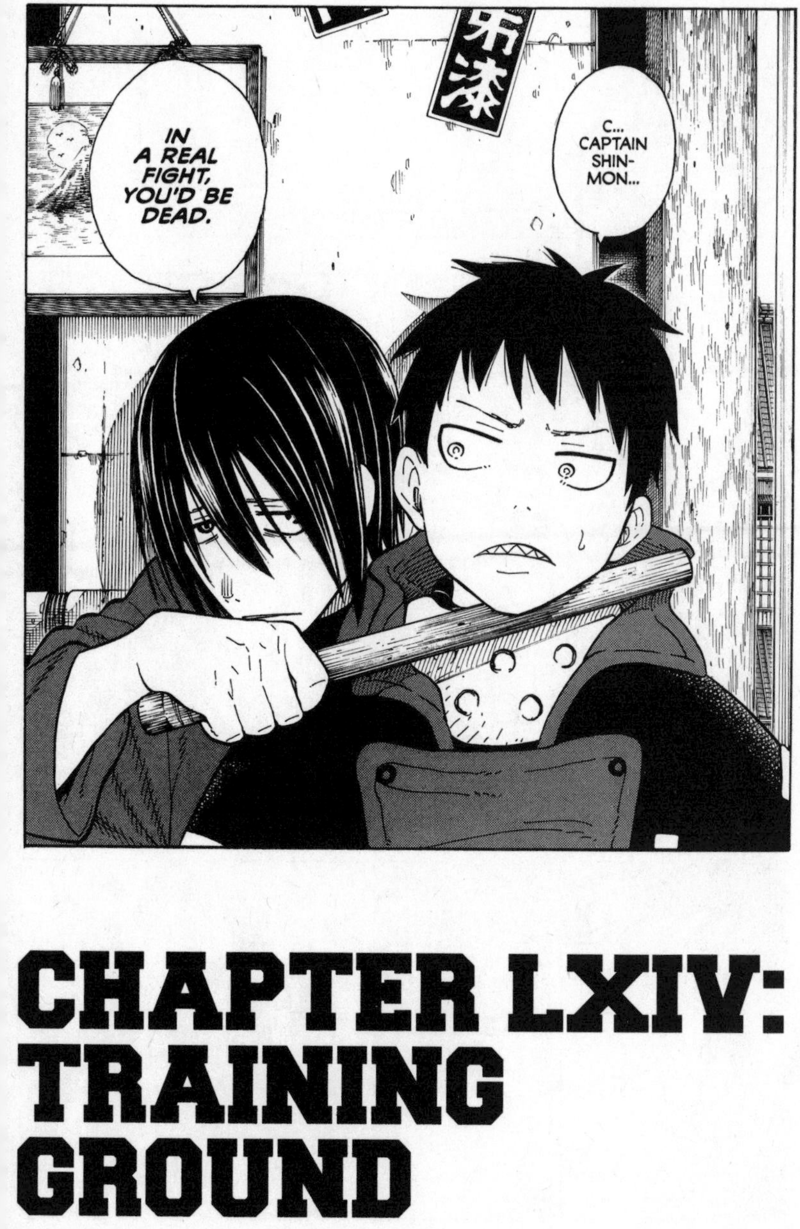
C... CAPTAIN SHIN-MON...
IN A REAL FIGHT, YOU'D BE DEAD.

CHAPTER LXIV: TRAINING GROUND

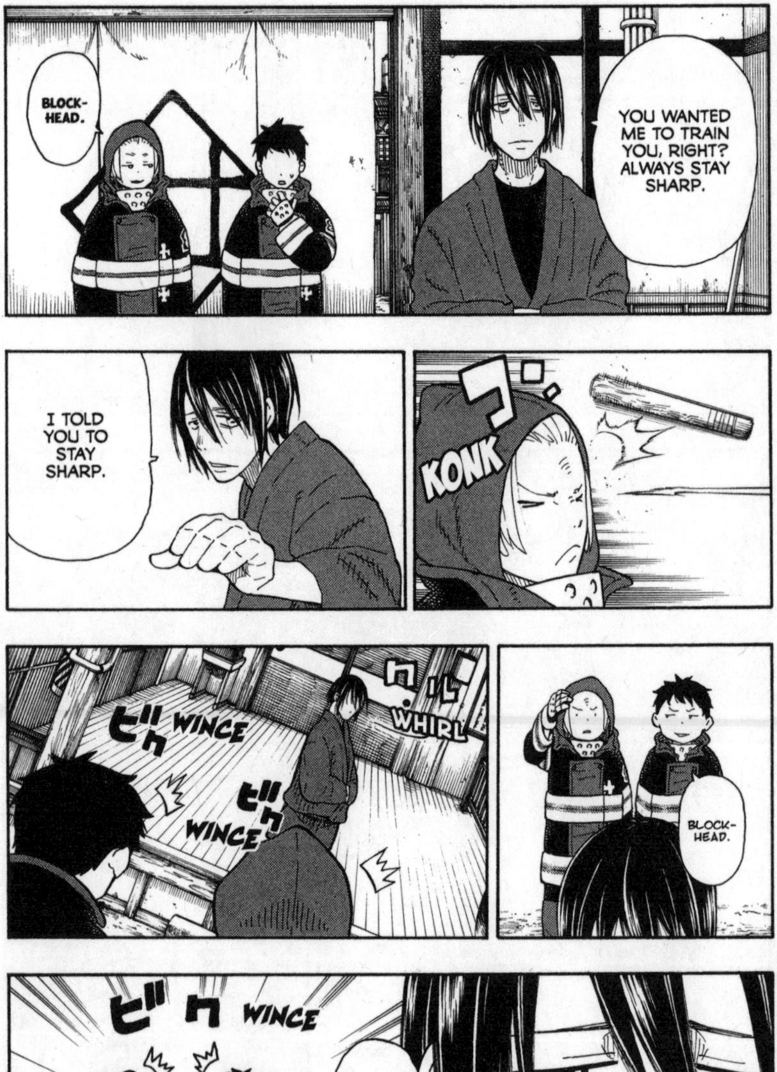
YOU WANTED ME TO TRAIN YOU, RIGHT? ALWAYS STAY SHARP.
BLOCK-HEAD.
KONK
I TOLD YOU TO STAY SHARP.
BLOCK-HEAD.
WHIRL
WINCE
WINCE
HEH.
WINCE

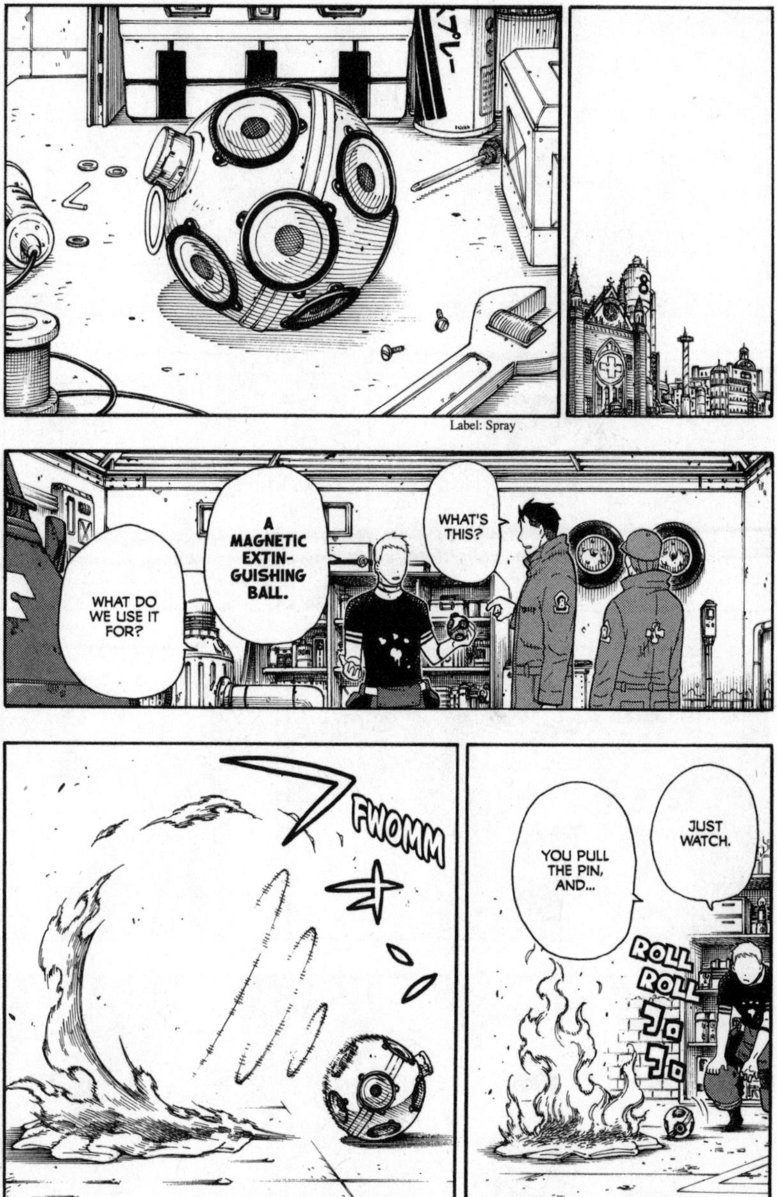
Label: Spray
WHAT'S THIS?
A MAGNETIC EXTIN-GUISHING BALL.
WHAT DO WE USE IT FOR?
JUST WATCH.
YOU PULL THE PIN, AND...
ROLL ROLL
コロコロ
FWOMM

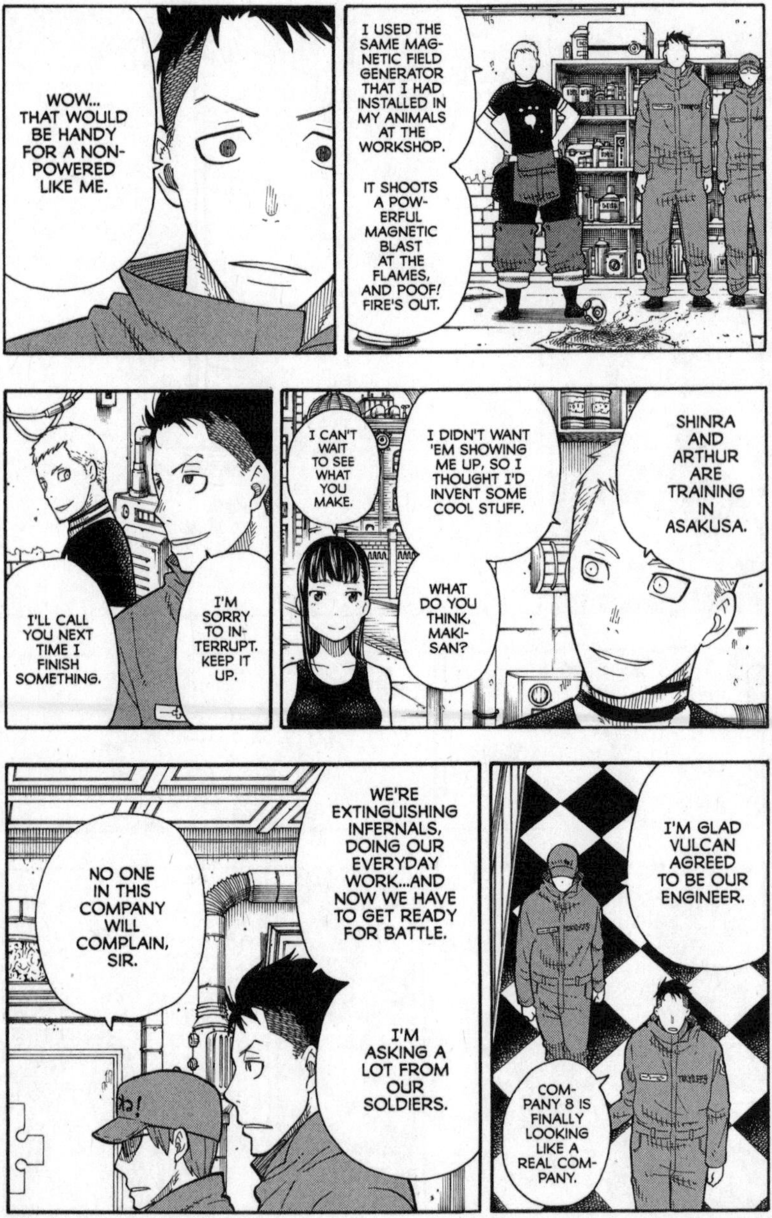
I USED THE SAME MAGNETIC FIELD GENERATOR THAT I HAD INSTALLED IN MY ANIMALS AT THE WORKSHOP.
IT SHOOTS A POWERFUL MAGNETIC BLAST AT THE FLAMES, AND POOF! FIRE'S OUT.
WOW... THAT WOULD BE HANDY FOR A NON-POWERED LIKE ME.
SHINRA AND ARTHUR ARE TRAINING IN ASAKUSA.
I DIDN'T WANT 'EM SHOWING ME UP, SO I THOUGHT I'D INVENT SOME COOL STUFF.
WHAT DO YOU THINK, MAKI-SAN?
I CAN'T WAIT TO SEE WHAT YOU MAKE.
I'M SORRY TO INTERRUPT. KEEP IT UP.
I'LL CALL YOU NEXT TIME I FINISH SOMETHING.
I'M GLAD VULCAN AGREED TO BE OUR ENGINEER.
COMPANY 8 IS FINALLY LOOKING LIKE A REAL COMPANY.
WE'RE EXTINGUISHING INFERNALS, DOING OUR EVERYDAY WORK...AND NOW WE HAVE TO GET READY FOR BATTLE.
I'M ASKING A LOT FROM OUR SOLDIERS.
NO ONE IN THIS COMPANY WILL COMPLAIN, SIR.

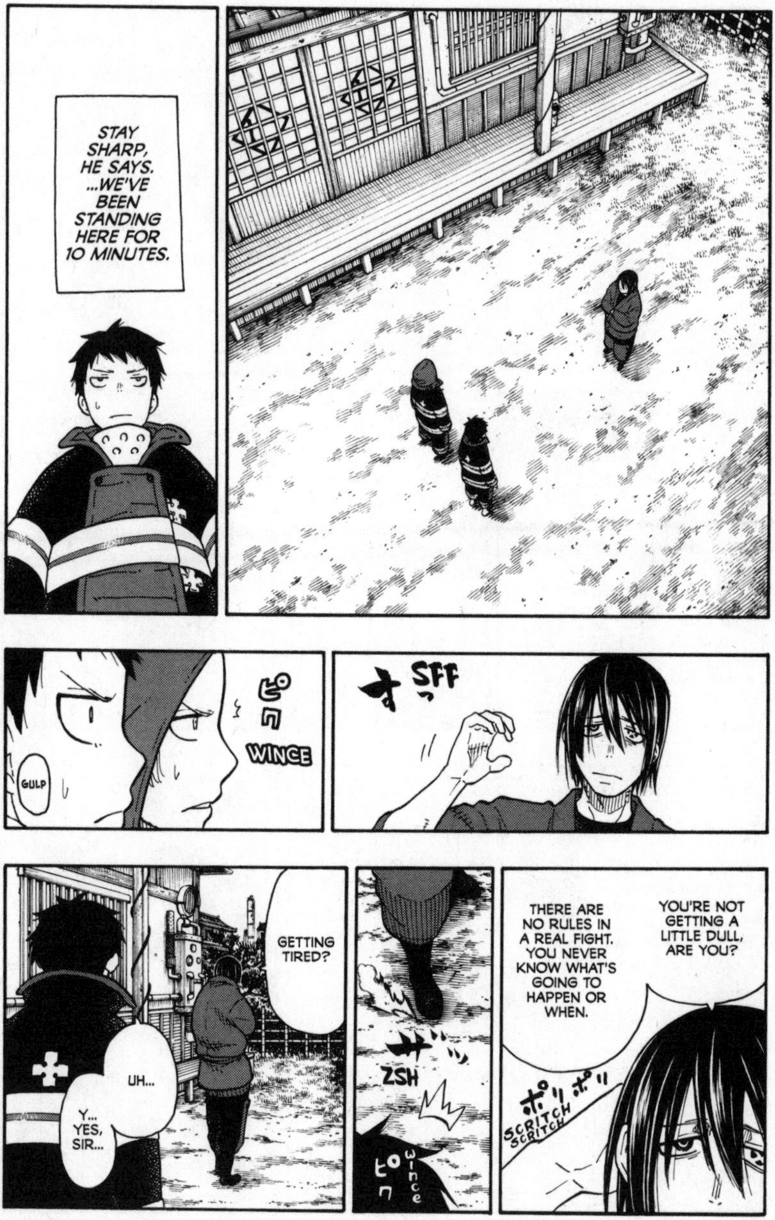
STAY SHARP, HE SAYS. ...WE'VE BEEN STANDING HERE FOR 10 MINUTES.
SFF
WINCE
GULP
YOU'RE NOT GETTING A LITTLE DULL, ARE YOU?
THERE ARE NO RULES IN A REAL FIGHT. YOU NEVER KNOW WHAT'S GOING TO HAPPEN OR WHEN.
SCRITCH SCRITCH
ZSH
ピク wince
GETTING TIRED?
UH...
Y... YES, SIR...

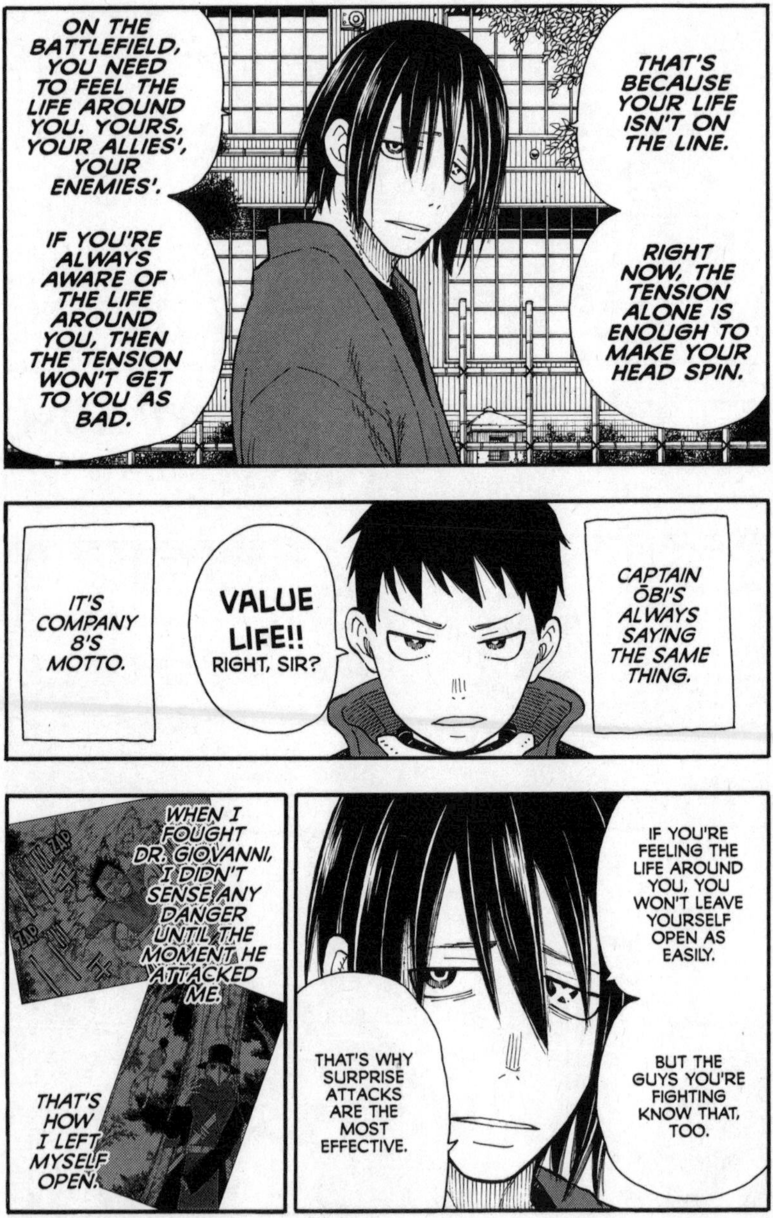
THAT'S BECAUSE YOUR LIFE ISN'T ON THE LINE.
RIGHT NOW, THE TENSION ALONE IS ENOUGH TO MAKE YOUR HEAD SPIN.
ON THE BATTLEFIELD, YOU NEED TO FEEL THE LIFE AROUND YOU. YOURS, YOUR ALLIES', YOUR ENEMIES'.
IF YOU'RE ALWAYS AWARE OF THE LIFE AROUND YOU, THEN THE TENSION WON'T GET TO YOU AS BAD.
CAPTAIN ŌBI'S ALWAYS SAYING THE SAME THING.
VALUE LIFE!! RIGHT, SIR?
IT'S COMPANY 8'S MOTTO.
IF YOU'RE FEELING THE LIFE AROUND YOU, YOU WON'T LEAVE YOURSELF OPEN AS EASILY.
BUT THE GUYS YOU'RE FIGHTING KNOW THAT, TOO.
THAT'S WHY SURPRISE ATTACKS ARE THE MOST EFFECTIVE.
WHEN I FOUGHT DR. GIOVANNI, I DIDN'T SENSE ANY DANGER UNTIL THE MOMENT HE ATTACKED ME.
ZAP
ZAP
THAT'S HOW I LEFT MYSELF OPEN.

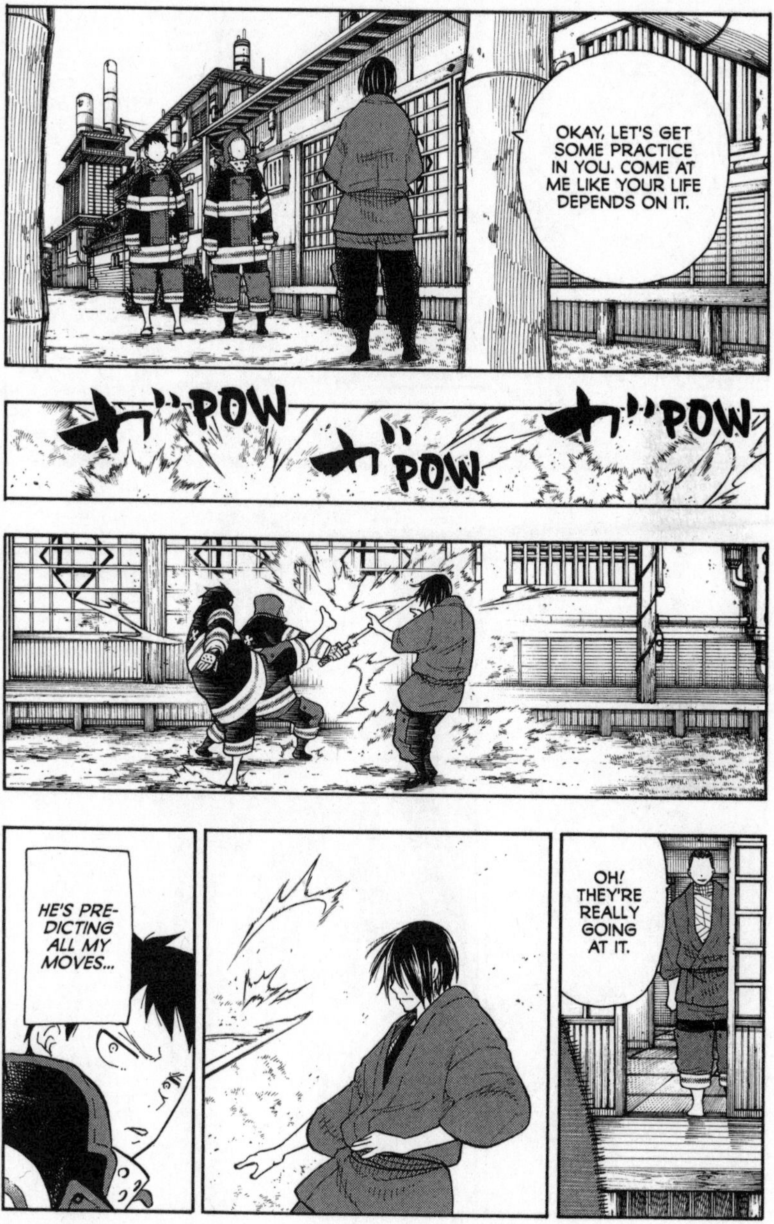
OKAY, LET'S GET SOME PRACTICE IN YOU. COME AT ME LIKE YOUR LIFE DEPENDS ON IT.
POW
POW
POW
OH! THEY'RE REALLY GOING AT IT.
HE'S PRE-DICTING ALL MY MOVES...

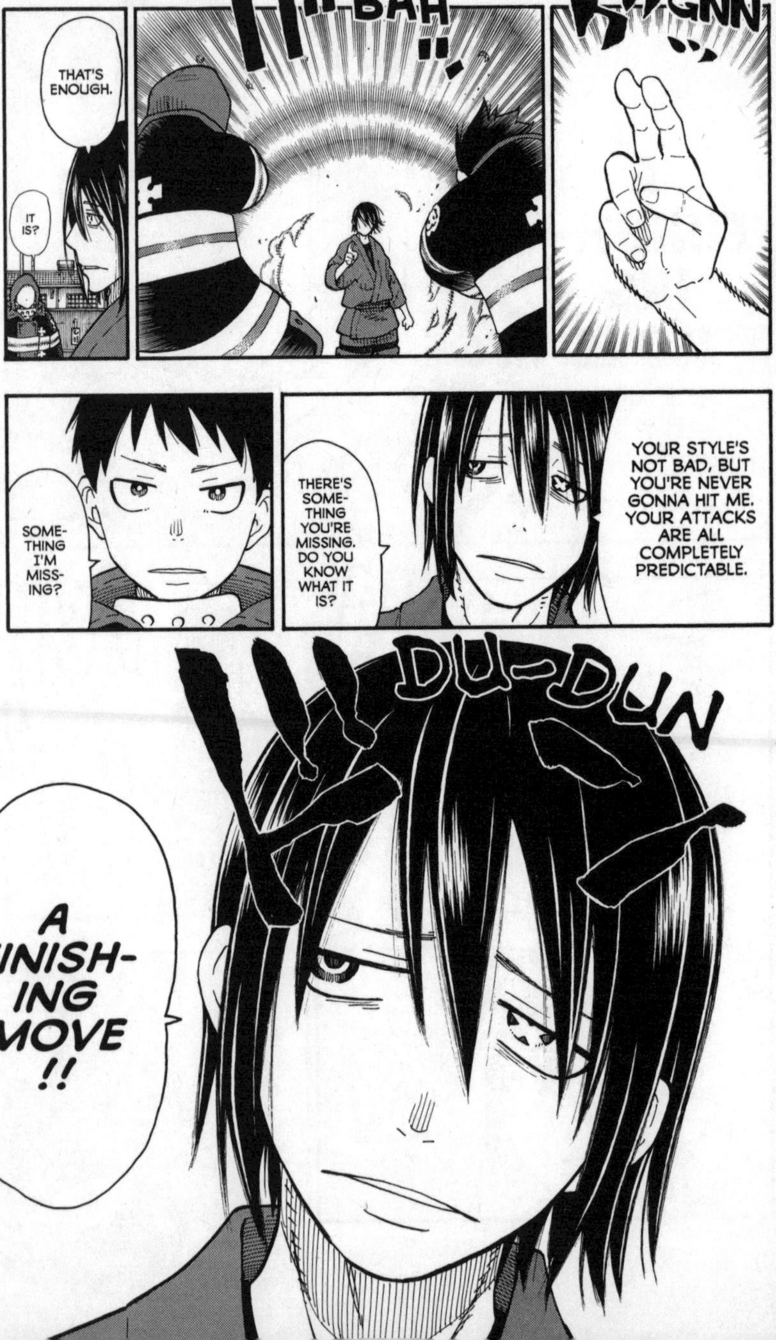
GNN
BAH
THAT'S ENOUGH.
IT IS?
YOUR STYLE'S NOT BAD, BUT YOU'RE NEVER GONNA HIT ME. YOUR ATTACKS ARE ALL COMPLETELY PREDICTABLE.
THERE'S SOME-THING YOU'RE MISSING. DO YOU KNOW WHAT IT IS?
SOME-THING I'M MISS-ING?
DU-DUN
A FINISH-ING MOVE !!

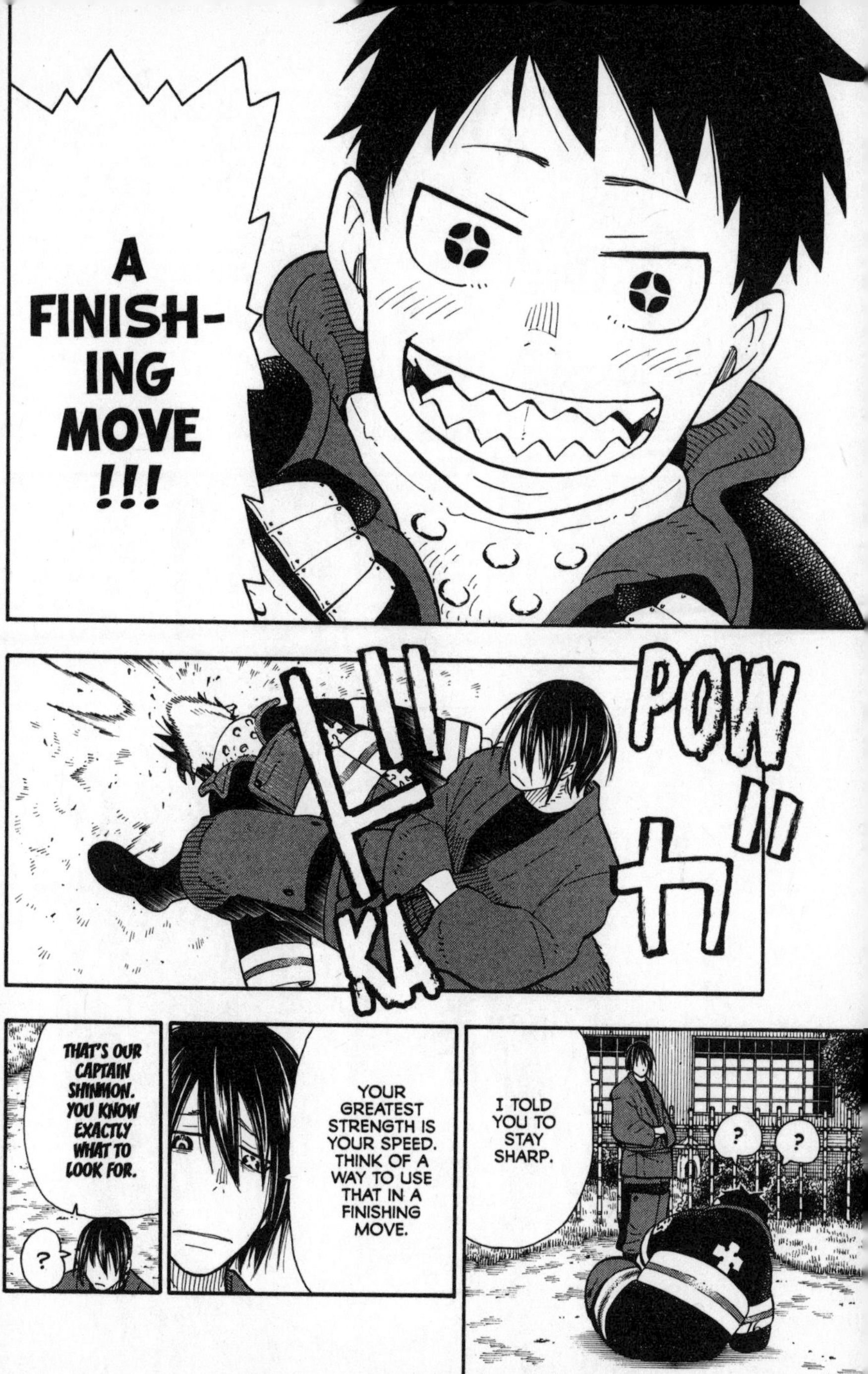
A FINISHING-ING MOVE!!!
POW
KA
I TOLD YOU TO STAY SHARP.
?
?
YOUR GREATEST STRENGTH IS YOUR SPEED. THINK OF A WAY TO USE THAT IN A FINISHING MOVE.
THAT'S OUR CAPTAIN SHINMON. YOU KNOW EXACTLY WHAT TO LOOK FOR.
?

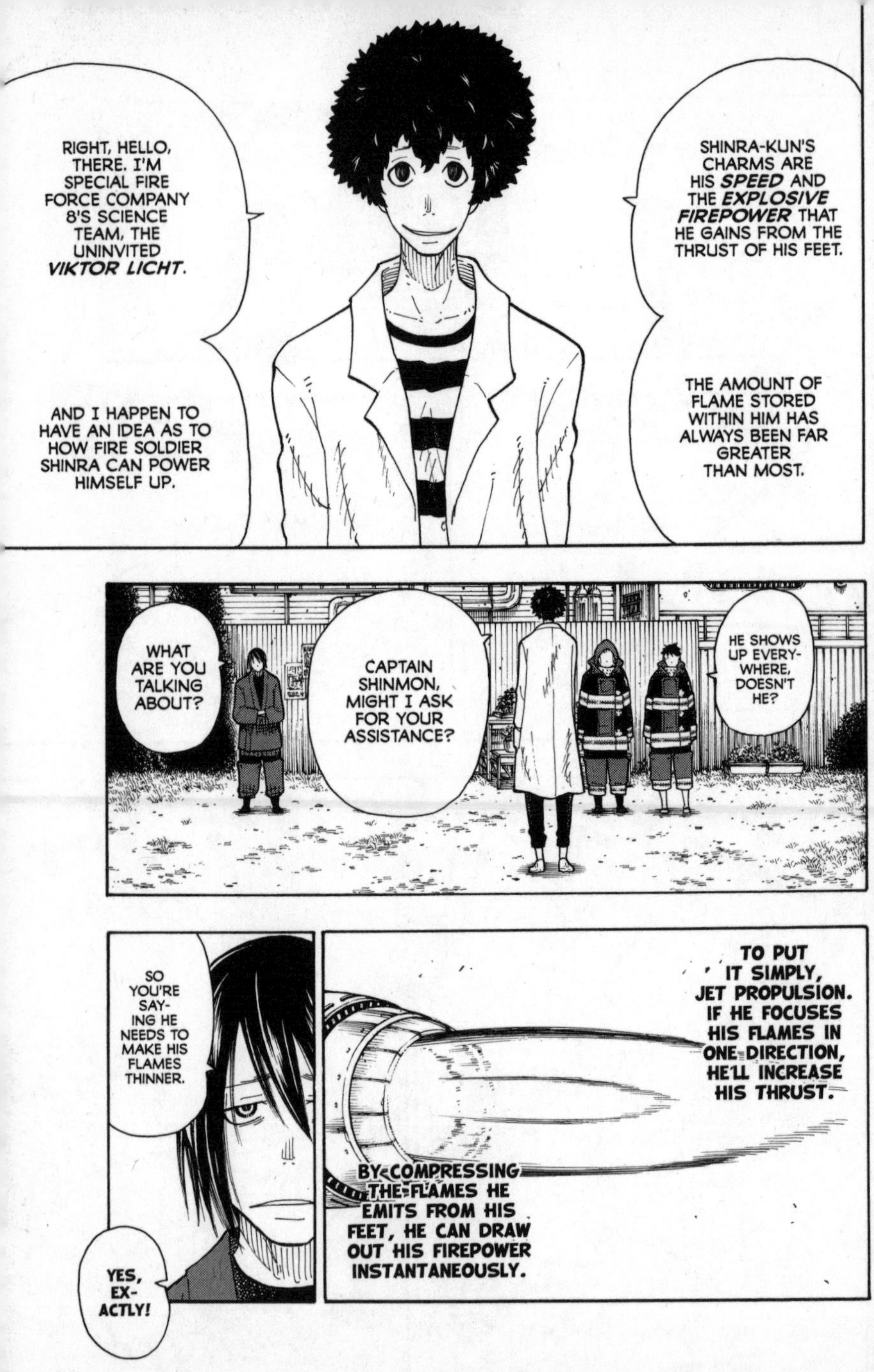
RIGHT, HELLO, THERE. I'M SPECIAL FIRE FORCE COMPANY 8'S SCIENCE TEAM, THE UNINVITED VIKTOR LICHT.
AND I HAPPEN TO HAVE AN IDEA AS TO HOW FIRE SOLDIER SHINRA CAN POWER HIMSELF UP.
SHINRA-KUN'S CHARMS ARE HIS SPEED AND THE EXPLOSIVE FIREPOWER THAT HE GAINS FROM THE THRUST OF HIS FEET.
THE AMOUNT OF FLAME STORED WITHIN HIM HAS ALWAYS BEEN FAR GREATER THAN MOST.
HE SHOWS UP EVERY-WHERE, DOESN'T HE?
CAPTAIN SHINMON, MIGHT I ASK FOR YOUR ASSISTANCE?
WHAT ARE YOU TALKING ABOUT?
TO PUT IT SIMPLY, JET PROPULSION. IF HE FOCUSES HIS FLAMES IN ONE DIRECTION, HE'LL INCREASE HIS THRUST.
BY COMPRESSING THE FLAMES HE EMITS FROM HIS FEET, HE CAN DRAW OUT HIS FIREPOWER INSTANTANEOUSLY.
SO YOU'RE SAY-ING HE NEEDS TO MAKE HIS FLAMES THINNER.
YES, EX-ACTLY!

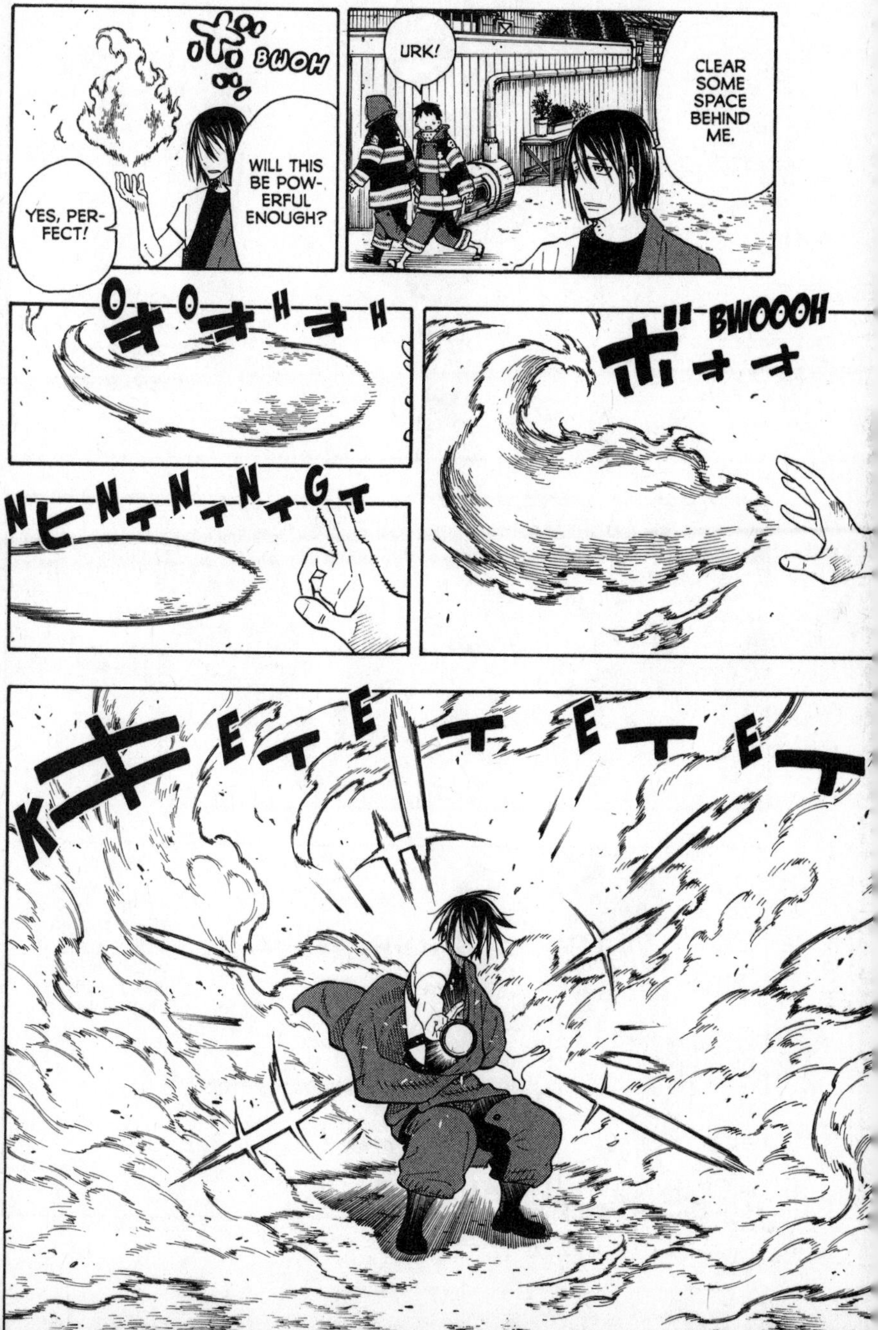
CLEAR SOME SPACE BEHIND ME.
URK!
BWOH
WILL THIS BE POW-ERFUL ENOUGH?
YES, PER-FECT!
BWOOOH
OOHH
NNNG
KEEEE

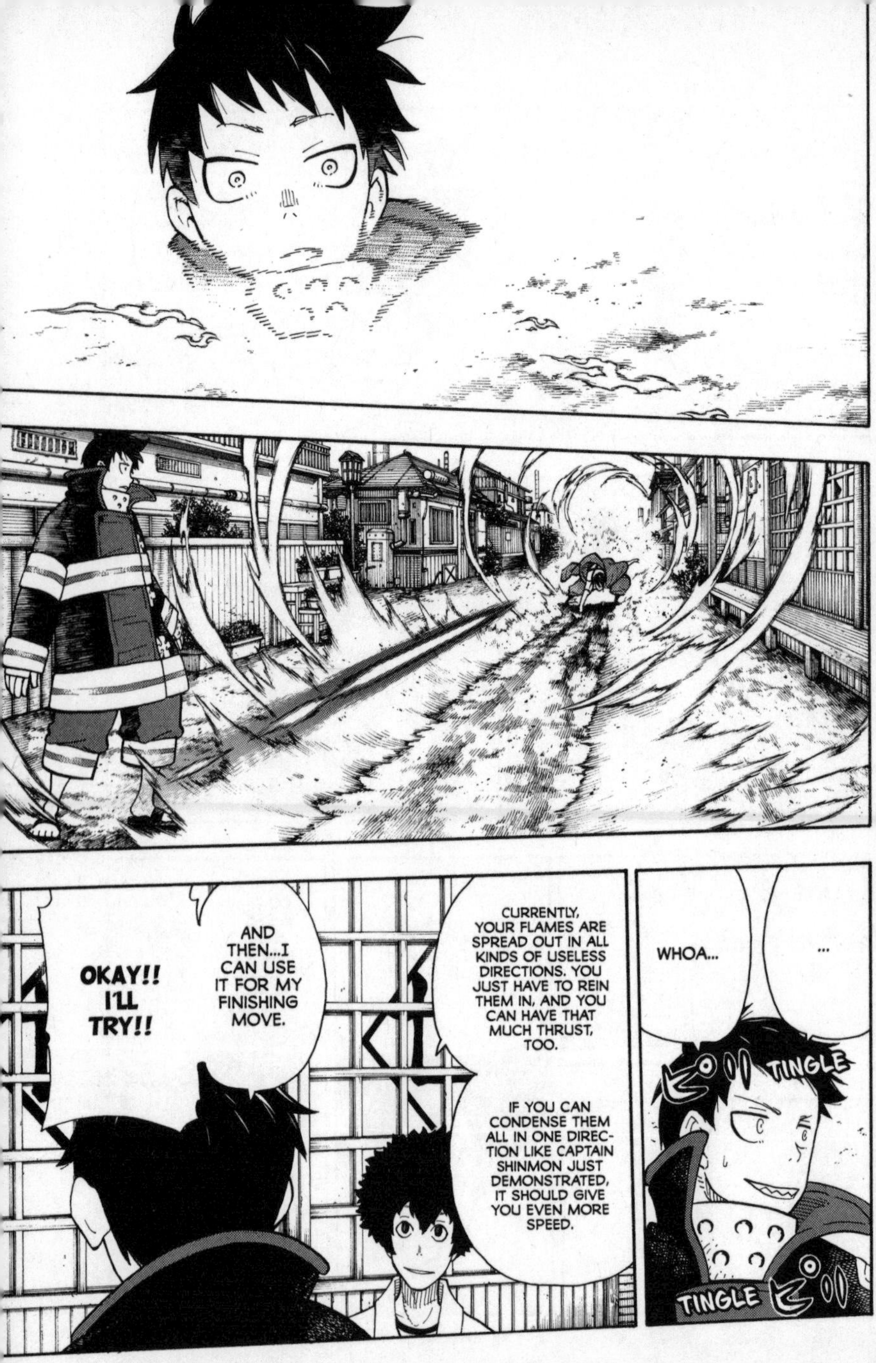
...
WHOA...
TINGLE
TINGLE
CURRENTLY, YOUR FLAMES ARE SPREAD OUT IN ALL KINDS OF USELESS DIRECTIONS. YOU JUST HAVE TO REIN THEM IN, AND YOU CAN HAVE THAT MUCH THRUST, TOO.
IF YOU CAN CONDENSE THEM ALL IN ONE DIRECTION LIKE CAPTAIN SHINMON JUST DEMONSTRATED, IT SHOULD GIVE YOU EVEN MORE SPEED.
AND THEN...I CAN USE IT FOR MY FINISHING MOVE.
OKAY!! I'LL TRY!!

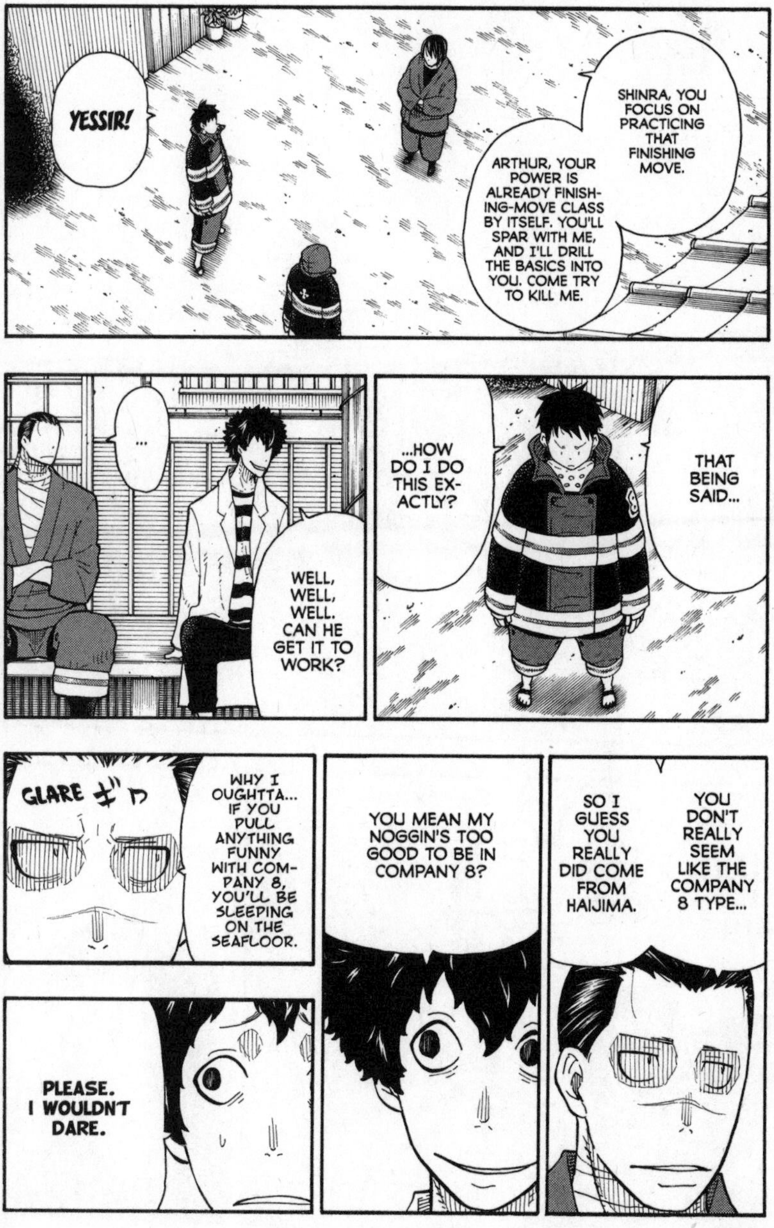
SHINRA, YOU FOCUS ON PRACTICING THAT FINISHING MOVE.
ARTHUR, YOUR POWER IS ALREADY FINISHING-MOVE CLASS BY ITSELF. YOU'LL SPAR WITH ME, AND I'LL DRILL THE BASICS INTO YOU. COME TRY TO KILL ME.
YESSIR!
THAT BEING SAID...
...HOW DO I DO THIS EXACTLY?
...
WELL, WELL, WELL. CAN HE GET IT TO WORK?
YOU DON'T REALLY SEEM LIKE THE COMPANY 8 TYPE...
SO I GUESS YOU REALLY DID COME FROM HAIJIMA.
YOU MEAN MY NOGGIN'S TOO GOOD TO BE IN COMPANY 8?
WHY I OUGHTTA... IF YOU PULL ANYTHING FUNNY WITH COMPANY 8, YOU'LL BE SLEEPING ON THE SEAFLOOR.
GLARE ギロ
PLEASE. I WOULDN'T DARE.

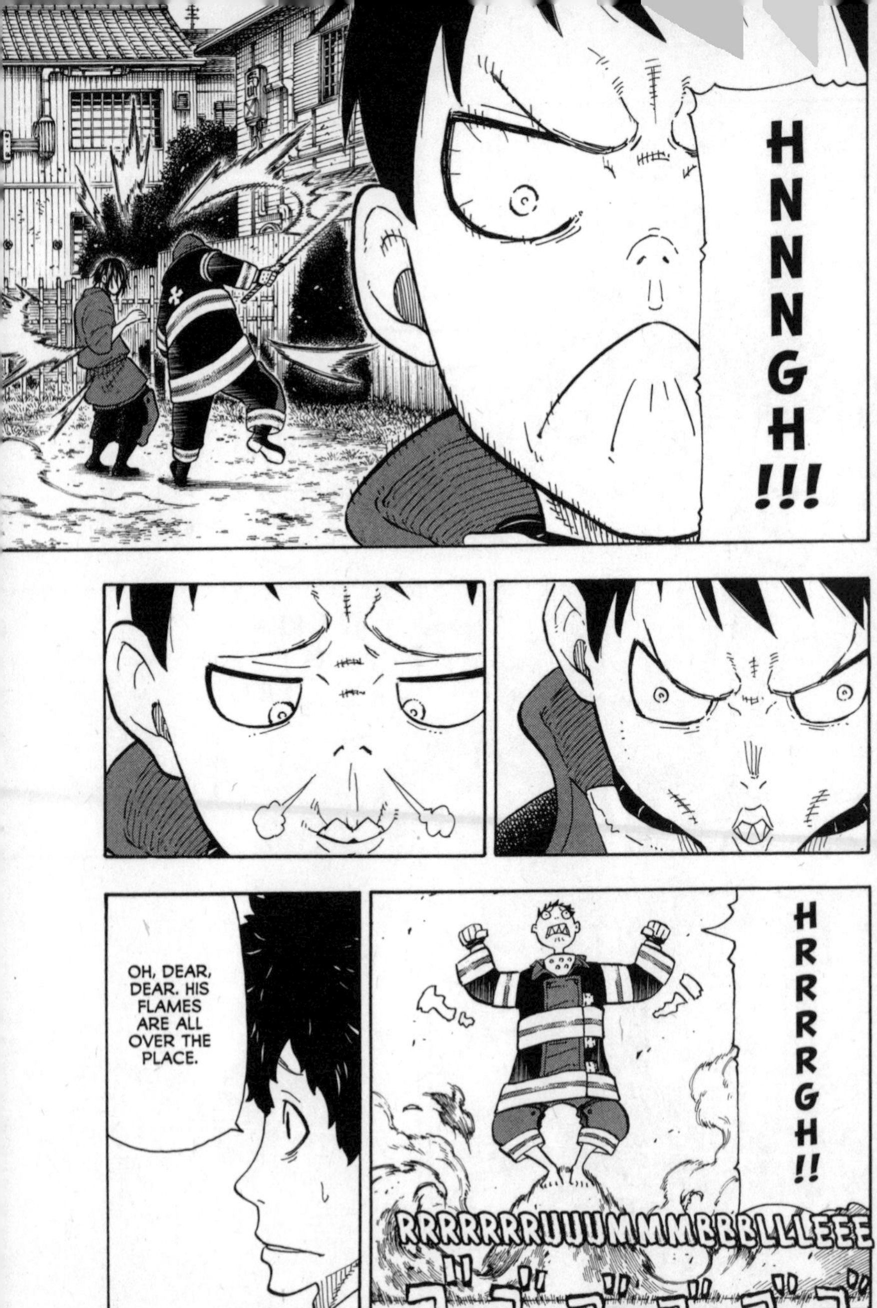
HNNNGH!!!
HRRRRRGH!!
OH, DEAR, DEAR. HIS FLAMES ARE ALL OVER THE PLACE.
RRRRRRRUUUMMMBBBLLLEEE!!
ゴゴゴゴゴゴ

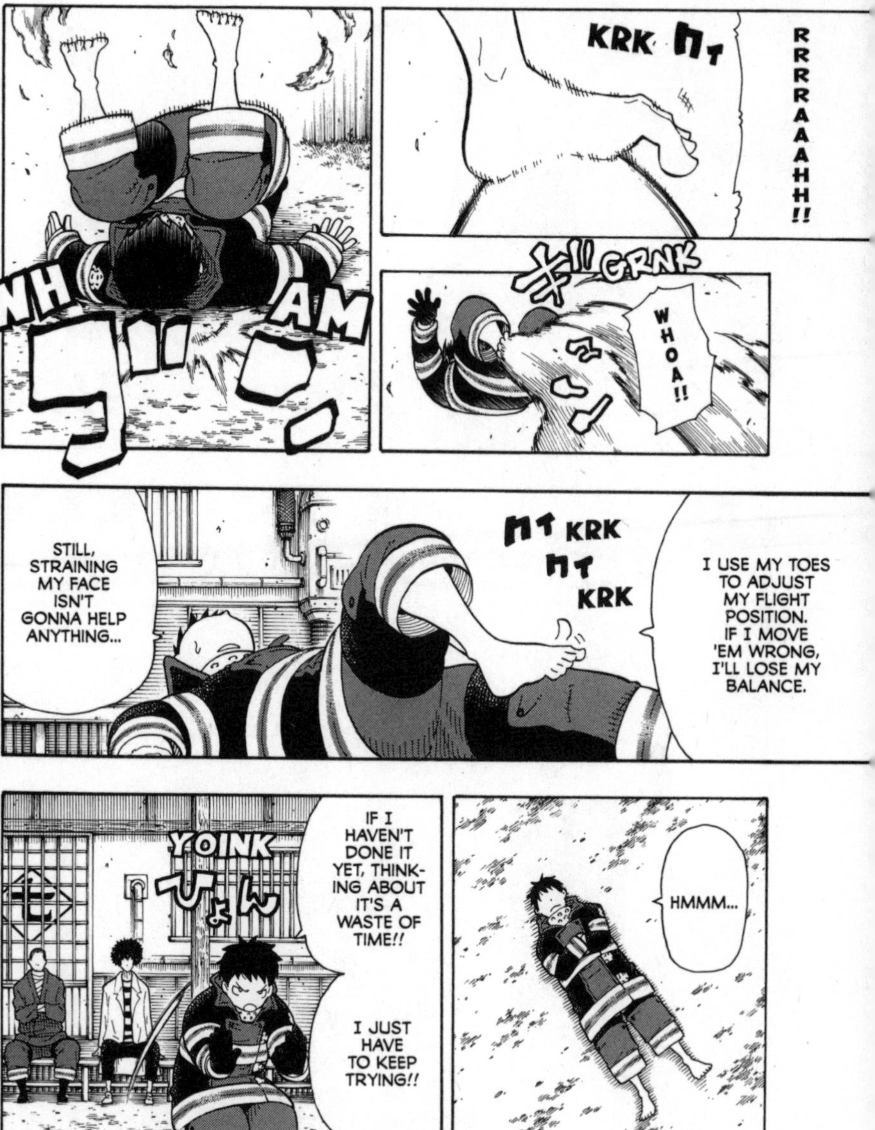
KRK
RRRRAAAAHH!!
GRNK
WHOA!!
WHAM
I USE MY TOES TO ADJUST MY FLIGHT POSITION. IF I MOVE 'EM WRONG, I'LL LOSE MY BALANCE.
KRK
KRK
STILL, STRAINING MY FACE ISN'T GONNA HELP ANYTHING...
HMMM...
IF I HAVEN'T DONE IT YET, THINKING ABOUT IT'S A WASTE OF TIME!!
I JUST HAVE TO KEEP TRYING!!
YOINK

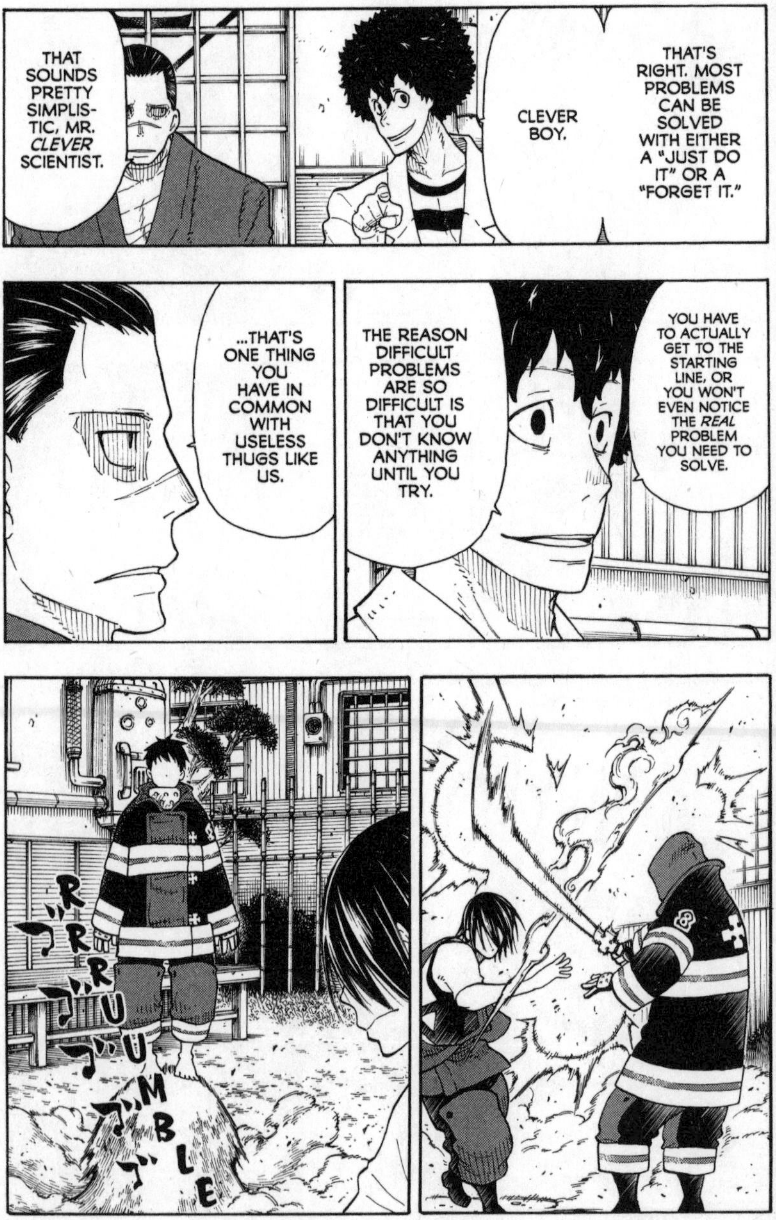
THAT'S RIGHT. MOST PROBLEMS CAN BE SOLVED WITH EITHER A "JUST DO IT" OR A "FORGET IT."
CLEVER BOY.
THAT SOUNDS PRETTY SIMPLISTIC, MR. *CLEVER* SCIENTIST.
YOU HAVE TO ACTUALLY GET TO THE STARTING LINE, OR YOU WON'T EVEN NOTICE THE *REAL* PROBLEM YOU NEED TO SOLVE.
THE REASON DIFFICULT PROBLEMS ARE SO DIFFICULT IS THAT YOU DON'T KNOW ANYTHING UNTIL YOU TRY.
...THAT'S ONE THING YOU HAVE IN COMMON WITH USELESS THUGS LIKE US.
RRRUUMBLE

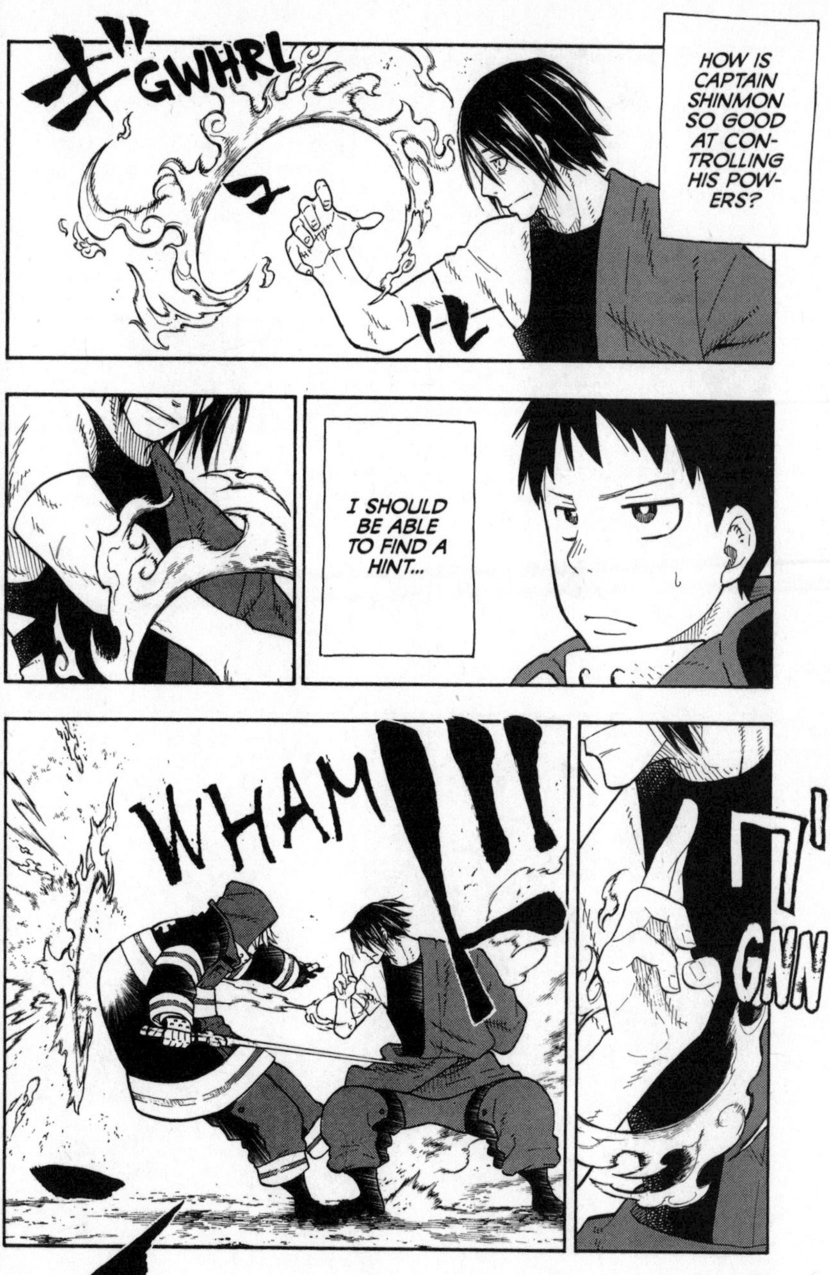
HOW IS CAPTAIN SHINMON SO GOOD AT CONTROLLING HIS POWERS?
GWHRL
I SHOULD BE ABLE TO FIND A HINT...
GNN
WHAM

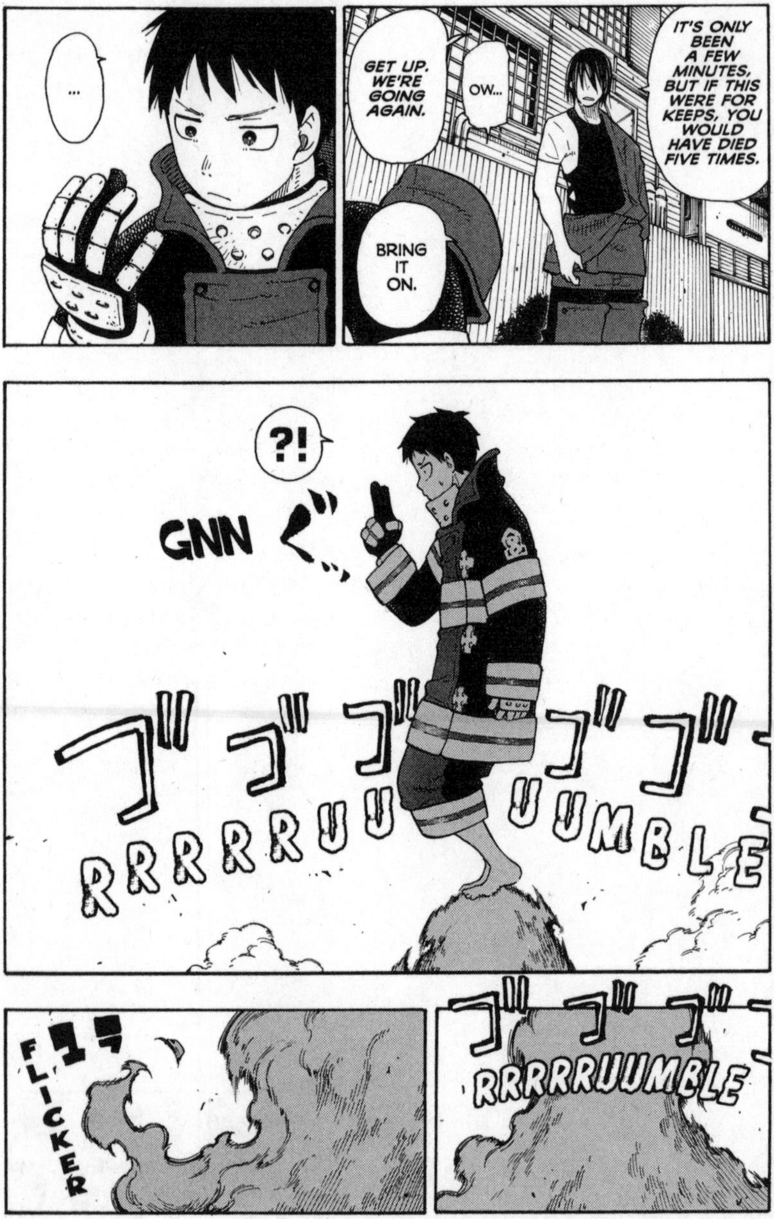
IT'S ONLY BEEN A FEW MINUTES, BUT IF THIS WERE FOR KEEPS, YOU WOULD HAVE DIED FIVE TIMES.
OW...
GET UP. WE'RE GOING AGAIN.
BRING IT ON.
...
?!
GNN
RRRRRUU UUMBLE
RRRRRUUMBLE
FLICKER

FIRE FORCE

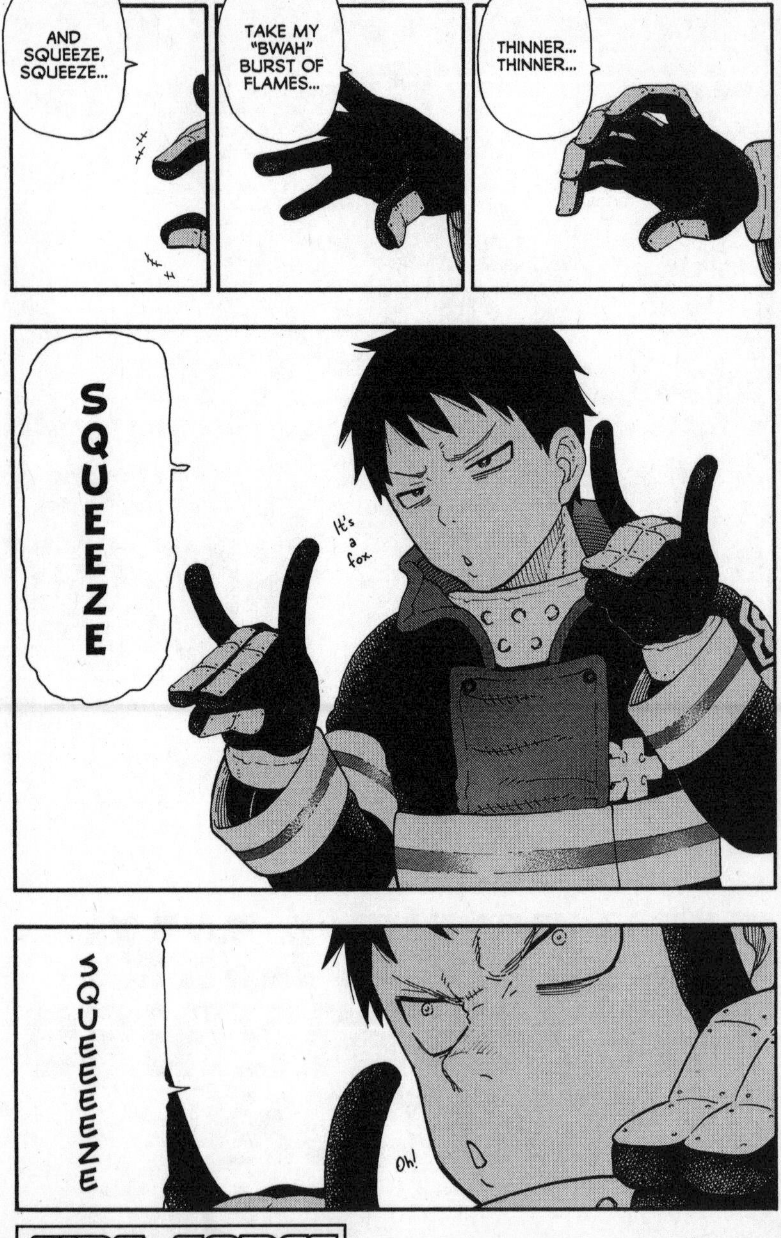
THINNER... THINNER...
TAKE MY "BWAH" BURST OF FLAMES...
AND SQUEEZE, SQUEEZE...
SQUEEZE
It's a fox.
SQUEEEEZE
Oh!

FIRE FORCE

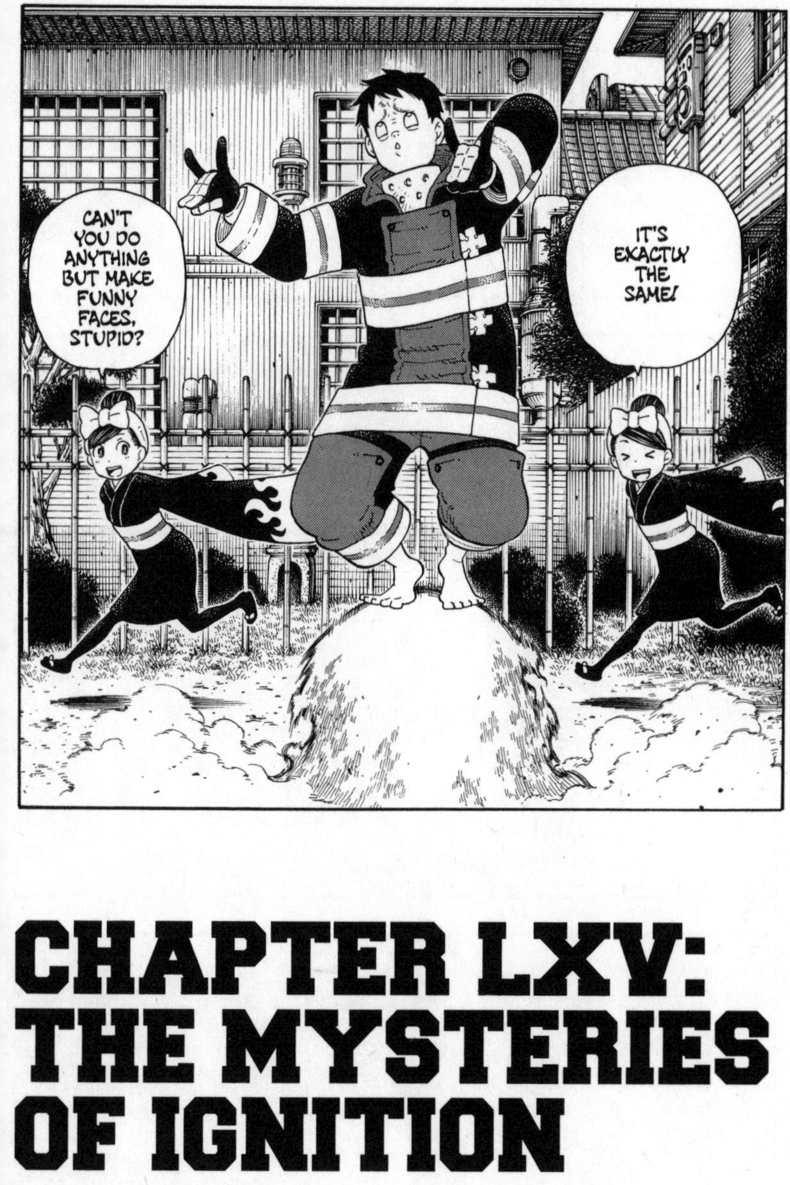
IT'S EXACTLY THE SAME!
CAN'T YOU DO ANYTHING BUT MAKE FUNNY FACES, STUPID?

CHAPTER LXV: THE MYSTERIES OF IGNITION

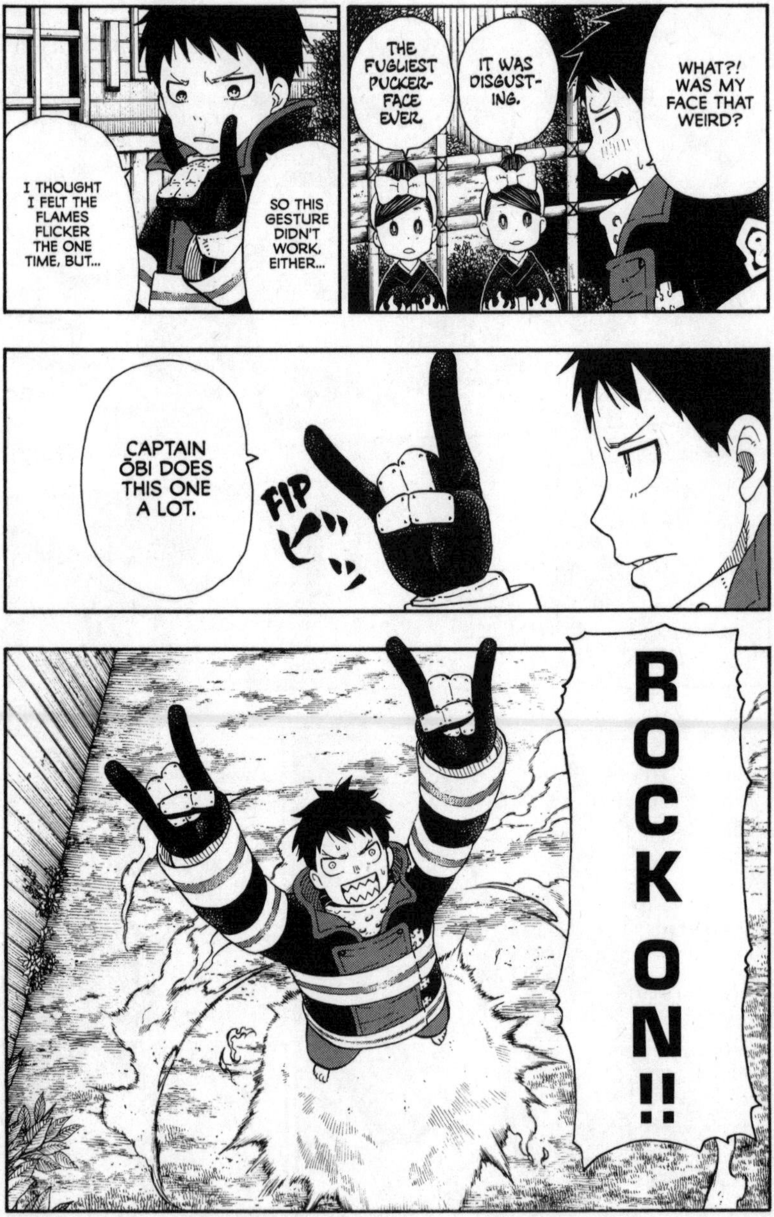
WHAT?! WAS MY FACE THAT WEIRD?
IT WAS DISGUST-ING.
THE FUGLIEST PUCKER-FACE EVER
SO THIS GESTURE DIDN'T WORK, EITHER...
I THOUGHT I FELT THE FLAMES FLICKER THE ONE TIME, BUT...
FIP
ピッ
CAPTAIN ŌBI DOES THIS ONE A LOT.
ROCK ON!!

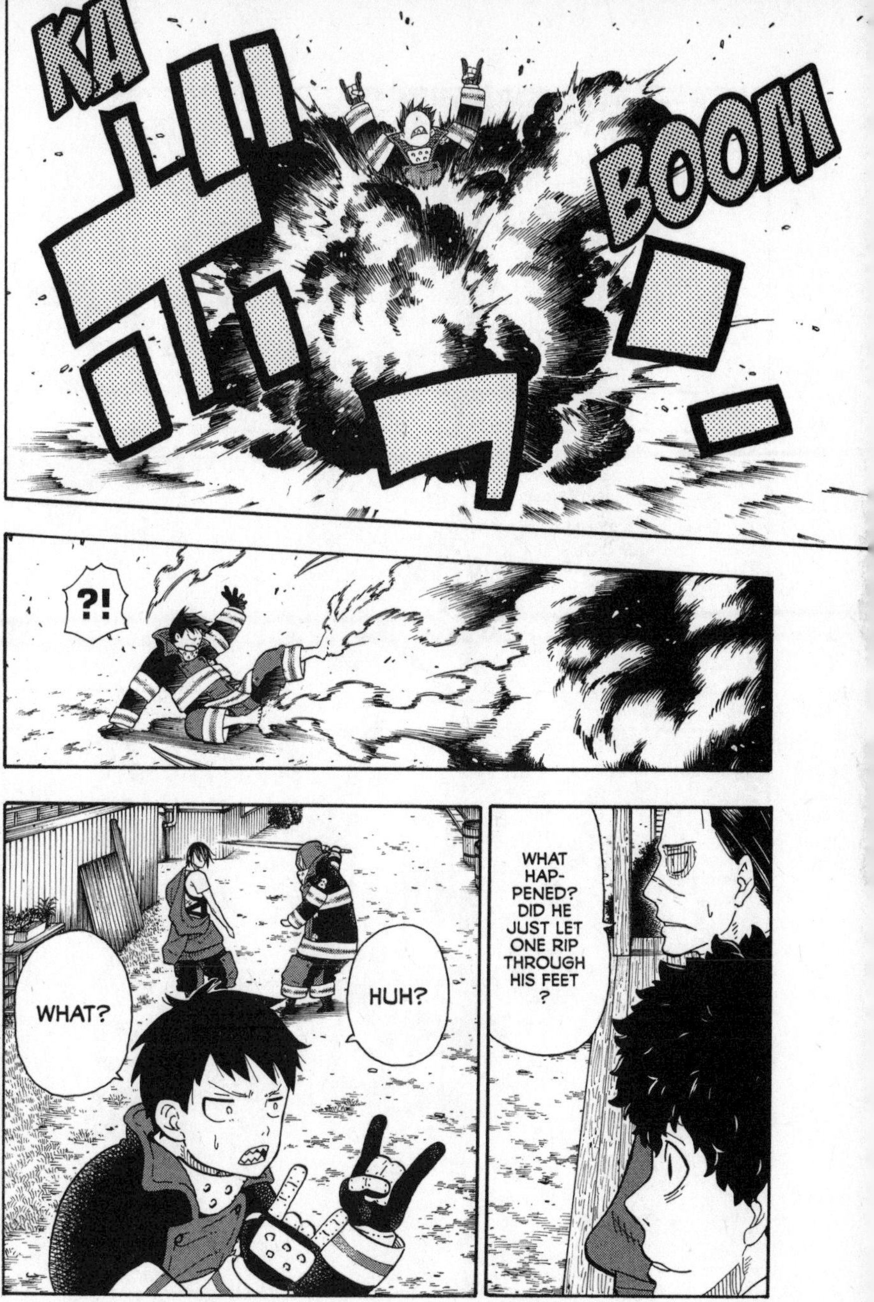
KA
BOOM
?!
WHAT HAP-PENED? DID HE JUST LET ONE RIP THROUGH HIS FEET?
HUH?
WHAT?

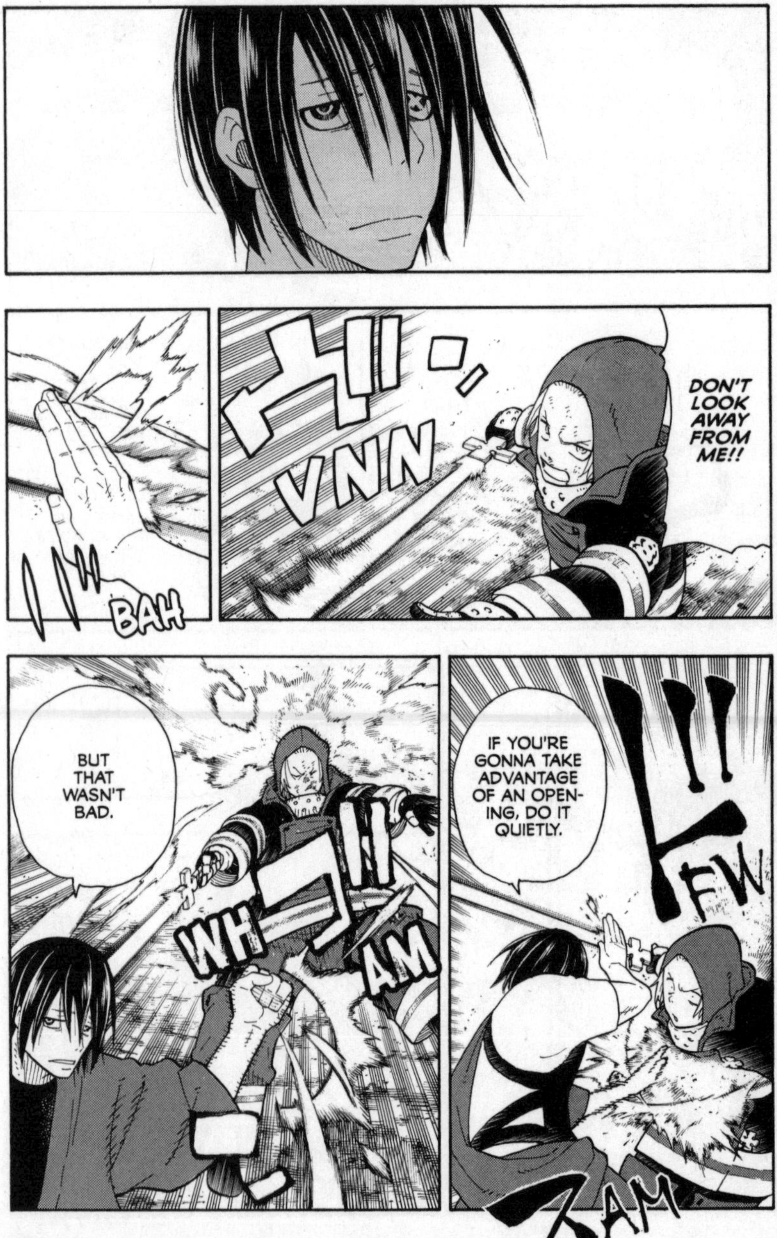
VNN
DON'T LOOK AWAY FROM ME!!
BAH
IF YOU'RE GONNA TAKE ADVANTAGE OF AN OPEN-ING, DO IT QUIETLY.
FW
AM
BUT THAT WASN'T BAD.
WH
AM

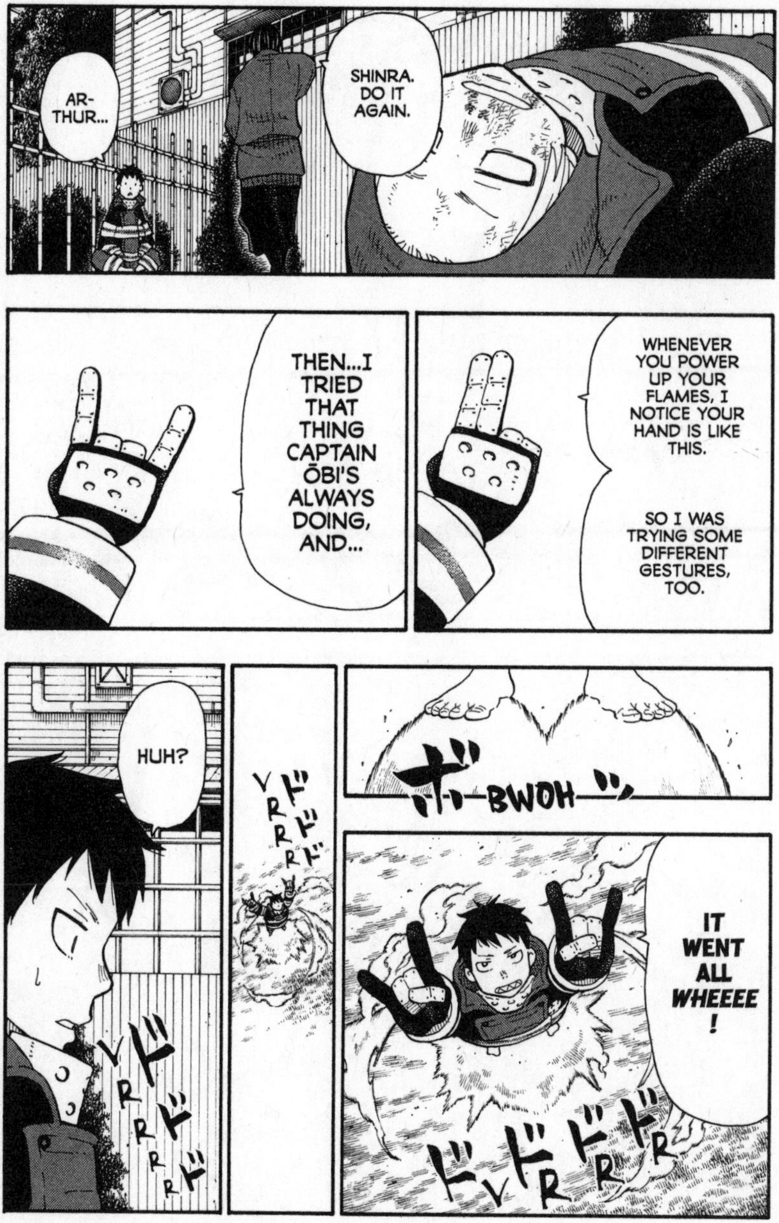
SHINRA. DO IT AGAIN.
AR-THUR...
WHENEVER YOU POWER UP YOUR FLAMES, I NOTICE YOUR HAND IS LIKE THIS.
SO I WAS TRYING SOME DIFFERENT GESTURES, TOO.
THEN...I TRIED THAT THING CAPTAIN ŌBI'S ALWAYS DOING, AND...
BWOH
IT WENT ALL WHEEEE!
VRRR
VRRR
HUH?
VRRR

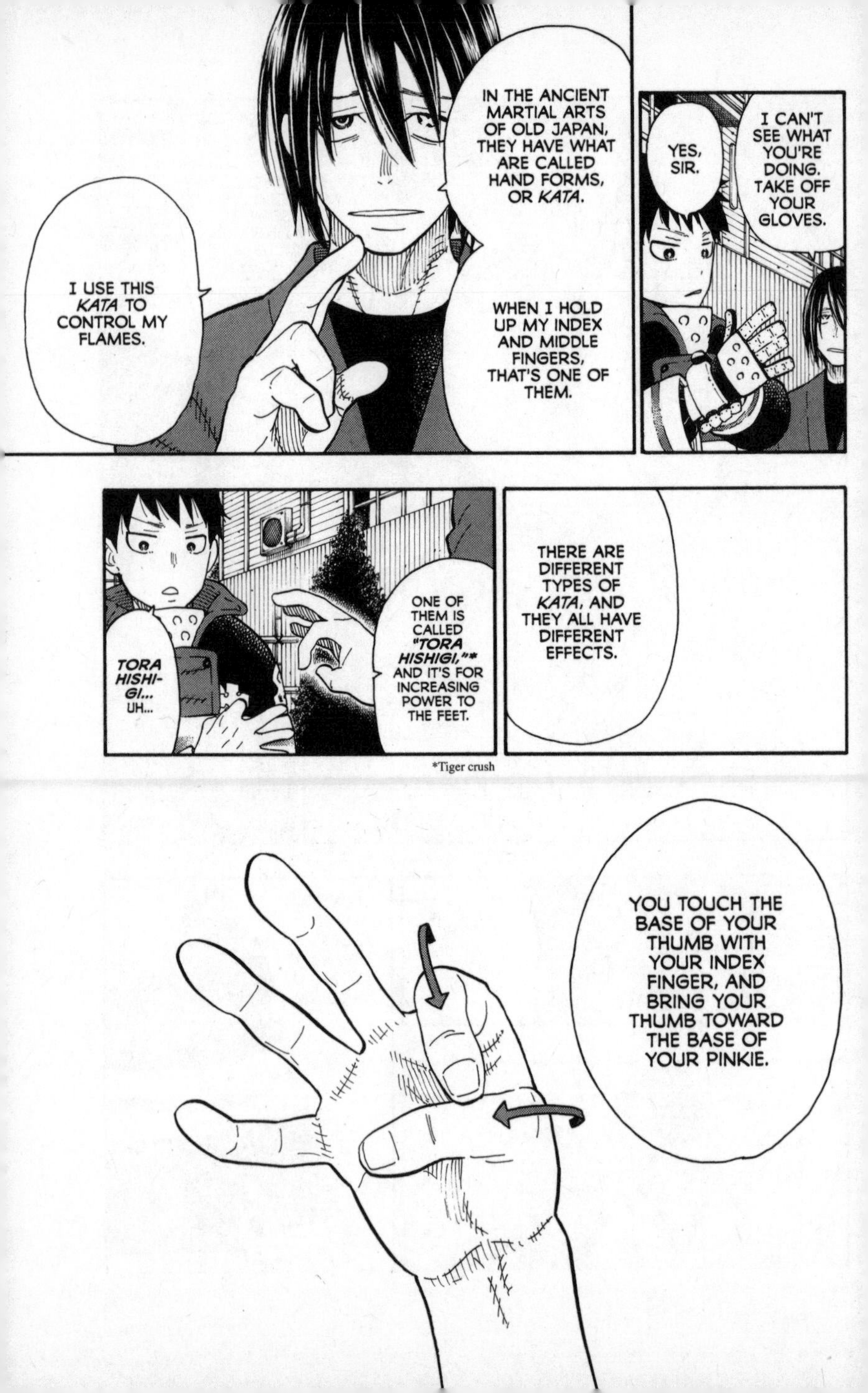
I CAN'T SEE WHAT YOU'RE DOING. TAKE OFF YOUR GLOVES.
YES, SIR.
IN THE ANCIENT MARTIAL ARTS OF OLD JAPAN, THEY HAVE WHAT ARE CALLED HAND FORMS, OR *KATA*.
WHEN I HOLD UP MY INDEX AND MIDDLE FINGERS, THAT'S ONE OF THEM.
I USE THIS *KATA* TO CONTROL MY FLAMES.
THERE ARE DIFFERENT TYPES OF *KATA*, AND THEY ALL HAVE DIFFERENT EFFECTS.
ONE OF THEM IS CALLED *"TORA HISHIGI,"** AND IT'S FOR INCREASING POWER TO THE FEET.
TORA HISHI-GI... UH...
YOU TOUCH THE BASE OF YOUR THUMB WITH YOUR INDEX FINGER, AND BRING YOUR THUMB TOWARD THE BASE OF YOUR PINKIE.

*Tiger crush

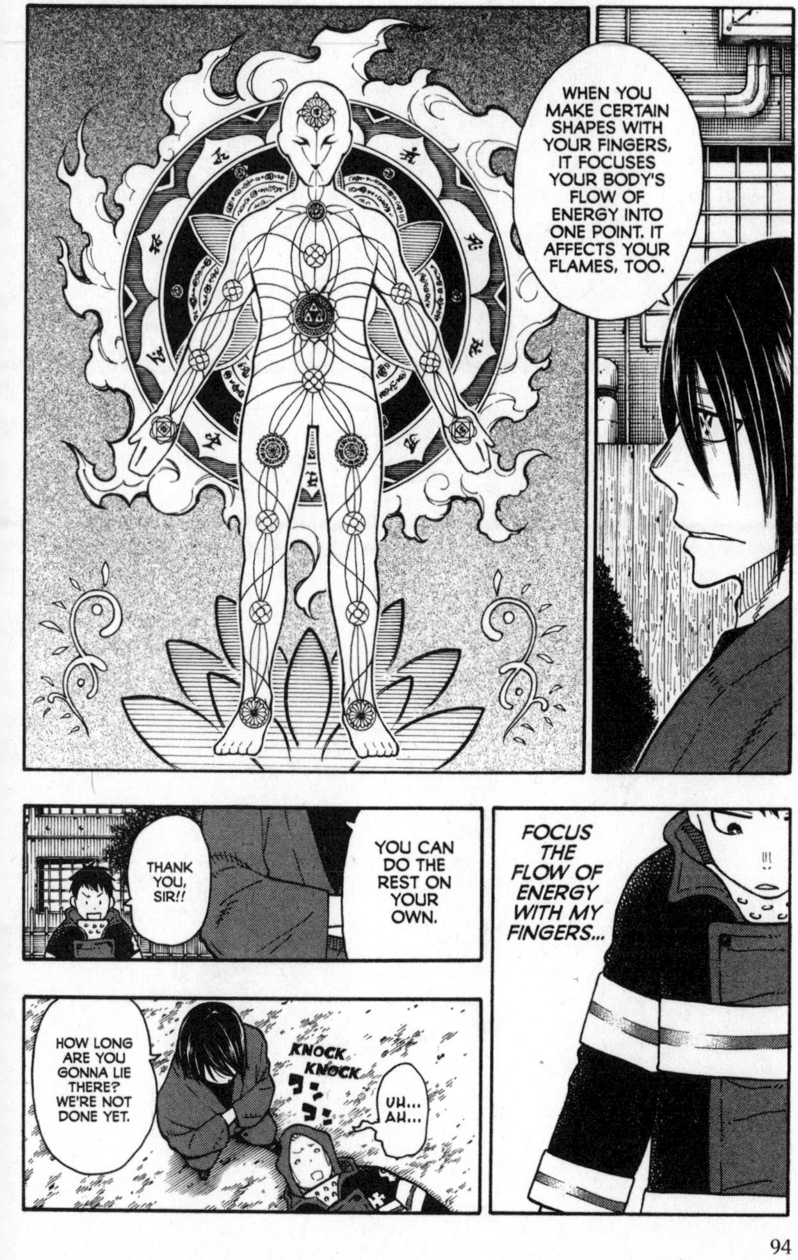
WHEN YOU MAKE CERTAIN SHAPES WITH YOUR FINGERS, IT FOCUSES YOUR BODY'S FLOW OF ENERGY INTO ONE POINT. IT AFFECTS YOUR FLAMES, TOO.
FOCUS THE FLOW OF ENERGY WITH MY FINGERS...
YOU CAN DO THE REST ON YOUR OWN.
THANK YOU, SIR!!
KNOCK KNOCK
UH... AH...
HOW LONG ARE YOU GONNA LIE THERE? WE'RE NOT DONE YET.

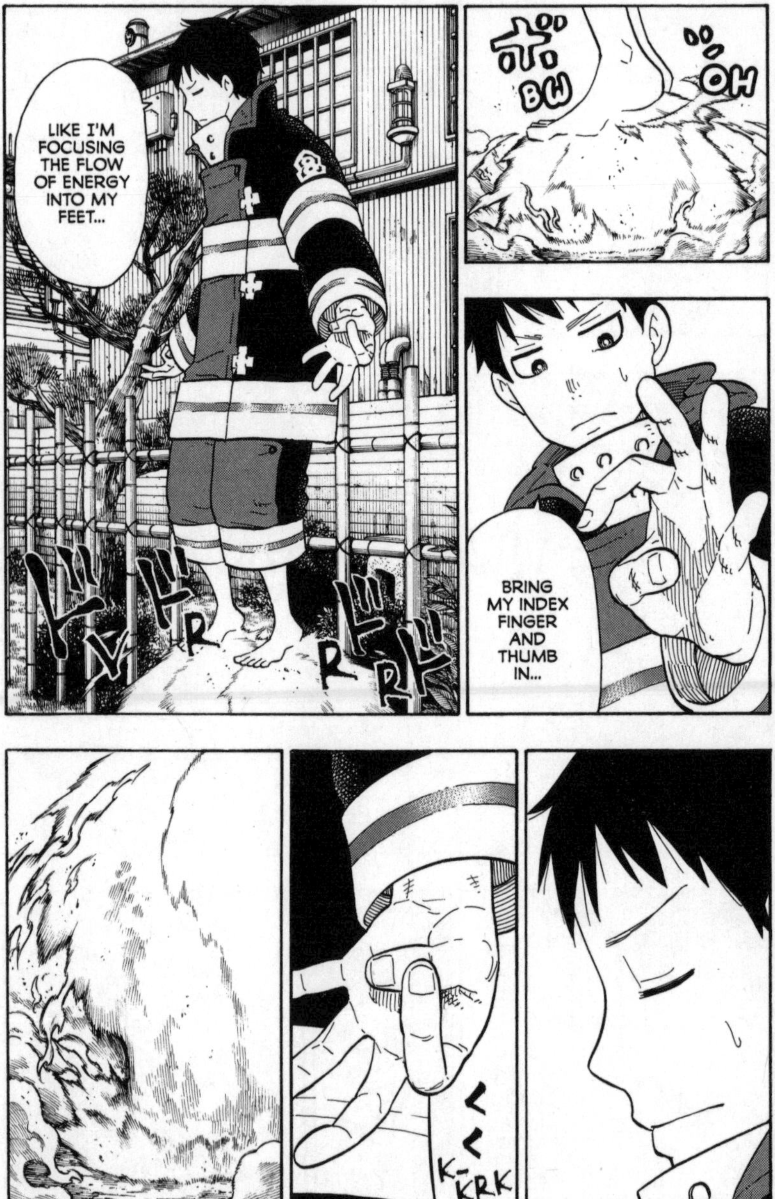
BW
OH
BRING MY INDEX FINGER AND THUMB IN...
LIKE I'M FOCUSING THE FLOW OF ENERGY INTO MY FEET...
K-KRK

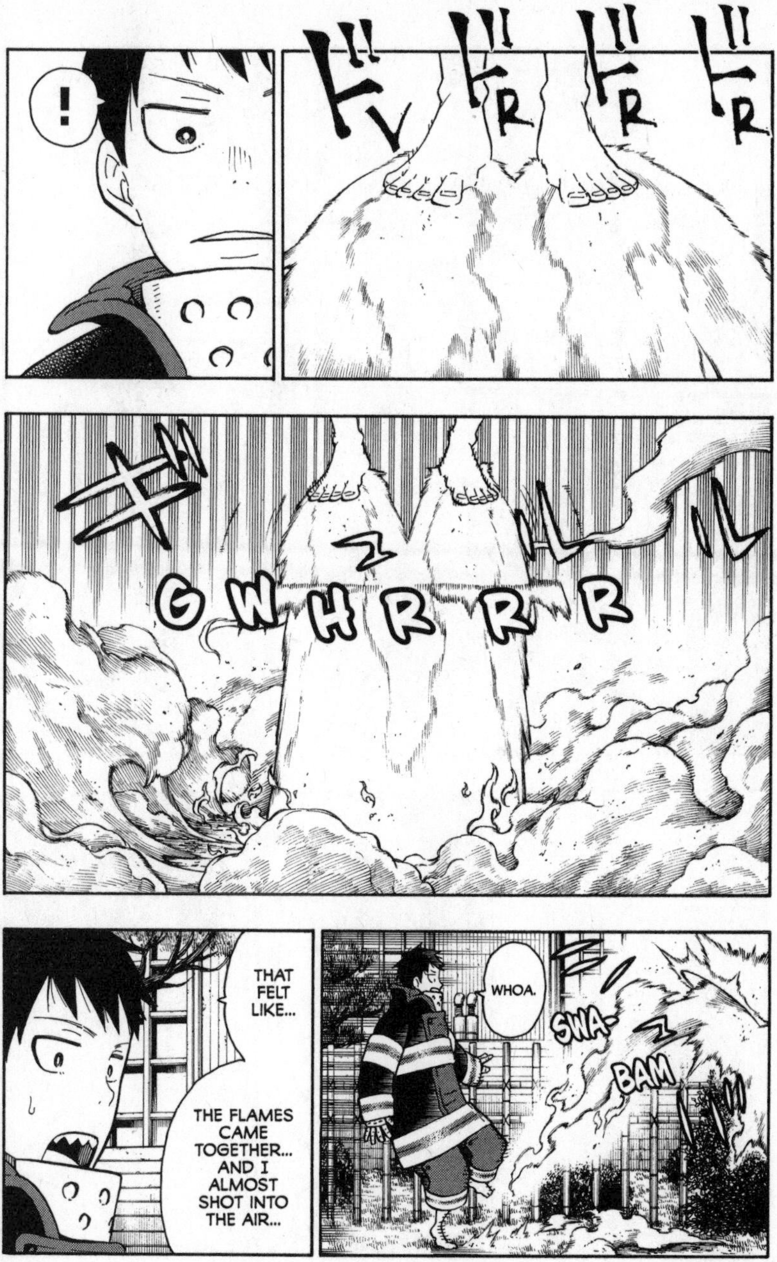
ドドドド
R R R
!
ギュルル
GWHRRR
SWA-BAM
WHOA.
THAT FELT LIKE...
THE FLAMES CAME TOGETHER... AND I ALMOST SHOT INTO THE AIR...

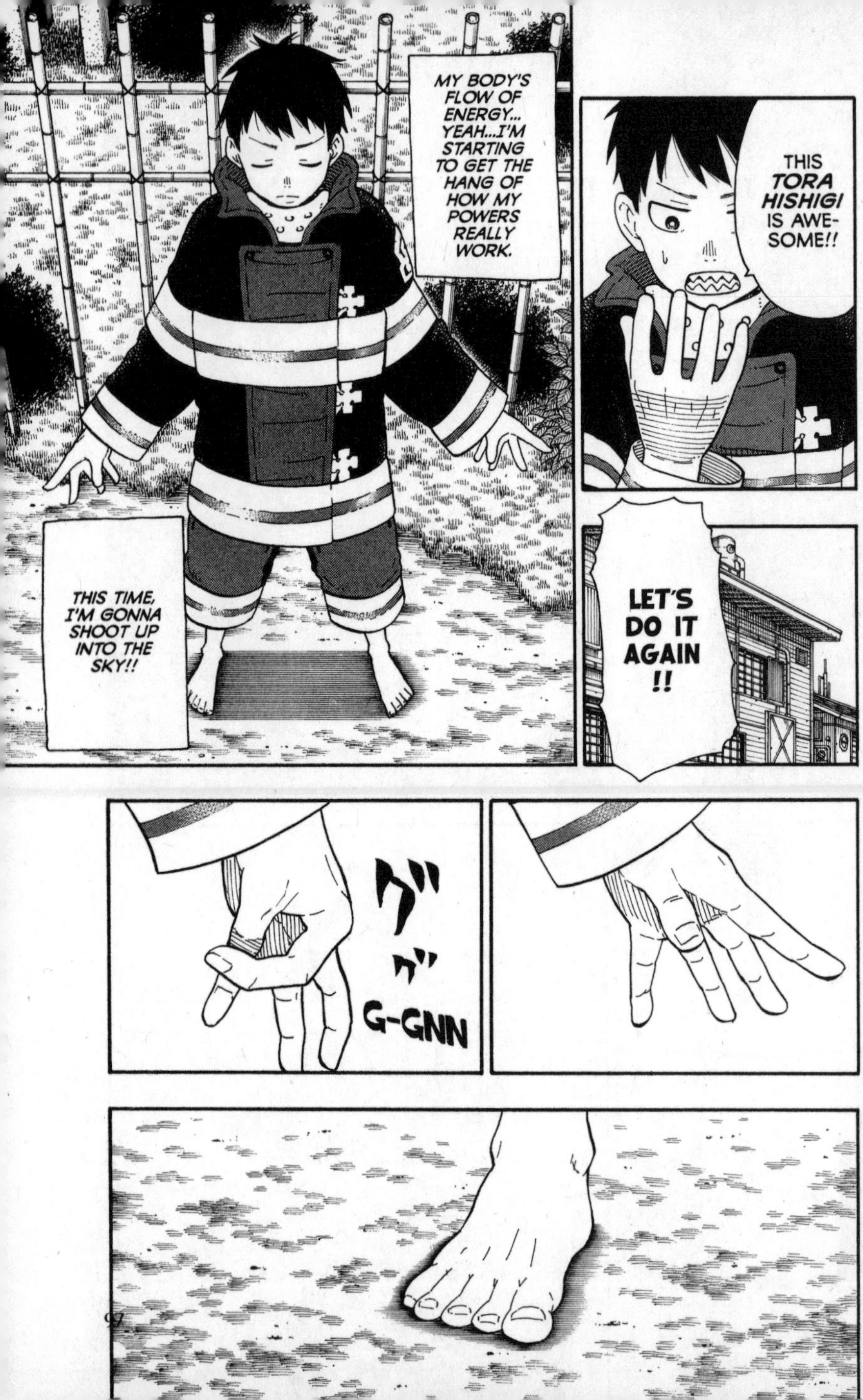
THIS TORA HISHIGI IS AWE-SOME!!
LET'S DO IT AGAIN!!
MY BODY'S FLOW OF ENERGY... YEAH...I'M STARTING TO GET THE HANG OF HOW MY POWERS REALLY WORK.
THIS TIME, I'M GONNA SHOOT UP INTO THE SKY!!
グッ
G-GNN

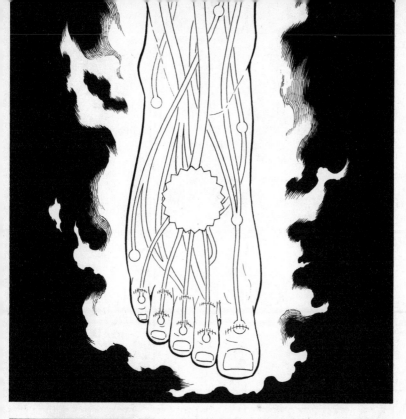

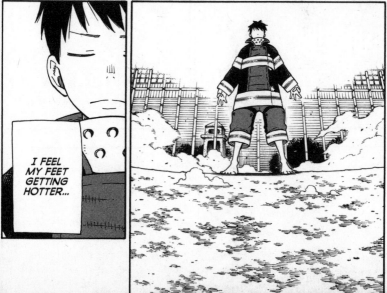

I FEEL
MY FEET
GETTING
HOTTER...

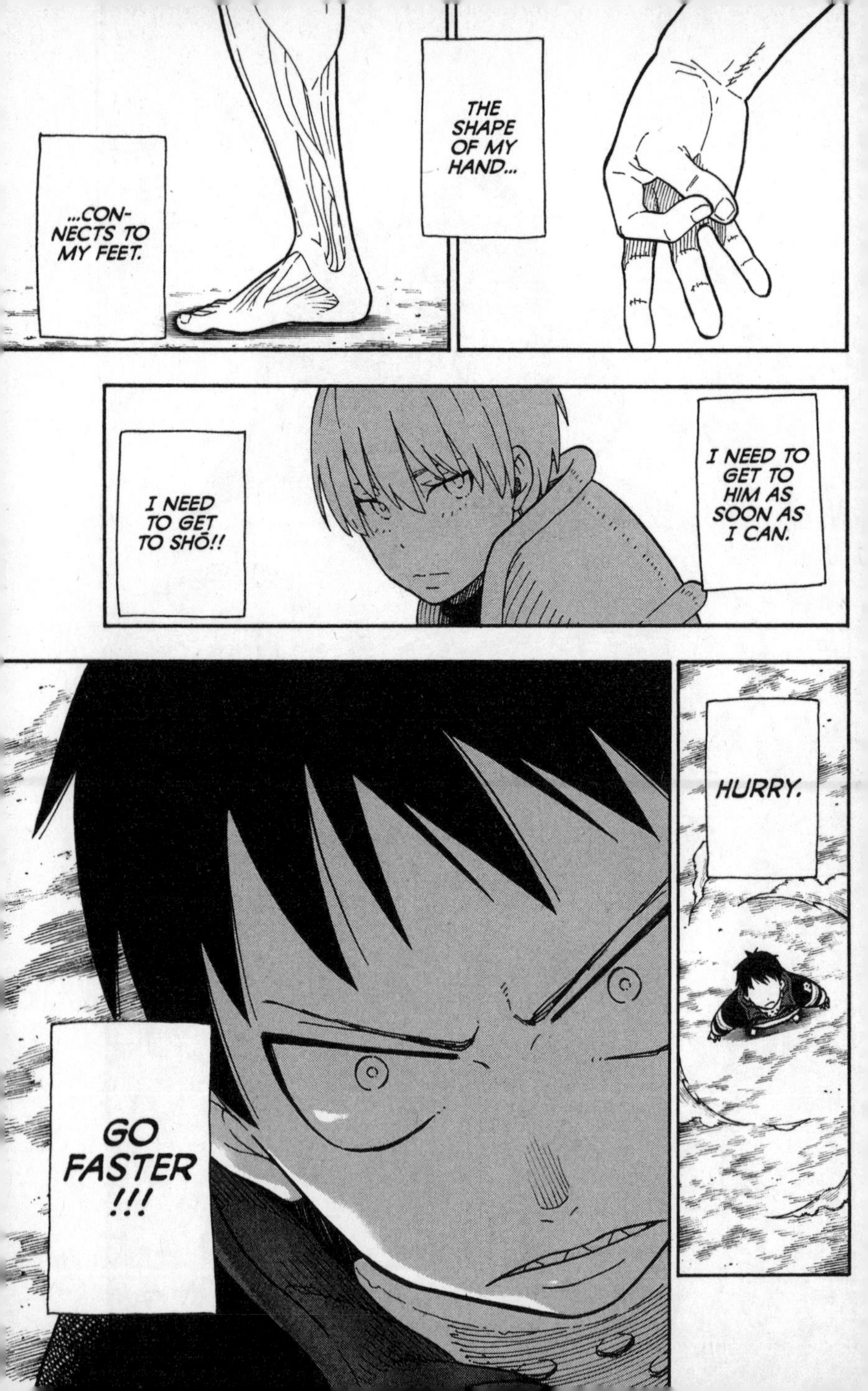
THE SHAPE OF MY HAND...
...CON-NECTS TO MY FEET.
I NEED TO GET TO HIM AS SOON AS I CAN.
I NEED TO GET TO SHŌ!!
HURRY.
GO FASTER!!!

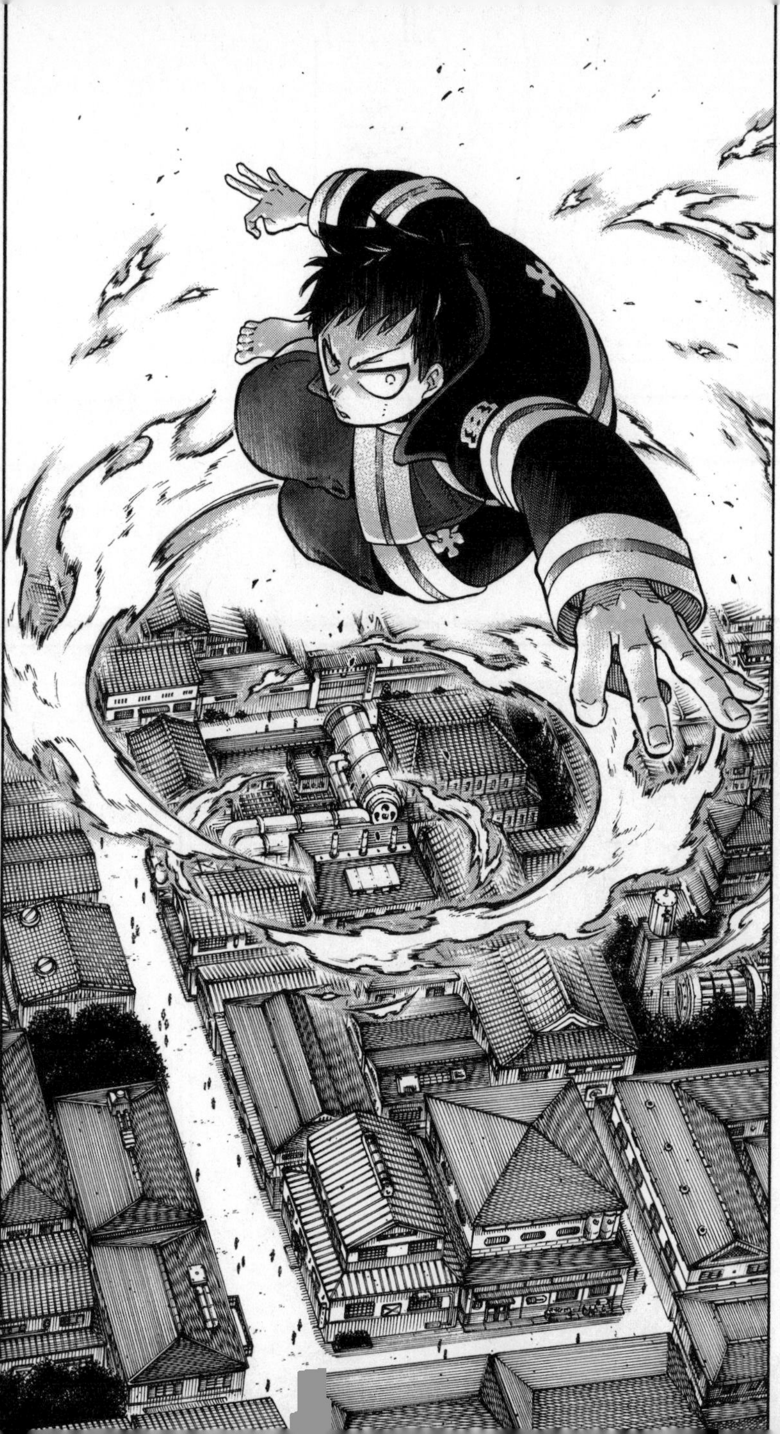

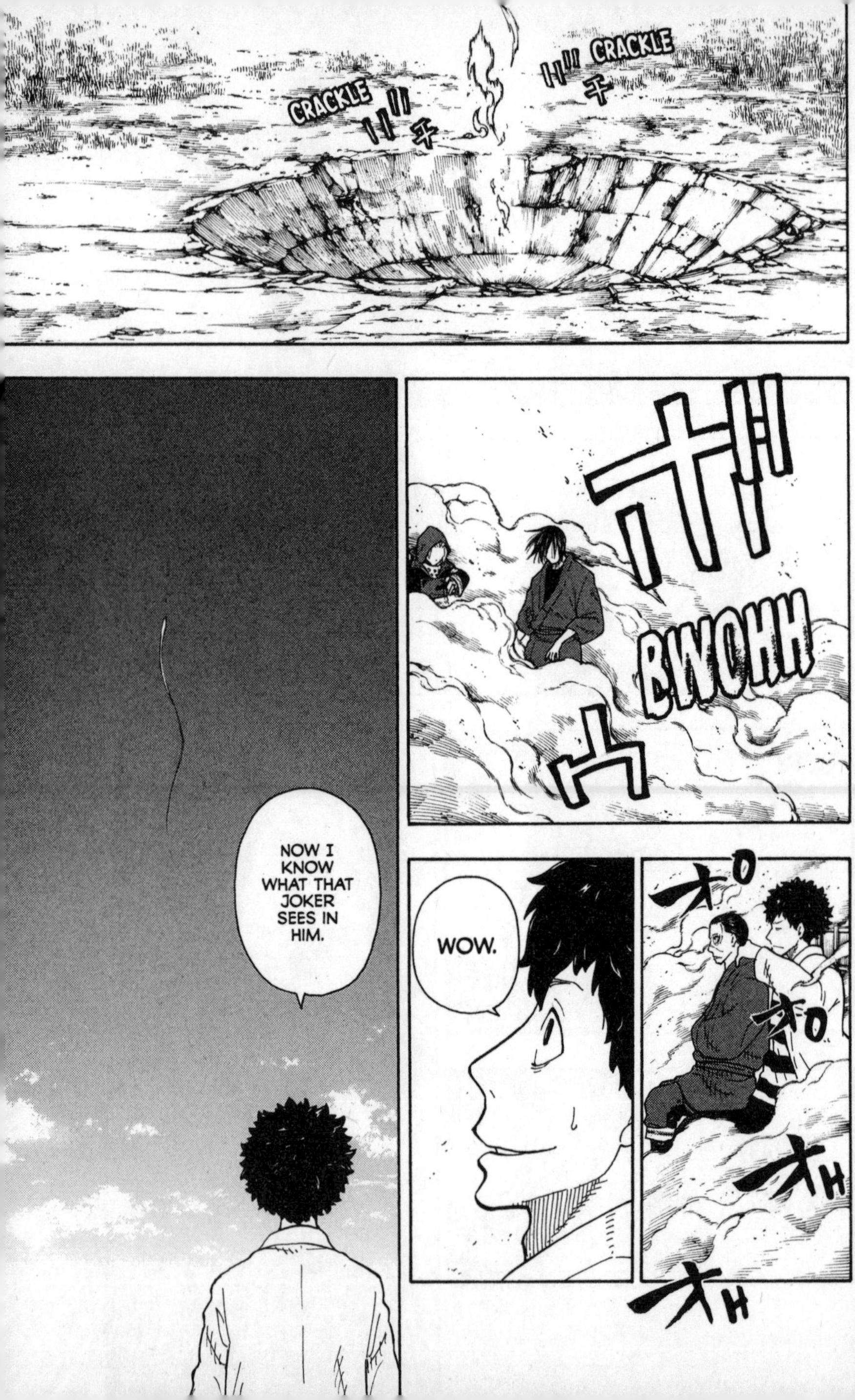

CRACKLE
CRACKLE
BWOHH
WOW.
NOW I KNOW WHAT THAT JOKER SEES IN HIM.

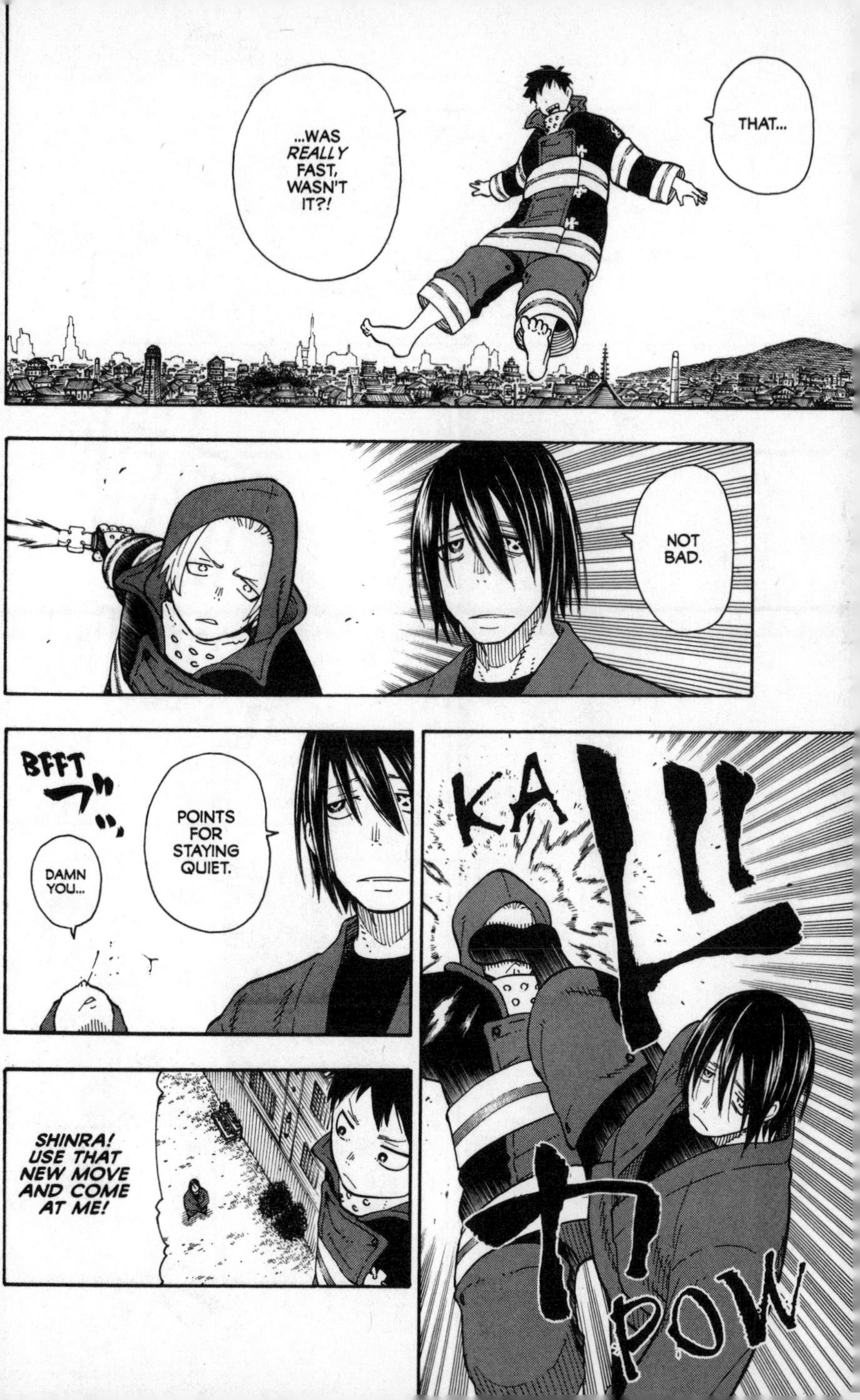
THAT...
...WAS *REALLY* FAST, WASN'T IT?!
NOT BAD.
KA
POW
POINTS FOR STAYING QUIET.
BFFT
DAMN YOU...
SHINRA! USE THAT NEW MOVE AND COME AT ME!

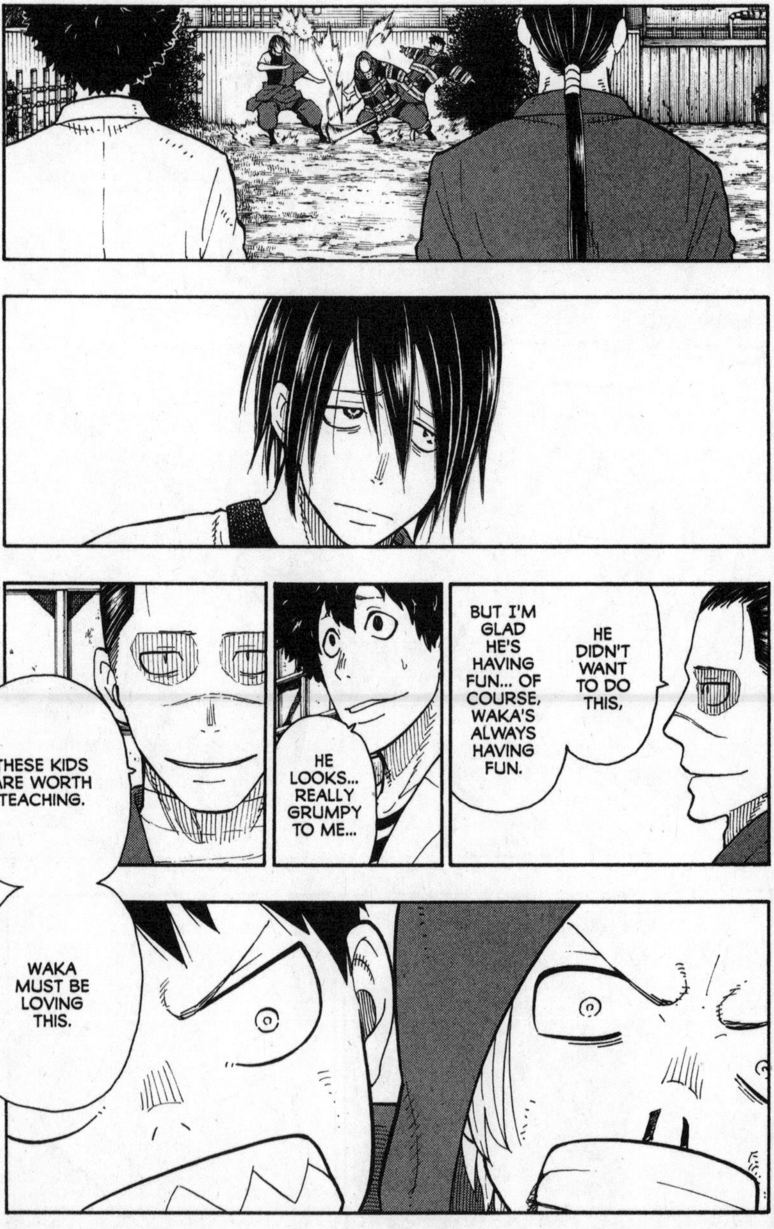
HE DIDN'T WANT TO DO THIS,
BUT I'M GLAD HE'S HAVING FUN... OF COURSE, WAKA'S ALWAYS HAVING FUN.
HE LOOKS... REALLY GRUMPY TO ME...
THESE KIDS ARE WORTH TEACHING.
WAKA MUST BE LOVING THIS.

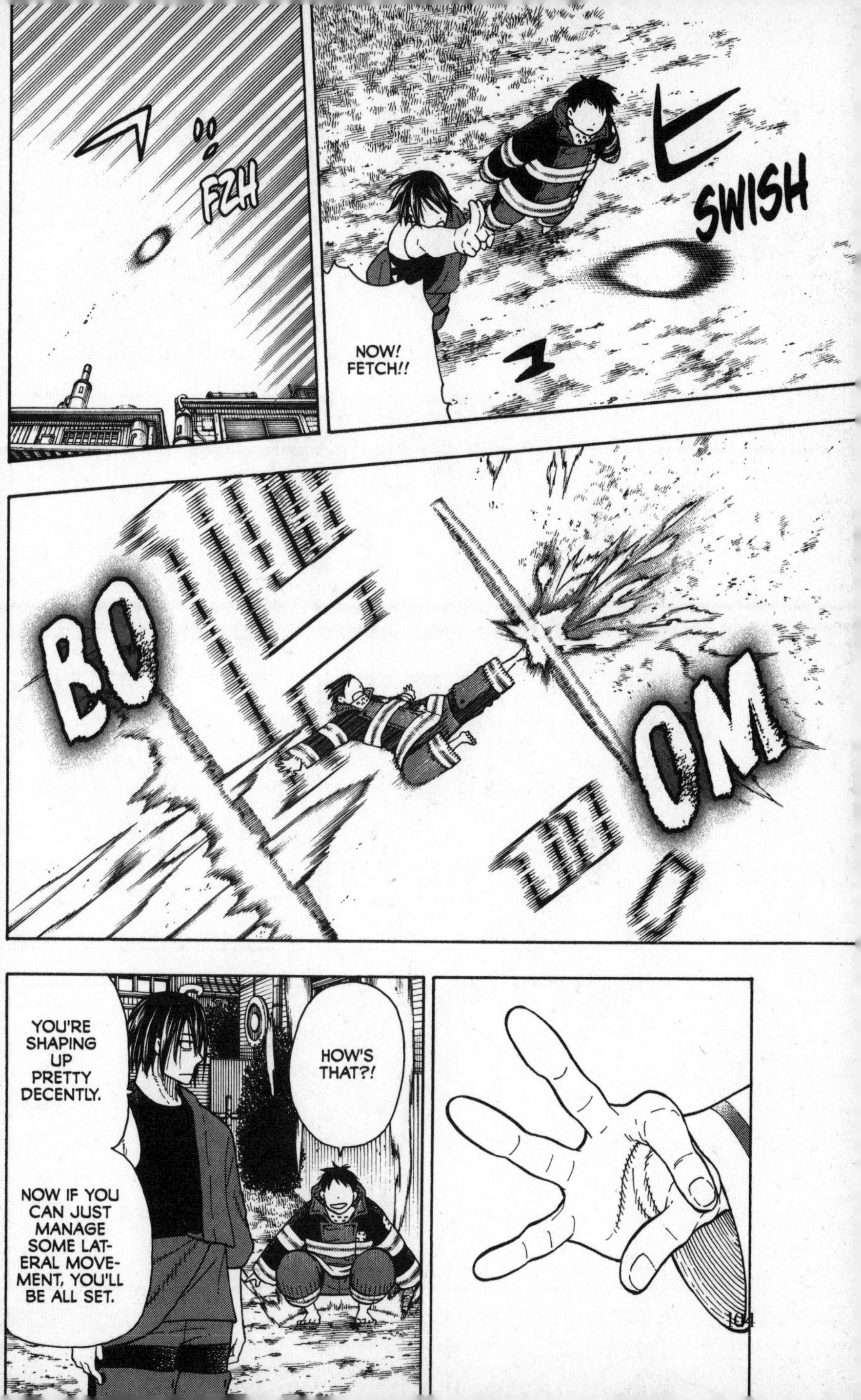
NOW! FETCH!!
SWISH
FZH
BO
OM
HOW'S THAT?!
YOU'RE SHAPING UP PRETTY DECENTLY.
NOW IF YOU CAN JUST MANAGE SOME LATERAL MOVEMENT, YOU'LL BE ALL SET.

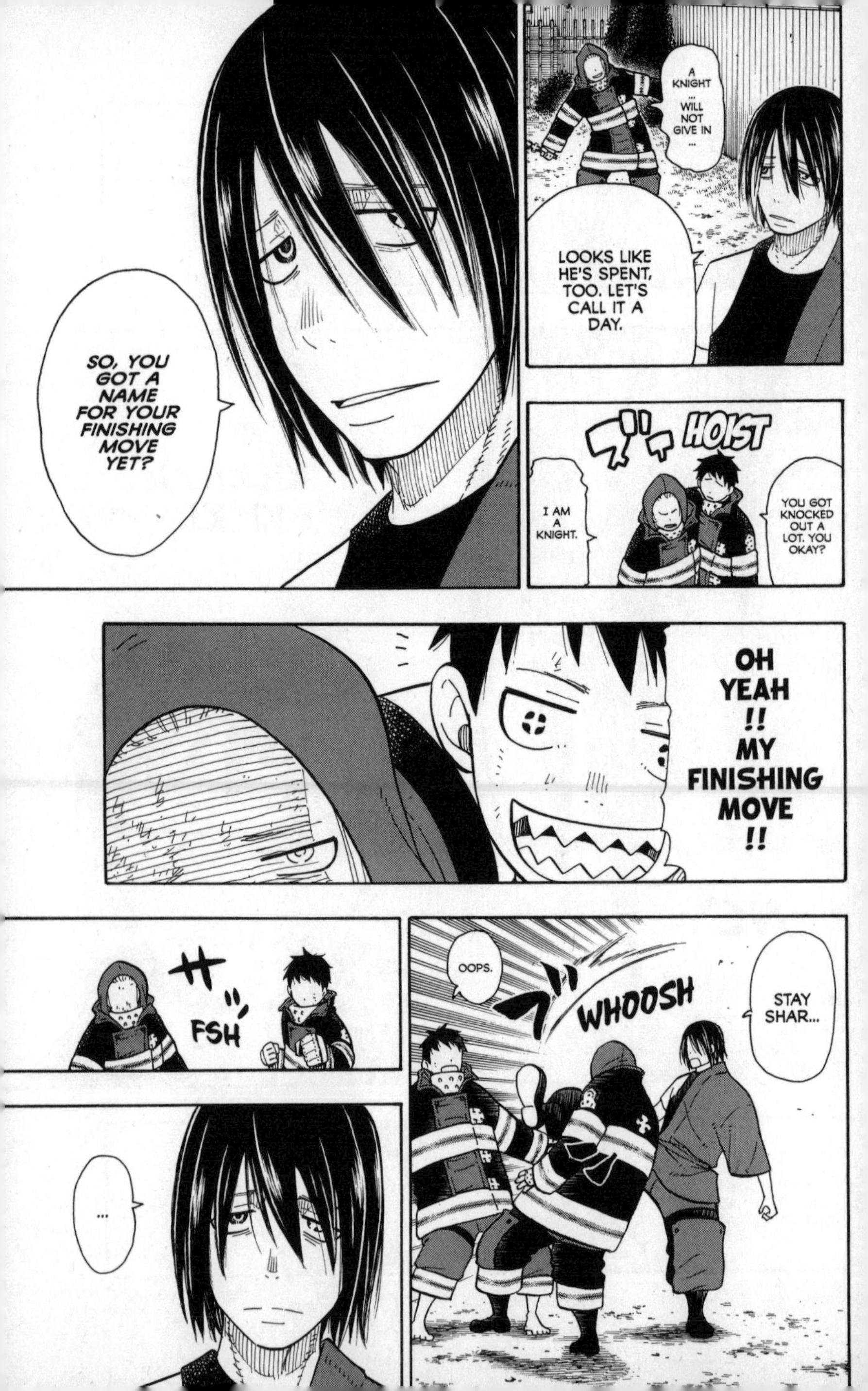
A KNIGHT ... WILL NOT GIVE IN ...
LOOKS LIKE HE'S SPENT, TOO. LET'S CALL IT A DAY.
HOIST
YOU GOT KNOCKED OUT A LOT. YOU OKAY?
I AM A KNIGHT.
SO, YOU GOT A NAME FOR YOUR FINISHING MOVE YET?
OH YEAH!! MY FINISHING MOVE!!
STAY SHAR...
WHOOSH
OOPS.
FSH
...

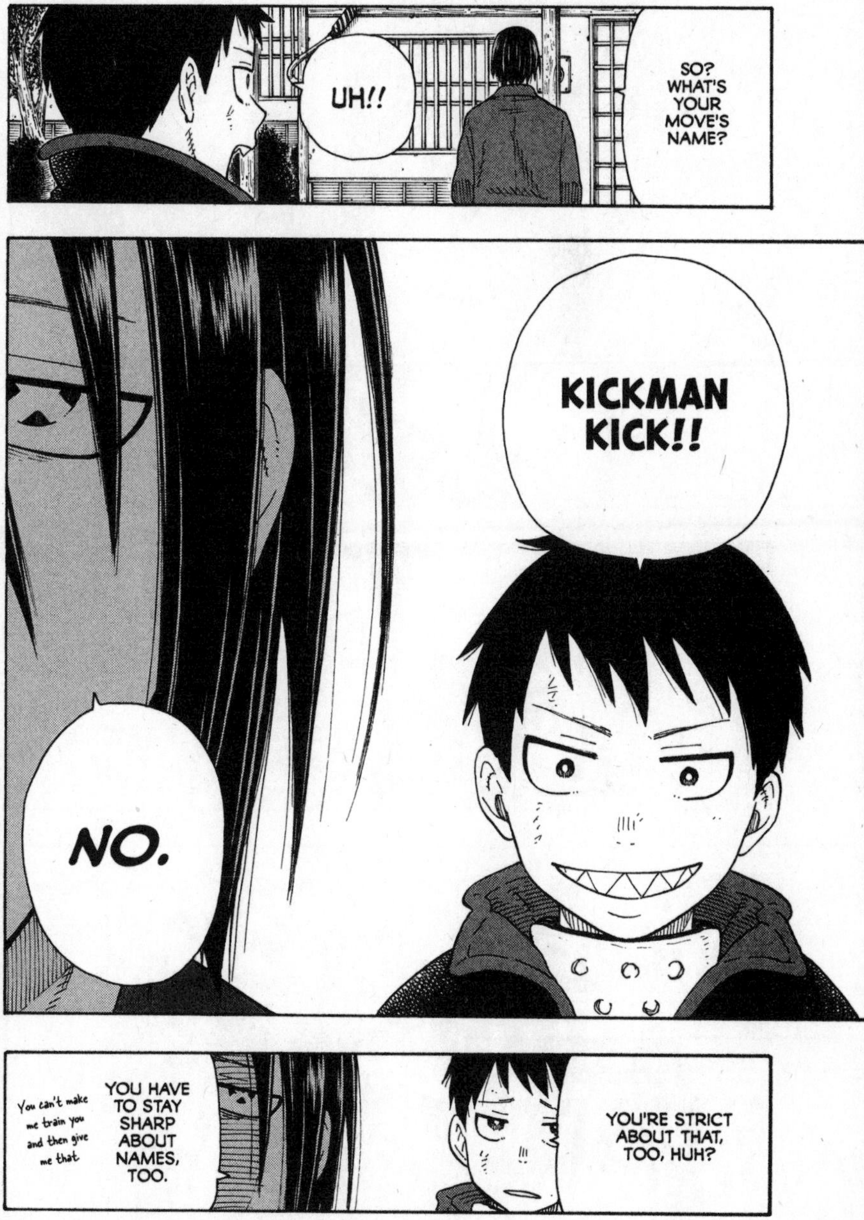
SO? WHAT'S YOUR MOVE'S NAME?
UH!!
KICKMAN KICK!!
NO.
YOU'RE STRICT ABOUT THAT, TOO, HUH?
YOU HAVE TO STAY SHARP ABOUT NAMES, TOO.
You can't make me train you and then give me that.

A WITCH'S FAMILIAR
DRAWS NEAR!
▶FIGHT
RUN
PET
EXTINGUISH
SPUTTER

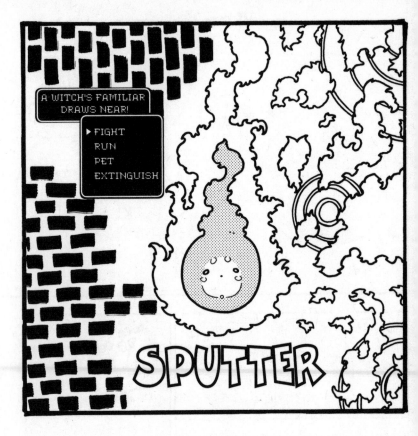

CHAPTER LXVI: VARIOUS RESULTS

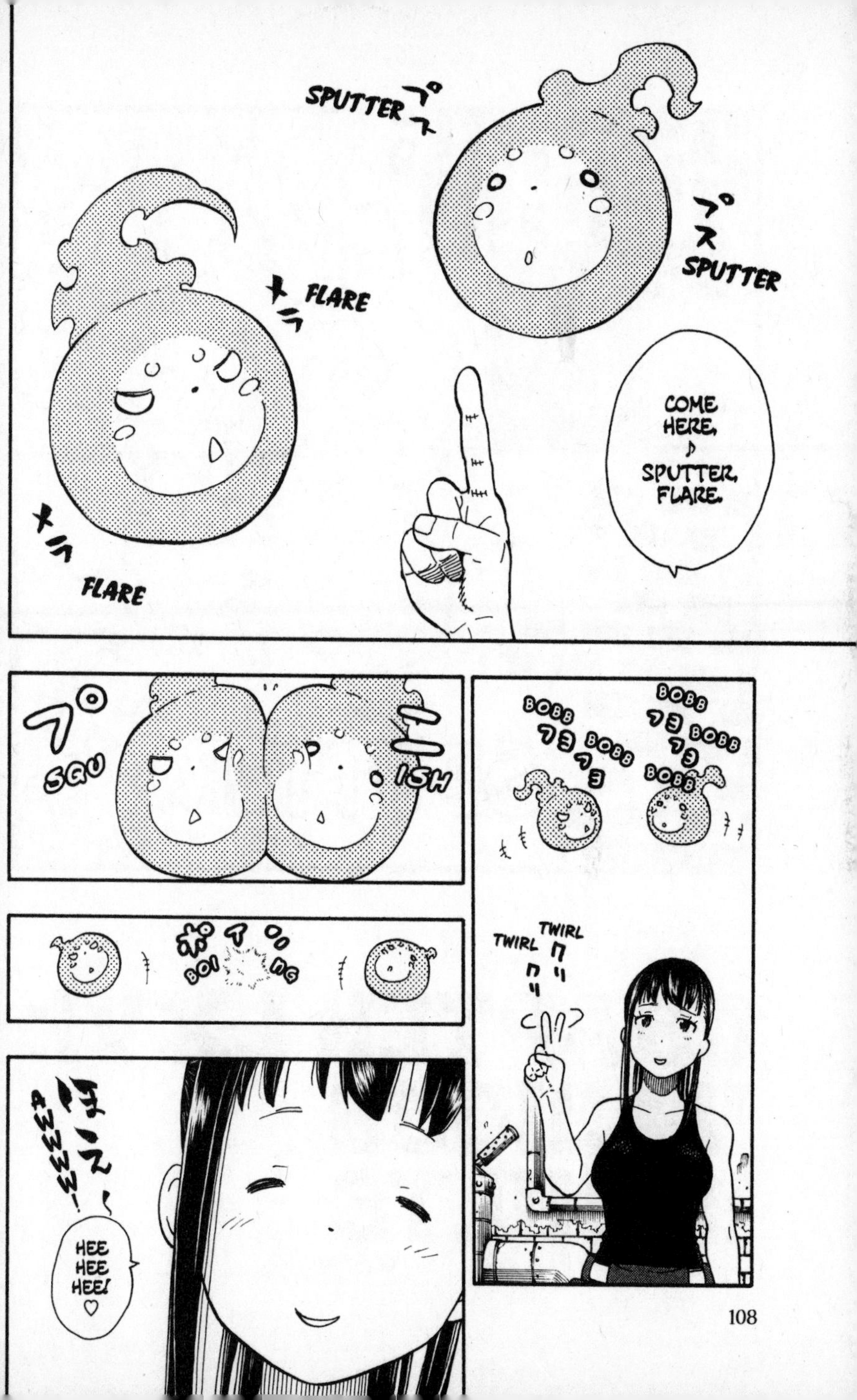
プス SPUTTER
COME HERE. ♪ SPUTTER. FLARE.
SPUTTER プス
FLARE
FLARE
BOBB BOBB BOBB BOBB BOBB
TWIRL TWIRL
SQUISH
BOING
AWWWW!
HEE HEE HEE! ♡

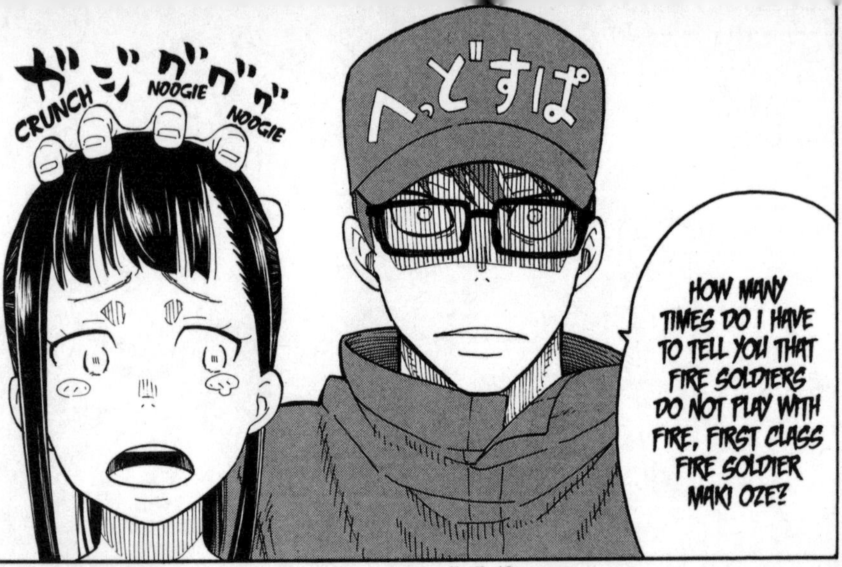
HOW MANY TIMES DO I HAVE TO TELL YOU THAT FIRE SOLDIERS DO NOT PLAY WITH FIRE, FIRST CLASS FIRE SOLDIER MAKI OZE?
へっどすぱ
ガジググ
CRUNCH
NOOGIE
NOOGIE

Hat: Head Spa

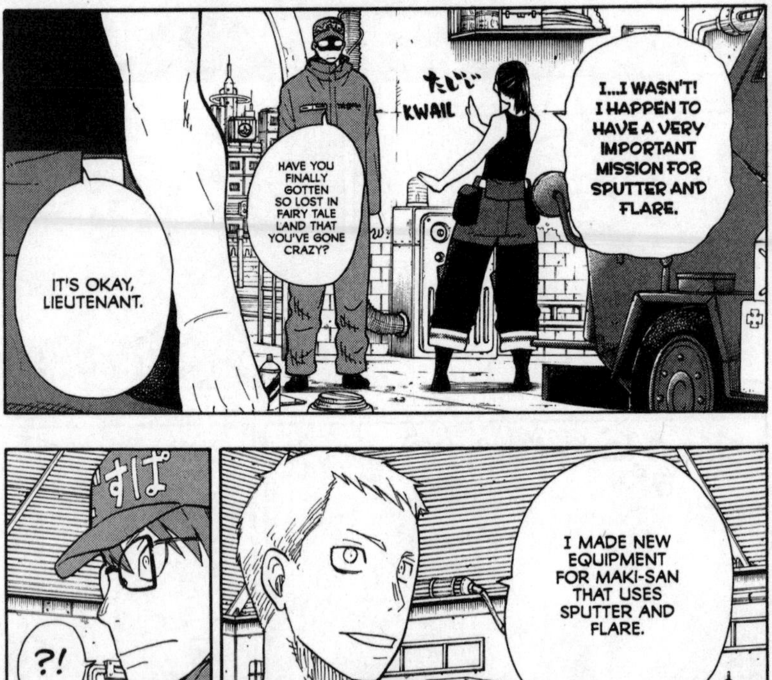
I...I WASN'T! I HAPPEN TO HAVE A VERY IMPORTANT MISSION FOR SPUTTER AND FLARE.
たじじ
KWAIL
HAVE YOU FINALLY GOTTEN SO LOST IN FAIRY TALE LAND THAT YOU'VE GONE CRAZY?
IT'S OKAY, LIEUTENANT.
I MADE NEW EQUIPMENT FOR MAKI-SAN THAT USES SPUTTER AND FLARE.
すぱ
?!

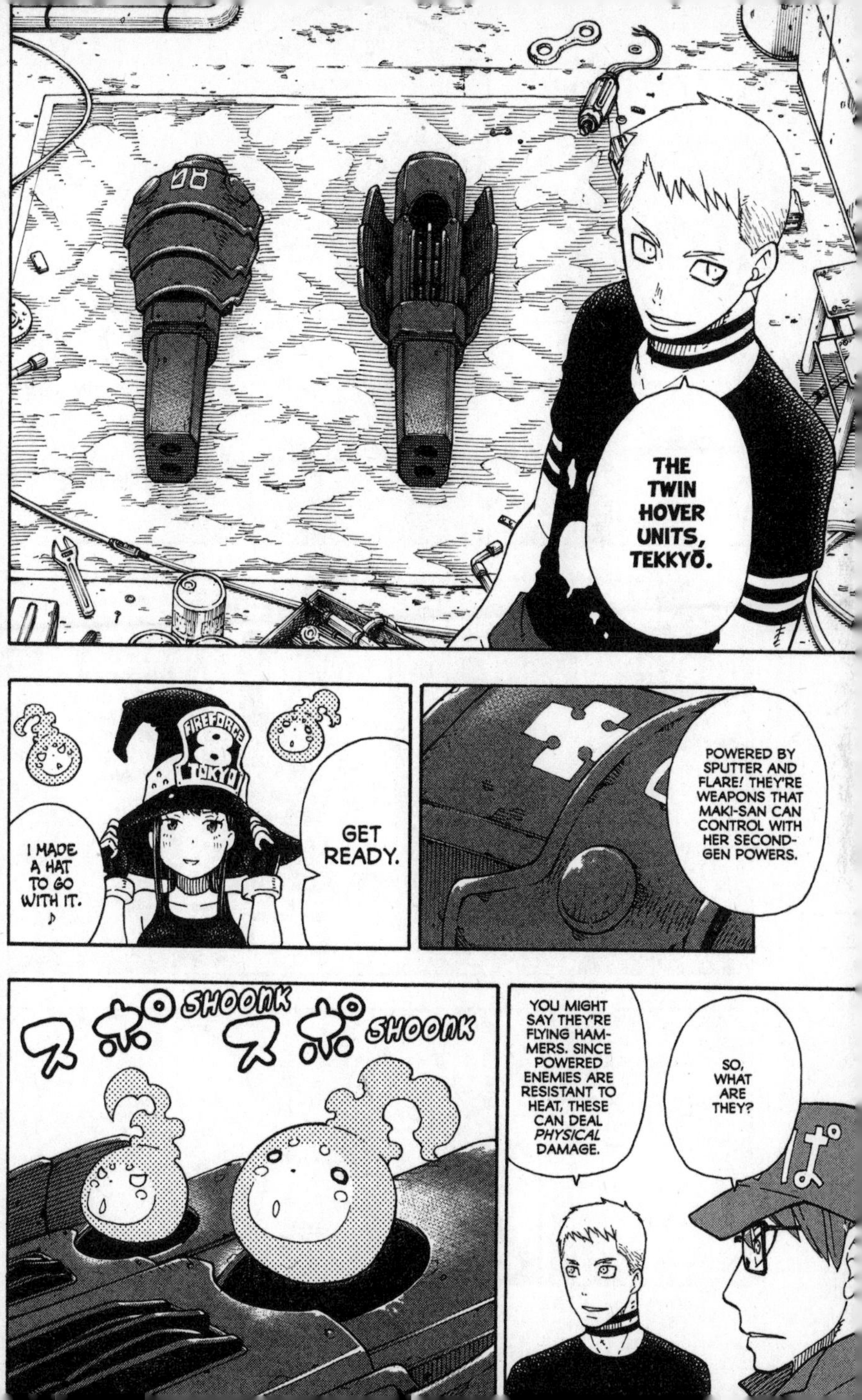
THE TWIN HOVER UNITS, TEKKYŌ.
POWERED BY SPUTTER AND FLARE! THEY'RE WEAPONS THAT MAKI-SAN CAN CONTROL WITH HER SECOND-GEN POWERS.
FIRE FORCE 8 TOKYO
GET READY.
I MADE A HAT TO GO WITH IT. ♪
SO, WHAT ARE THEY?
YOU MIGHT SAY THEY'RE FLYING HAMMERS. SINCE POWERED ENEMIES ARE RESISTANT TO HEAT, THESE CAN DEAL *PHYSICAL* DAMAGE.
SHOONK
SHOONK

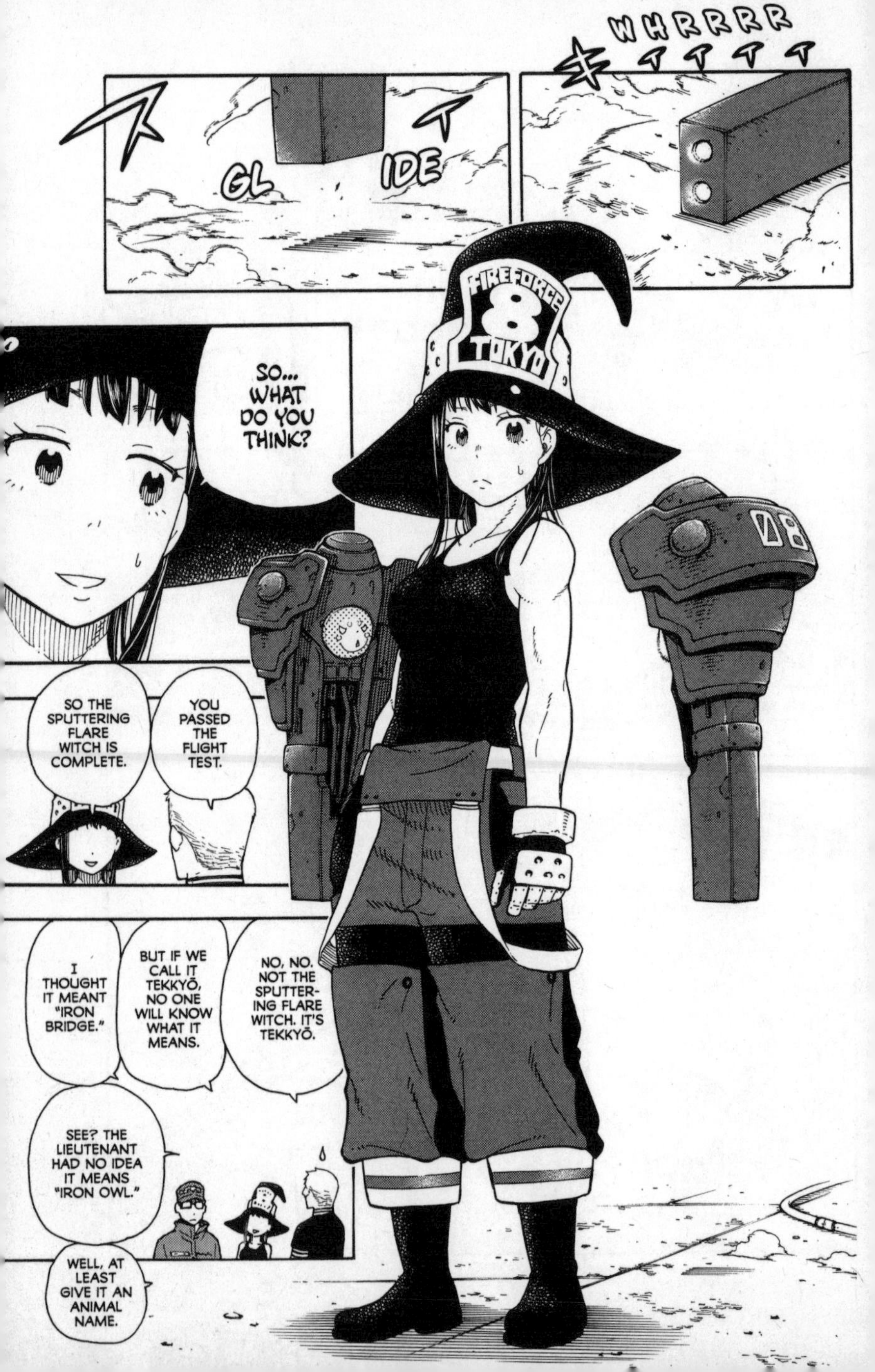
WHRRRRT
GL IDE
SO... WHAT DO YOU THINK?
YOU PASSED THE FLIGHT TEST.
SO THE SPUTTERING FLARE WITCH IS COMPLETE.
NO, NO. NOT THE SPUTTERING FLARE WITCH. IT'S TEKKYŌ.
BUT IF WE CALL IT TEKKYŌ, NO ONE WILL KNOW WHAT IT MEANS.
I THOUGHT IT MEANT "IRON BRIDGE."
SEE? THE LIEUTENANT HAD NO IDEA IT MEANS "IRON OWL."
WELL, AT LEAST GIVE IT AN ANIMAL NAME.
FIREFORCE 8 TOKYO
08

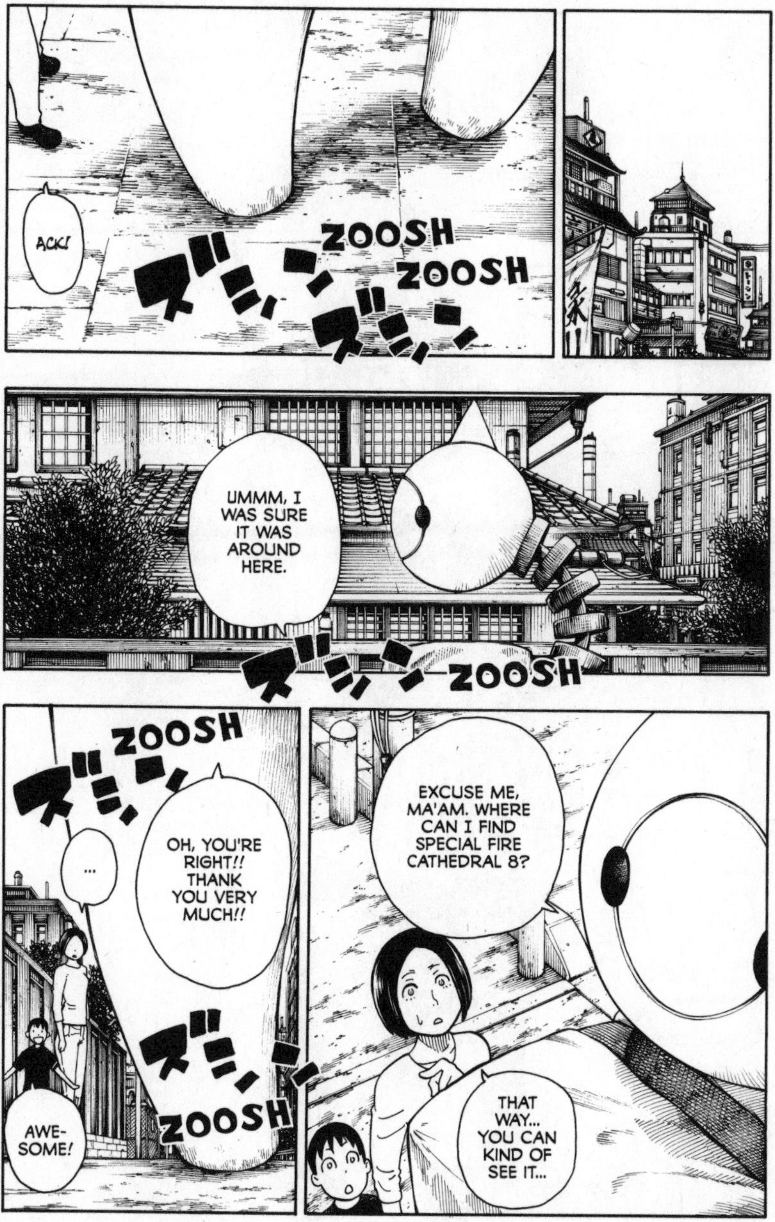
ZOOSH
ZOOSH
ACK!
UMMM, I WAS SURE IT WAS AROUND HERE.
ZOOSH
EXCUSE ME, MA'AM. WHERE CAN I FIND SPECIAL FIRE CATHEDRAL 8?
THAT WAY... YOU CAN KIND OF SEE IT...
ZOOSH
OH, YOU'RE RIGHT!! THANK YOU VERY MUCH!!
...
ZOOSH
AWE-SOME!

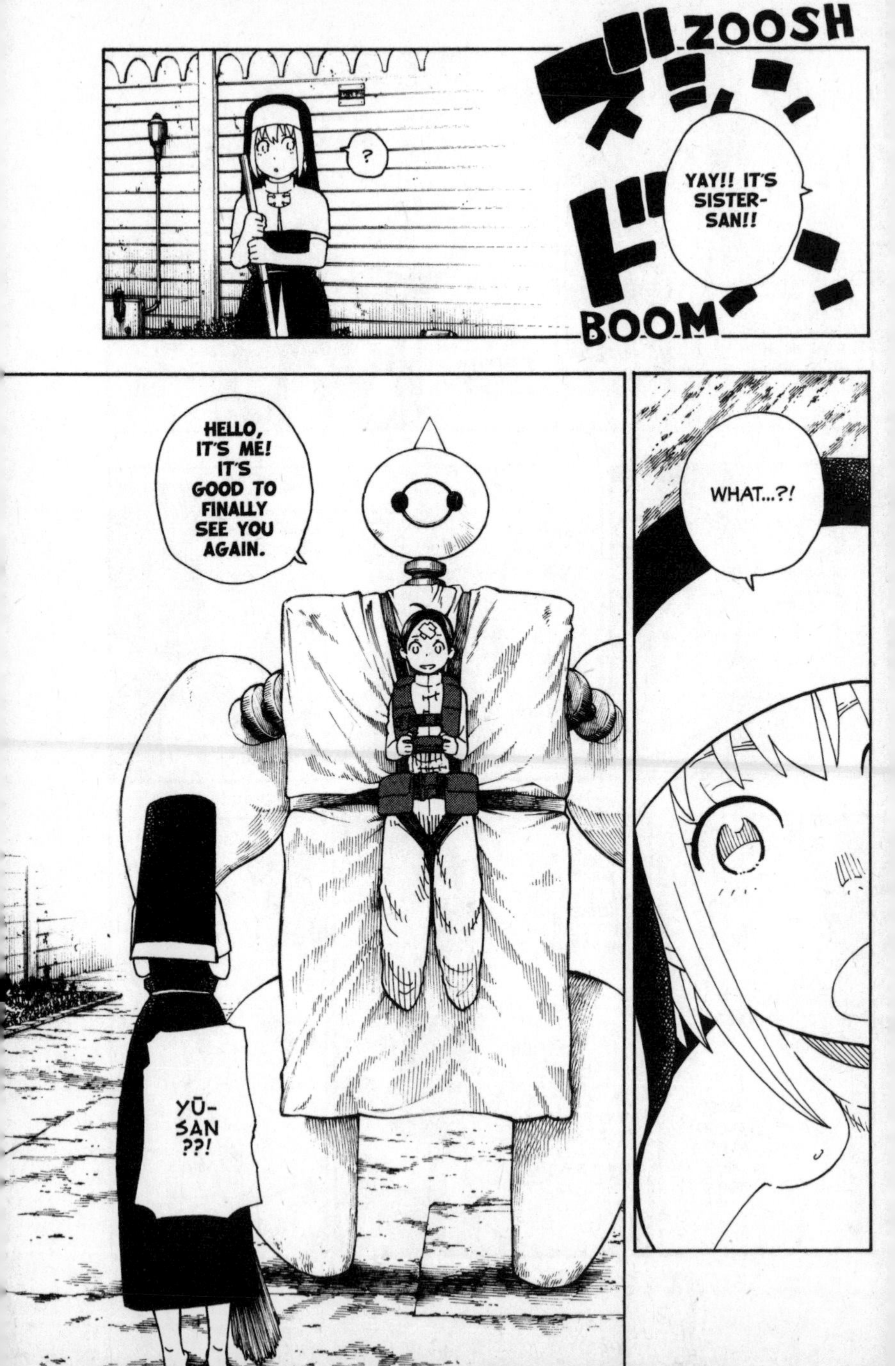
ZOOSH
YAY!! IT'S SISTER-SAN!!
BOOM
?
WHAT...?!
HELLO, IT'S ME! IT'S GOOD TO FINALLY SEE YOU AGAIN.
YŪ-SAN??!

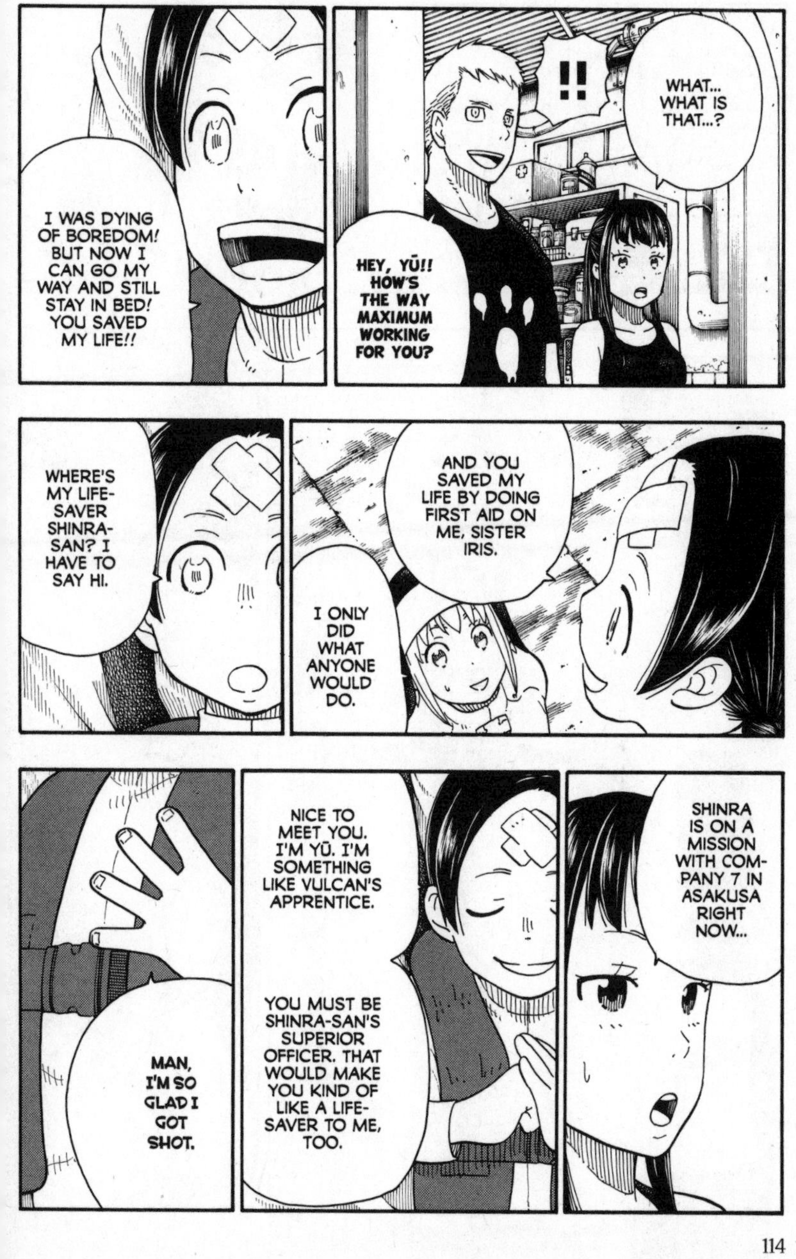
WHAT... WHAT IS THAT...?
!!
HEY, YŪ!! HOW'S THE WAY MAXIMUM WORKING FOR YOU?
I WAS DYING OF BOREDOM! BUT NOW I CAN GO MY WAY AND STILL STAY IN BED! YOU SAVED MY LIFE!!
AND YOU SAVED MY LIFE BY DOING FIRST AID ON ME, SISTER IRIS.
I ONLY DID WHAT ANYONE WOULD DO.
WHERE'S MY LIFE-SAVER SHINRA-SAN? I HAVE TO SAY HI.
SHINRA IS ON A MISSION WITH COMPANY 7 IN ASAKUSA RIGHT NOW...
NICE TO MEET YOU. I'M YŪ. I'M SOMETHING LIKE VULCAN'S APPRENTICE.
YOU MUST BE SHINRA-SAN'S SUPERIOR OFFICER. THAT WOULD MAKE YOU KIND OF LIKE A LIFE-SAVER TO ME, TOO.
MAN, I'M SO GLAD I GOT SHOT.

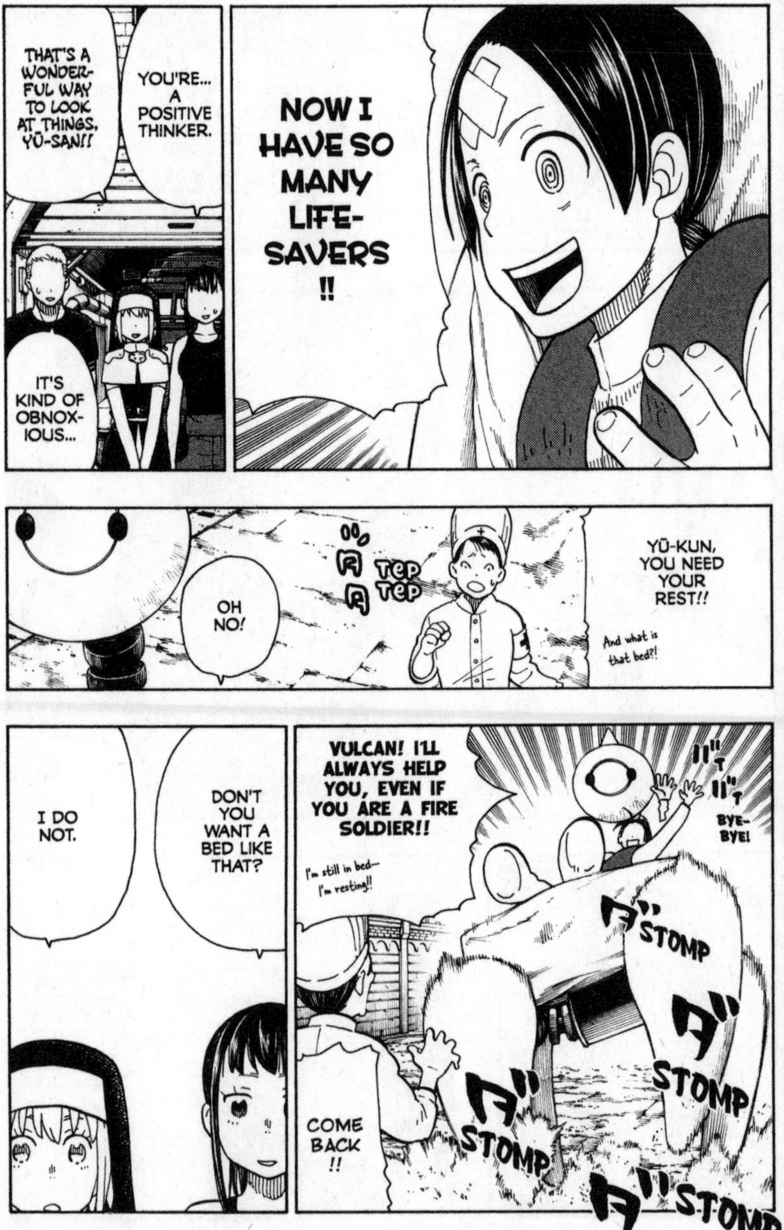
NOW I HAVE SO MANY LIFE-SAVERS!!
YOU'RE... A POSITIVE THINKER.
THAT'S A WONDERFUL WAY TO LOOK AT THINGS, YŪ-SAN!!
IT'S KIND OF OBNOXIOUS...
YŪ-KUN, YOU NEED YOUR REST!!
And what is that bed?!
TEP TEP
OH NO!
VULCAN! I'LL ALWAYS HELP YOU, EVEN IF YOU ARE A FIRE SOLDIER!!
BYE-BYE!
I'm still in bed— I'm resting!!
STOMP
STOMP
STOMP
STOMP
COME BACK!!
DON'T YOU WANT A BED LIKE THAT?
I DO NOT.

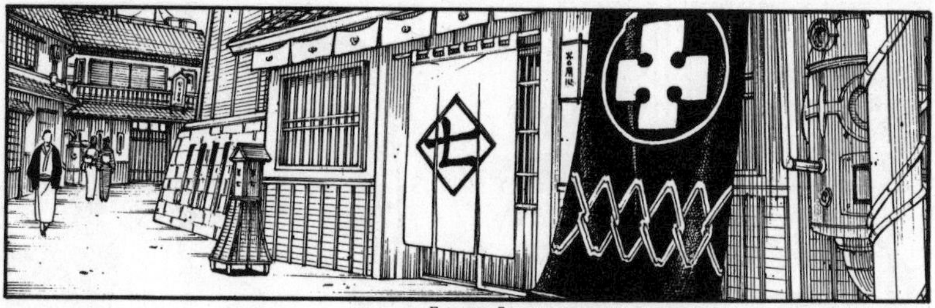
Entryway: 7

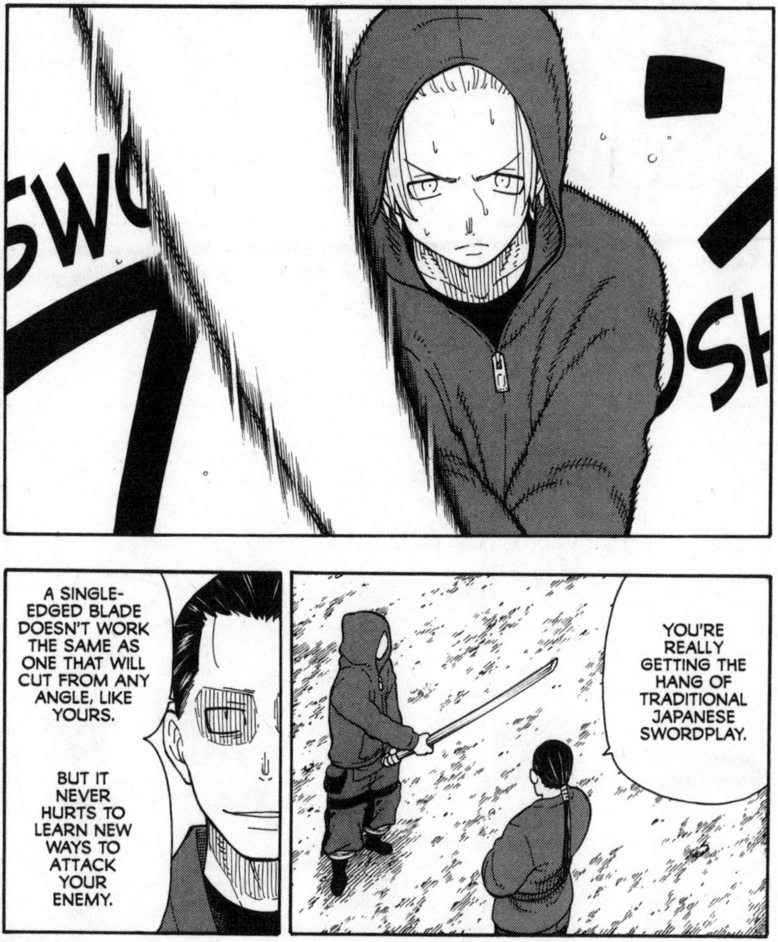
SWO
OSH
YOU'RE REALLY GETTING THE HANG OF TRADITIONAL JAPANESE SWORDPLAY.
A SINGLE-EDGED BLADE DOESN'T WORK THE SAME AS ONE THAT WILL CUT FROM ANY ANGLE, LIKE YOURS.
BUT IT NEVER HURTS TO LEARN NEW WAYS TO ATTACK YOUR ENEMY.

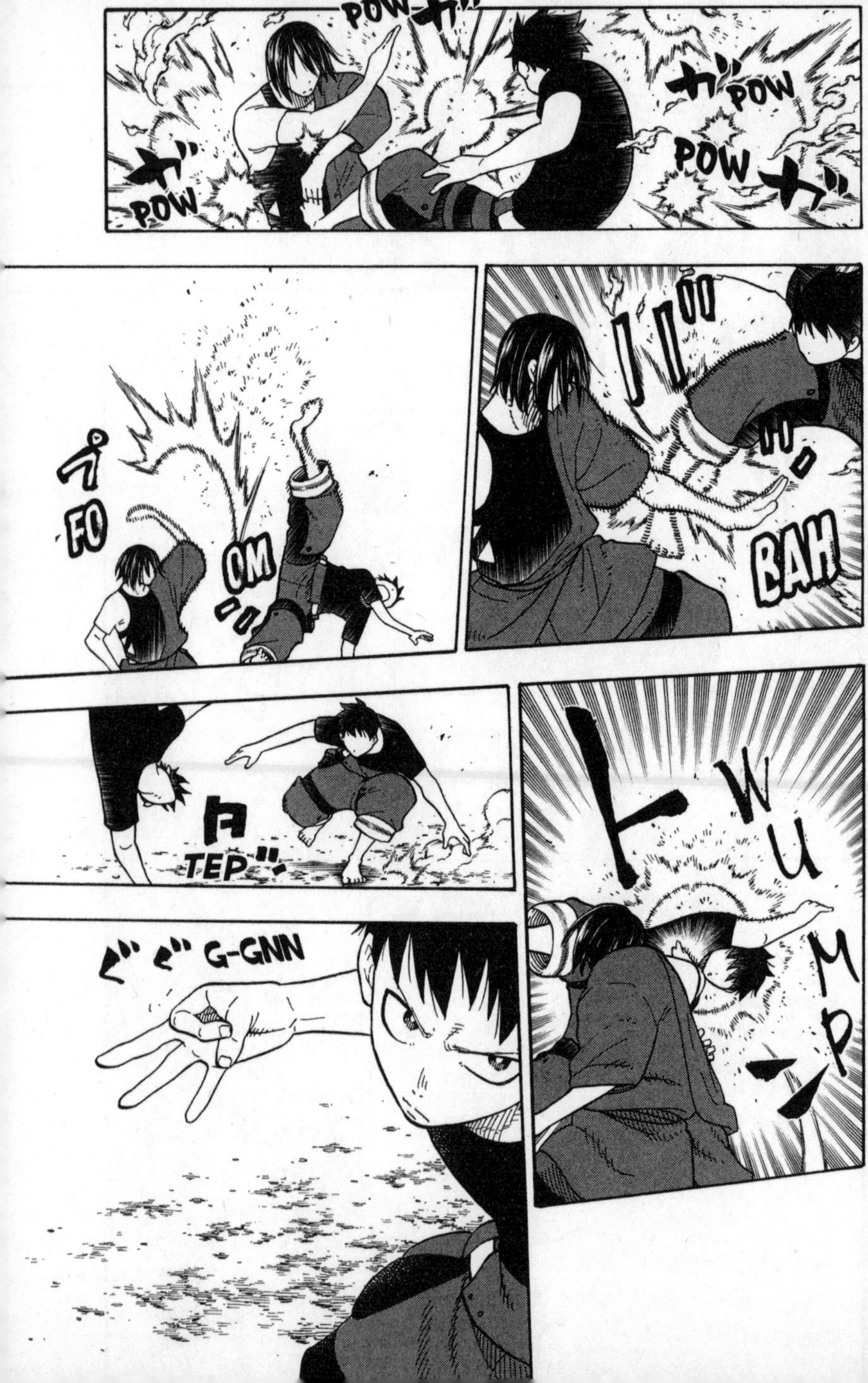
POW
POW
POW
POW
BAH
FO
OM
WUMP
TEP
G-GNN

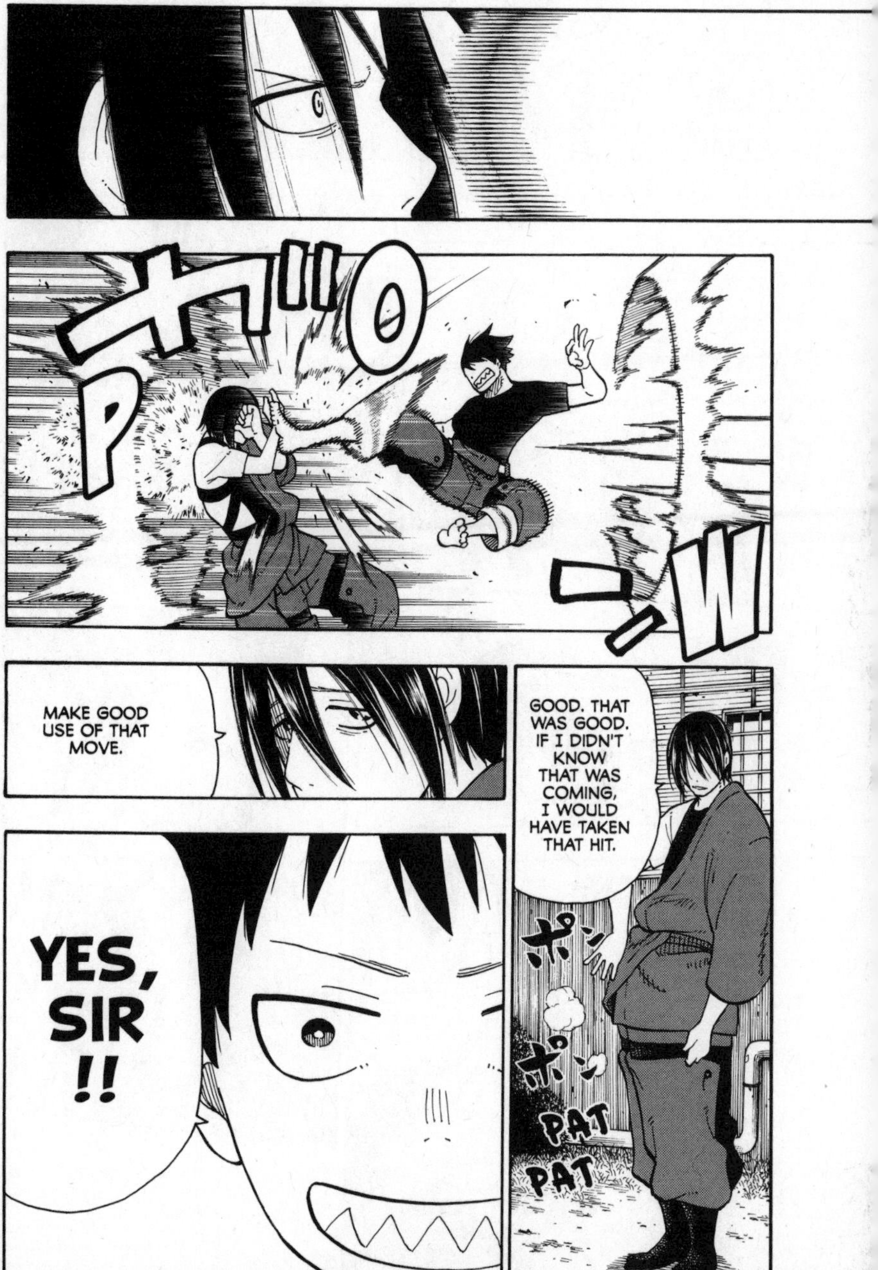

GOOD. THAT WAS GOOD. IF I DIDN'T KNOW THAT WAS COMING, I WOULD HAVE TAKEN THAT HIT.
PAT PAT
MAKE GOOD USE OF THAT MOVE.
YES, SIR!!

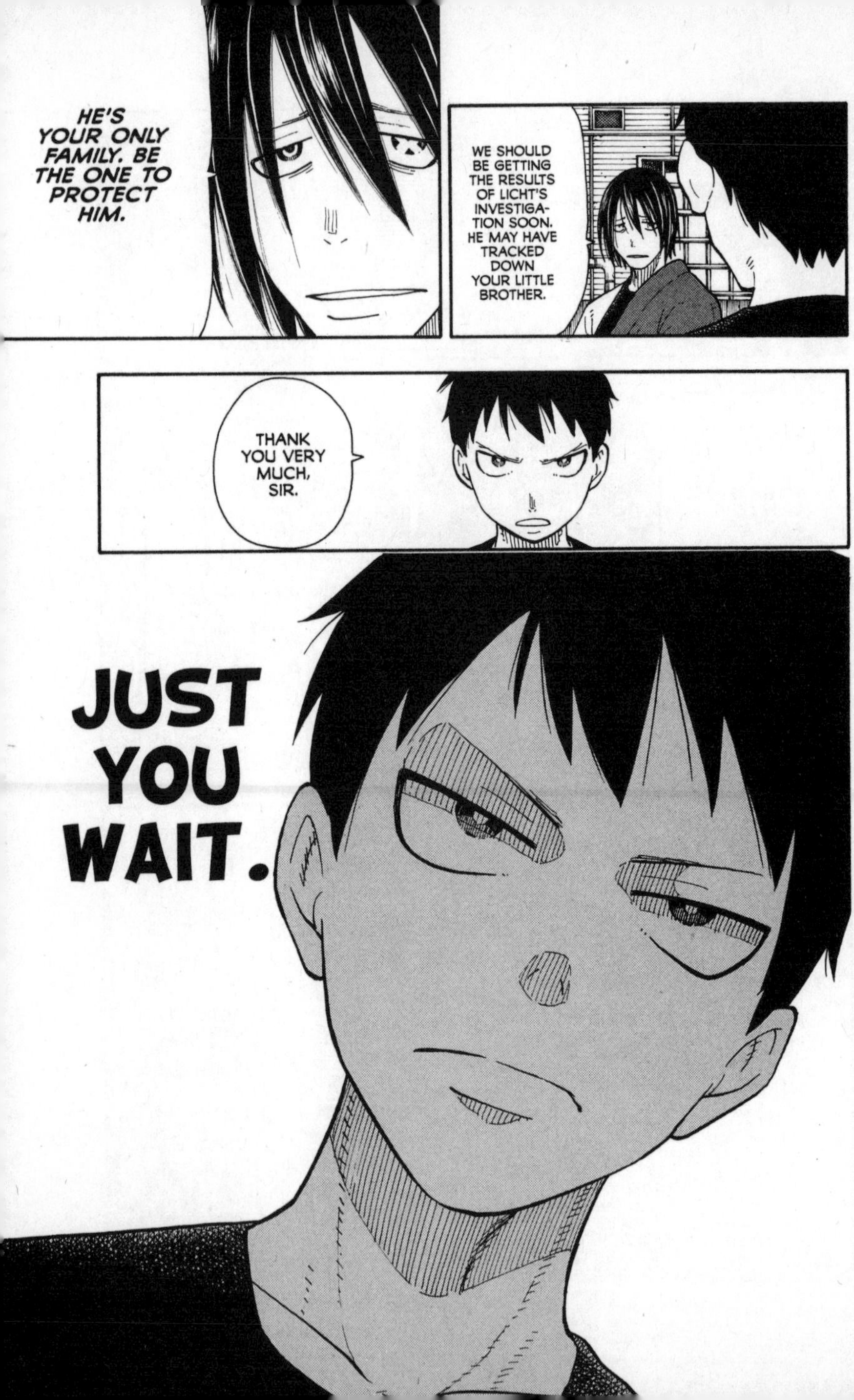
WE SHOULD BE GETTING THE RESULTS OF LICHT'S INVESTIGATION SOON. HE MAY HAVE TRACKED DOWN YOUR LITTLE BROTHER.
HE'S YOUR ONLY FAMILY. BE THE ONE TO PROTECT HIM.
THANK YOU VERY MUCH, SIR.
JUST YOU WAIT.

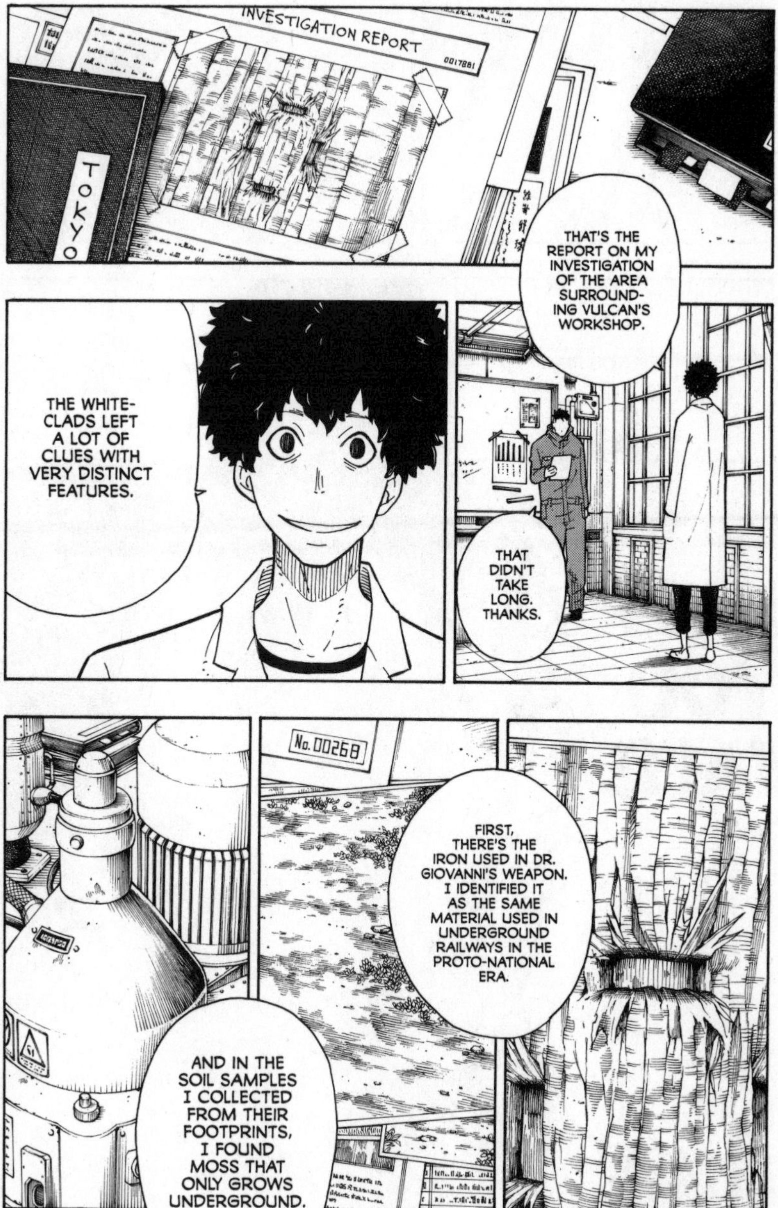
INVESTIGATION REPORT
0017881
TOKYO
THAT'S THE REPORT ON MY INVESTIGATION OF THE AREA SURROUNDING VULCAN'S WORKSHOP.
THAT DIDN'T TAKE LONG. THANKS.
THE WHITE-CLADS LEFT A LOT OF CLUES WITH VERY DISTINCT FEATURES.
FIRST, THERE'S THE IRON USED IN DR. GIOVANNI'S WEAPON. I IDENTIFIED IT AS THE SAME MATERIAL USED IN UNDERGROUND RAILWAYS IN THE PROTO-NATIONAL ERA.
No. 00268
AND IN THE SOIL SAMPLES I COLLECTED FROM THEIR FOOTPRINTS, I FOUND MOSS THAT ONLY GROWS UNDERGROUND.

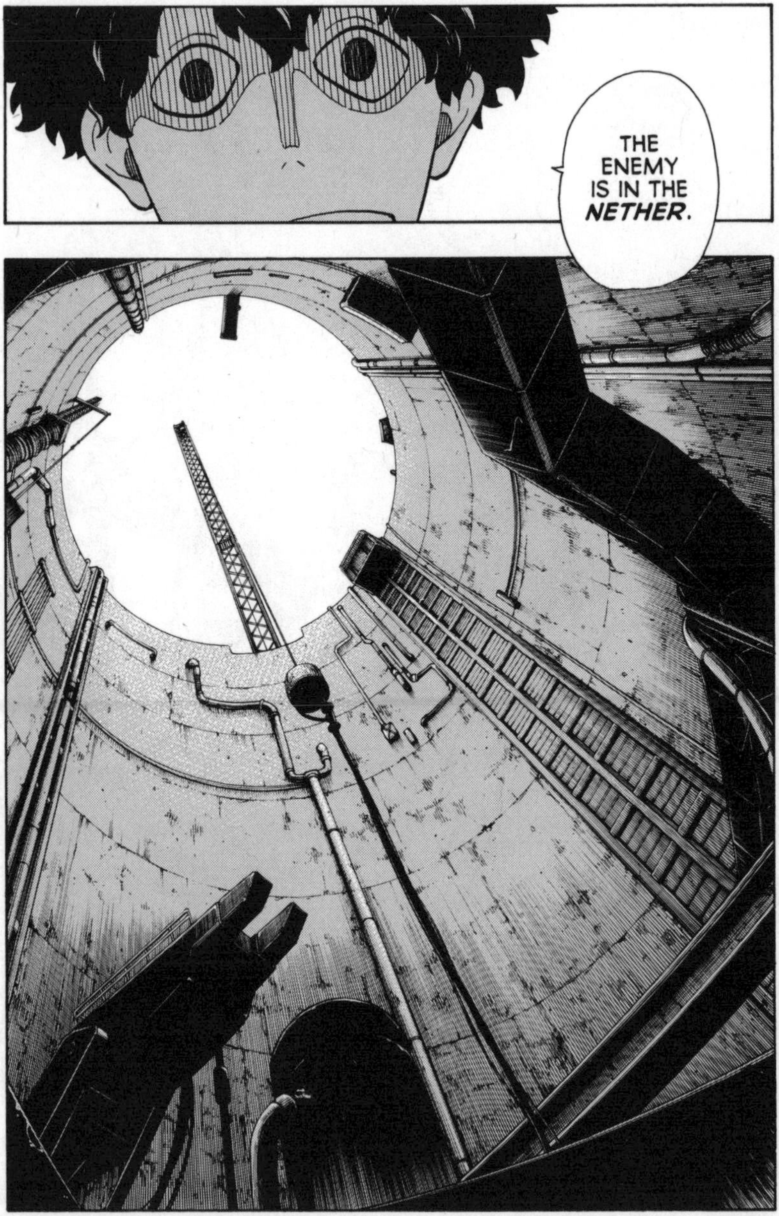
THE ENEMY IS IN THE **NETHER**.

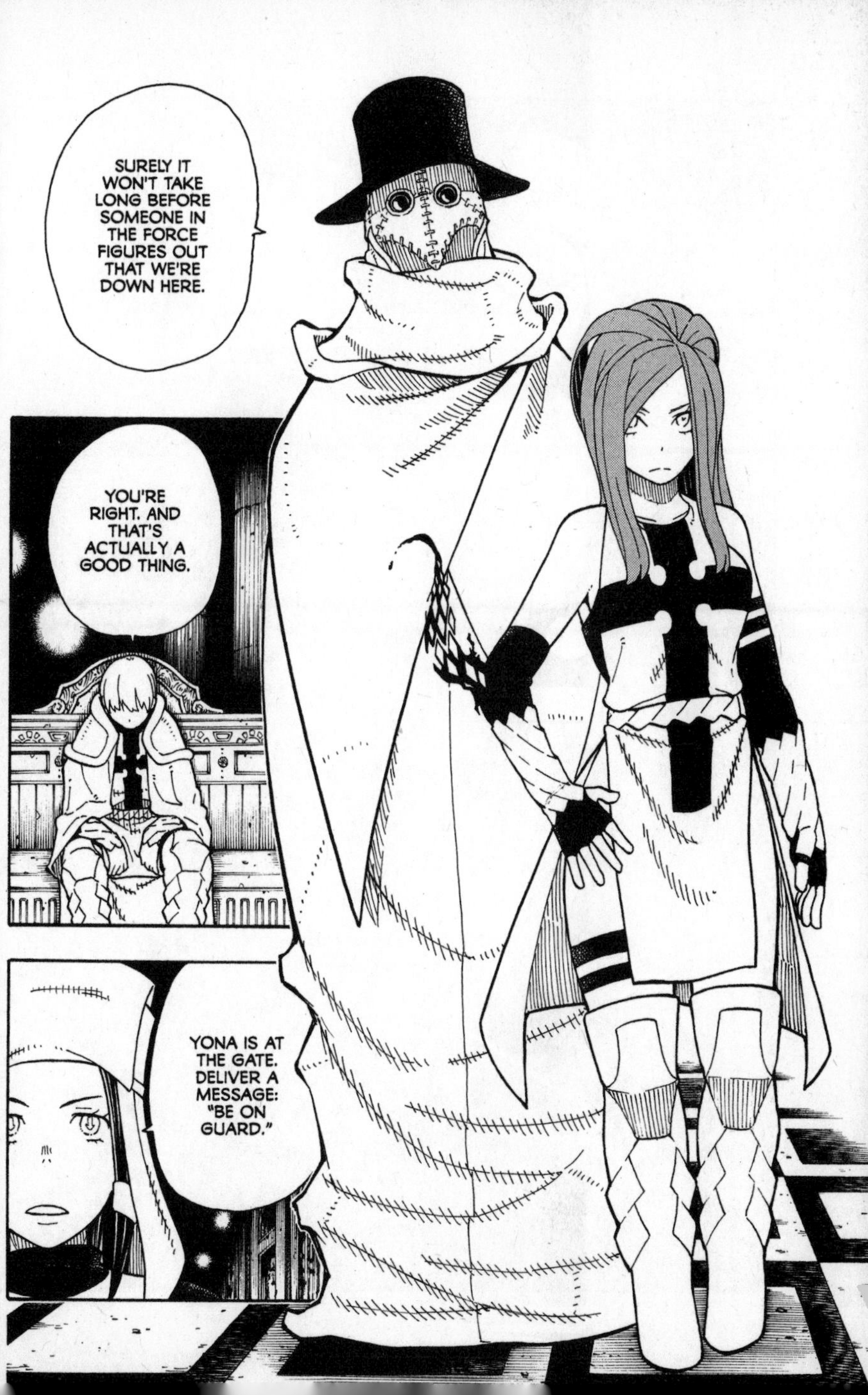
SURELY IT WON'T TAKE LONG BEFORE SOMEONE IN THE FORCE FIGURES OUT THAT WE'RE DOWN HERE.
YOU'RE RIGHT. AND THAT'S ACTUALLY A GOOD THING.
YONA IS AT THE GATE. DELIVER A MESSAGE: "BE ON GUARD."

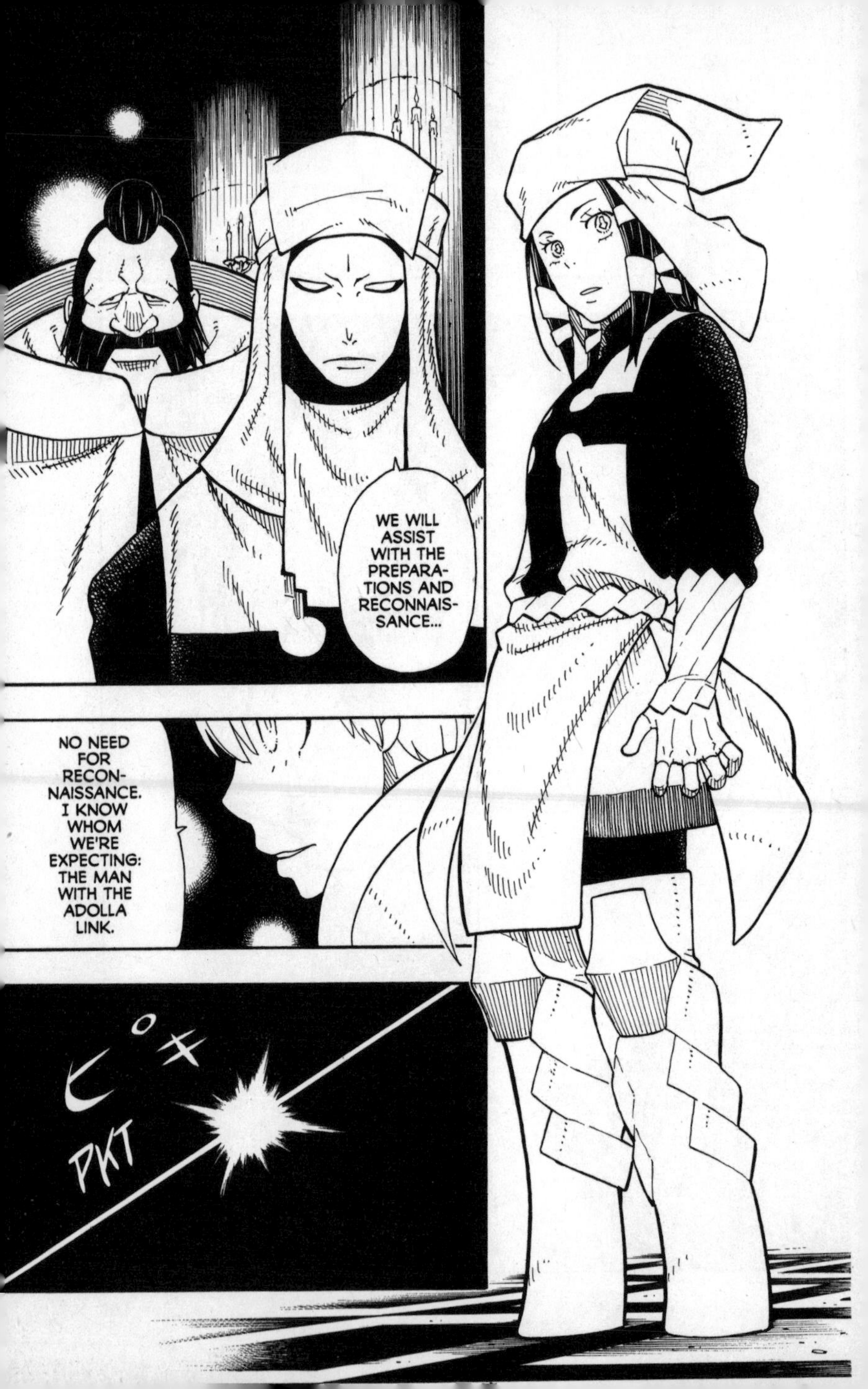
WE WILL ASSIST WITH THE PREPARATIONS AND RECONNAISSANCE...
NO NEED FOR RECONNAISSANCE. I KNOW WHOM WE'RE EXPECTING: THE MAN WITH THE ADOLLA LINK.
PKT

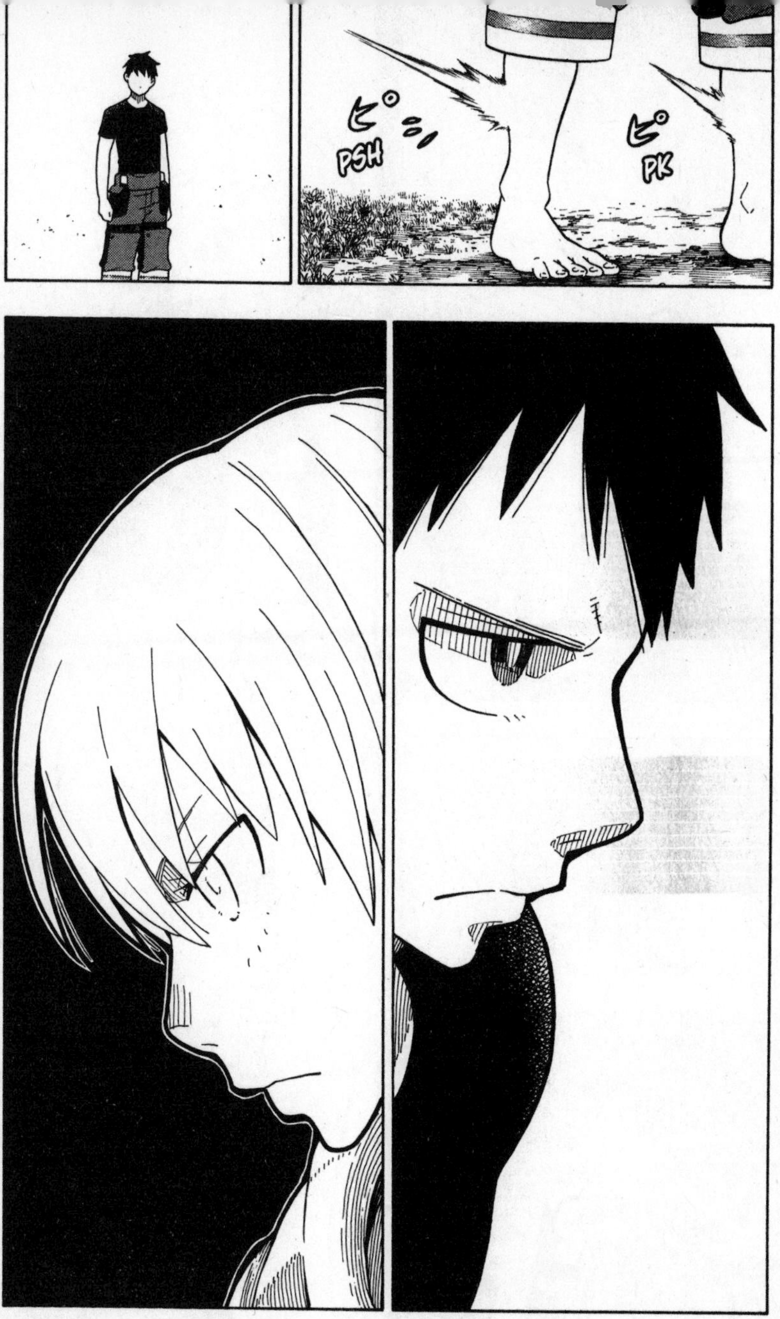
ピ
PK
ピ
PSH

FIRE FORCE

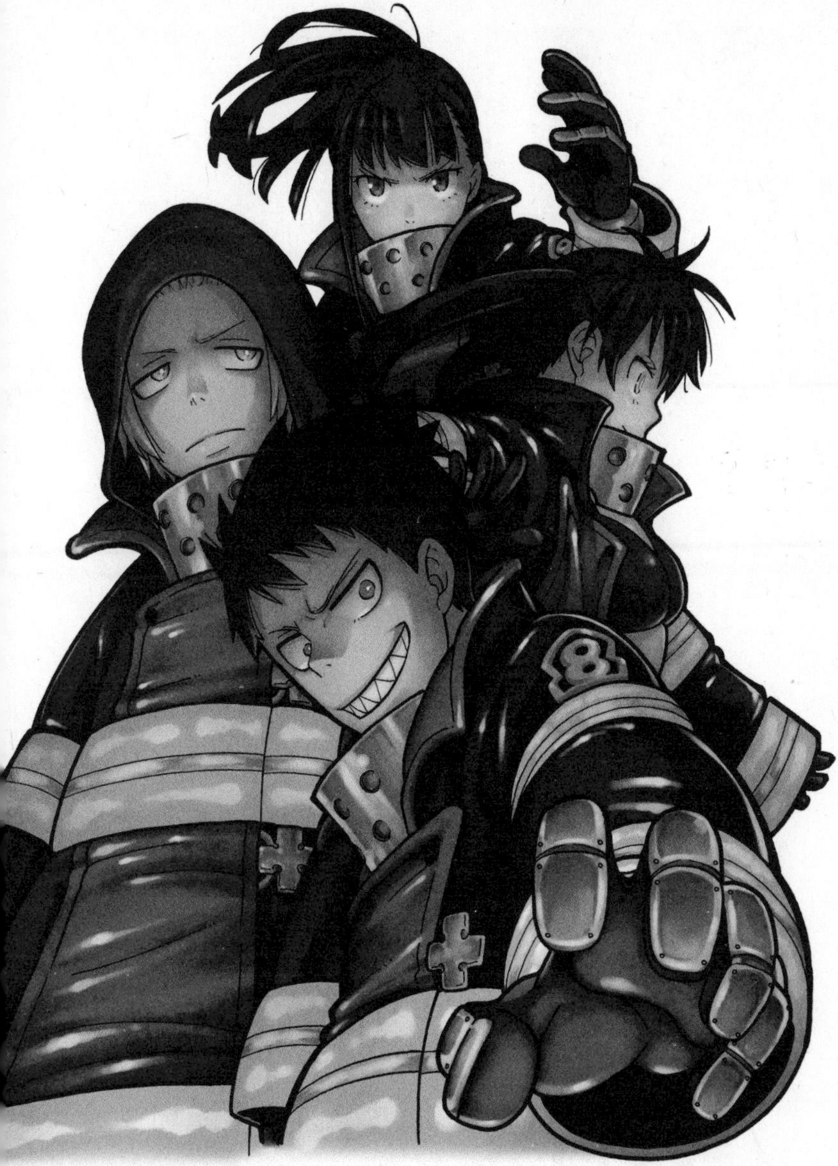

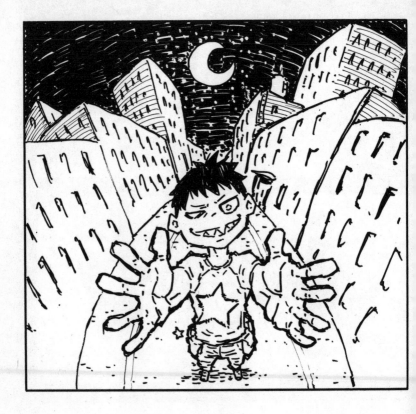

CHAPTER LXVII: TO THE NETHER

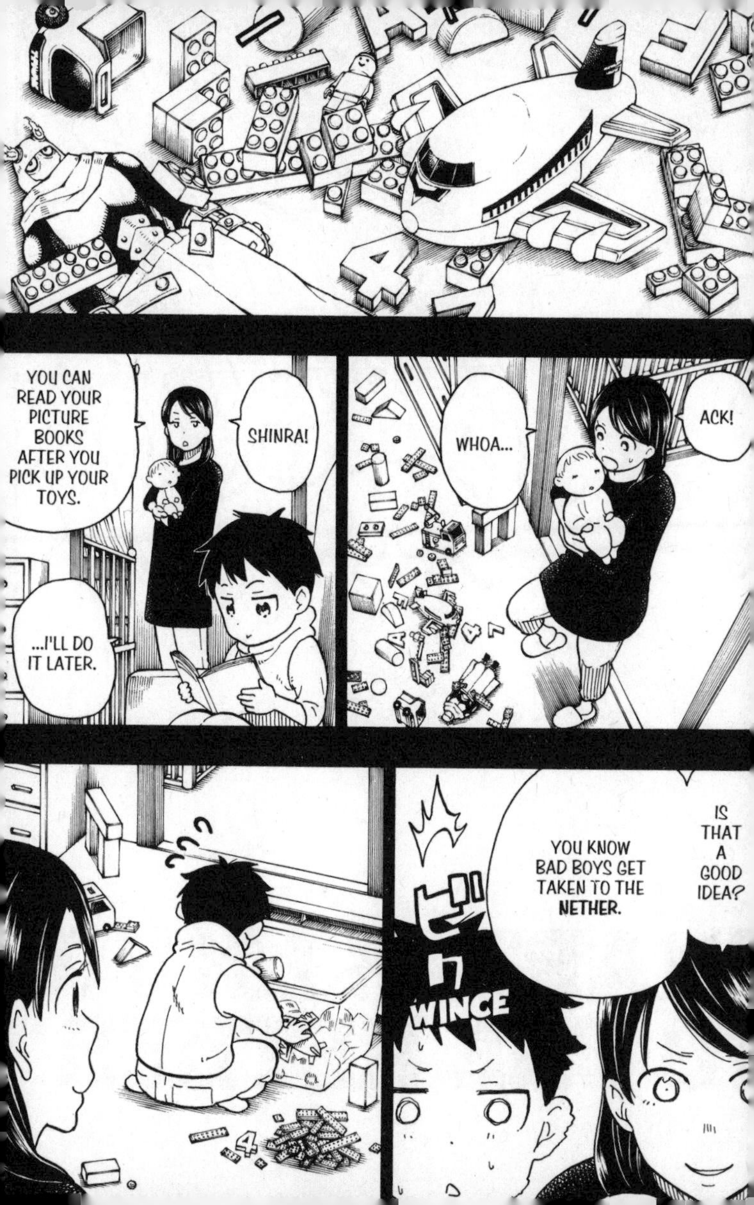
ACK!
WHOA...
SHINRA!
YOU CAN READ YOUR PICTURE BOOKS AFTER YOU PICK UP YOUR TOYS.
...I'LL DO IT LATER.
IS THAT A GOOD IDEA?
YOU KNOW BAD BOYS GET TAKEN TO THE **NETHER.**
WINCE

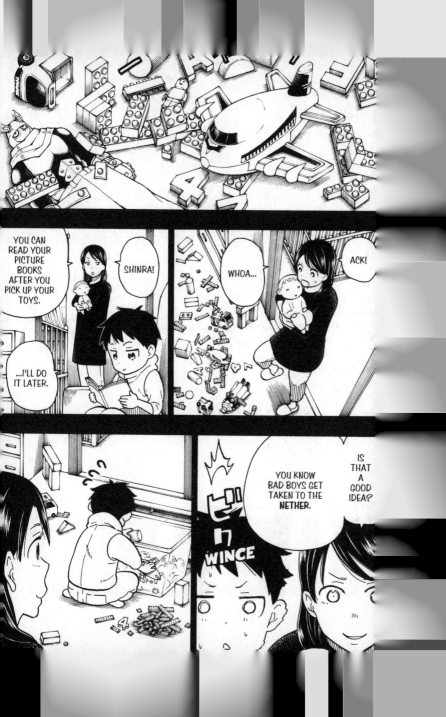

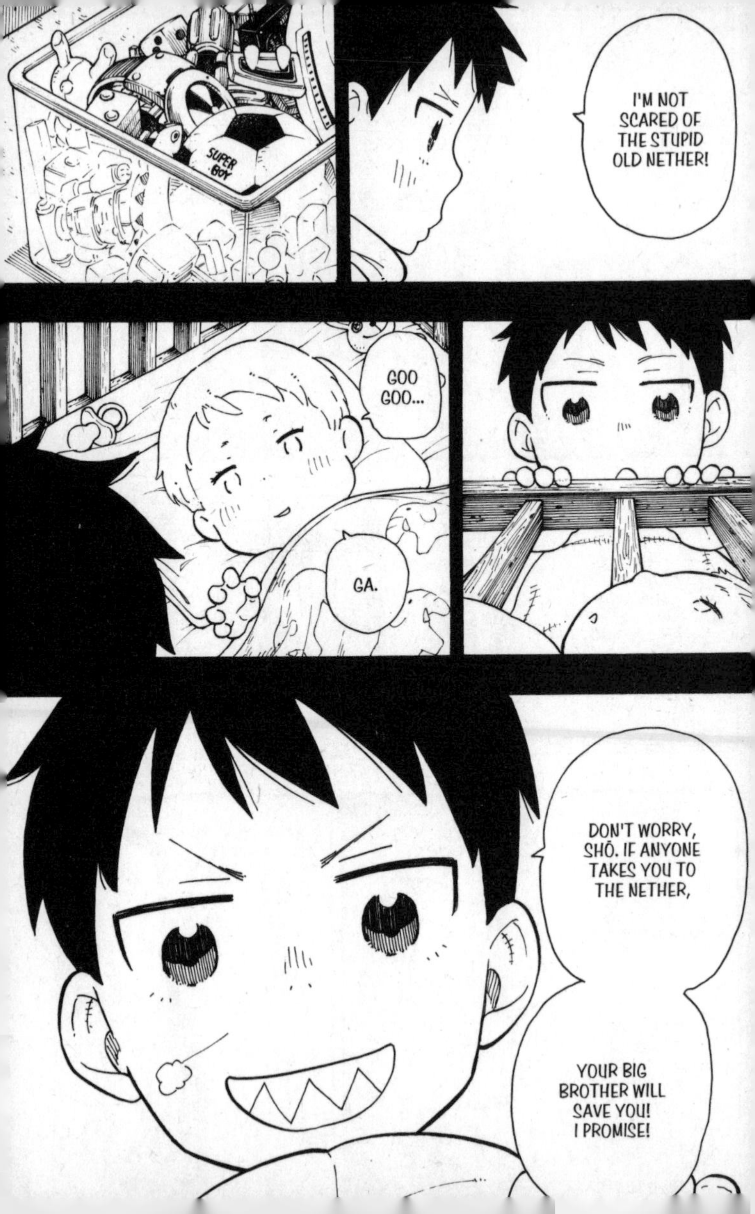
I'M NOT SCARED OF THE STUPID OLD NETHER!
SUPER BOY
GOO GOO...
GA.
DON'T WORRY, SHŌ. IF ANYONE TAKES YOU TO THE NETHER,
YOUR BIG BROTHER WILL SAVE YOU! I PROMISE!

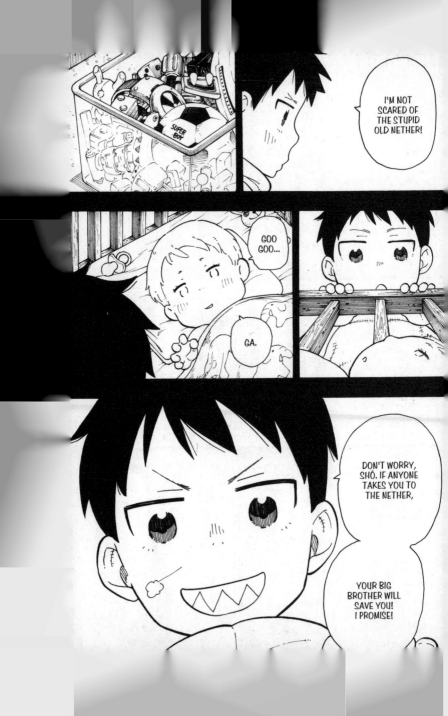

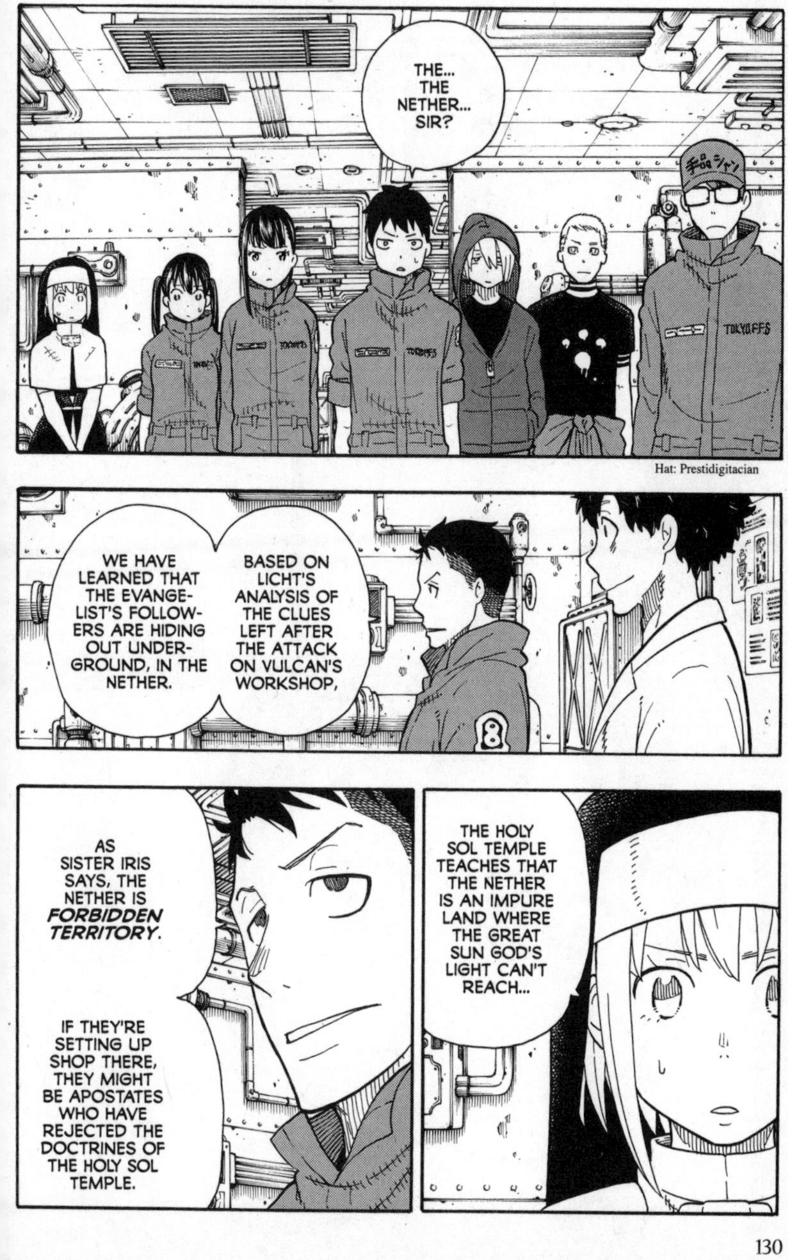
THE... THE NETHER... SIR?
BASED ON LICHT'S ANALYSIS OF THE CLUES LEFT AFTER THE ATTACK ON VULCAN'S WORKSHOP,
WE HAVE LEARNED THAT THE EVANGE-LIST'S FOLLOW-ERS ARE HIDING OUT UNDER-GROUND, IN THE NETHER.
THE HOLY SOL TEMPLE TEACHES THAT THE NETHER IS AN IMPURE LAND WHERE THE GREAT SUN GOD'S LIGHT CAN'T REACH...
AS SISTER IRIS SAYS, THE NETHER IS *FORBIDDEN TERRITORY*.
IF THEY'RE SETTING UP SHOP THERE, THEY MIGHT BE APOSTATES WHO HAVE REJECTED THE DOCTRINES OF THE HOLY SOL TEMPLE.

Hat: Prestidigitacian

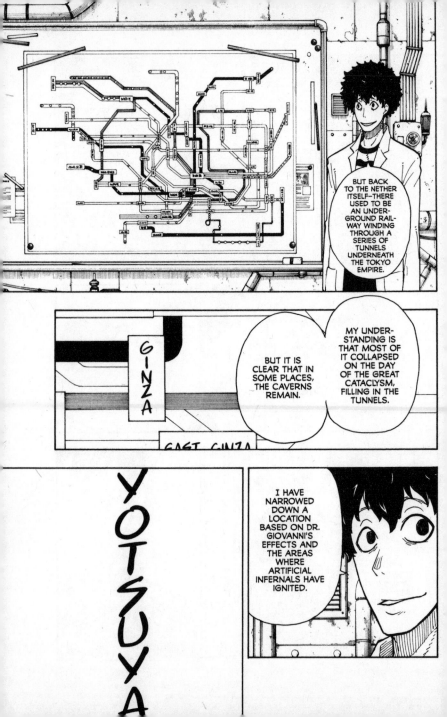

BUT BACK TO THE NETHER ITSELF—THERE USED TO BE AN UNDERGROUND RAILWAY WINDING THROUGH A SERIES OF TUNNELS UNDERNEATH THE TOKYO EMPIRE.

MY UNDERSTANDING IS THAT MOST OF IT COLLAPSED ON THE DAY OF THE GREAT CATACLYSM, FILLING IN THE TUNNELS.

BUT IT IS CLEAR THAT IN SOME PLACES, THE CAVERNS REMAIN.

GINZA

EAST GINZA

YOTSUYA

I HAVE NARROWED DOWN A LOCATION BASED ON DR. GIOVANNI'S EFFECTS AND THE AREAS WHERE ARTIFICIAL INFERNALS HAVE IGNITED.

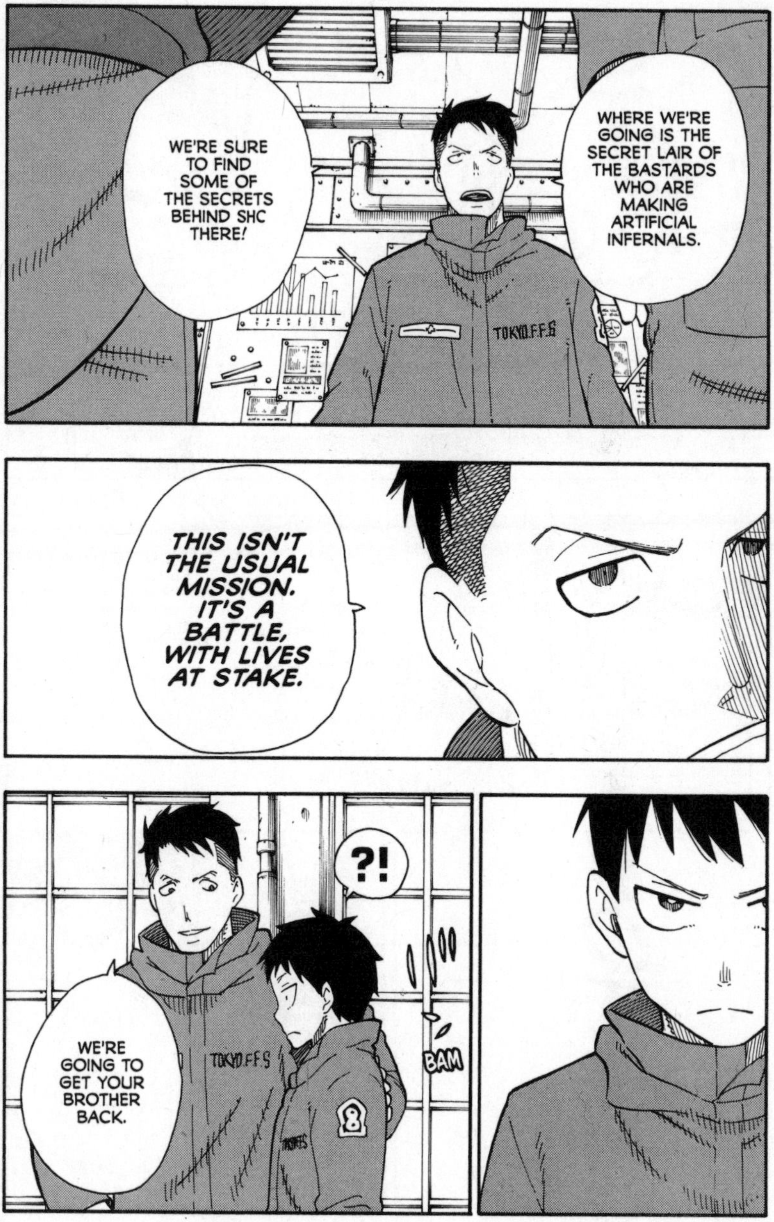
WHERE WE'RE GOING IS THE SECRET LAIR OF THE BASTARDS WHO ARE MAKING ARTIFICIAL INFERNALS.
WE'RE SURE TO FIND SOME OF THE SECRETS BEHIND SHC THERE!
THIS ISN'T THE USUAL MISSION. IT'S A BATTLE, WITH LIVES AT STAKE.
?!
BAM
WE'RE GOING TO GET YOUR BROTHER BACK.

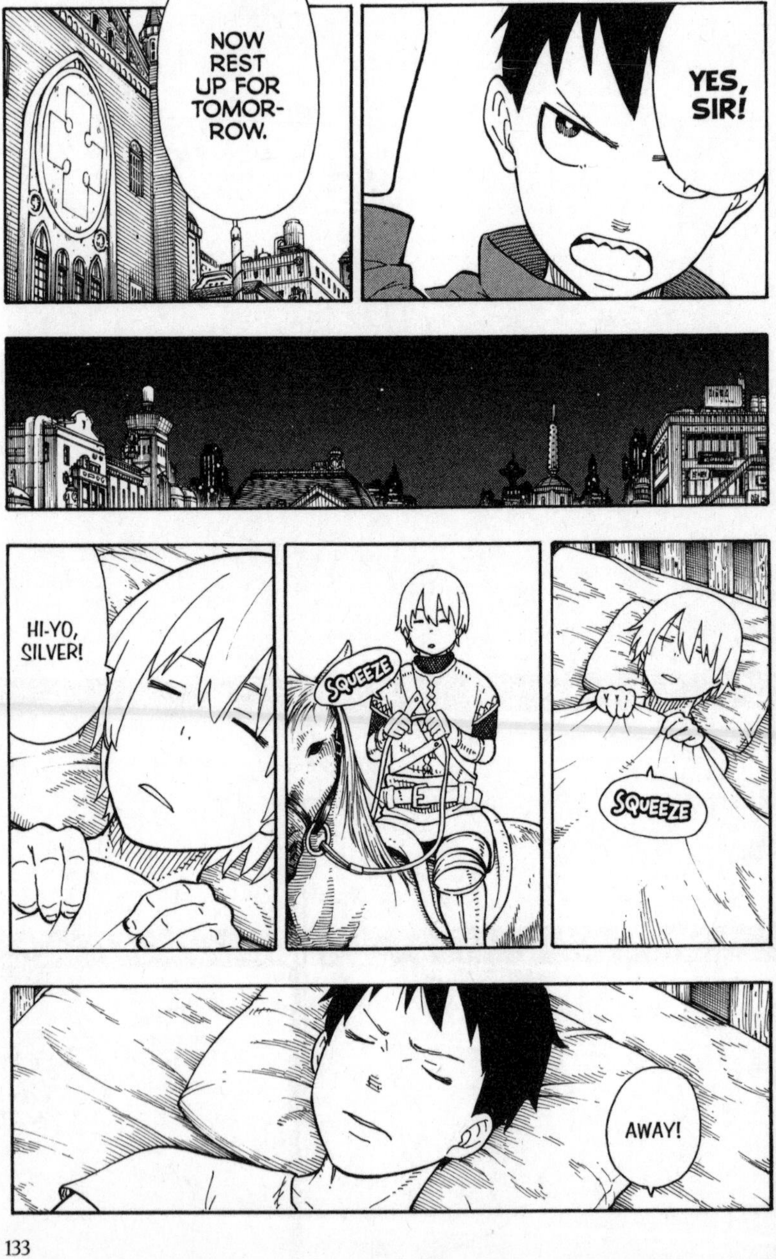
YES, SIR!
NOW REST UP FOR TOMORROW.
SQUEEZE
SQUEEZE
HI-YO, SILVER!
AWAY!

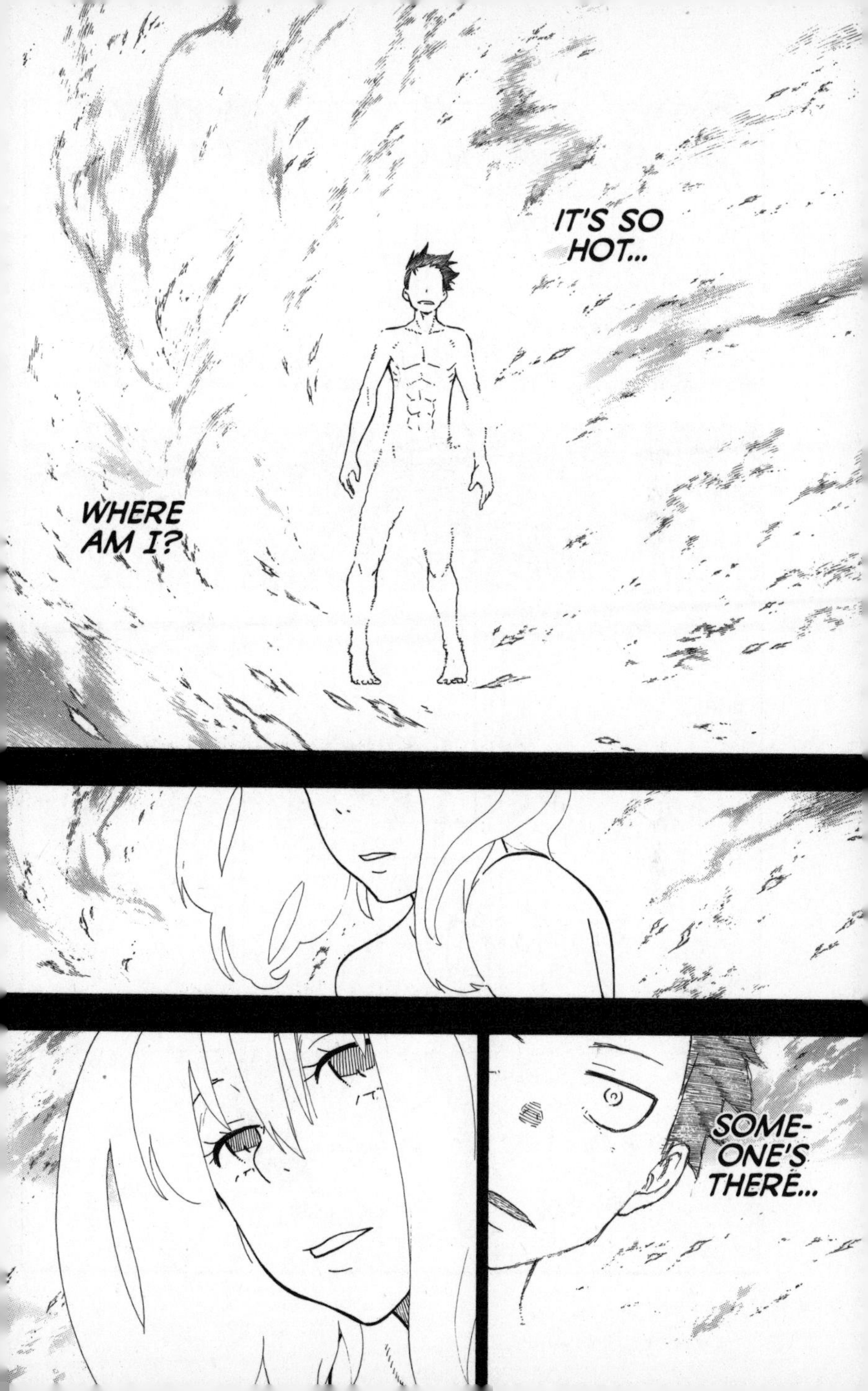
IT'S SO HOT...
WHERE AM I?
SOME-ONE'S THERE...

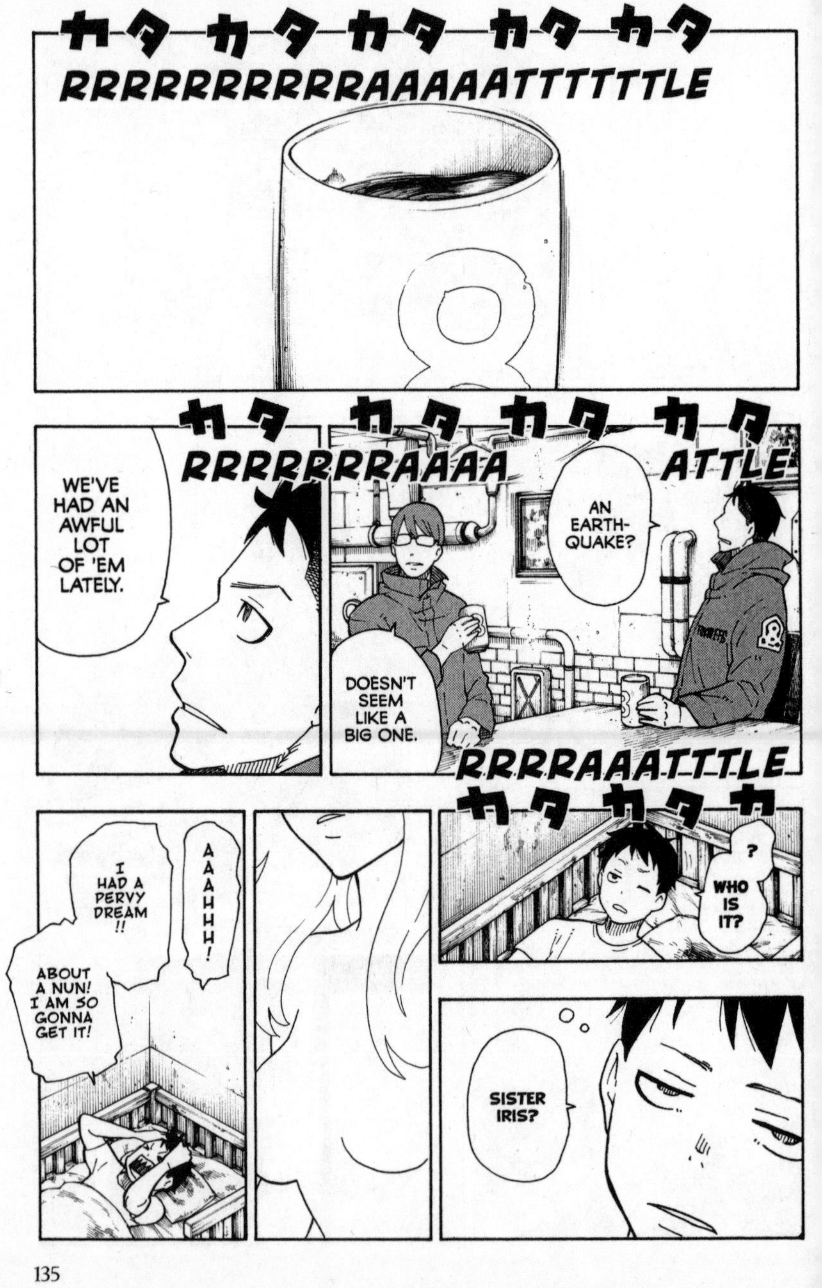
カタカタカタ カタカタ
RRRRRRRRRRAAAAATTTTTTLE
カタ カタ カタ カタ
RRRRRRRAAAAA ATTLE
AN EARTH-QUAKE?
DOESN'T SEEM LIKE A BIG ONE.
WE'VE HAD AN AWFUL LOT OF 'EM LATELY.
RRRRAAATTTLE
カタカタカ
?
WHO IS IT?
SISTER IRIS?
AAAHHH!
I HAD A PERVY DREAM!!
ABOUT A NUN! I AM SO GONNA GET IT!

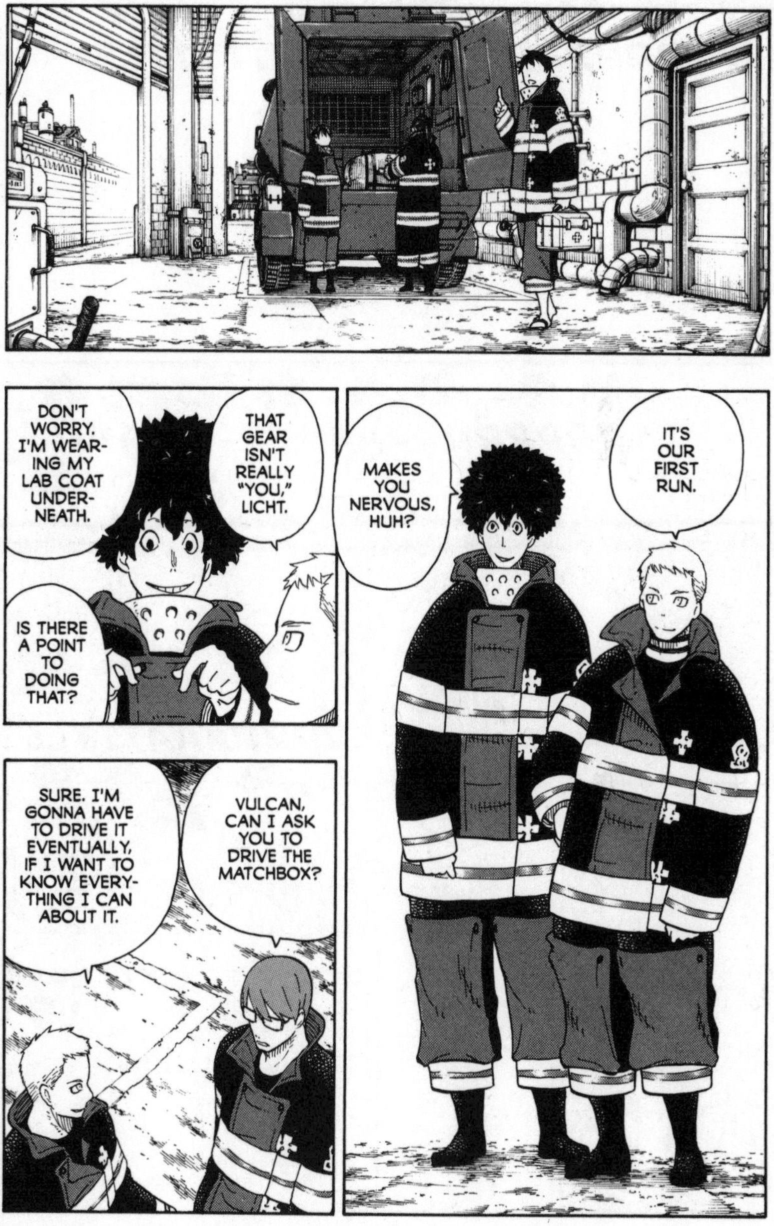
IT'S OUR FIRST RUN.
MAKES YOU NERVOUS, HUH?
THAT GEAR ISN'T REALLY "YOU," LICHT.
DON'T WORRY. I'M WEAR-ING MY LAB COAT UNDER-NEATH.
IS THERE A POINT TO DOING THAT?
VULCAN, CAN I ASK YOU TO DRIVE THE MATCHBOX?
SURE. I'M GONNA HAVE TO DRIVE IT EVENTUALLY, IF I WANT TO KNOW EVERY-THING I CAN ABOUT IT.

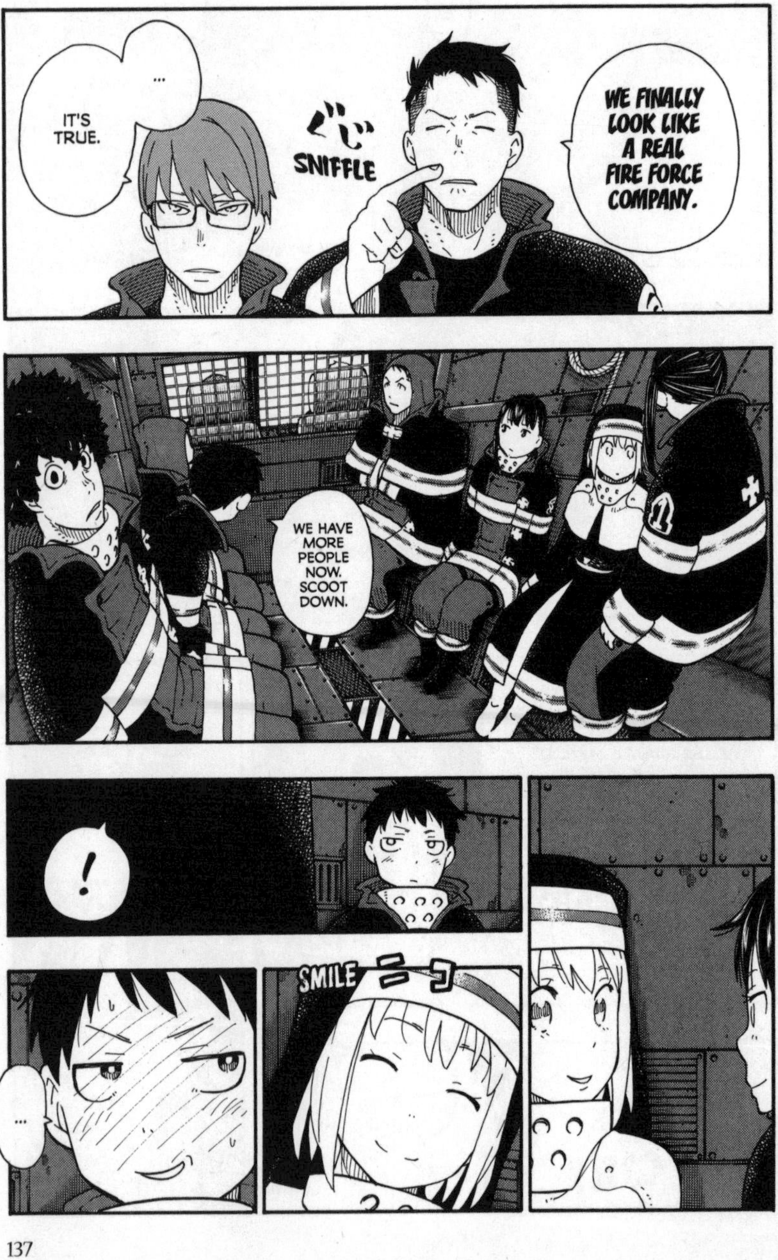
WE FINALLY LOOK LIKE A REAL FIRE FORCE COMPANY.
ぐじ
SNIFFLE
... IT'S TRUE.
WE HAVE MORE PEOPLE NOW. SCOOT DOWN.
!
ニコ
SMILE
...

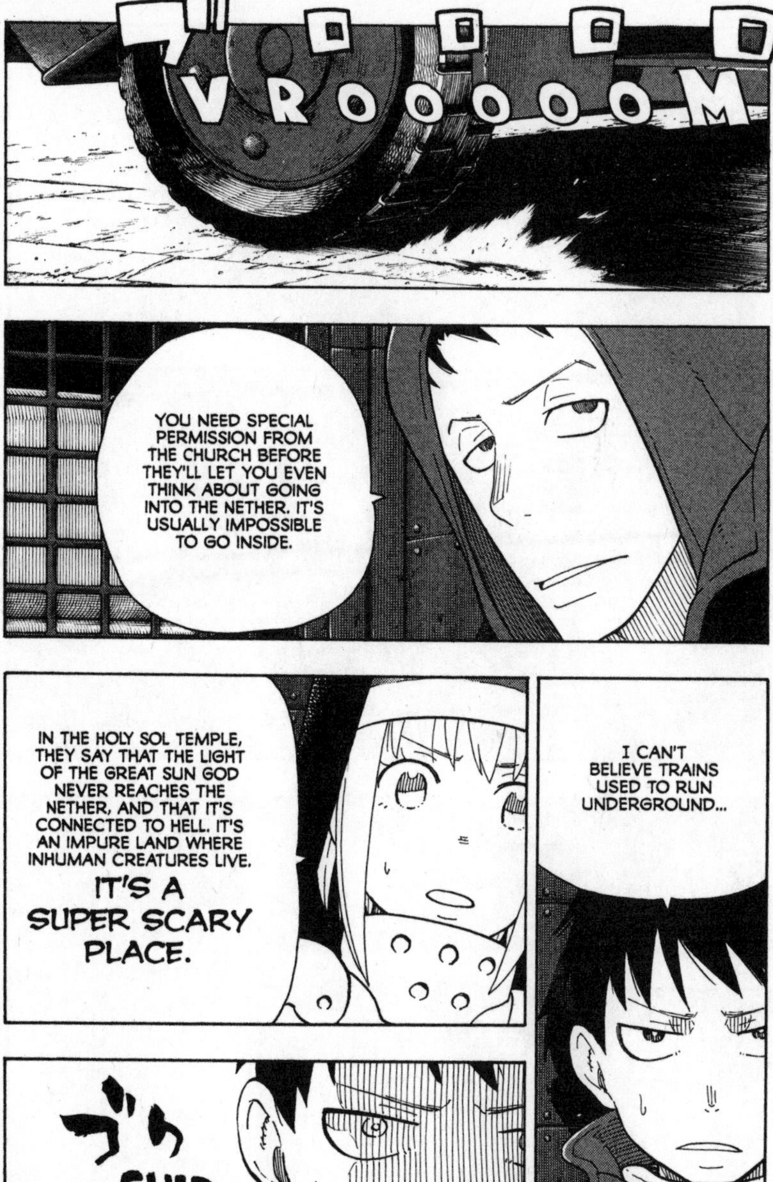
VROOOOOM
YOU NEED SPECIAL PERMISSION FROM THE CHURCH BEFORE THEY'LL LET YOU EVEN THINK ABOUT GOING INTO THE NETHER. IT'S USUALLY IMPOSSIBLE TO GO INSIDE.
I CAN'T BELIEVE TRAINS USED TO RUN UNDERGROUND...
IN THE HOLY SOL TEMPLE, THEY SAY THAT THE LIGHT OF THE GREAT SUN GOD NEVER REACHES THE NETHER, AND THAT IT'S CONNECTED TO HELL. IT'S AN IMPURE LAND WHERE INHUMAN CREATURES LIVE.
IT'S A SUPER SCARY PLACE.
ゴク
GULP

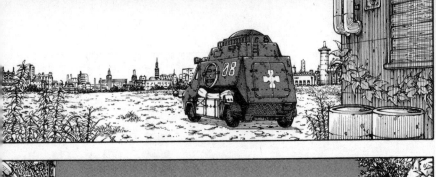

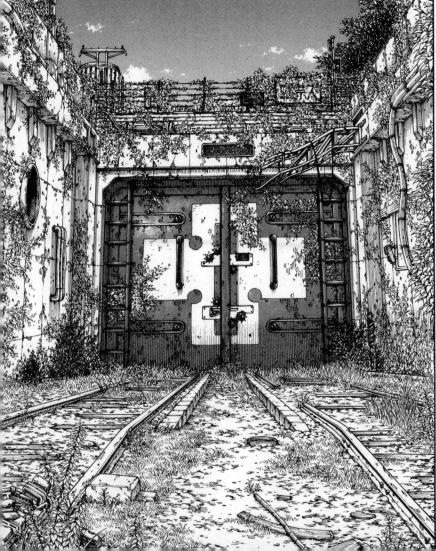

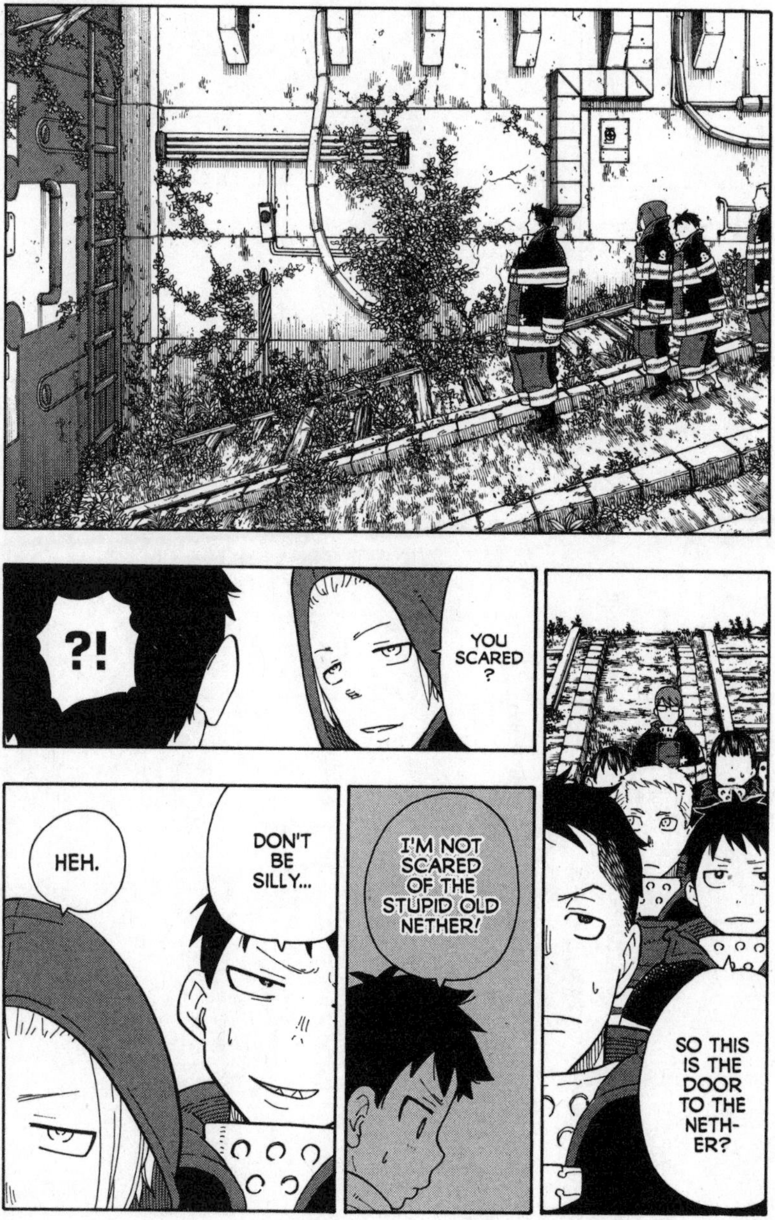
SO THIS IS THE DOOR TO THE NETHER?
YOU SCARED?
?!
I'M NOT SCARED OF THE STUPID OLD NETHER!
DON'T BE SILLY...
HEH.

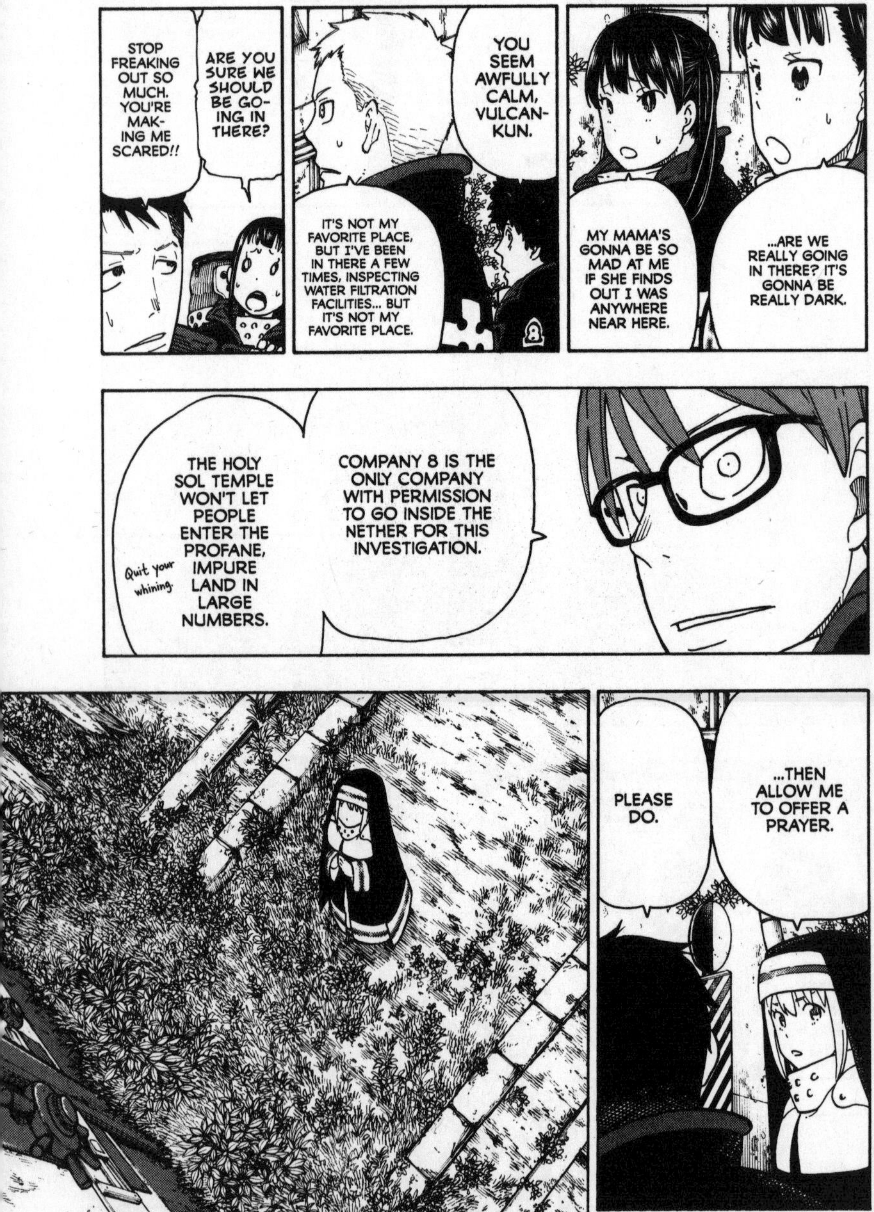
...ARE WE REALLY GOING IN THERE? IT'S GONNA BE REALLY DARK.
MY MAMA'S GONNA BE SO MAD AT ME IF SHE FINDS OUT I WAS ANYWHERE NEAR HERE.
YOU SEEM AWFULLY CALM, VULCAN-KUN.
IT'S NOT MY FAVORITE PLACE, BUT I'VE BEEN IN THERE A FEW TIMES, INSPECTING WATER FILTRATION FACILITIES... BUT IT'S NOT MY FAVORITE PLACE.
ARE YOU SURE WE SHOULD BE GO-ING IN THERE?
STOP FREAKING OUT SO MUCH. YOU'RE MAK-ING ME SCARED!!
COMPANY 8 IS THE ONLY COMPANY WITH PERMISSION TO GO INSIDE THE NETHER FOR THIS INVESTIGATION.
THE HOLY SOL TEMPLE WON'T LET PEOPLE ENTER THE PROFANE, IMPURE LAND IN LARGE NUMBERS.
Quit your whining.
...THEN ALLOW ME TO OFFER A PRAYER.
PLEASE DO.

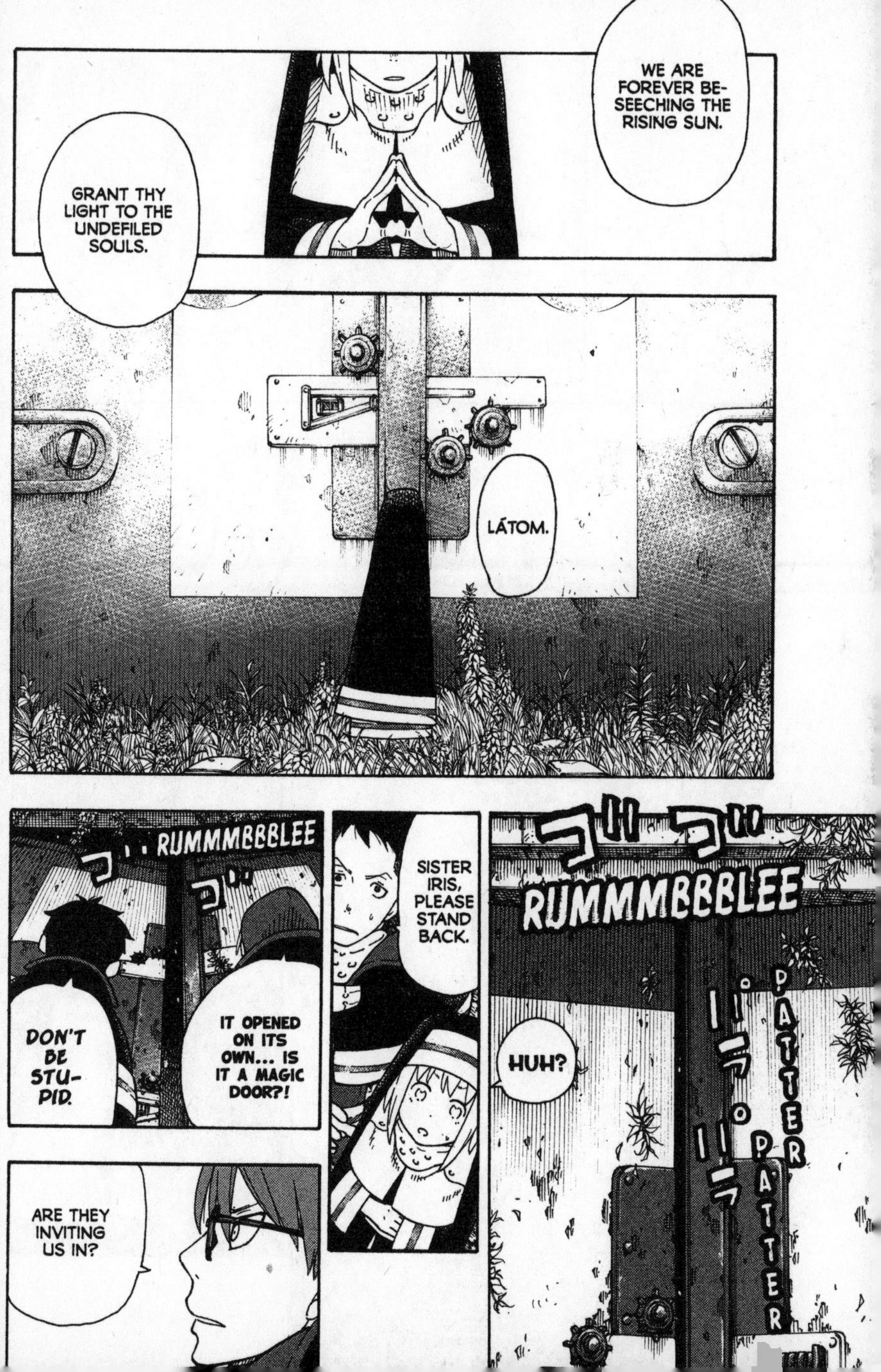
WE ARE FOREVER BE-SEECHING THE RISING SUN.
GRANT THY LIGHT TO THE UNDEFILED SOULS.
LÁTOM.
RUMMMBBBLEE
HUH?
PATTER PATTER
SISTER IRIS, PLEASE STAND BACK.
RUMMMBBBLEE
IT OPENED ON ITS OWN... IS IT A MAGIC DOOR?!
DON'T BE STU-PID.
ARE THEY INVITING US IN?

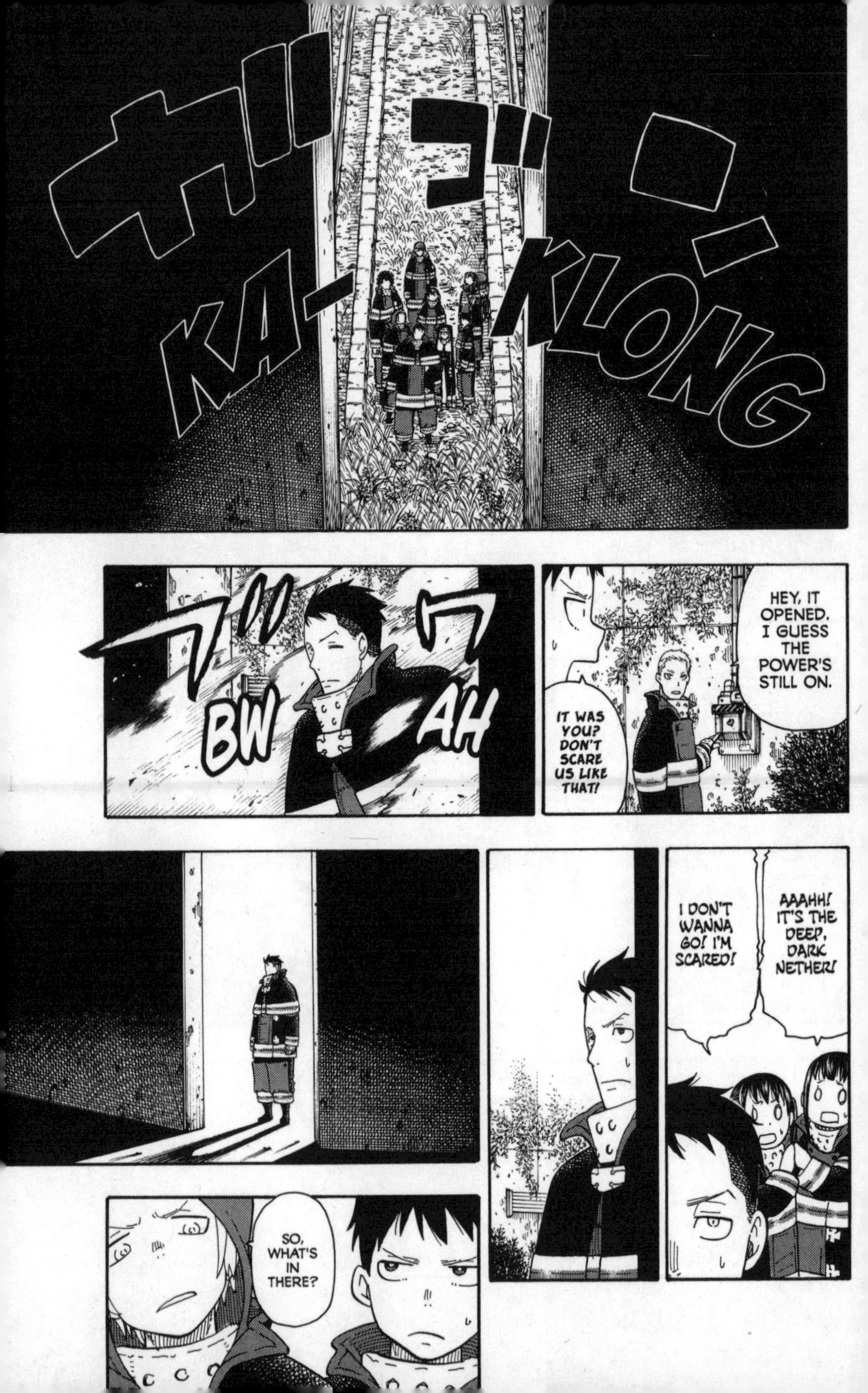
KA-KLONG
HEY, IT OPENED. I GUESS THE POWER'S STILL ON.
IT WAS YOU? DON'T SCARE US LIKE THAT!
BWAH
AAAHH! IT'S THE DEEP, DARK NETHER!
I DON'T WANNA GO! I'M SCARED!
SO, WHAT'S IN THERE?

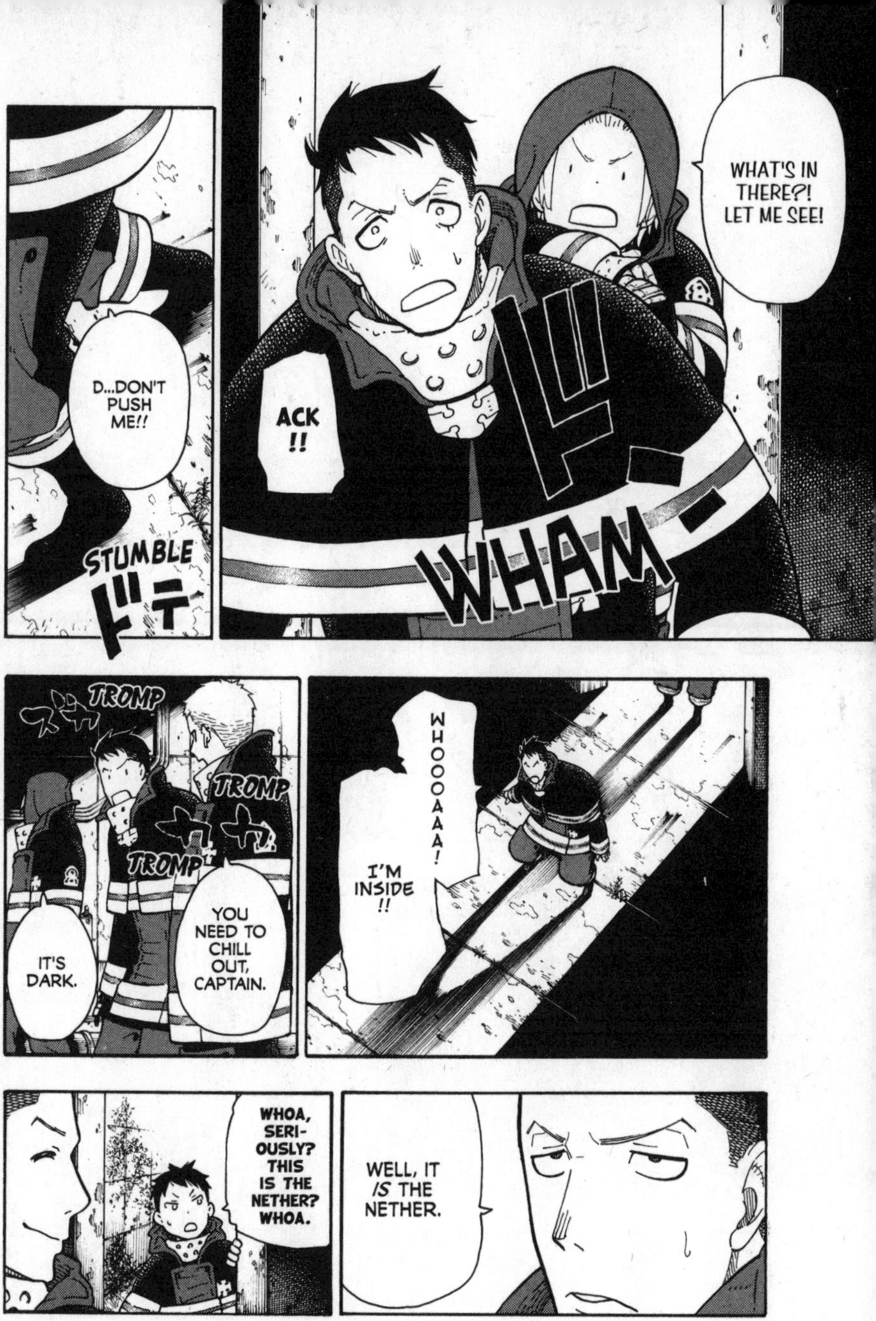
WHAT'S IN THERE?! LET ME SEE!
ACK !!
WHAM
D...DON'T PUSH ME!!
STUMBLE
ドテ
WHOOOAAA!
I'M INSIDE !!
TROMP
TROMP
TROMP
YOU NEED TO CHILL OUT, CAPTAIN.
IT'S DARK.
WELL, IT *IS* THE NETHER.
WHOA, SERIOUSLY? THIS IS THE NETHER? WHOA.

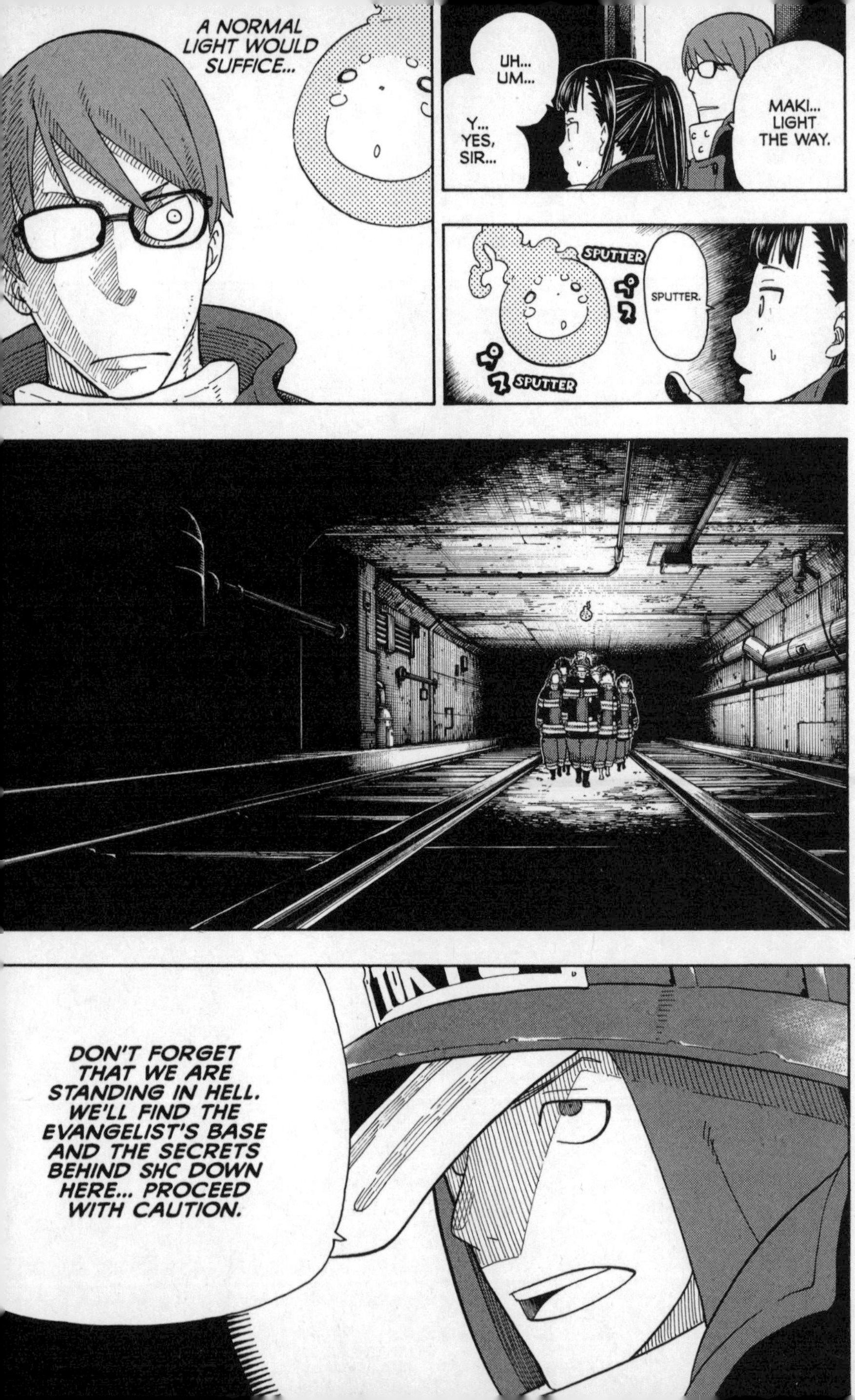
MAKI... LIGHT THE WAY.
UH... UM...
Y... YES, SIR...
SPUTTER
SPUTTER.
SPUTTER
A NORMAL LIGHT WOULD SUFFICE...
DON'T FORGET THAT WE ARE STANDING IN HELL. WE'LL FIND THE EVANGELIST'S BASE AND THE SECRETS BEHIND SHC DOWN HERE... PROCEED WITH CAUTION.

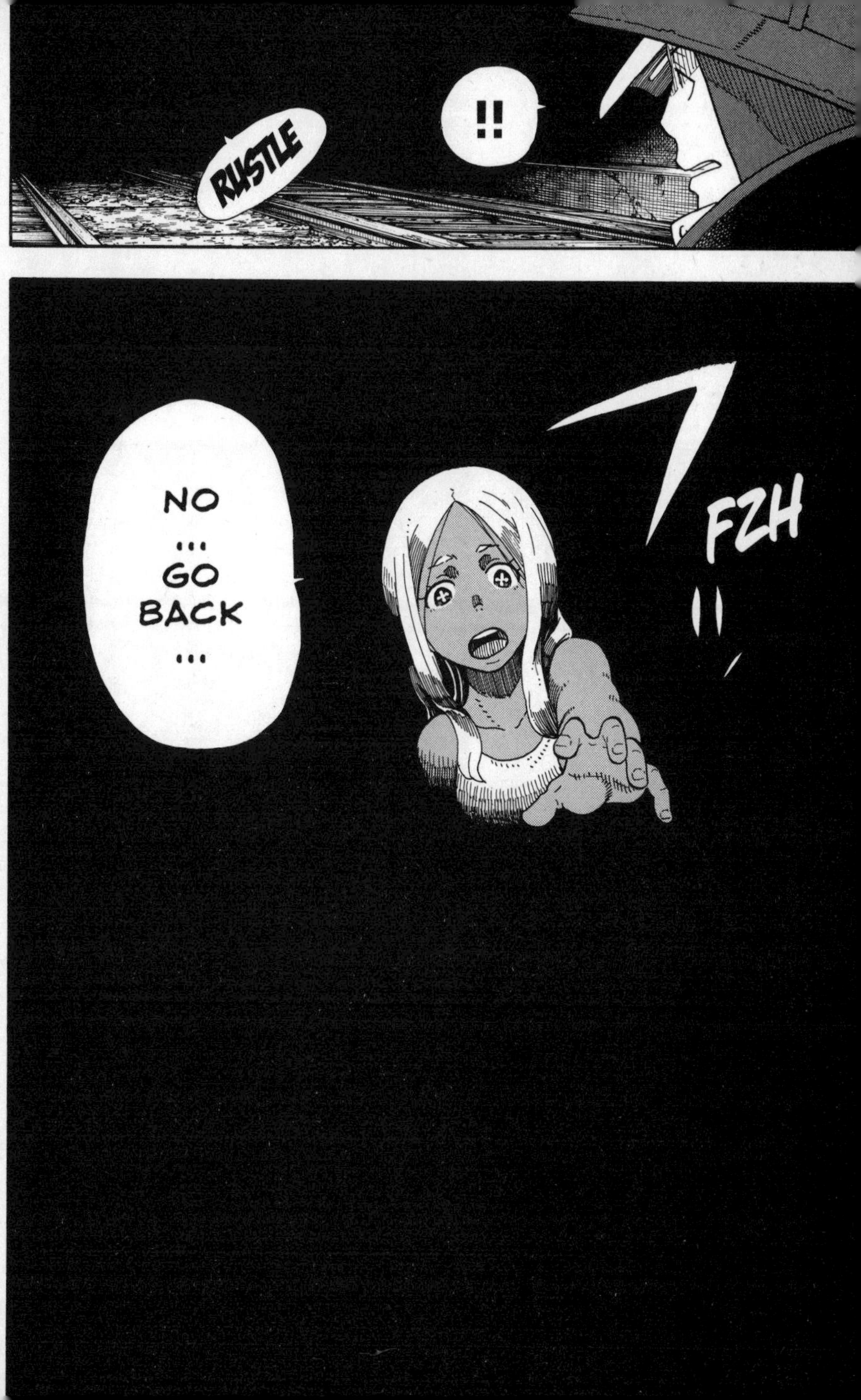

!!
RUSTLE
NO ... GO BACK ...
FZH

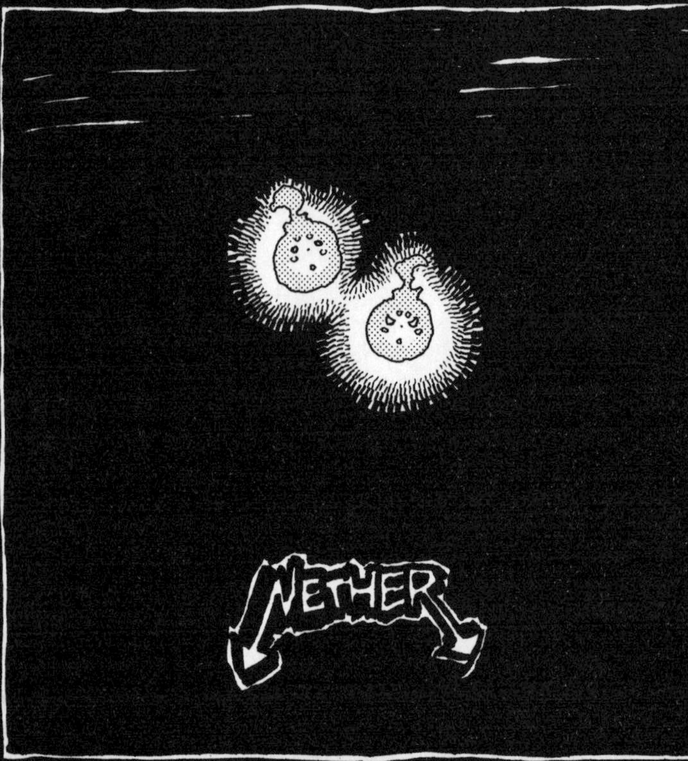
NETHER

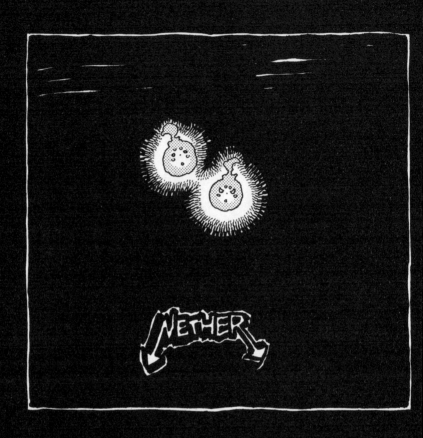

CHAPTER LXVIII: LOST IN THE DARK

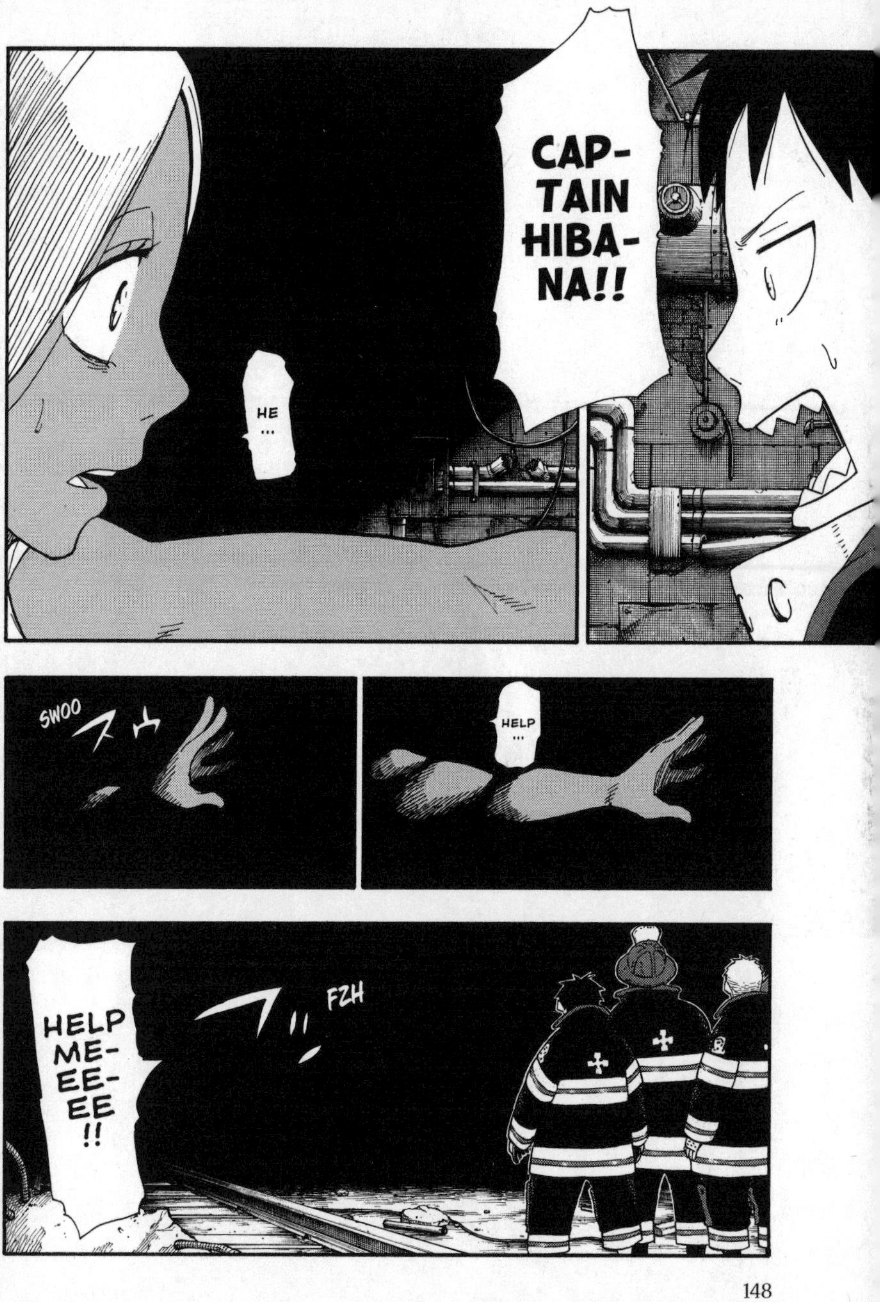
CAP-
TAIN
HIBA-
NA!!
HE
...
HELP
...
SWOO
FZH
HELP
ME-
EE-
EE
!!

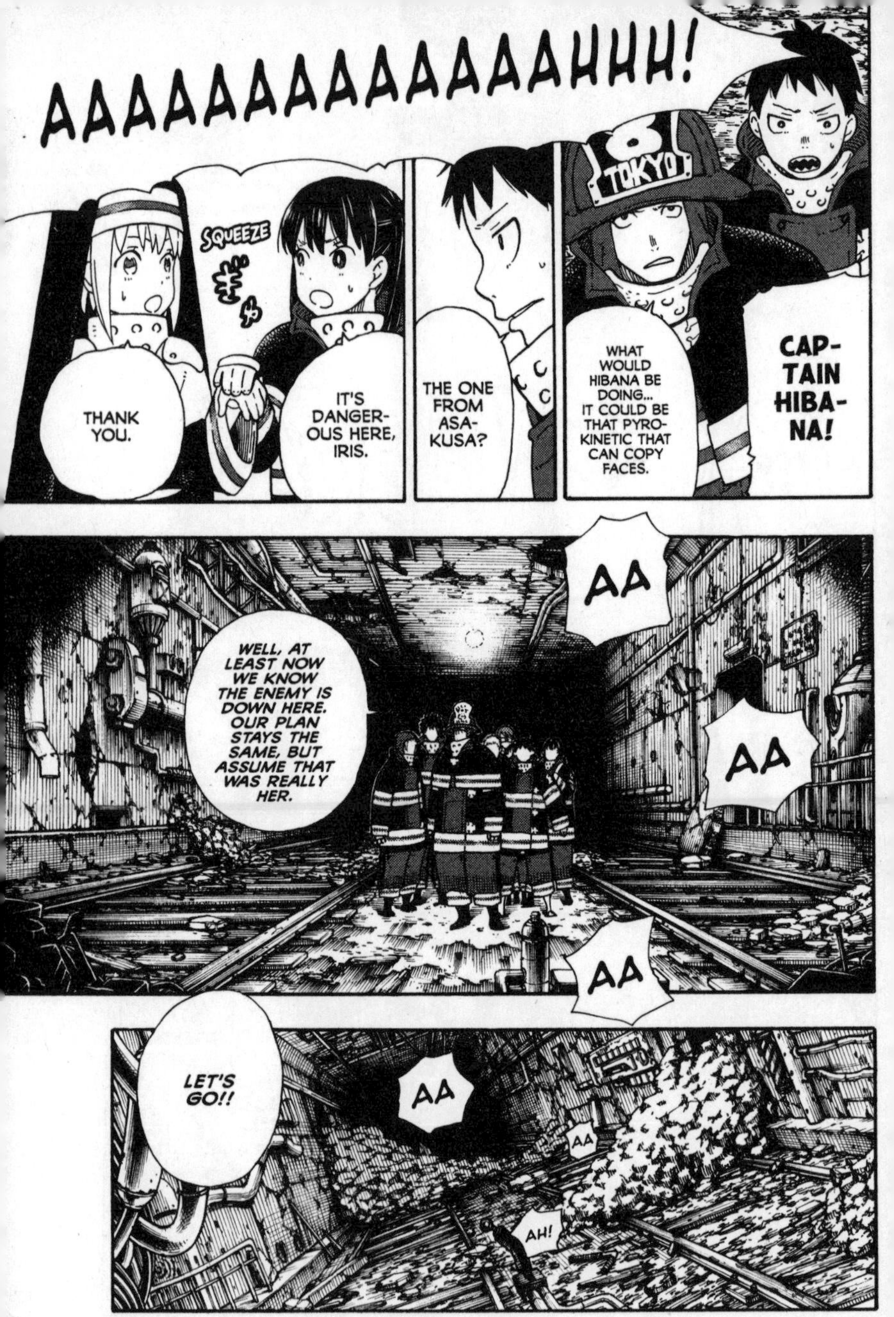

AAAAAAAAAAAAAHHH!
CAPTAIN HIBANA!
WHAT WOULD HIBANA BE DOING... IT COULD BE THAT PYROKINETIC THAT CAN COPY FACES.
THE ONE FROM ASAKUSA?
IT'S DANGEROUS HERE, IRIS.
SQUEEZE
THANK YOU.
AA
WELL, AT LEAST NOW WE KNOW THE ENEMY IS DOWN HERE. OUR PLAN STAYS THE SAME, BUT ASSUME THAT WAS REALLY HER.
AA
AA
LET'S GO!!
AA
AA
AH!

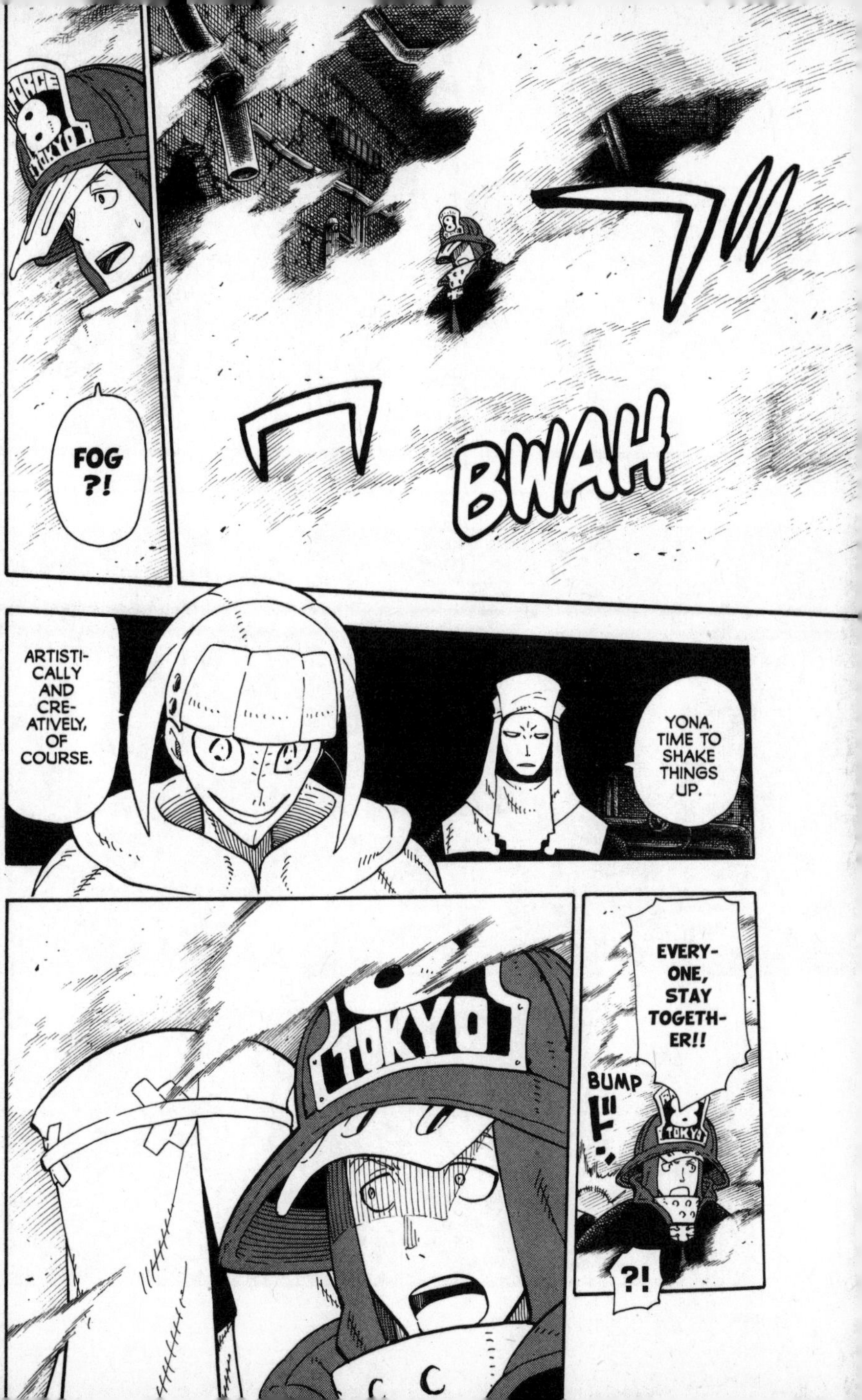
BWAH
FOG ?!
YONA. TIME TO SHAKE THINGS UP.
ARTISTICALLY AND CREATIVELY, OF COURSE.
EVERYONE, STAY TOGETHER!!
BUMP
?!

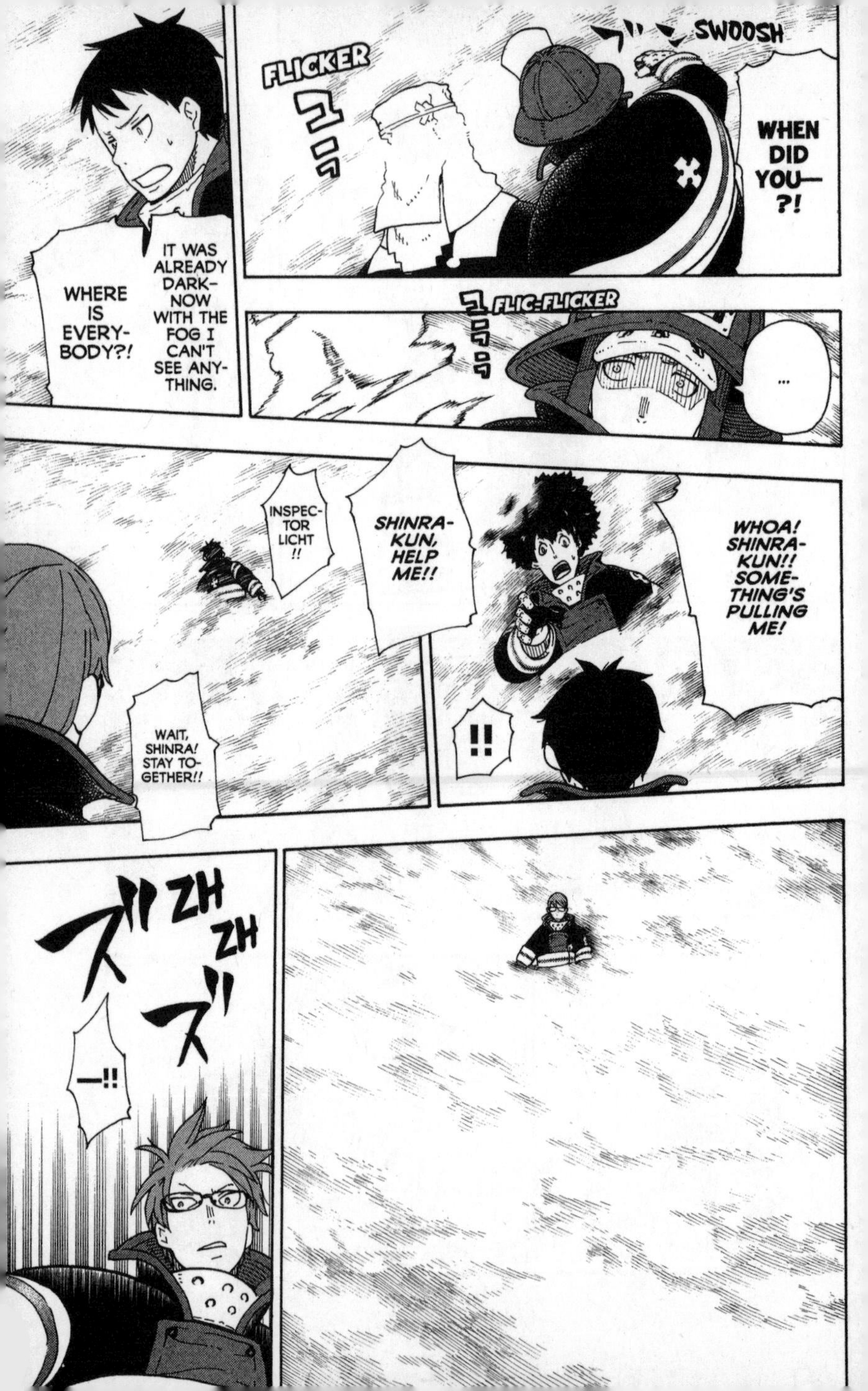
SWOOSH
WHEN DID YOU—?!
FLICKER
FLIC-FLICKER
...
IT WAS ALREADY DARK—NOW WITH THE FOG I CAN'T SEE ANYTHING.
WHERE IS EVERYBODY?!
WHOA! SHINRA-KUN!! SOMETHING'S PULLING ME!
SHINRA-KUN, HELP ME!!
!!
INSPECTOR LICHT!!
WAIT, SHINRA! STAY TOGETHER!!
ZH
ZH
—!!

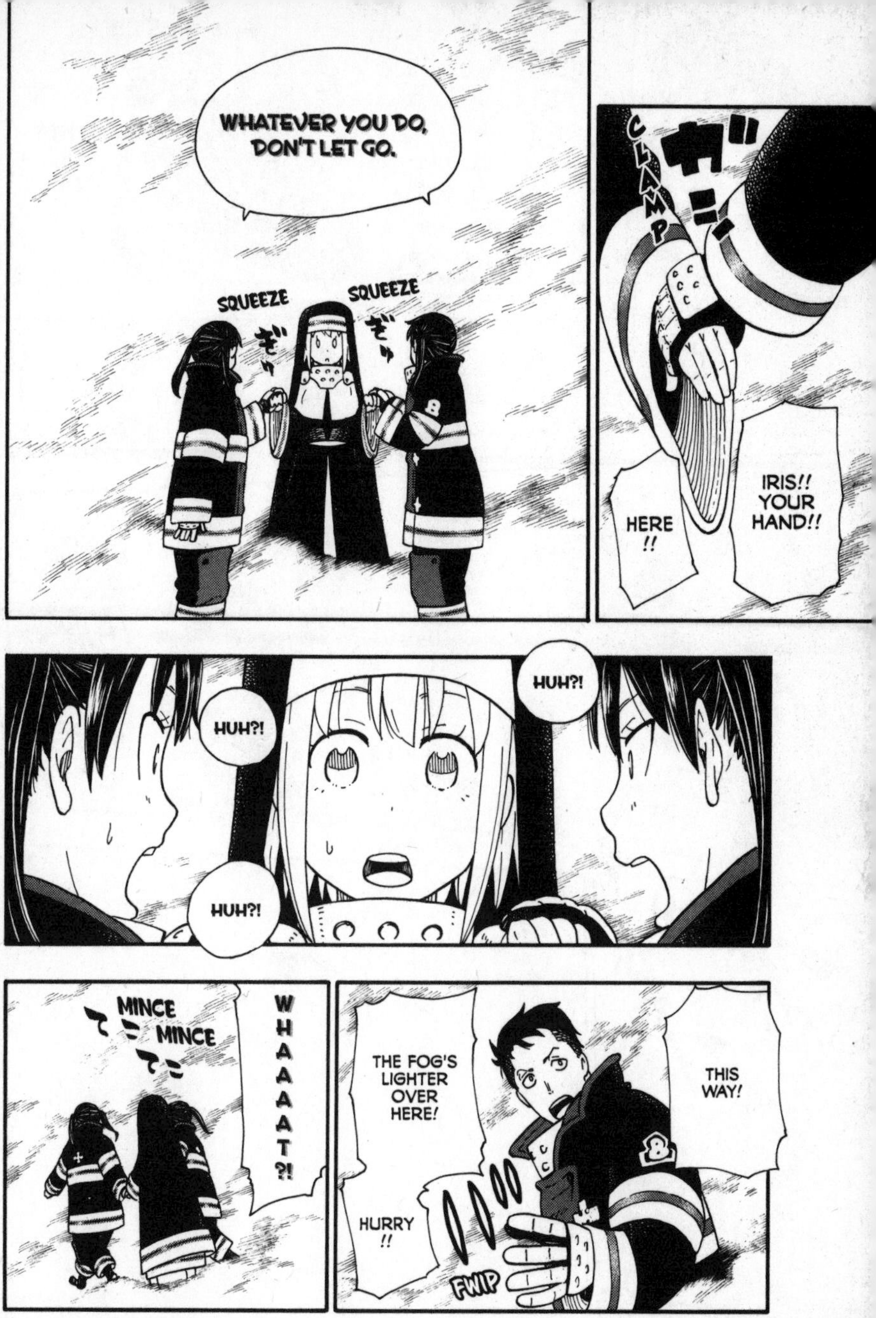
CLAMP
IRIS!! YOUR HAND!!
HERE!!
WHATEVER YOU DO, DON'T LET GO.
SQUEEZE
SQUEEZE
HUH?!
HUH?!
HUH?!
THIS WAY!
THE FOG'S LIGHTER OVER HERE!
HURRY!!
FWIP
WHAAAAAT?!
MINCE
MINCE

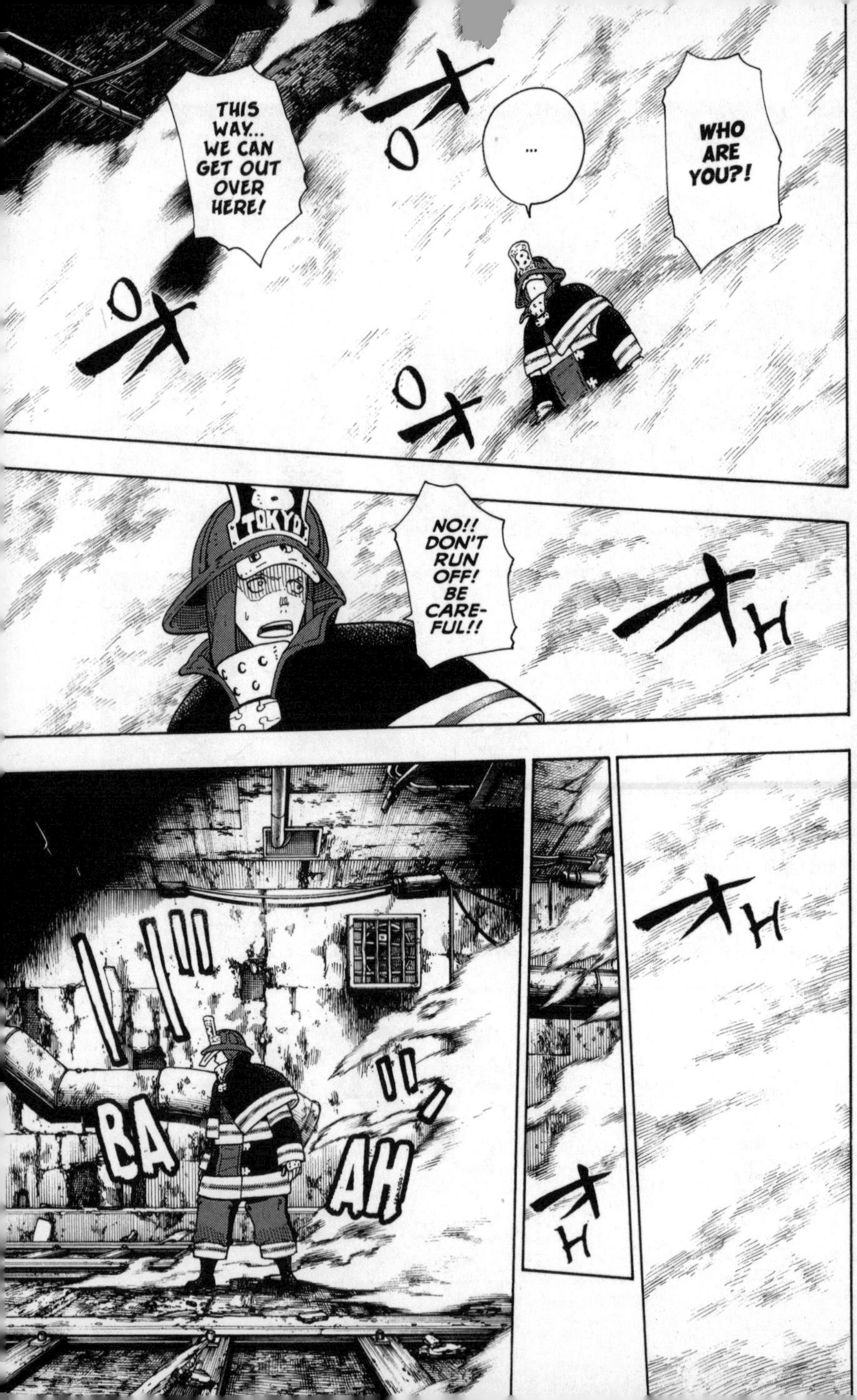
WHO ARE YOU?!
...
THIS WAY... WE CAN GET OUT OVER HERE!
NO!! DON'T RUN OFF! BE CAREFUL!!
BA AH

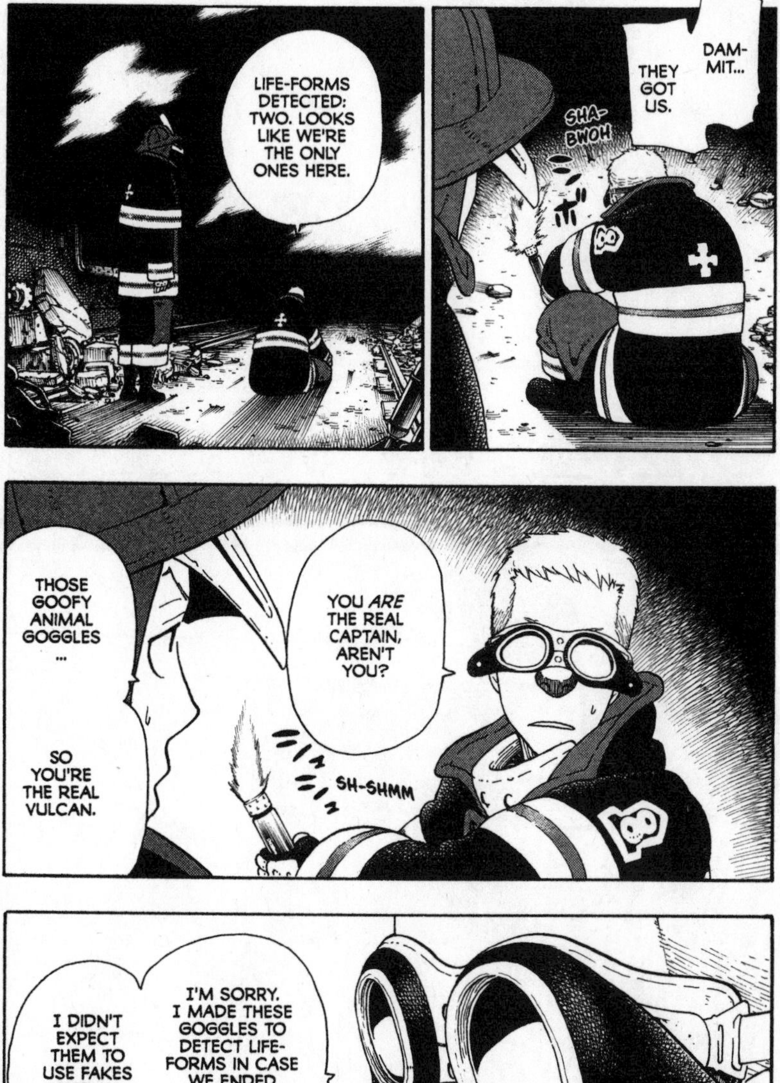
DAM-MIT...
THEY GOT US.
SHA-BWOH
LIFE-FORMS DETECTED: TWO. LOOKS LIKE WE'RE THE ONLY ONES HERE.
YOU *ARE* THE REAL CAPTAIN, AREN'T YOU?
SH-SHMM
THOSE GOOFY ANIMAL GOGGLES...
SO YOU'RE THE REAL VULCAN.
I'M SORRY. I MADE THESE GOGGLES TO DETECT LIFE-FORMS IN CASE WE ENDED UP FIGHTING MIRAGE.
I DIDN'T EXPECT THEM TO USE FAKES *AND* ALL THIS FOG AT THE SAME TIME.
Based on a sloth.

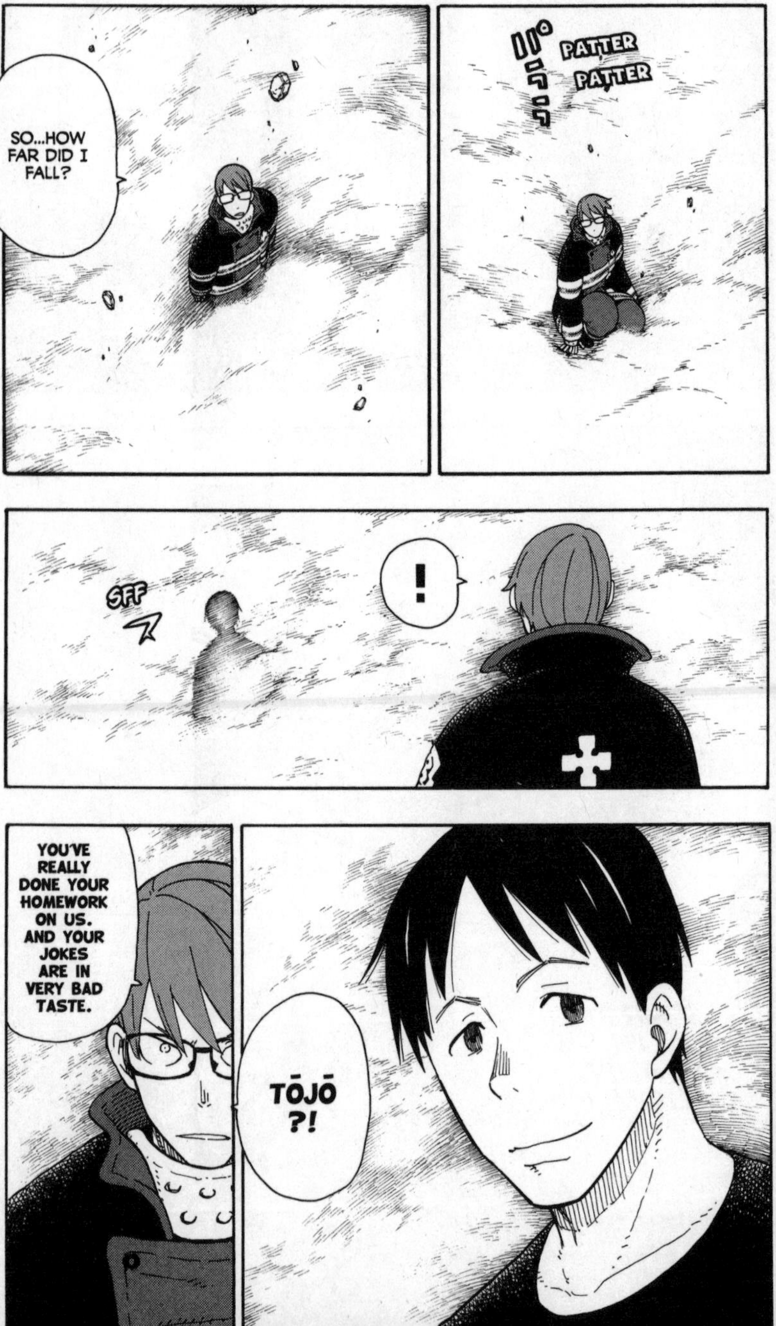
パラ パラ
PATTER PATTER
SO...HOW FAR DID I FALL?
!
SFF
TŌJŌ ?!
YOU'VE REALLY DONE YOUR HOMEWORK ON US. AND YOUR JOKES ARE IN VERY BAD TASTE.

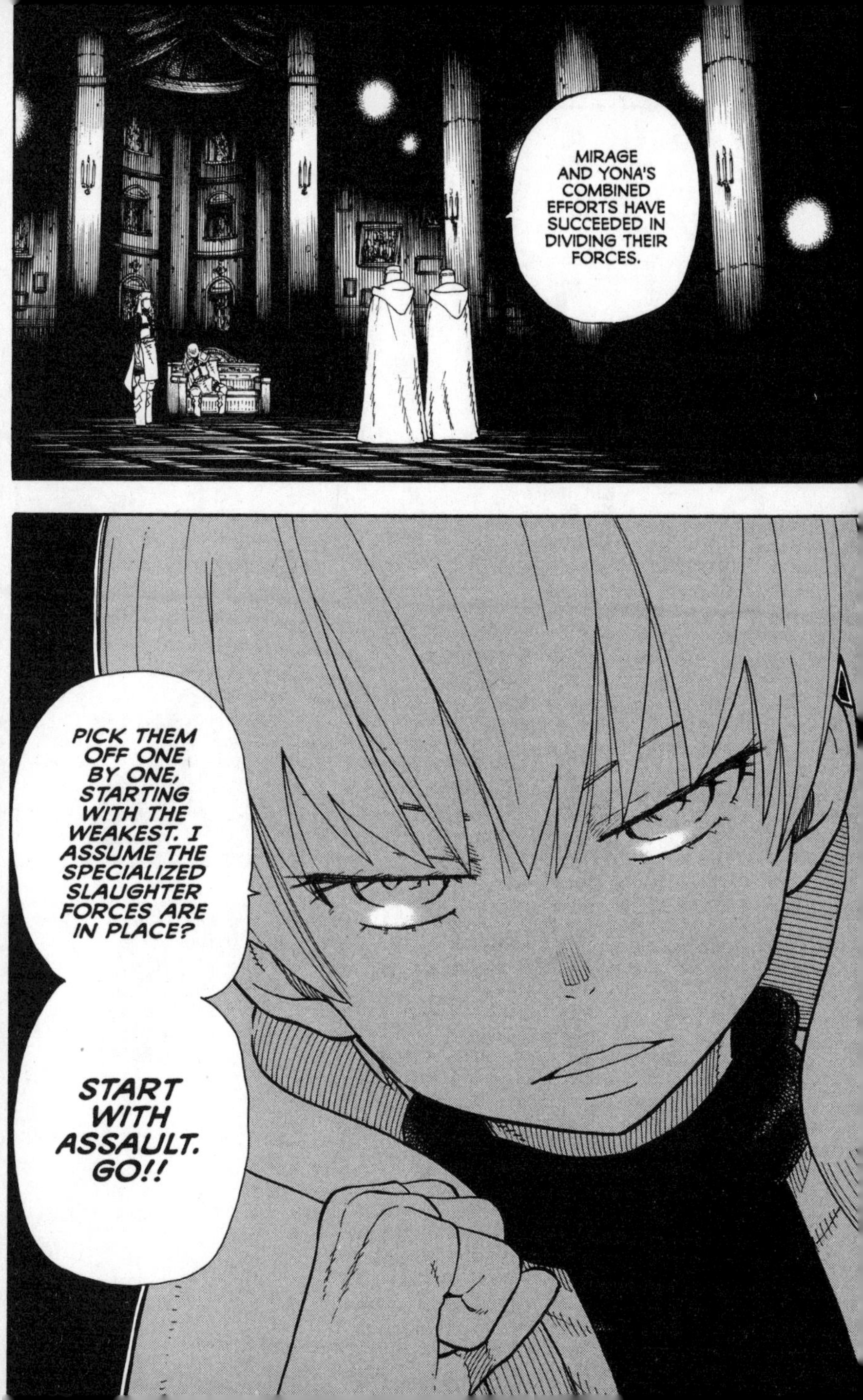
MIRAGE AND YONA'S COMBINED EFFORTS HAVE SUCCEEDED IN DIVIDING THEIR FORCES.
PICK THEM OFF ONE BY ONE, STARTING WITH THE WEAKEST. I ASSUME THE SPECIALIZED SLAUGHTER FORCES ARE IN PLACE?
START WITH ASSAULT. GO!!

IRIS, I'M TELLING YOU, I'M THE REAL ONE!
SHAKE
SHAKE
NO, I AM!
ER...UH, HMMM.
WHY DO YOU EVEN NEED TO THINK ABOUT IT?! SHE IS OBVIOUSLY FAKE!
THAT'S NOT EVEN TRUE!! SHE'S THE FAKE!
I'm hurt! Hmph!
BWOH
COME ON, YOU KNOW I WAS HOLDING YOUR LEFT HAND!! I EVEN HAVE FIRE EARS, SEE?!
THAT'S A GOOD POINT...
THAT'S NOT FAIR! YOU'RE TRYING TO TRICK HER BY DOING SOME-THING I CAN'T DO! YOU'RE SO MEAN! YOU'RE MAKING ME CRY!
IT MIGHT BE A VERY CLEVER TRAP.
YOU CAN SEE MY EARS!!
AARRGH!! FINE! YOU'RE STUPID, IRIS!!
AND SHE TOTALLY SOUNDS LIKE AN OLD MAN!!
MEEP...
FIP

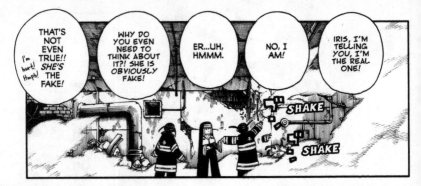

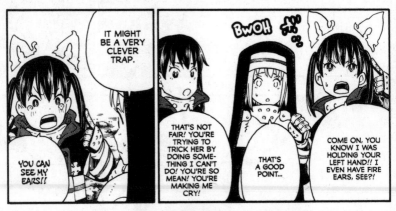

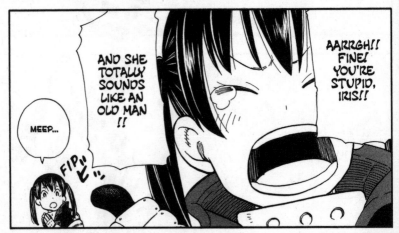

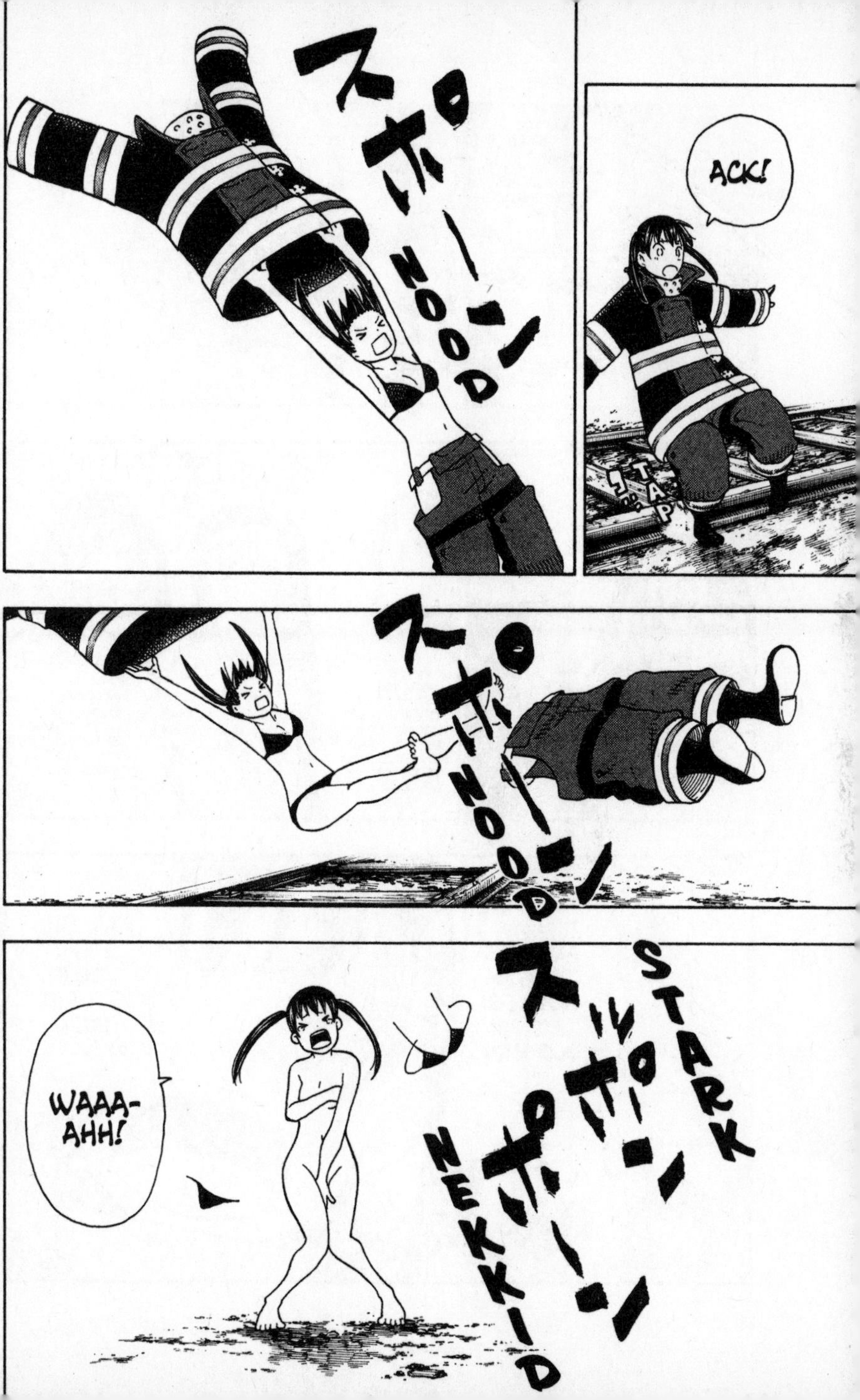
ACK!
TAP
NOOOD
NOOOD
STARK
NEKKID
WAAA-
AHH!

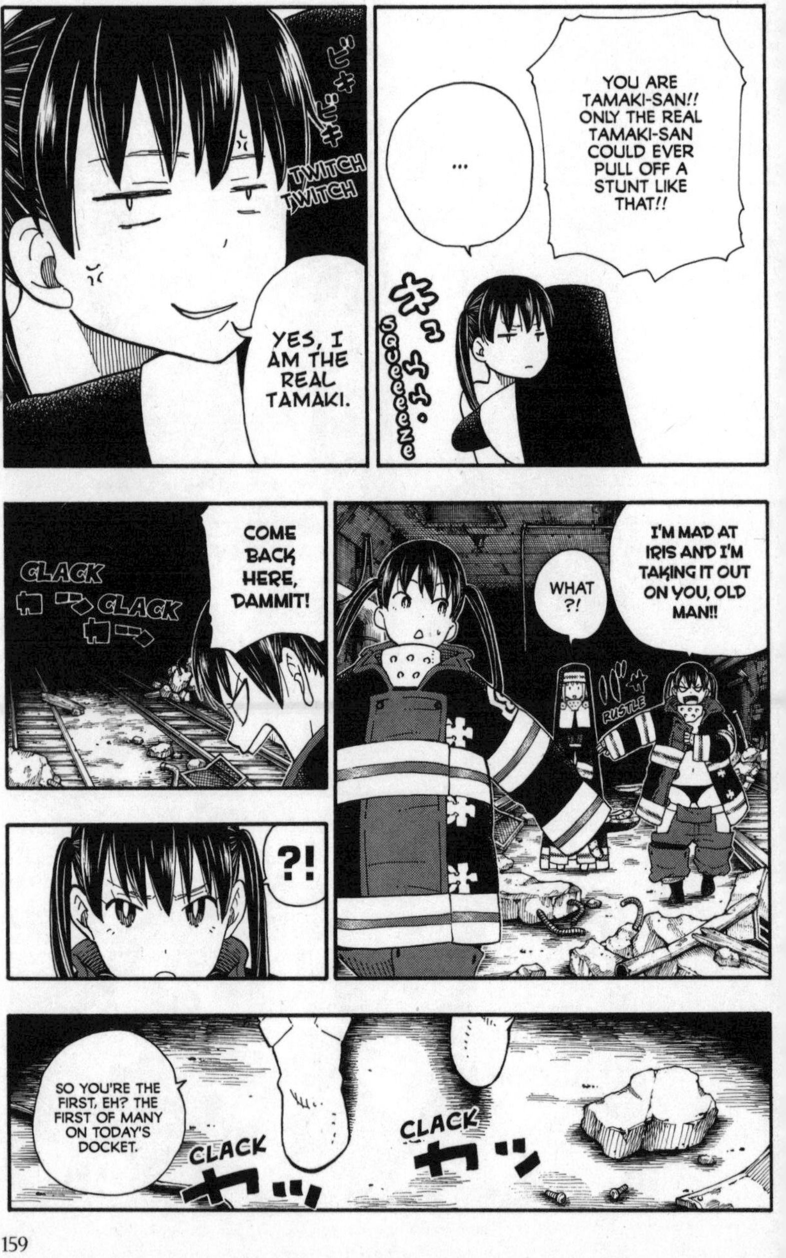
YOU ARE TAMAKI-SAN!! ONLY THE REAL TAMAKI-SAN COULD EVER PULL OFF A STUNT LIKE THAT!!
...
SQUEEEEZE
TWITCH TWITCH
YES, I AM THE REAL TAMAKI.
I'M MAD AT IRIS AND I'M TAKING IT OUT ON YOU, OLD MAN!!
WHAT?!
RUSTLE
COME BACK HERE, DAMMIT!
CLACK
CLACK
?!
CLACK
CLACK
SO YOU'RE THE FIRST, EH? THE FIRST OF MANY ON TODAY'S DOCKET.

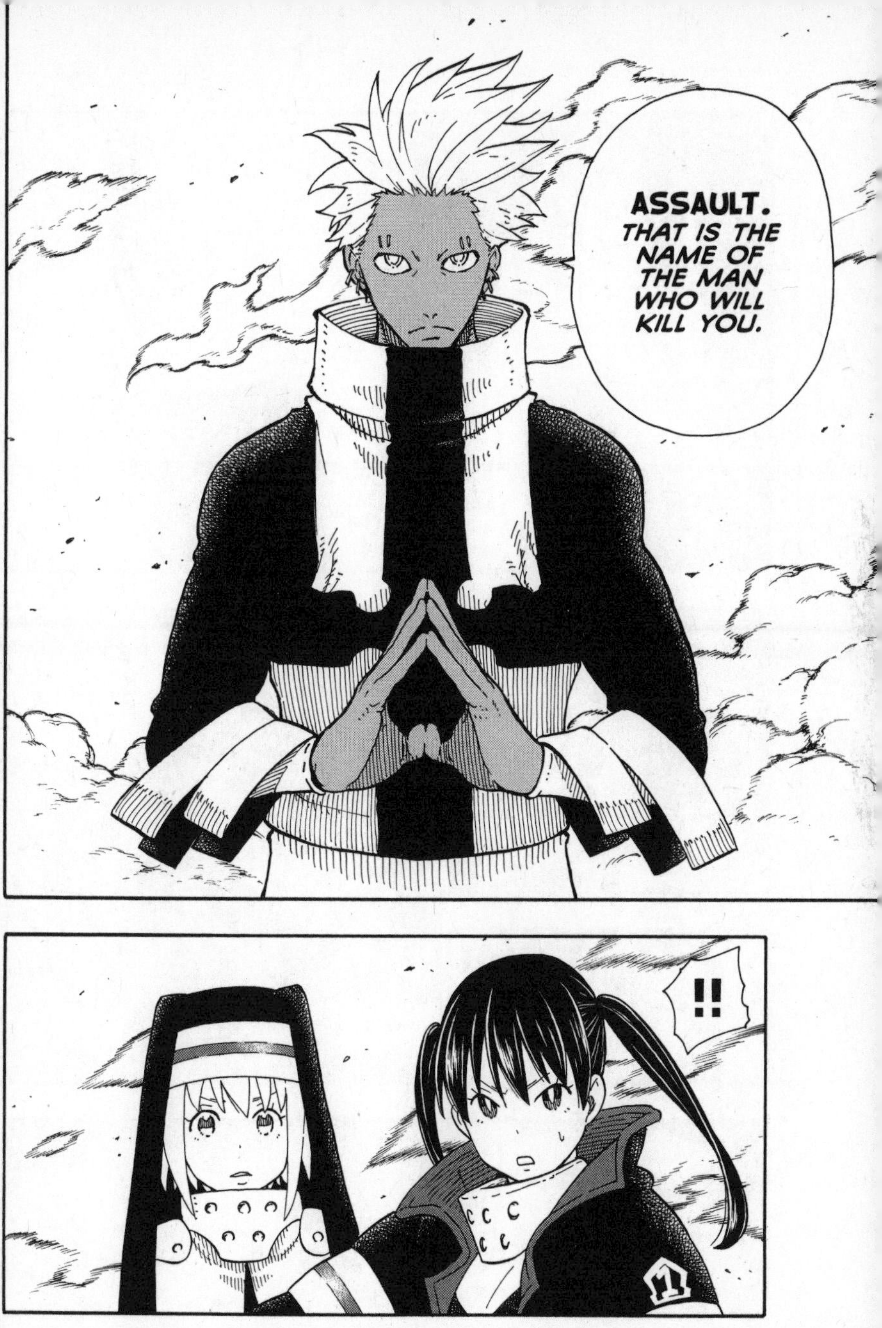
ASSAULT. THAT IS THE NAME OF THE MAN WHO WILL KILL YOU.
!!

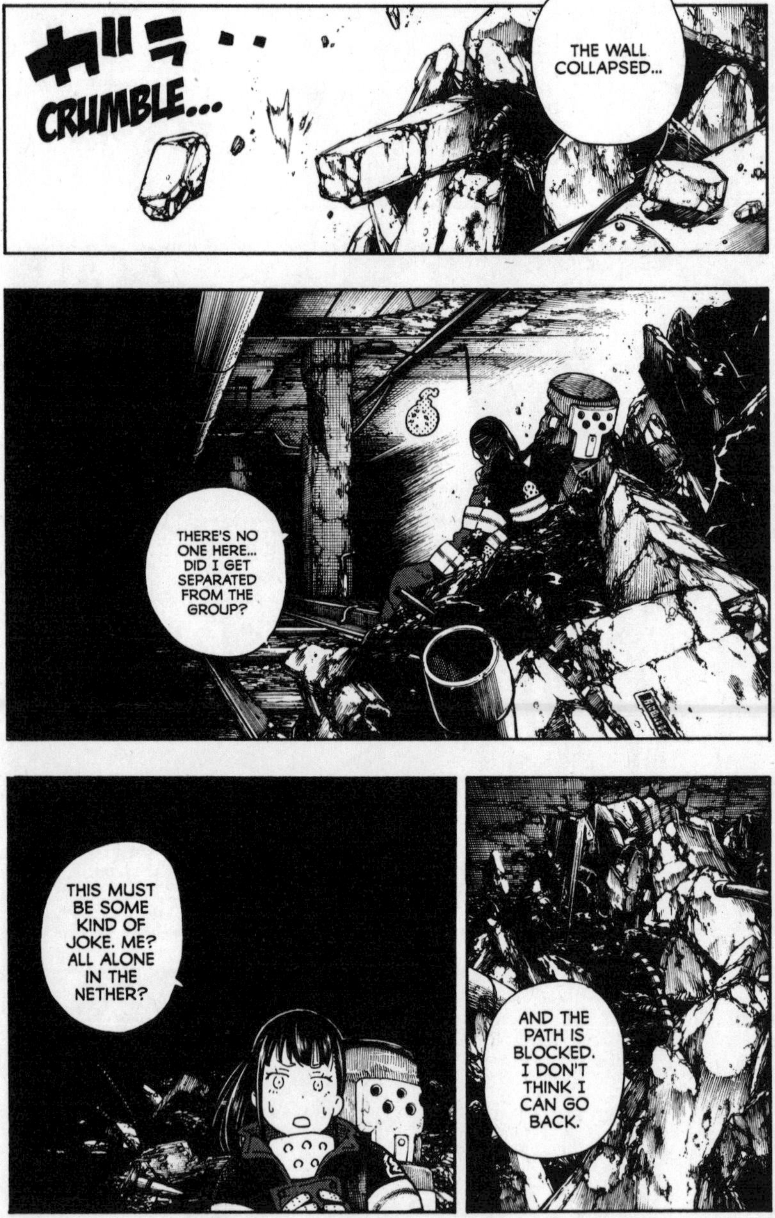

THE WALL COLLAPSED...
カラ・・
CRUMBLE...
THERE'S NO ONE HERE... DID I GET SEPARATED FROM THE GROUP?
AND THE PATH IS BLOCKED. I DON'T THINK I CAN GO BACK.
THIS MUST BE SOME KIND OF JOKE. ME? ALL ALONE IN THE NETHER?

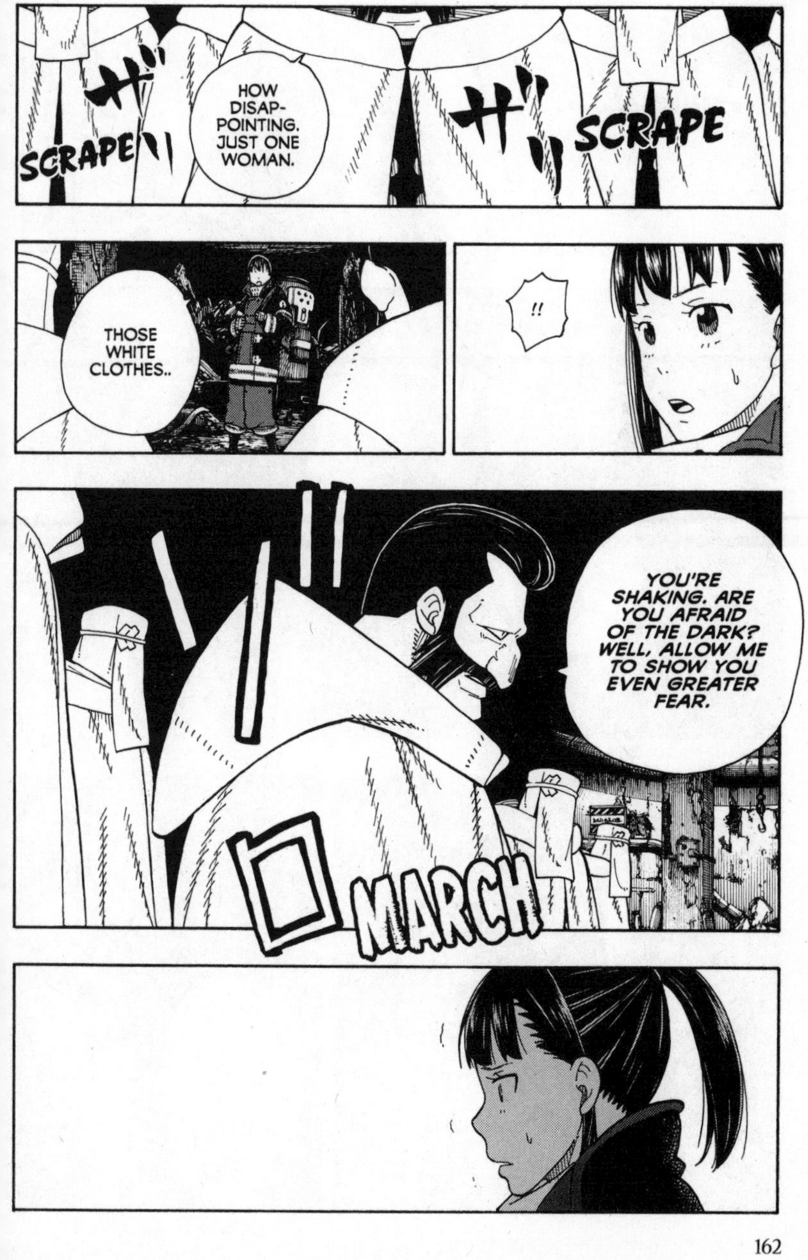
SCRAPE
HOW DISAP-POINTING. JUST ONE WOMAN.
SCRAPE
!!
THOSE WHITE CLOTHES..
YOU'RE SHAKING. ARE YOU AFRAID OF THE DARK? WELL, ALLOW ME TO SHOW YOU EVEN GREATER FEAR.
MARCH

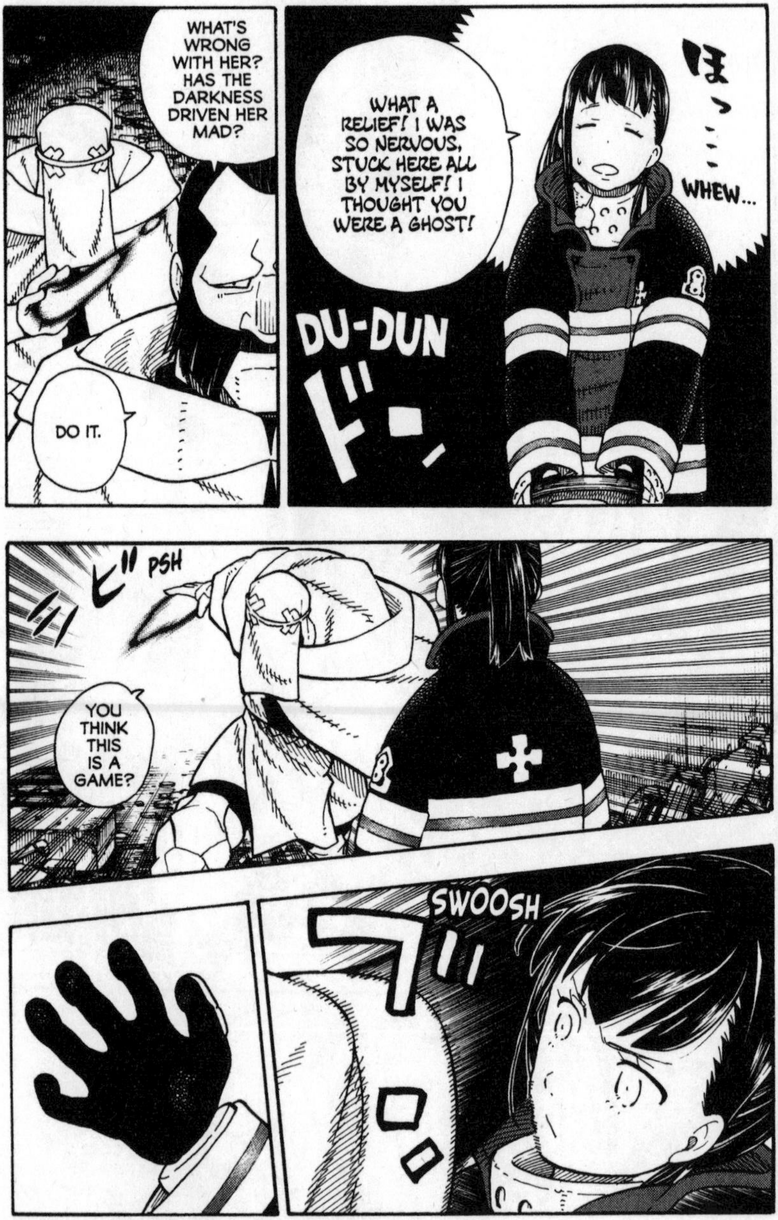
WHEW...
WHAT A RELIEF! I WAS SO NERVOUS, STUCK HERE ALL BY MYSELF! I THOUGHT YOU WERE A GHOST!
DU-DUN
WHAT'S WRONG WITH HER? HAS THE DARKNESS DRIVEN HER MAD?
DO IT.
PSH
YOU THINK THIS IS A GAME?
SWOOSH

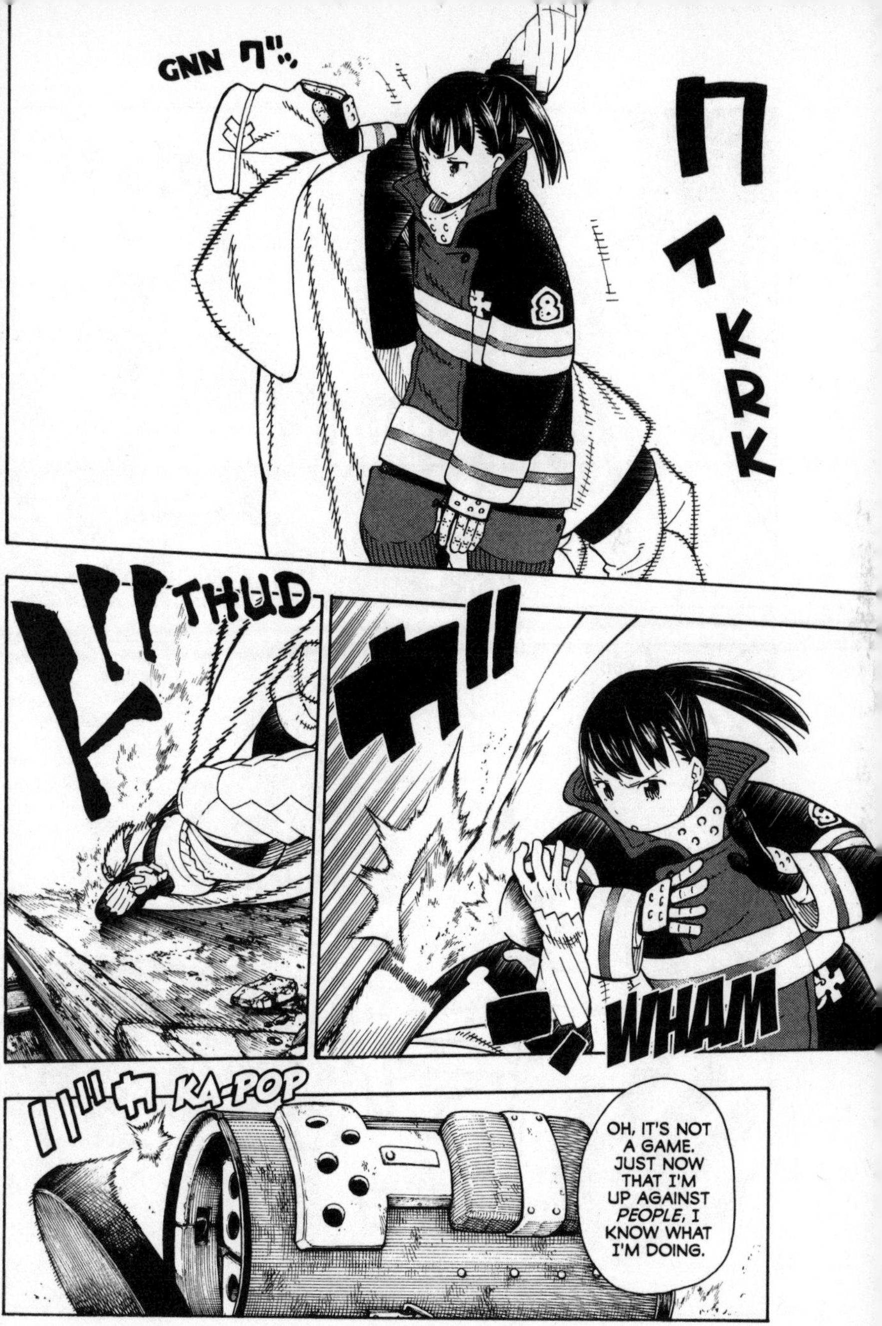
KRK
GNN
WHAM
THUD
KA-POP
OH, IT'S NOT A GAME. JUST NOW THAT I'M UP AGAINST *PEOPLE*, I KNOW WHAT I'M DOING.

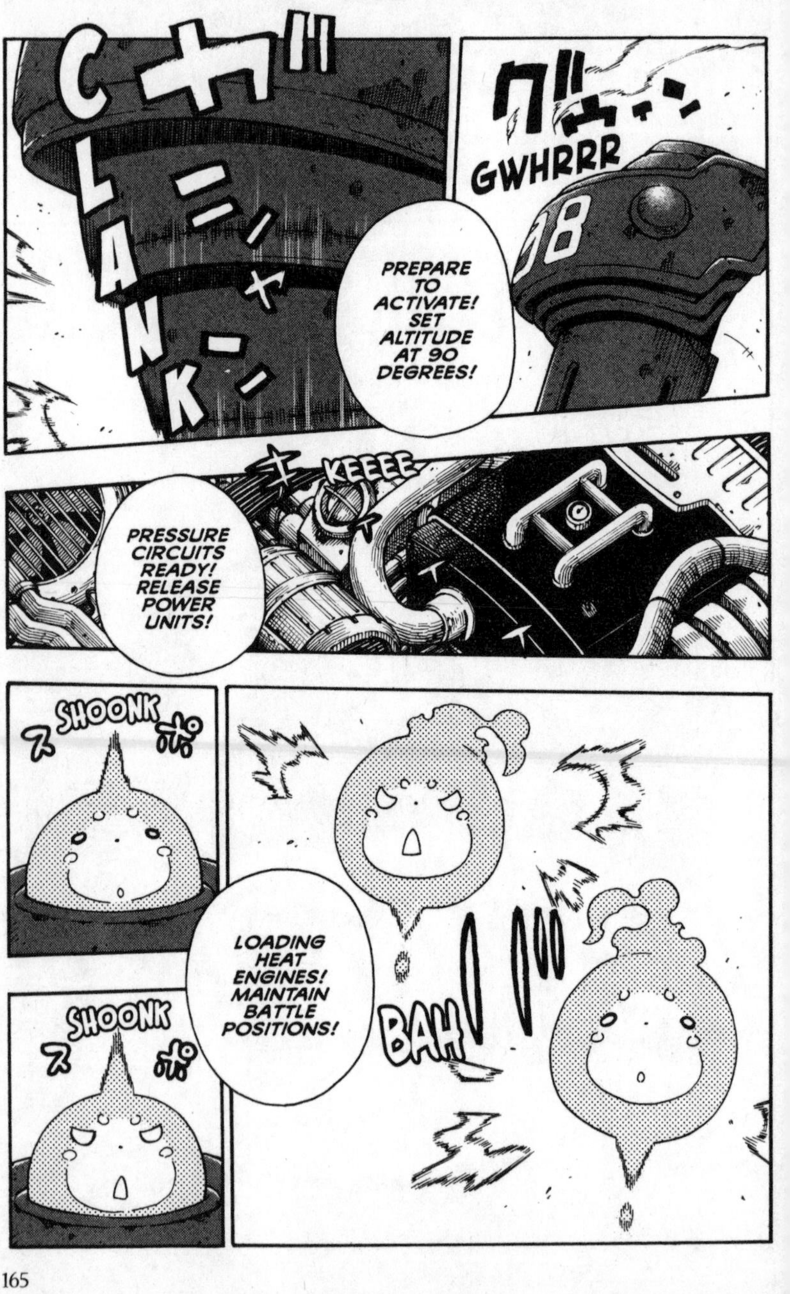
GWHRRR
PREPARE TO ACTIVATE! SET ALTITUDE AT 90 DEGREES!
CLANK
KEEEE
PRESSURE CIRCUITS READY! RELEASE POWER UNITS!
LOADING HEAT ENGINES! MAINTAIN BATTLE POSITIONS!
BAH
SHOONK
SHOONK

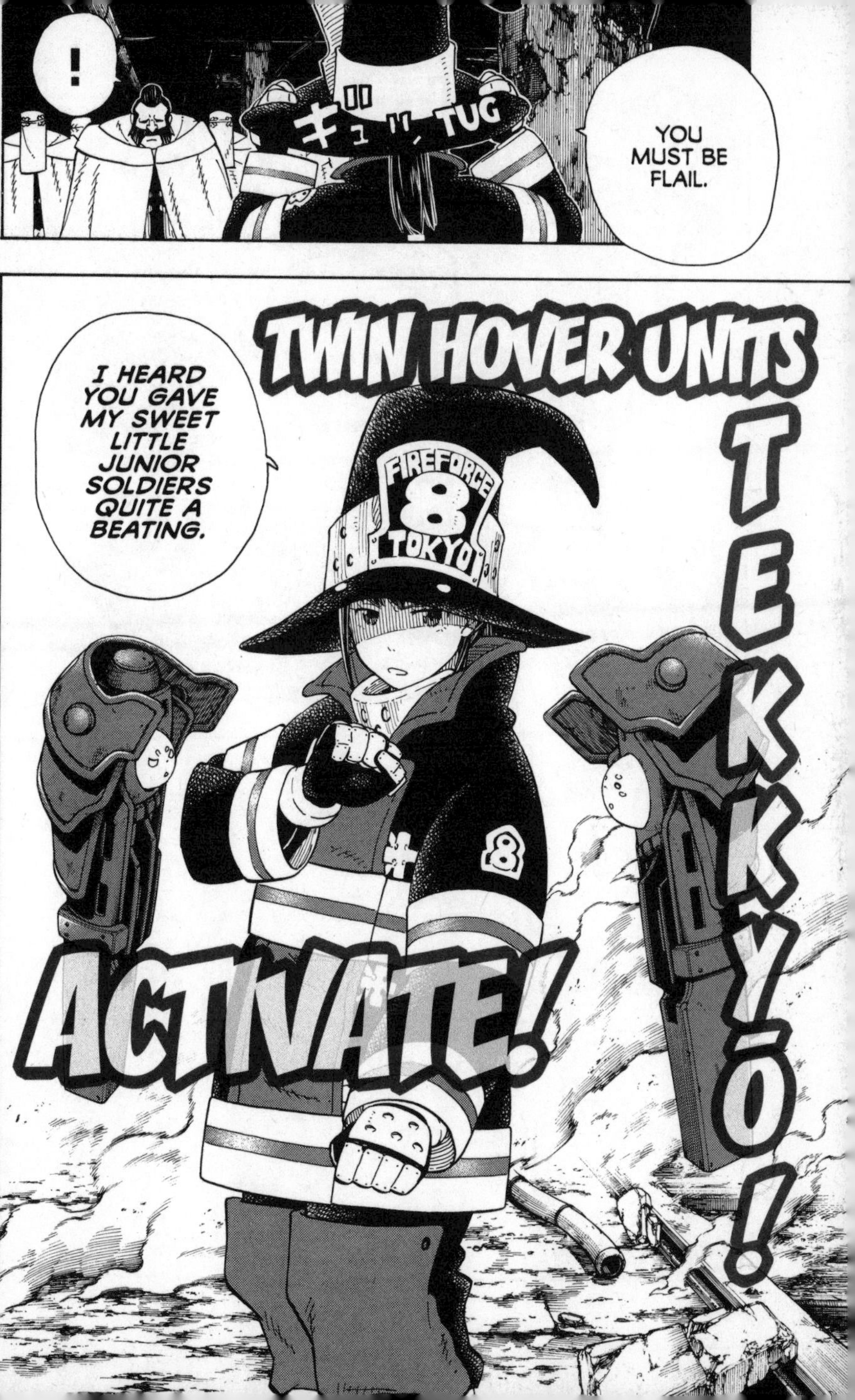
YOU MUST BE FLAIL.
TUG
!
TWIN HOVER UNITS
TEKKYŌ!
I HEARD YOU GAVE MY SWEET LITTLE JUNIOR SOLDIERS QUITE A BEATING.
ACTIVATE!

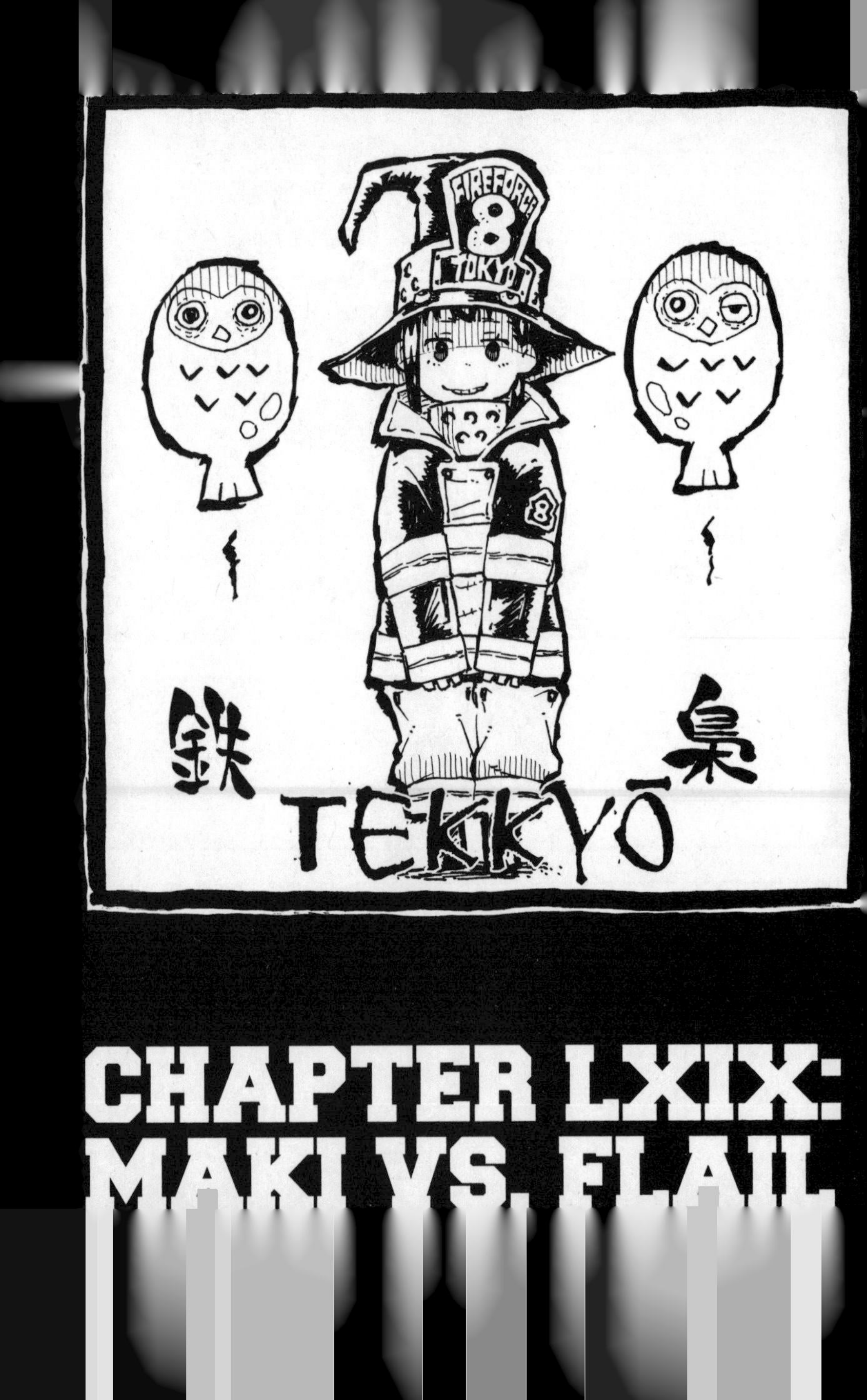
FIRE FORCE
8
TOKYO
鉄
梟
TEKKYŌ

CHAPTER LXIX: MAKI VS. FLAIL

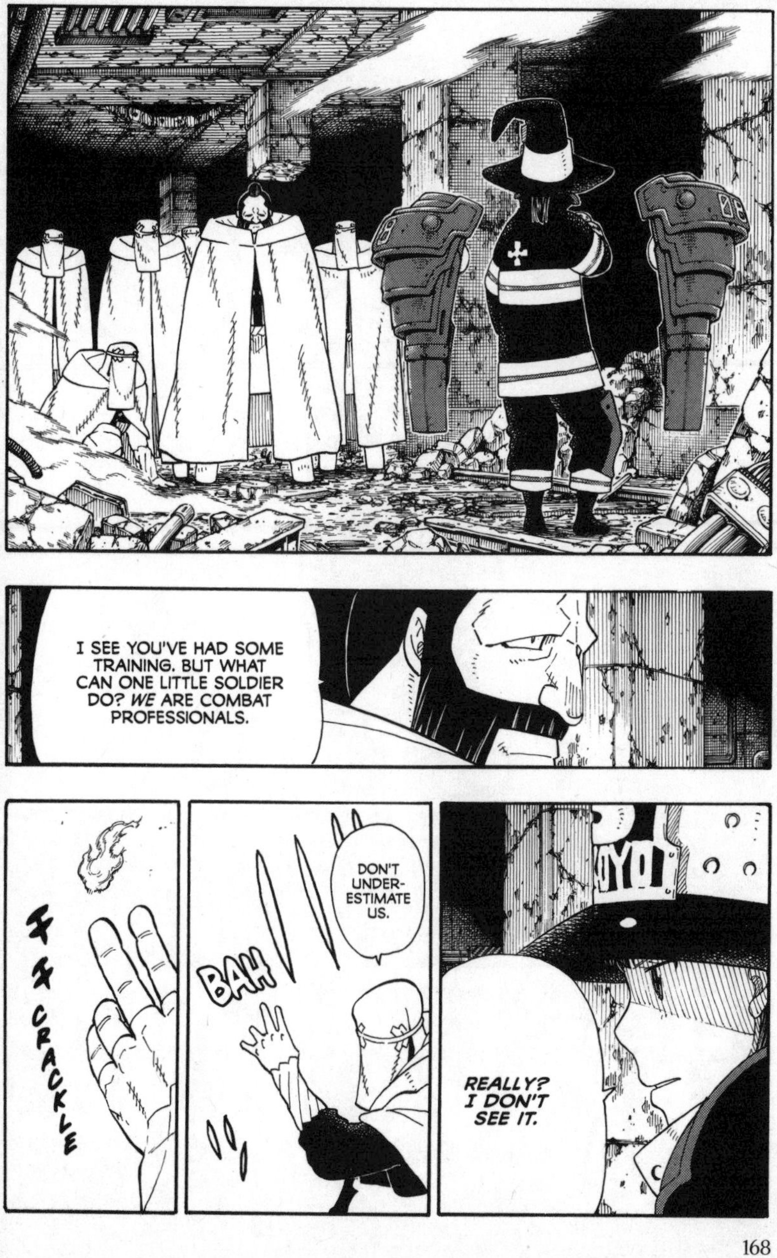
I SEE YOU'VE HAD SOME TRAINING. BUT WHAT CAN ONE LITTLE SOLDIER DO? *WE* ARE COMBAT PROFESSIONALS.
REALLY? I DON'T SEE IT.
DON'T UNDER-ESTIMATE US.
BAH
チチ
CRACKLE

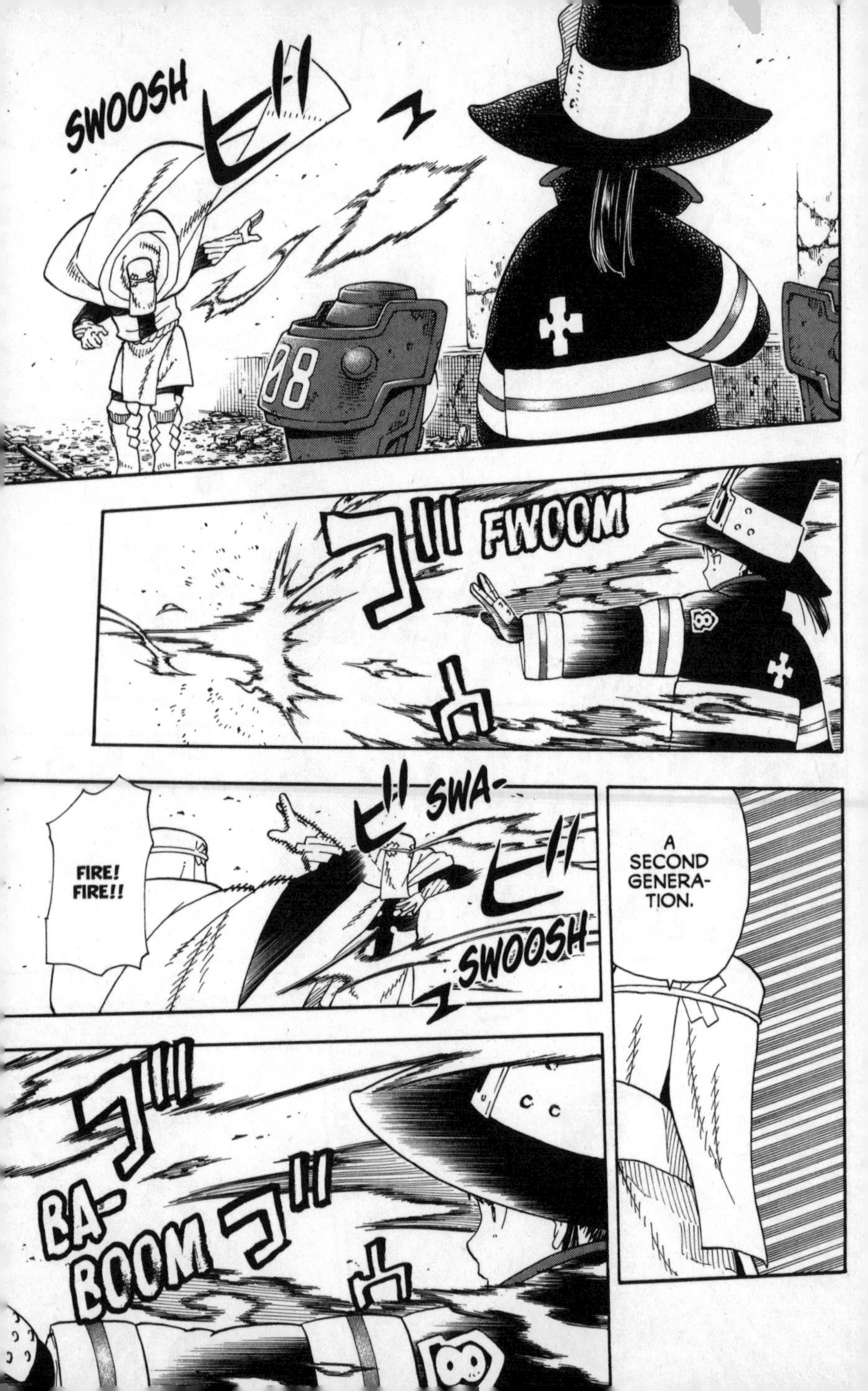
SWOOSH
FWOOM
A SECOND GENERATION.
SWA-
FIRE! FIRE!!
SWOOSH
BA-BOOM

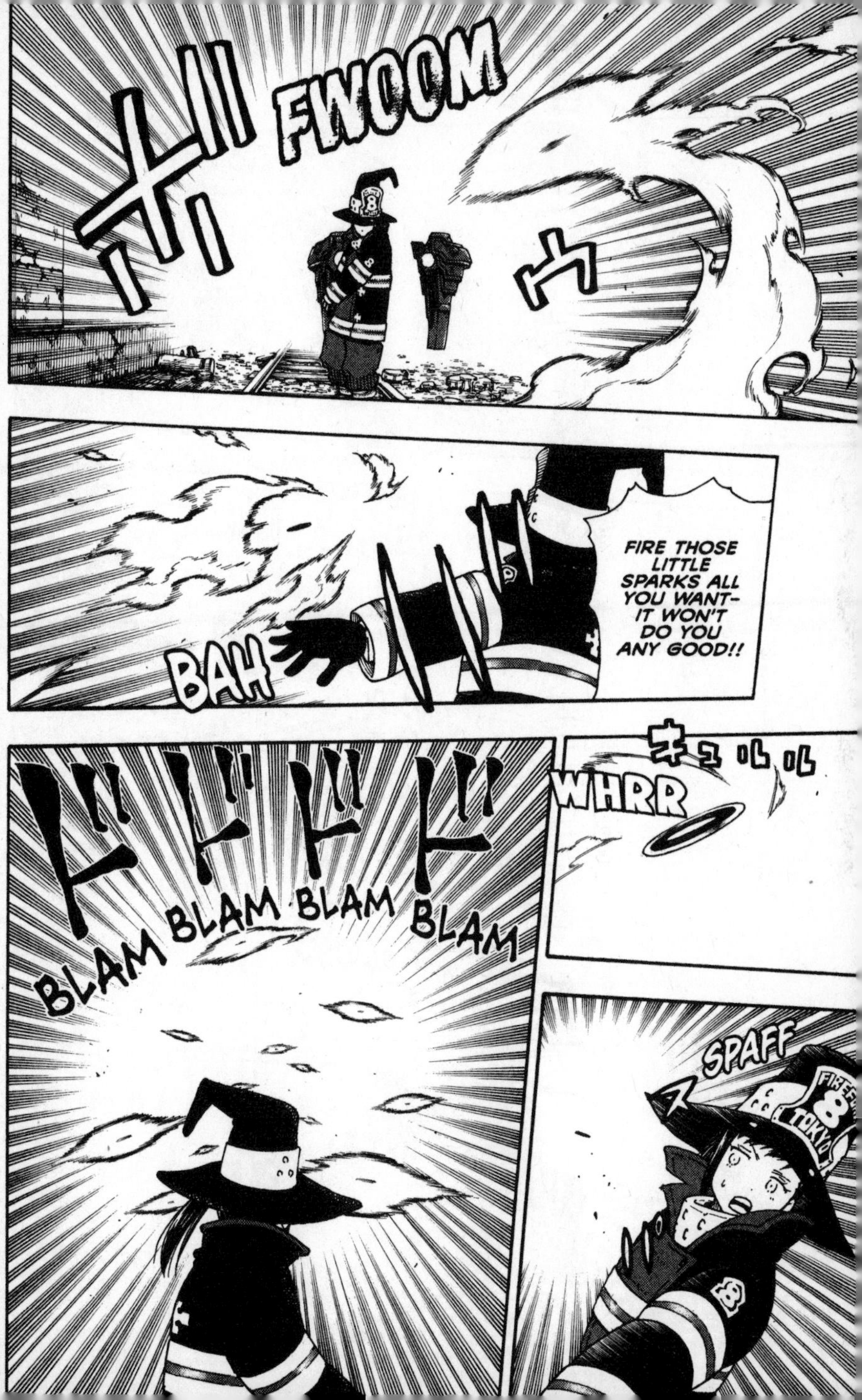
FWOOM
FIRE THOSE LITTLE SPARKS ALL YOU WANT-IT WON'T DO YOU ANY GOOD!!
BAH
キュルル
WHRR
ス
SPAFF
ドドドド
BLAM BLAM BLAM BLAM

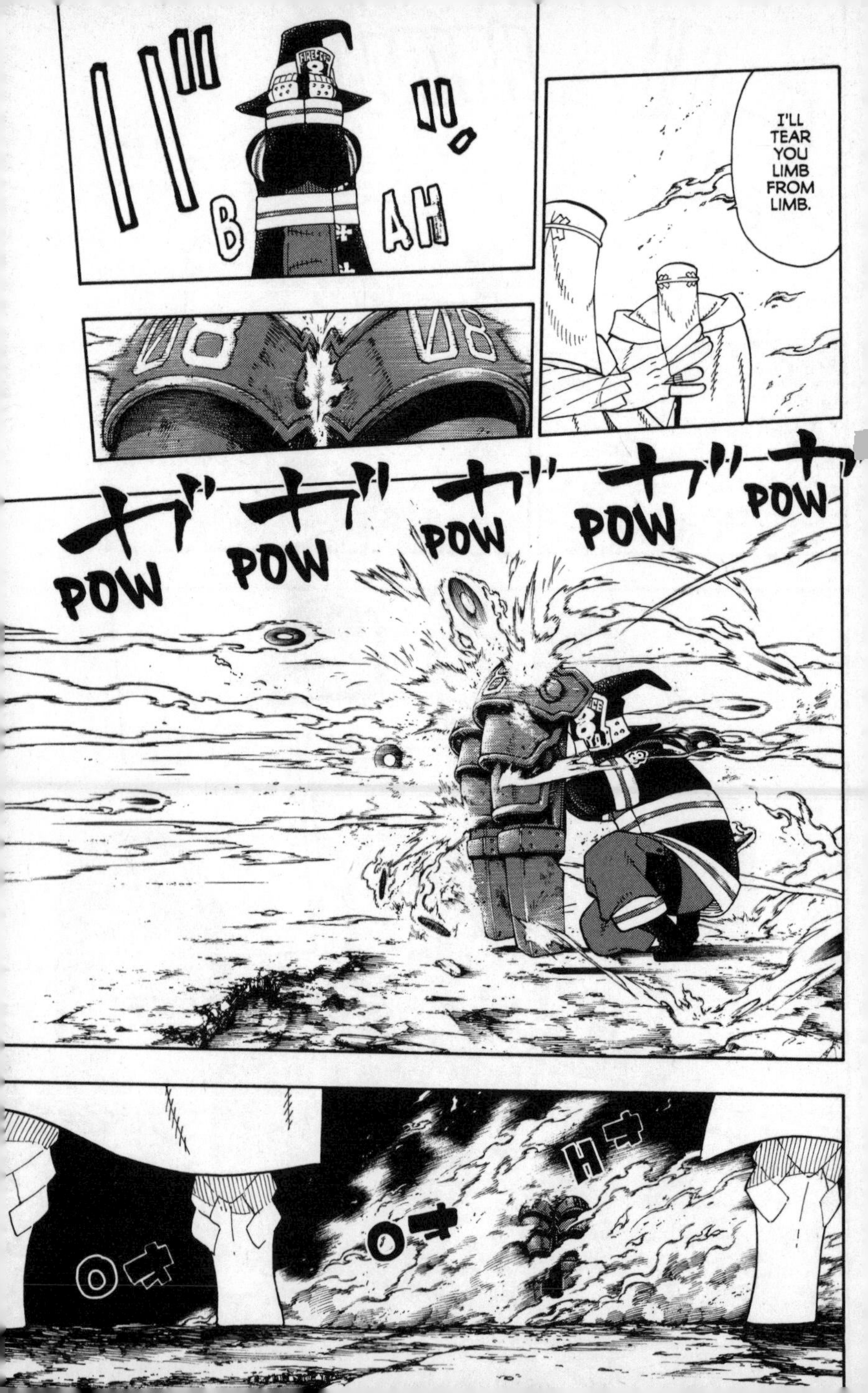
I'LL TEAR YOU LIMB FROM LIMB.
BAH
POW POW POW POW POW

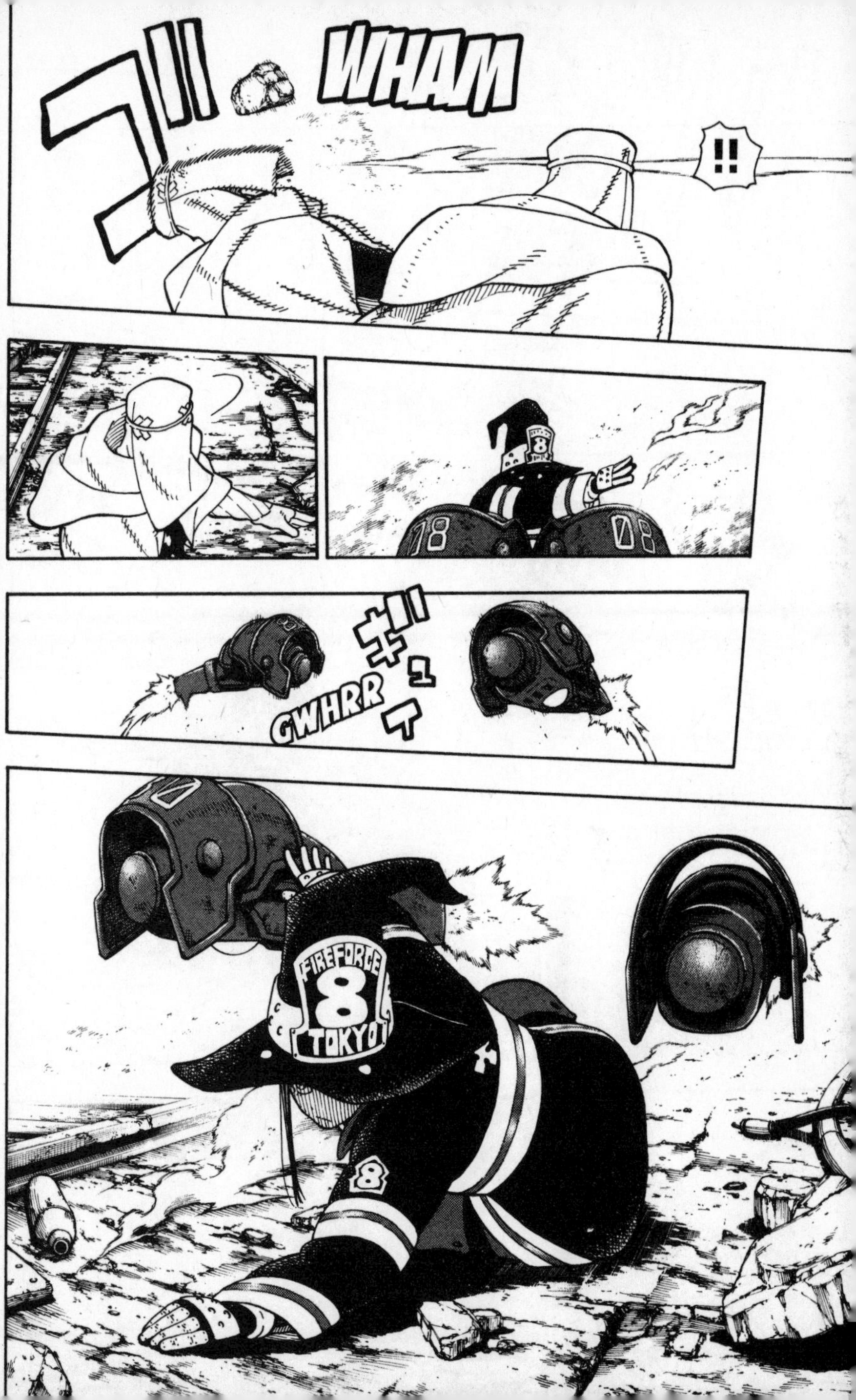
WHAM
!!
GWHRR

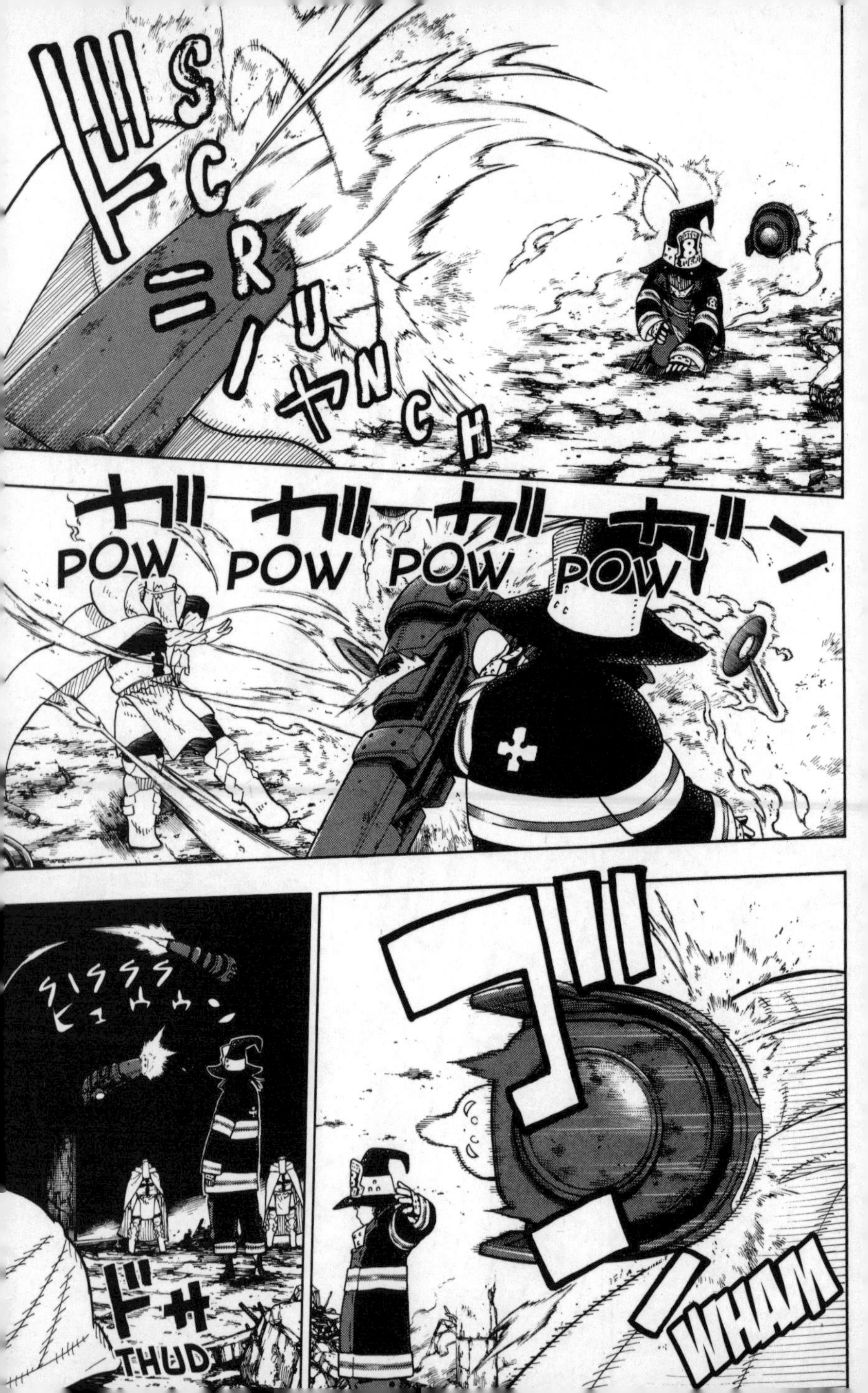

SCRUNCH
ガガガガン
POW POW POW POW
WHAM
SISSS
THUD

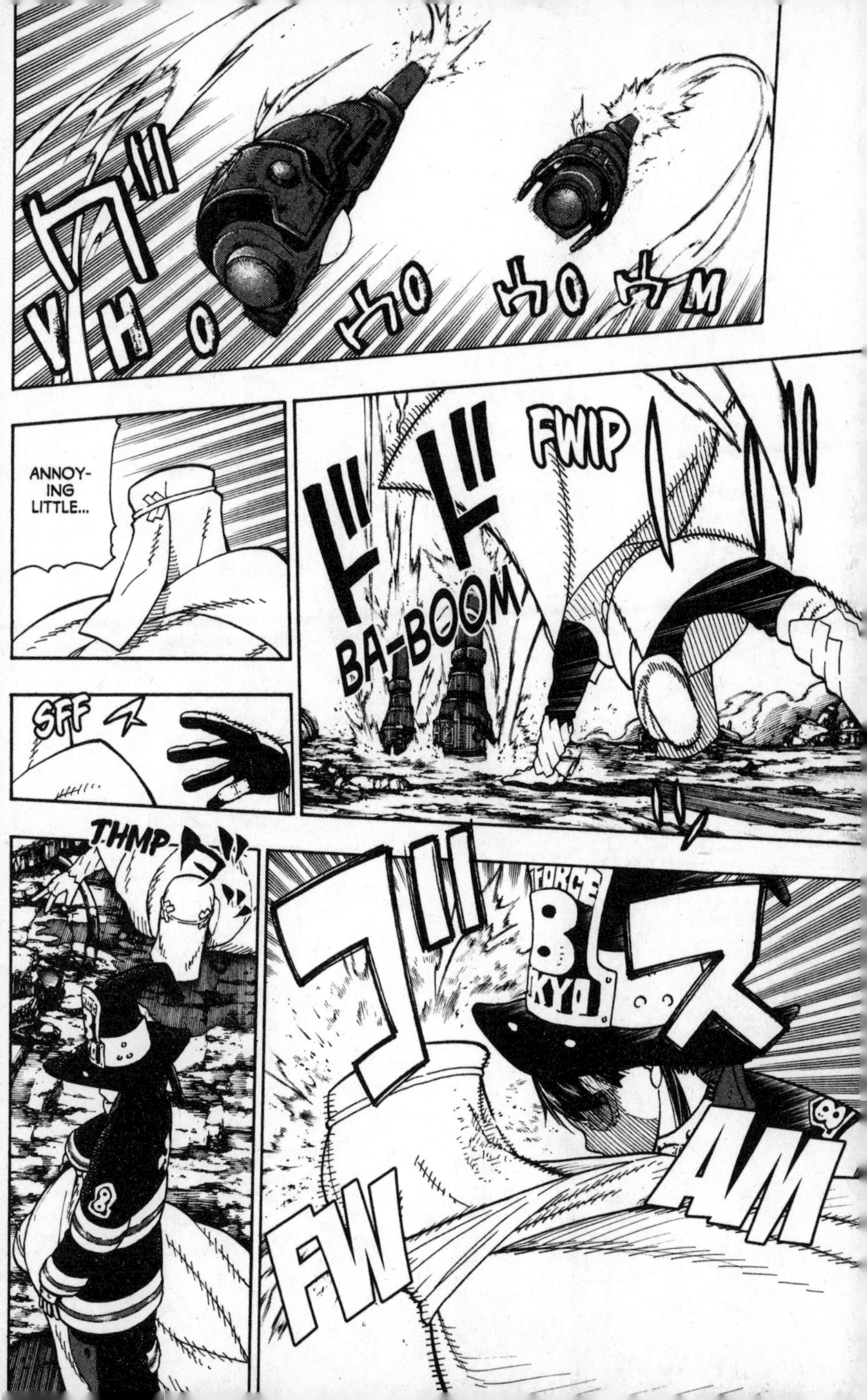
VHOOOM
FWIP
BA-BOOM
ANNOY-ING LITTLE...
SFF
FW
AM
THMP

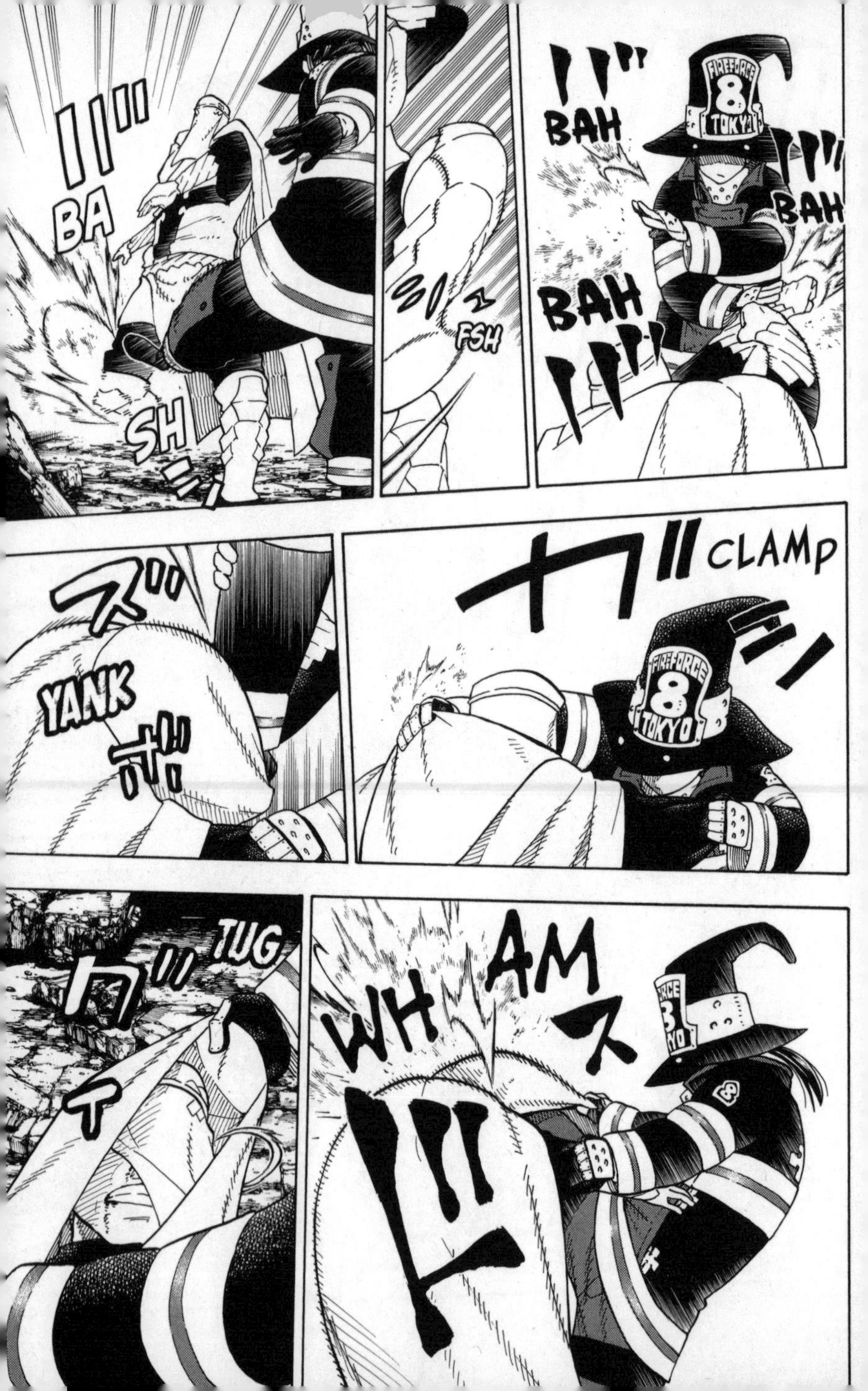
BAH
BAH
BAH
FSH
BA
SH
CLAMP
YANK
WHAM
TUG

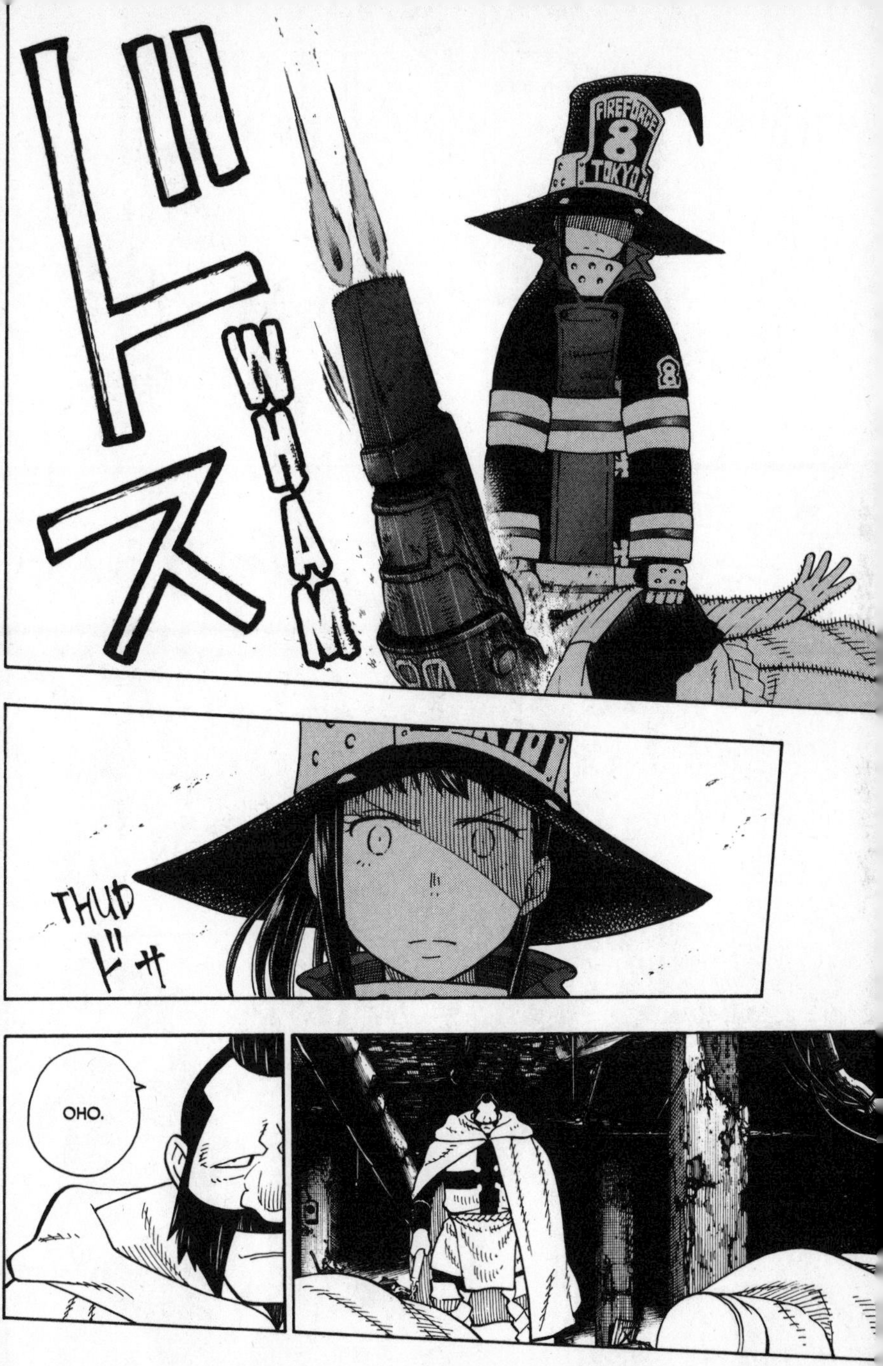
ドス
WHAM
FIREFORCE 8 TOKYO
THUD
ドサ
OHO.

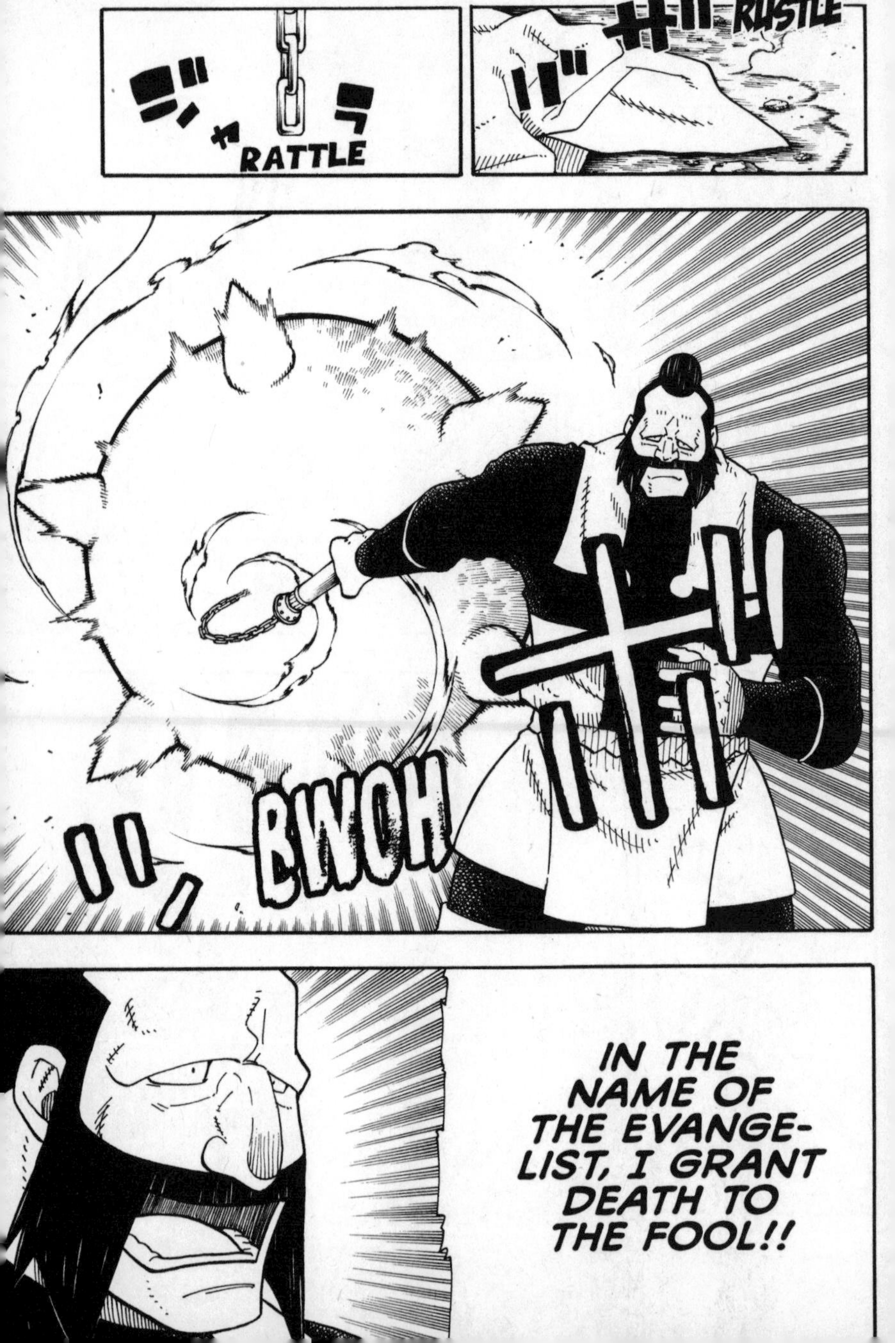
RUSTLE
RATTLE
BWOH
IN THE NAME OF THE EVANGE-LIST, I GRANT DEATH TO THE FOOL!!

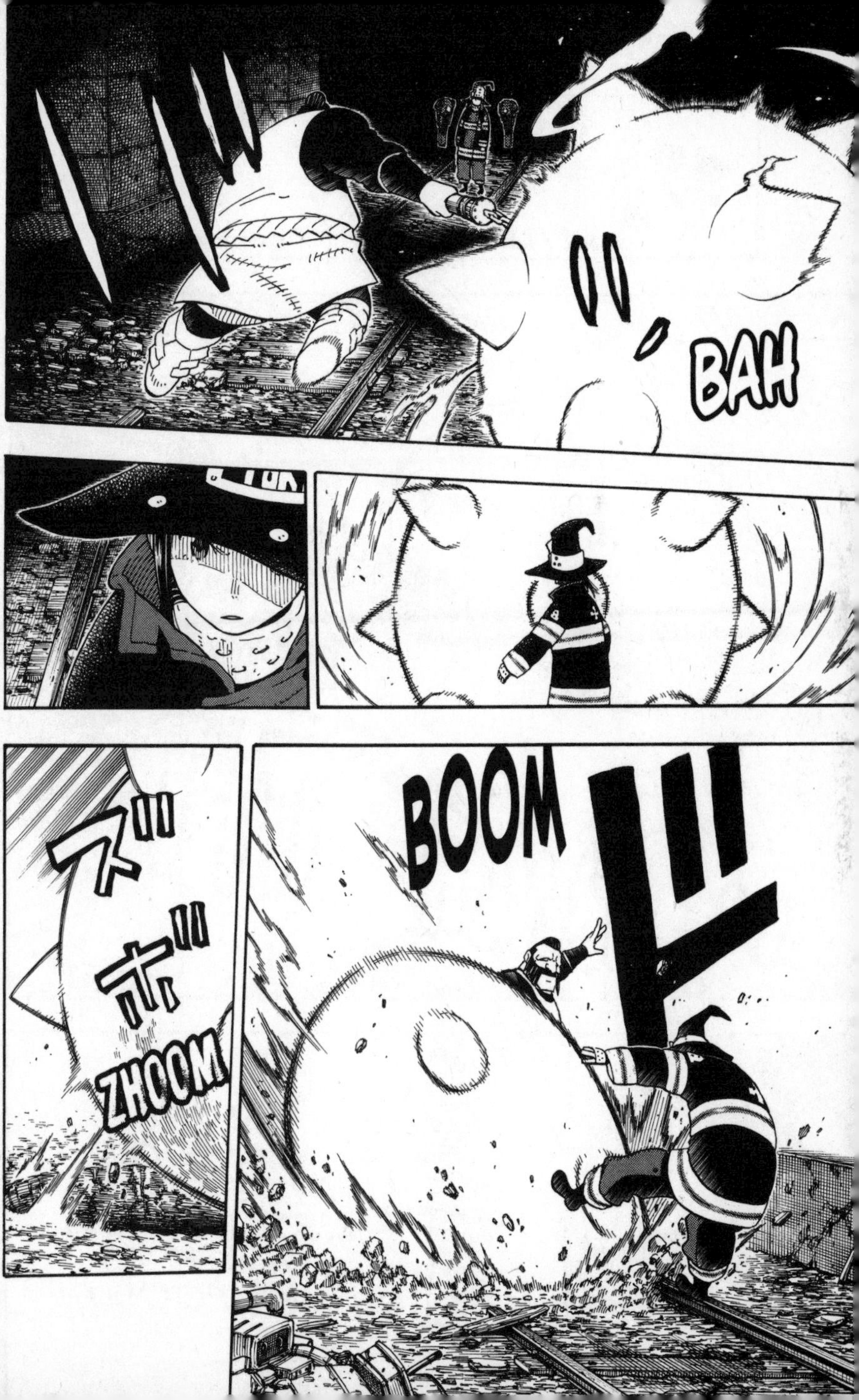
BAH
BOOM
ド
ズボ
ZHOOM

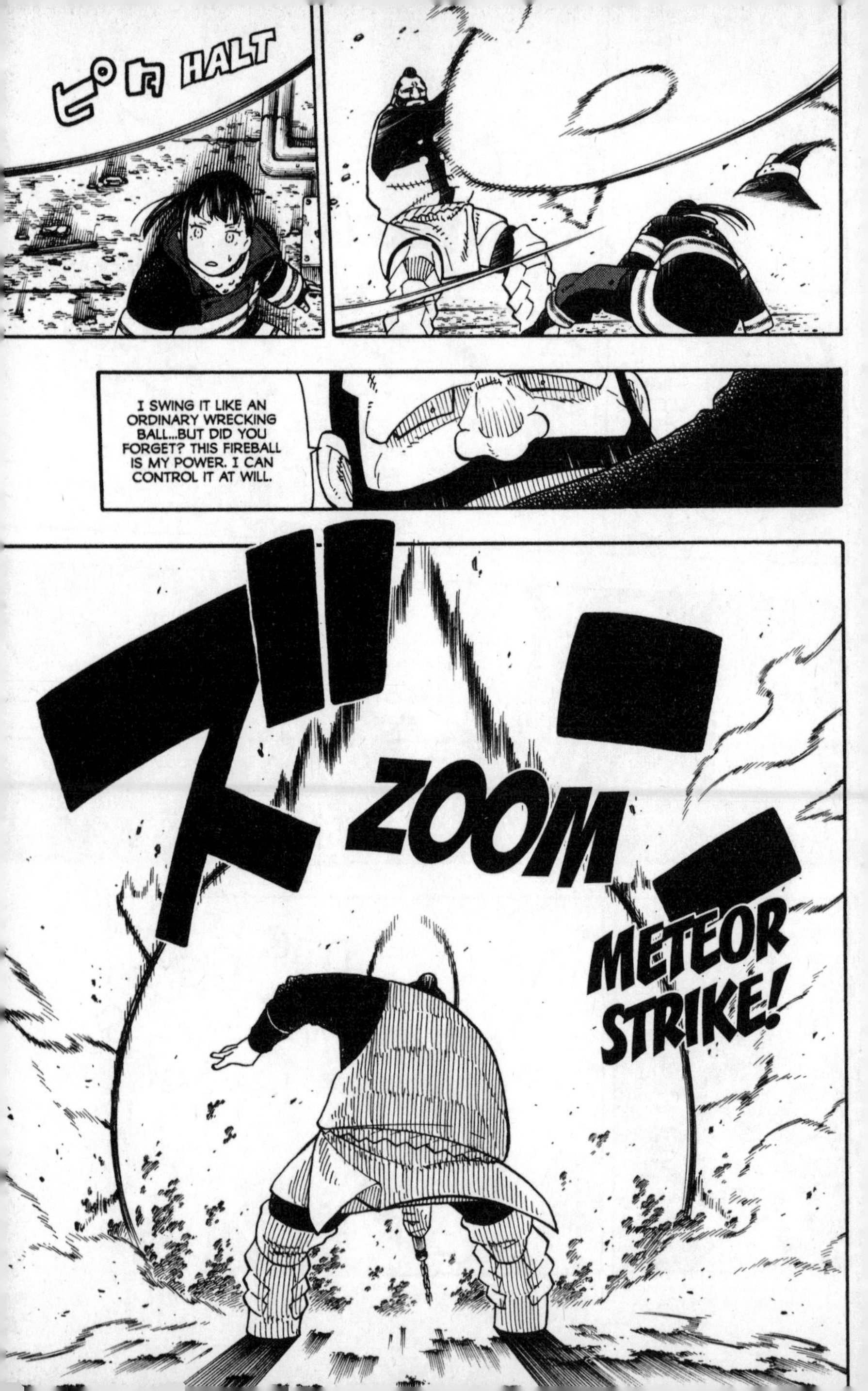

HALT
I SWING IT LIKE AN ORDINARY WRECKING BALL...BUT DID YOU FORGET? THIS FIREBALL IS MY POWER. I CAN CONTROL IT AT WILL.
ZOOM
METEOR STRIKE!

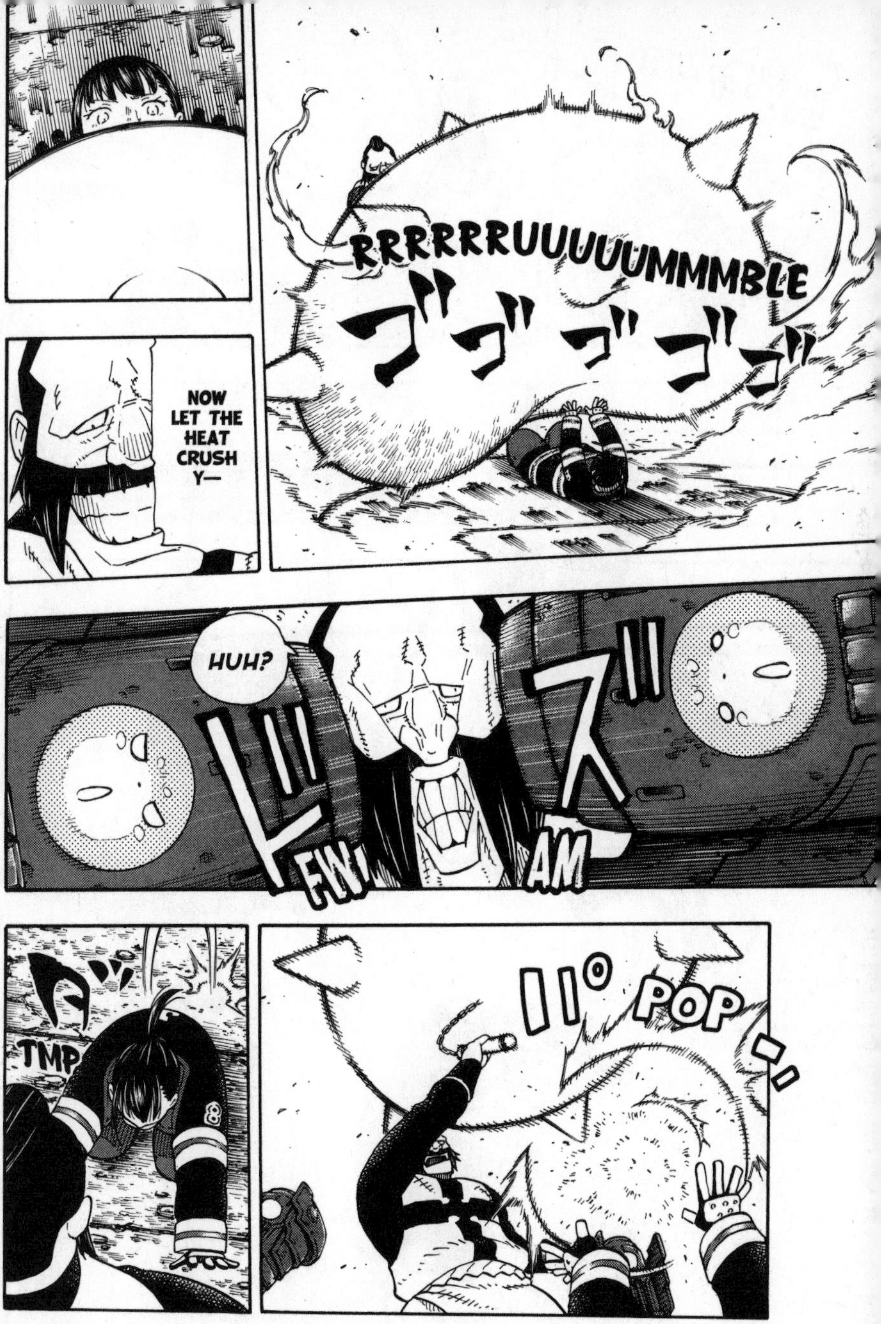
RRRRRRUUUUUUMMMBLE
ゴゴゴゴゴ
NOW LET THE HEAT CRUSH Y—
HUH?
ドズ
FW
AM
POP
TMP

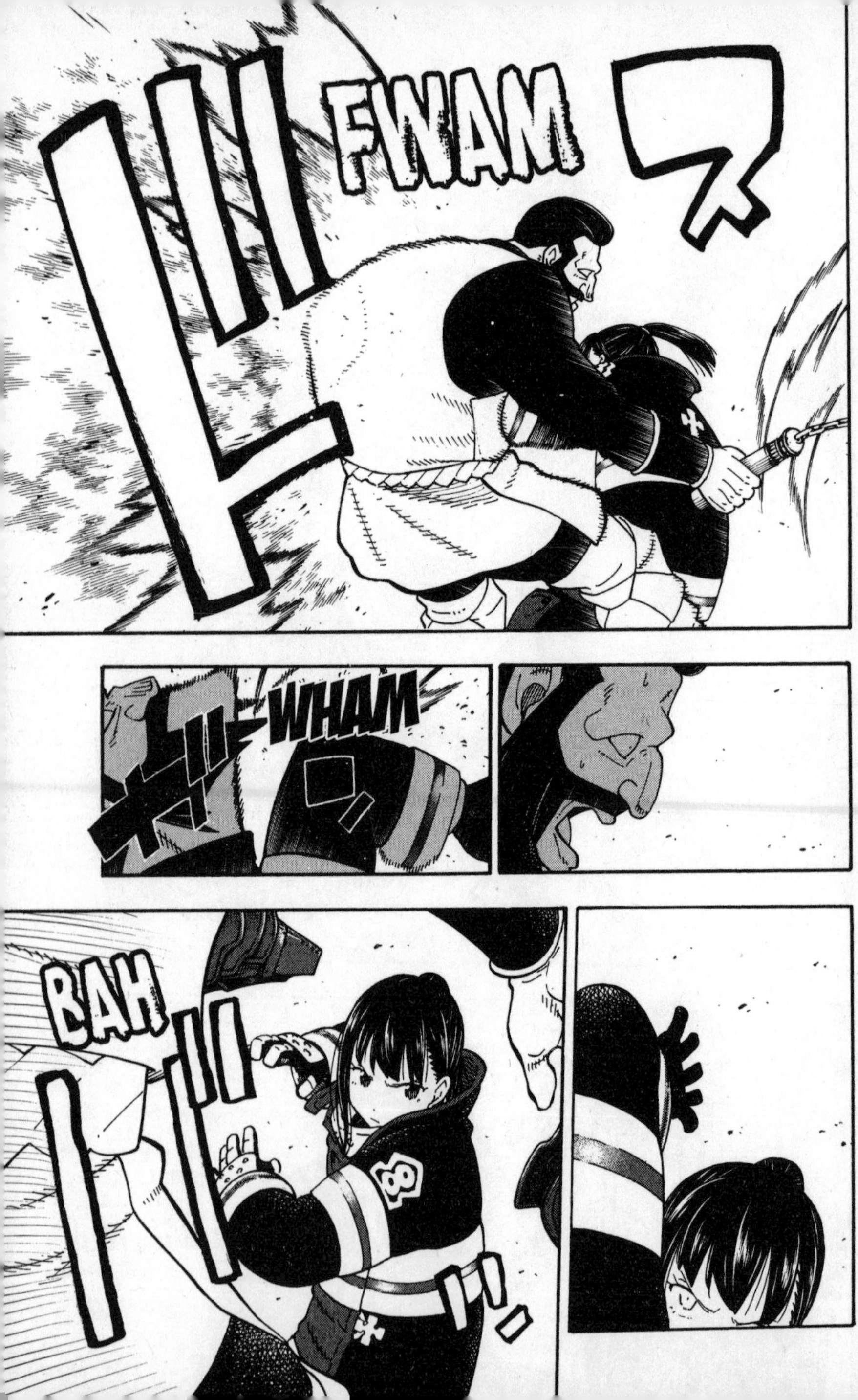
FWAM
WHAM
BAH

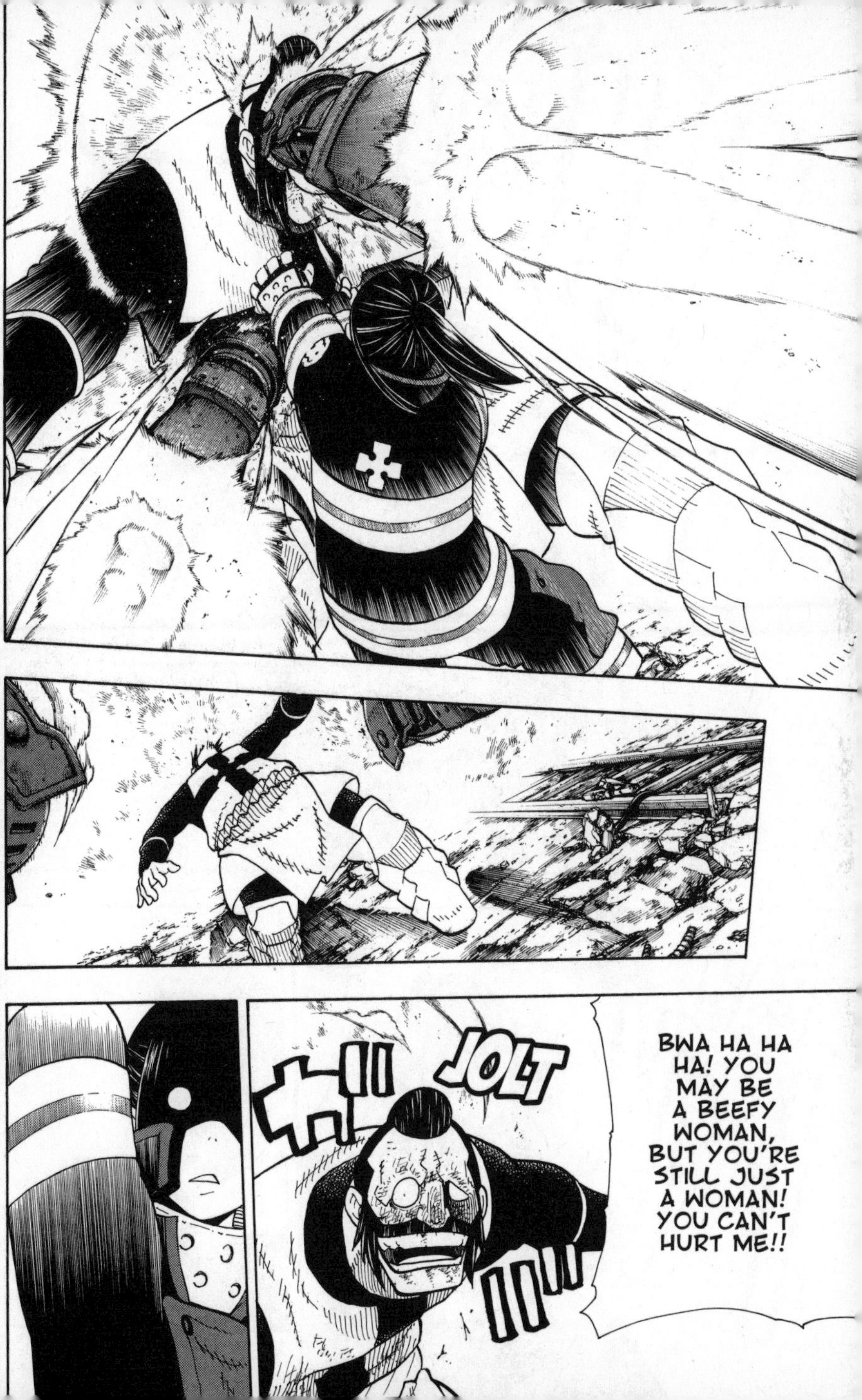
JOLT
BWA HA HA HA! YOU MAY BE A BEEFY WOMAN, BUT YOU'RE STILL JUST A WOMAN! YOU CAN'T HURT ME!!

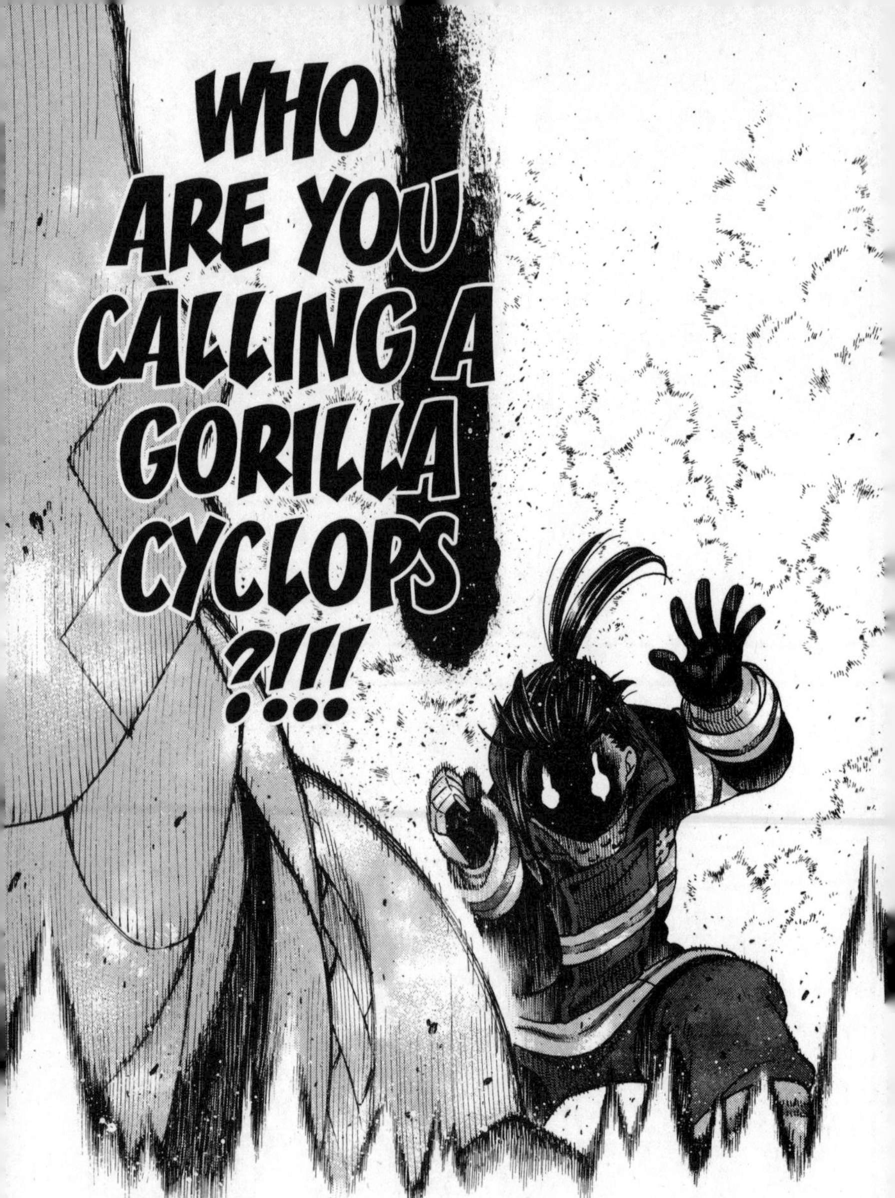
WHO ARE YOU CALLING A GORILLA CYCLOPS ?!!!

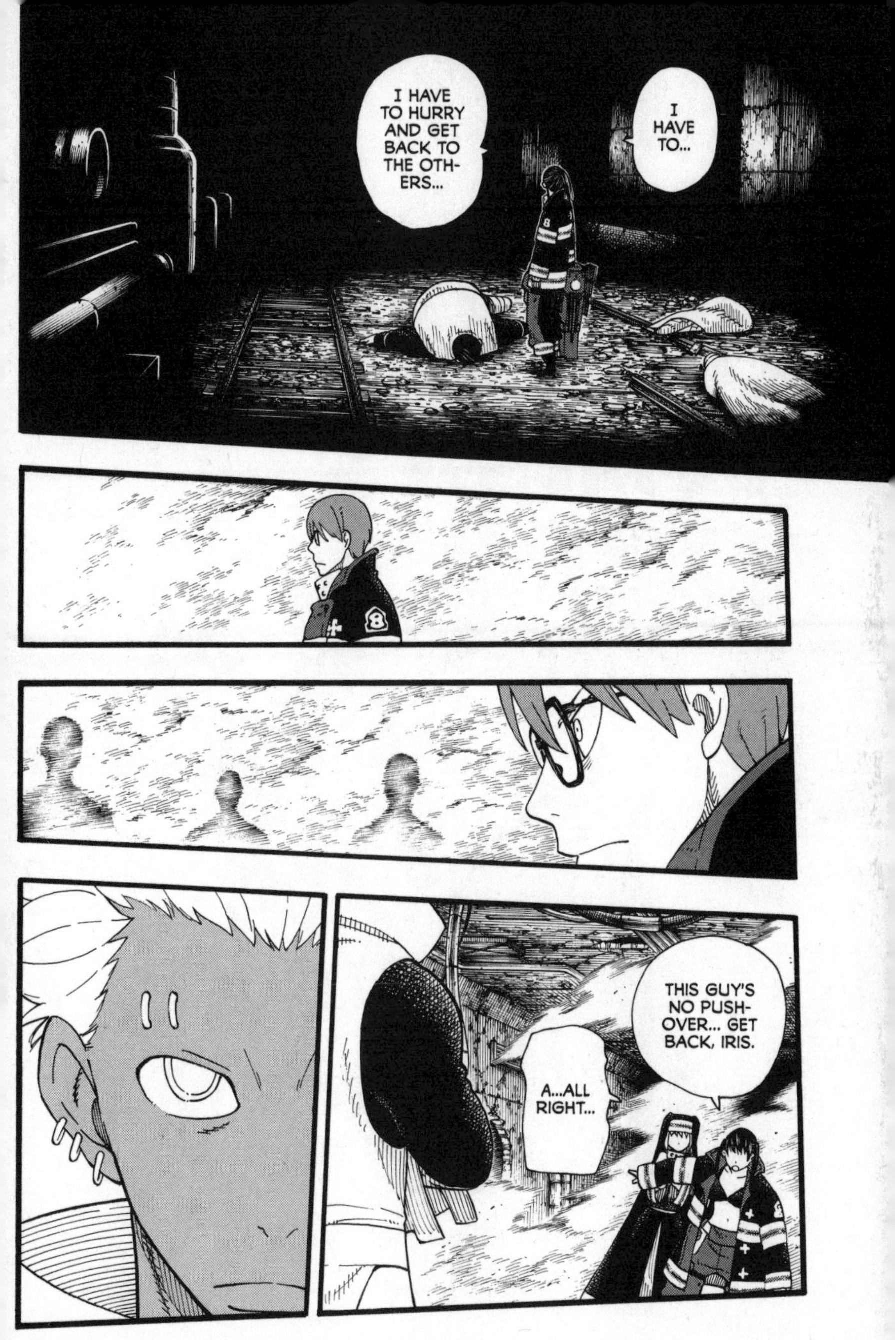
I HAVE TO...
I HAVE TO HURRY AND GET BACK TO THE OTH- ERS...
THIS GUY'S NO PUSH- OVER... GET BACK, IRIS.
A...ALL RIGHT...

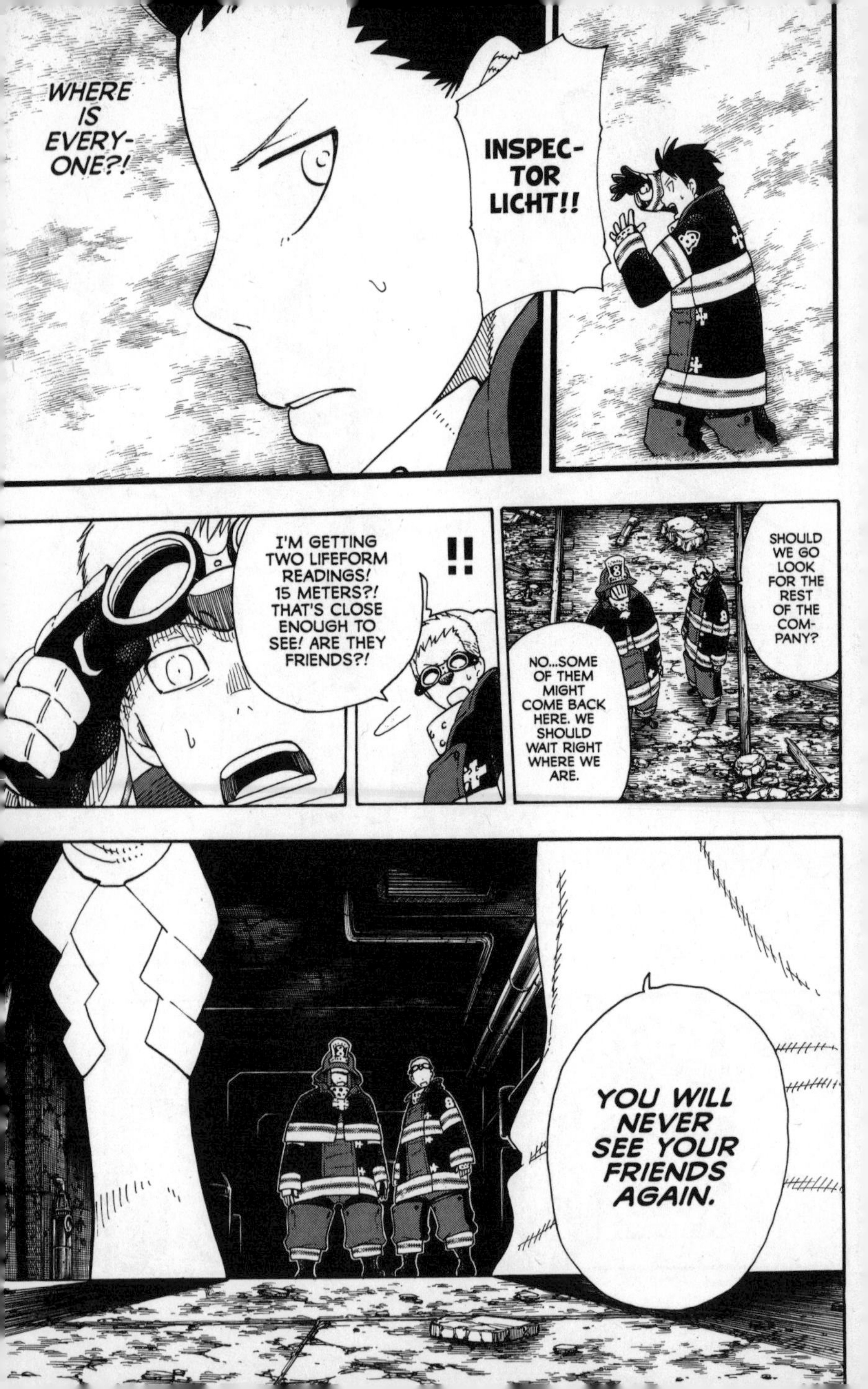
INSPECTOR LICHT!!
WHERE IS EVERYONE?!
SHOULD WE GO LOOK FOR THE REST OF THE COMPANY?
NO...SOME OF THEM MIGHT COME BACK HERE. WE SHOULD WAIT RIGHT WHERE WE ARE.
!!
I'M GETTING TWO LIFEFORM READINGS! 15 METERS?! THAT'S CLOSE ENOUGH TO SEE! ARE THEY FRIENDS?!
YOU WILL NEVER SEE YOUR FRIENDS AGAIN.

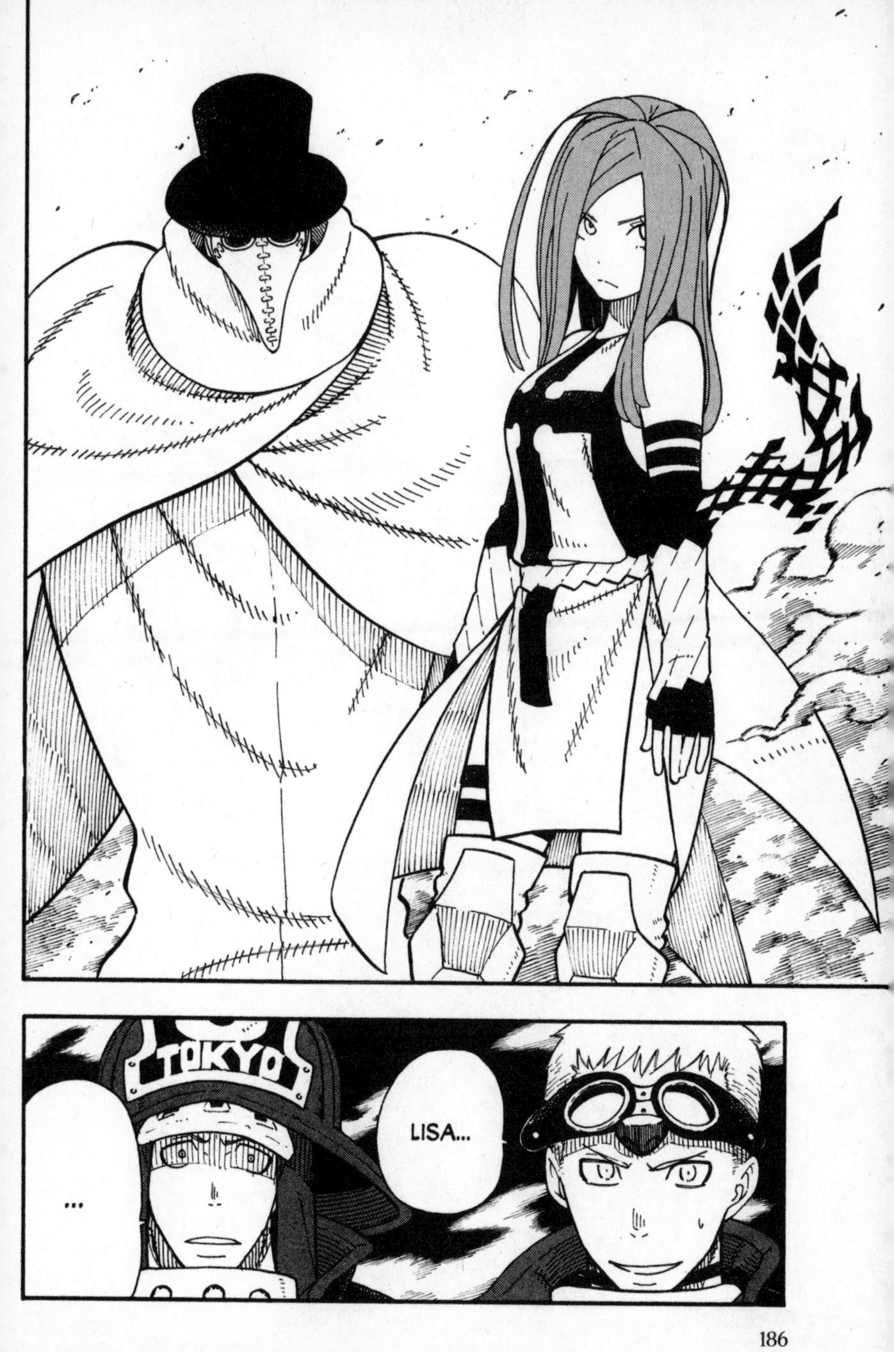
LISA...
...

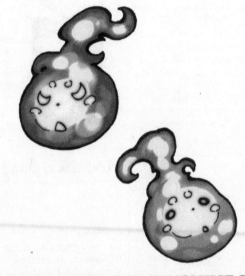

TO BE CONTINUED IN VOLUME 9!!

Translation Notes:

More feminine, page 40

The term *joshi-ryoku* (literally: "girl power") has a different connotation in Japanese than the phrase "girl power" in English. It refers to the ability to do things that are typically considered to be feminine, such as creating delicious meals, making a living space a pleasant place to be, developing a fashion sense, etc.

Silburro, page 53

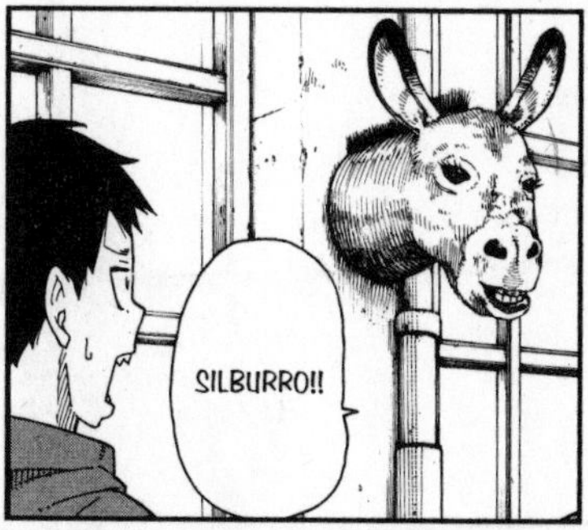
SILBURRO!!

Even in the original Japanese, Arthur's name for the steed he so longs to find is the English word "Silver," but because of the way the Japanese writing system works, it actually sounds more like "shirubaa." By trading the "ru" for a "ro," Arthur has created a name, Shiroba, which includes the Japanese word for donkey, *roba*. To replicate the effect in English, the translators borrowed a word that the English language has in turn borrowed from Spanish. We'll just say that Arthur was channeling his inner Don Quixote.

Moosifer, page 54

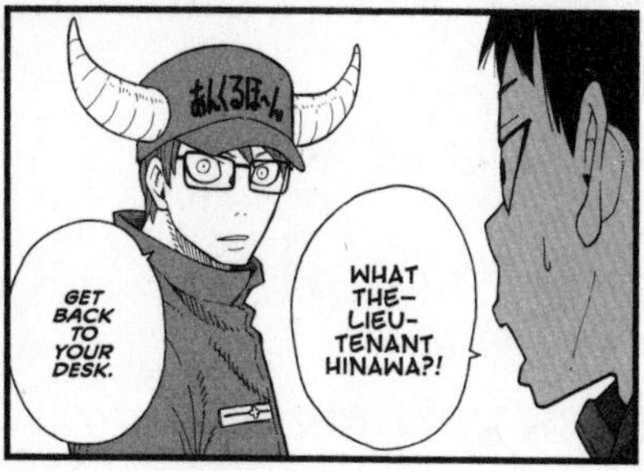
あんくるほーん
WHAT THE— LIEU-TENANT HINAWA?!
GET BACK TO YOUR DESK.

The name written on the Lieutenant's hat is actually Uncle Horn, which happens to be the name of a monster in *Dragon Quest*. In English versions of the game, the name is changed to Moosifer. While the reasons for the change are unknown to these translators, they feel it bears noting that the English rendition most likely comes from the sound bovine creatures make, and not from the antlered moose.

Tekkyō, page 111

In Japanese, it's fairly easy to make up words by taking two kanji characters with appropriate meanings and sticking them together, in this case *tetsu* for iron and *kyō* for owl. The problem here is that *tekkyō* is already a word that doesn't have very many other meanings, so when people hear it they are most likely to assume it means "iron bridge," as demonstrated by Lieutenant Hinawa.

Prestidigitacian, page 130

A combination of "prestidigitator," otherwise known as a party magician, and "magician." In Japan, there's a bit more of a pun, as *tejinashan* (prestidigitacian) sounds similar to *tekunishan* (technician).

CHARACTER PROFILE

FIRE FORCE

PRINCESS HIBANA

HOLY SOL NAME: **SISTER HIBANA**

AFFILIATION: **SPECIAL FIRE FORCE COMPANY 5**

RANK: **CAPTAIN**

ABILITY: **THIRD GENERATION PYROKINETIC (MANIPULATES HEAT TO CREATE SYNCOPE, ATTACKS WITH FLORAL FLAMES)**

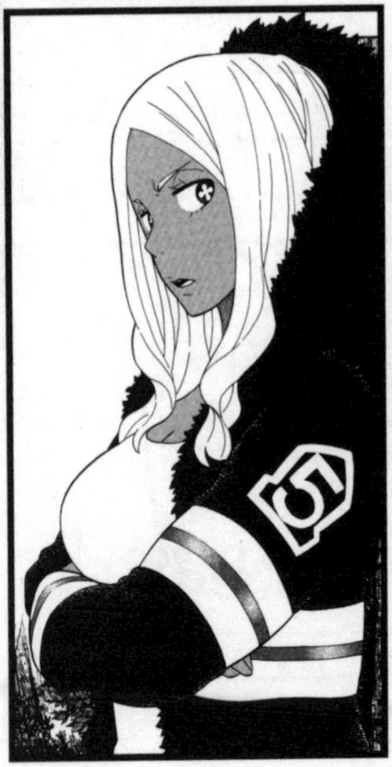
5

Height	A well-proportioned 169 cm [5'6.5'']
Weight	A nicely shaped 54 kg [119 lbs.]
Age	A different sort of 20
Birthday	The glorious day of March 3
Sign	The Sign of the Princess, naturally
Bloodtype	High-class type A
Nickname	Princess, Onē-sama
Self-Proclaimed	Muse, Venus
Favorite Foods	Anmitsu (jellied fruit dessert), anything decorated with flowers
Least Favorite Food	Spicy food
Favorite Music	I'm not really familiar with music
Favorite Animal	Guinea pigs
Favorite Color	The color of ethanol
Her Type	A man who aspires to be a hero ...I'm not talking about Shinra!
Who She Respects	My smart, strong, beautiful self
Who She Has Trouble Around	No one
Who She's Afraid Of	My too-perfect self
Hobbies	Research, video games
Daily Routine	Making lunches...not for Shinra!
Dream	Revenge against whoever burned down my convent and...I can't tell you that, stupid!
Shoe Size	A lovely 21 cm [5]
Eyesight	With perfectly round eyes, 0.5 [20/40]
Favorite Subject	Science!
Least Favorite Subject	Boring old language arts

AFTERWORD MANGA: ATSUSHIYA

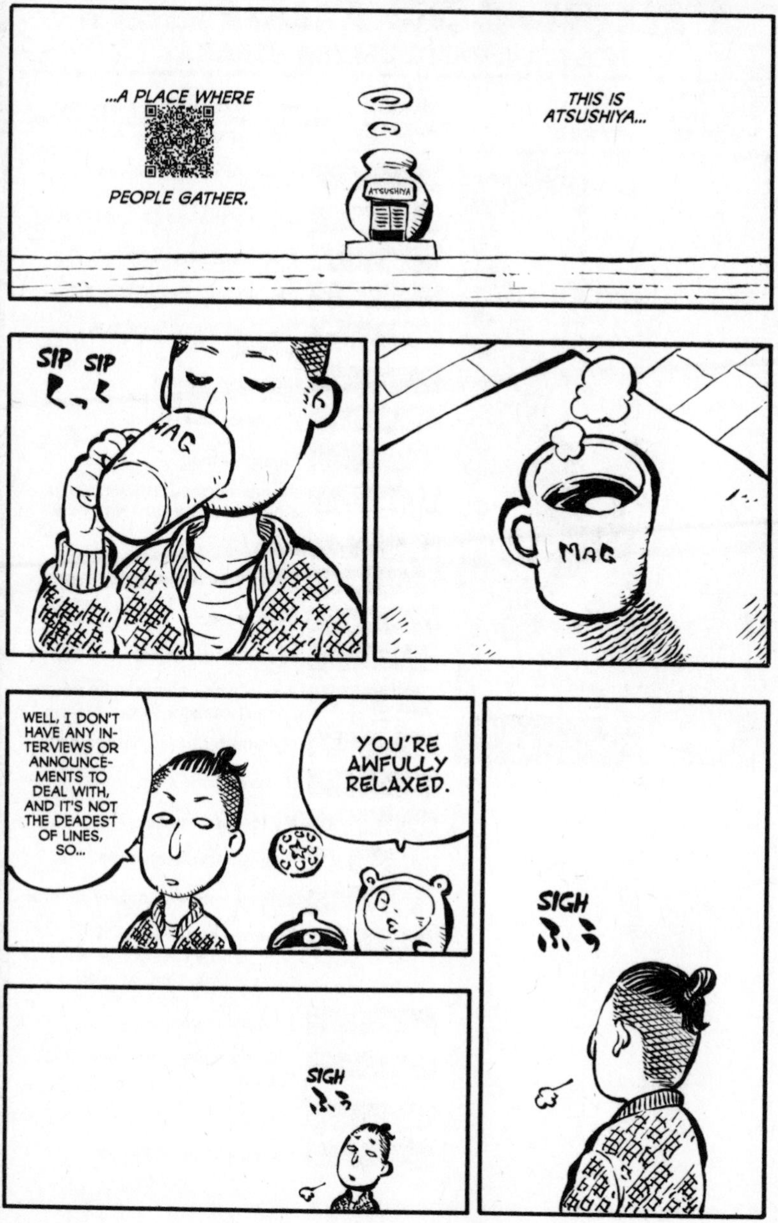

THIS IS ATSUSHIYA...
...A PLACE WHERE PEOPLE GATHER.
ATSUSHIYA
MAG
SIP SIP
MAG
SIGH
ふう
YOU'RE AWFULLY RELAXED.
WELL, I DON'T HAVE ANY INTERVIEWS OR ANNOUNCEMENTS TO DEAL WITH, AND IT'S NOT THE DEADEST OF LINES, SO...
SIGH
ふう

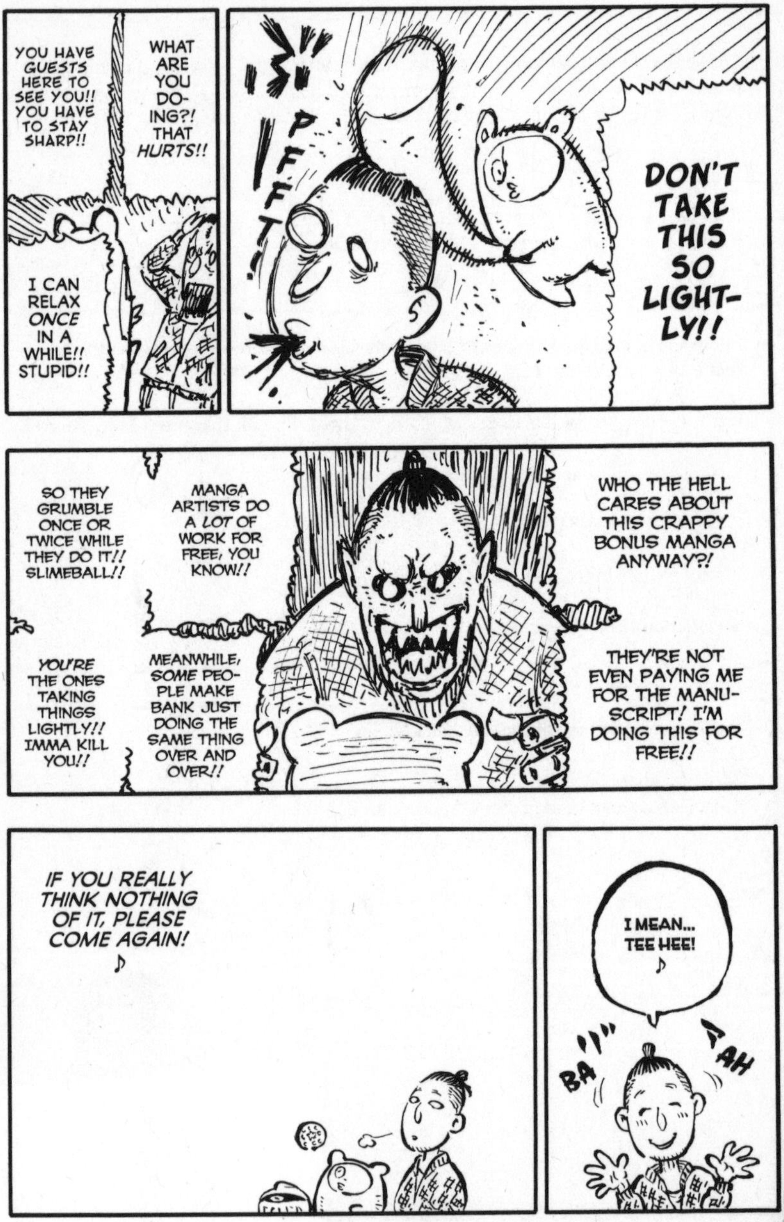
PFFFT!
DON'T TAKE THIS SO LIGHTLY!!
WHAT ARE YOU DOING?! THAT *HURTS!!*
YOU HAVE *GUESTS* HERE TO SEE YOU!! YOU HAVE TO STAY SHARP!!
I CAN RELAX *ONCE* IN A WHILE!! STUPID!!
WHO THE HELL CARES ABOUT THIS CRAPPY BONUS MANGA ANYWAY?!
THEY'RE NOT EVEN PAYING ME FOR THE MANUSCRIPT! I'M DOING THIS FOR FREE!!
MANGA ARTISTS DO A *LOT* OF WORK FOR FREE, YOU KNOW!!
MEANWHILE, *SOME* PEOPLE MAKE BANK JUST DOING THE SAME THING OVER AND OVER!!
SO THEY GRUMBLE ONCE OR TWICE WHILE THEY DO IT!! SLIMEBALL!!
YOU'RE THE ONES TAKING THINGS LIGHTLY!! IMMA KILL YOU!!
I MEAN... TEE HEE! ♪
BA-AH
IF YOU REALLY THINK NOTHING OF IT, PLEASE COME AGAIN! ♪

A Kodansha Comics Trade Paperback Original.

Fire Force volume 8 copyright © 2017 Atsushi Ohkubo
English translation copyright © 2017 Atsushi Ohkubo

All rights reserved.

Published in the United States by Kodansha Comics, an imprint of Kodansha USA Publishing, LLC, New York.

Publication rights for this English edition arranged through Kodansha Ltd., Tokyo.

First published in Japan in 2017 by Kodansha Ltd., Tokyo.

ISBN 978-1-63236-547-7

Printed in the United States of America.

www.kodanshacomics.com

9 8 7 6 5 4 3

Translation: Alethea Nibley & Athena Nibley
Lettering: AndWorld Design
Editing: Lauren Scanlan
Kodansha Comics edition cover design: Phil Balsman

D0180534